74114A

16
99BB

Anorexia Nervosa

Anorexia Nervosa

HELMUT THOMÄ

Translated by Gillian Brydone

INTERNATIONAL UNIVERSITIES PRESS, INC.

NEW YORK   NEW YORK

Contents

Anorexia Nervosa

Foreword to the English-Language Edition

As one critic put it, in referring to the German edition which appeared in Autumn 1961, "In some ways this is several books in one; it conveys the curious impression of an author with several personalities."

The symptomatology of anorexia nervosa is, in the truest sense of the word, psychosomatic. This has made it essential to describe both the physical and the mental side of the syndrome. At the same time, anorexia nervosa has been the subject of close study by every relevant branch of medicine for the last hundred years. The opportunity to compare methods of approach and theories of the origins of the disorder was too good to be missed. This is the source, no doubt, of the impression of "several books in one."

Many reviewers have also expressed curiosity about the author himself. I studied to become a psychiatrist in Germany and then spent a year as a postgraduate student at Yale. I trained as a psychoanalyst in Heidelberg. Since psychoanalysis is still in the earliest stages of a renaissance in Germany, in order to receive the *sit venia legendi* and to become a Reader in psychoanalysis, I had to prove its scientific value and validity. This is why I have felt it necessary to present chapter and verse for even the most familiar hypotheses, and to sketch in the general principles of the psychoanalytic theory of the neuroses, which have been household terms in most English-speaking countries for several decades. I must therefore beg the American or English reader to bear with me if he or she finds the case histories somewhat long-winded. I not only had to make my point—I had to defend it from every side!

The material collected in this book was gathered over the course of ten years in the Psychosomatic Department of Heidelberg University and discussed during a series of departmental seminars. What successes we achieved were the result of close and stimulating collaboration.

My thanks are due especially to the Rockefeller Foundation which originally made this work possible through a grant to the Department of Psychosomatic Medicine, founded in Heidelberg University in 1950. Further assistance on the part of the Rockefeller Foundation also enabled the German publishers to bring out this book in an unabridged form.

Of my colleagues, I wish to thank Professor Alexander Mitscherlich, who guided our discussions and contributed much constructive criticism during the course of the work. It was his special concern to eliminate the one-sidedness of "personal equations," and thus several physicians were involved in the psychotherapy. I am also extremely grateful to all of my colleagues who cheerfully undertook the onerous task of collating extensive case histories, especially Dr. M. Eicke-Spengler, Dr. L. von Kries, Dr. M. Mitscherlich-Nielsen, Dr. M. von Niederhöffer and Dr. H-J. Seeberger.

The book is dedicated to Dr. G. Ruffler, in memory of his efforts during the setting-up of the Department and his help with the project itself. His premature death was a great loss to us all.

The fact that the material was finally hammered into shape is due largely to the tireless labor of our secretaries, Mrs. Vilma Saler and Miss Rosemarie Schmich; Miss Käte Hügel gave us invaluable assistance with the French literature.

Since the first of January 1960, which was the closing date for this collection of case histories, 55 more cases of anorexia nervosa have been examined, and in some cases, treated in this Department. The addition of this large number of cases is undoubtedly due to our various publications on the subject. Any further experience we have gained coincides closely with the conclusions set out here, and no important revisions were found to be necessary. One section on pathological anatomy has been omitted, since it was only a survey of information readily available elsewhere, and the bibliography has been increased. Although nothing essential has been altered, the translation has, in my view, given the text a new lease on life. This is the result of the work of Miss Brydone, who has even succeeded in unraveling the critical discussion of existential analysis so that it will now, I hope, be comprehensible to the English-speaking reader.

Helmut Thomä
Heidelberg, 1964

✕ 1 ✕

A Historical Survey

Although myths and mysteries still surround its origins, the syndrome known as anorexia nervosa has been familiar to medical science for several centuries. As early as 1689, in England, Morton published a perceptive, graphic description of the symptoms, but the first medical account is said to have come from a Genoese physician, Simone Porta o Portio, in 1500 (Acconero, 1943; Baraldi, 1952). The revival of interest in the disease in more recent years was stimulated by the work of Gull (1868, 1873) in England, and Lasègue (1873) in France. These two authors published, simultaneously, comprehensive clinical descriptions of anorexia nervosa. Since that time, it has been frequently rediscovered by general practitioners, pediatricians, and psychiatrists—and as frequently renamed.

Before going on to a survey of the many and various interpretations that have been put forward since the pioneer work of Gull and Lasègue, it would be interesting to consider one of Morton's case histories. Without realizing it, Morton paints a vivid picture of the course and tragic outcome of a severe but typical anorexia nervosa.

> ... Mr. Duke's Daughter in St. Mary Axe, in the year 1684 and the eighteenth Year of her Age, in the month of July, fell into a total suppression of her Monthly Courses from a multitude of Cares and Passions of her Mind, but without any symptom of the Green-Sickness following upon it. From which time her Appetite began to abate, and her Digestion to be bad; her flesh also began to be flaccid

and loose, and her looks pale, with other Symptoms usual in an Universal Consumption of the Habit of the Body, and by the extream and memorable cold weather which happened the Winter following, this Consumption did seem to be not a little improved; for that she was wont by her studying at Night, and continual poring upon Books, to expose herself both Day and Night to the injuries of the Air, which was at that time extreamly cold, not without some manifest Predjudice to the System of her Nerves. The Spring following by the Prescription of some Emperick, she took a Vomit, and after that I know not what Steel Medicines, but without any Advantage. So from that time loathing all sorts of Medicaments, she wholly neglected the care of herself for two full Years, till at last being brought to the last degree of a Marasmus, or Consumption, and thereupon subject to Frequent Fainting Fits, she apply'd her self to me for Advice.

I do not remember that I did ever in all my Practice see one, that was conversant with the Living, so much wasted with the greatest degree of a Consumption (like a Skeleton only clad with skin); yet there was no Fever, but on the contrary a coldness of the whole body; no Cough, or difficulty of Breathing nor an appearance of any other distemper of the Lungs, or of any other Entrail; No looseness, or any other sign of a Colliquation, or Preternatural expence of the Nutritious Juices. Only her Appetite was diminished, and her Digestion uneasie, with Fainting Fits, which did frequently return upon her. Which Symptoms I did endeavour to relieve by the outward application of Aromatick Bags made to the Region of the Stomach, and by Stomack-Plaisters, as also by the internal use of Bitter Medicines, Chalybeates, and Juleps made of Cephalick and Antihysterick Waters, sufficiently impregnated with Spirit of Salt Aromoniack, and Tincture of Castor, and other things of that Nature. Upon the Use of which she seemed to be much better, but being quickly tired with Medicines, she beg'd that the whole Affair might be committed again to Nature, whereupon consuming every day more and more, she was after three months taken with a Fainting Fit and dyed [quoted in Bliss and Branch, 1960].

None of the essential features of the illness escaped Morton's experienced eye: he noted the amenorrhea, loss of appetite, constipation, loss of weight, and the patient's constant application to her books in spite of the severe cachexia, which she regarded with indifference.

Apart from the subnormal temperature, Morton could not discover any symptoms of physical illness, but he did remark on the strange decrease in appetite. The way in which the patient rejected treatment is also characteristic, and we can be sure that she was not ill-pleased to have someone prescribe an emetic. At the beginning of the "Nervous Consumption," Morton mentions that his patient was full of cares and worries, but it is a matter of conjecture whether he attributes any etiological importance to them.

Some years later, Whytt (1767), a famous neurologist in his time, and Naudeau (1789), an unknown French doctor, published further descriptions of the syndrome. However, it seems doubtful (or at least a question of definition) whether Naudeau's 35-year-old patient, who was suffering from epigastric pain and refused food and medicine for only a short period, could truly be said to have been suffering from anorexia nervosa. It was not until the second half of the last century that Morton's "Nervous Consumption" was brought to light once again; before long, however, the clinical picture of anorexia nervosa had been assigned its now permanent position in the annals of Anglo-American and French medicine. In Germany, the work of Gull and Lasègue was either soon forgotten or completely ignored. After Simmonds had published his "Über Hypophysisschwund mit tödlichen Ausgang" (1914) and "Über Kachexie hypophysären Ursprungs" (1916), cachectic anorexia nervosa cases were often diagnosed as pituitary cachexias, particularly in circles where the clinical picture of anorexia nervosa was still unknown. Suffice it to say for the moment that alarming photographs of extremely emaciated patients, who must in many cases have been suffering from anorexia nervosa, did more than a little to link cachexia with pituitary cachexia and Simmonds' disease in the medical mind.

Gull gave the first hint of his discovery in a paper read before the English Medical Society in 1868: "Thus we avoid the error of supposing the presence of mesenteric disease in young women emaciated to the last degree through *hysterica apepsia,* by our knowledge of the latter affection and by the absence of tubercular disease elsewhere" (Gull's italics). This fleeting reference gives Gull precedence over Lasègue, but he did not publish a detailed description until five years later, when it appeared in the *Medical Times and Gazette,* side by side with a translation of Lasègue's work. Gull followed up this account with two other papers on the subject in 1874 and 1888. Both he and Lasègue agreed in essence with Morton, and explained the symptoms as "anorectic emaciation as the consequence of chronic starvation." Stimulated by his colleague's work, Gull (1873a) wrote: "In fact the clinical characteristics were those of starvation only, without any signs of visceral disease. It was remarkable how long this condition often continued, and with how little change in the vital functions, the pulsation and respirations remaining at the low standard named for a year or two or more (namely: temperature ½° to a degree below normal, respirations 12, pulse 56-60). Such patients, though extremely wasted, complained of no pain, nor indeed of any malaise, but often were singularly restless and wayward if the prostration had not reached its extremest point" (p. 534).

Gull insisted that the diagnosis should be based upon the slow pulse and respiration rate, the slightly subnormal temperature, and the absence of any signs of internal thoracic or abdominal disease, all of which indicated that the emaciation could be explained only as the result of chronic starvation. Since any nourishment taken was digested well, except in extreme cases, and there was no apparent stomach disorder which could have caused the loss of appetite, Gull suggested that it would be better to speak not of apepsia hysterica, but of anorexia nervosa.

Gull's patients were three adolescent girls between 14 and 18 years of age; one died subsequently of inanition and thrombosis. In his opinion, the illness was most frequently found in young girls between 15 and 23 (Lasègue gives the critical age as 15-20). He added constipation and amenorrhea to the clinical picture, which can hardly be improved upon today. In fact, we can add only the observation that the amenorrhea does not always appear in the third stage of physical debility, as Gull supposed, but often as a preliminary symptom, before there is any noticeable loss of weight.

The reports of Gull and Lasègue merit consideration not only because of their clinical precision, their excellent descriptions of the course of the illness, and their fundamentally accurate pathogenic speculations; their contributions are also extremely valuable in pointing up their attitude toward the illness as a whole, and in distinguishing among the different forms the illness can take.

Lasègue seems to have thought that the clinical picture of "anorexia hysterica," as he called it, was invariable. The regularity of the symptoms, he said, made it perfectly possible to test the accuracy of his description; any doctor who had not come across it in his practice previously could not fail to recognize it. He also questioned whether the name "anorexia" was appropriate, or whether it would be better to speak of "hysterical inanition." His feeling was that "anorexia" put too great an emphasis on the phenomenology, and that there were several distinct types of this disturbance of appetite. In Lasègue's (1873) own words:

> Of the different stages of which digestion consists the best analyzed by patients and the least easily investigated by the physician, is the appetite for food. If the term "anorexia" is generally adopted to represent the pathological condition, it has no physiological correspondent and the word "orexia" does not exist in our language.
> The consequence is that we are defective in expression for the degrees or varieties of inappetence—the poverty of our vocabulary corresponding to the insufficiency of our knowledge [p. 144].

Lasègue distinguished among the following forms of anorexia: (1) loss of appetite without distaste, so that the patient complains of a lack of need for food; (2) distaste for certain kinds of food; (3) disgust with all kinds of nourishment, but in varying degrees; (4) loss of appetite of an illusionary nature. These patients believe that their illness is the result of inanition, and that it could be alleviated by the ingestion of food (Lasègue mentions diabetics in this group, implying that this list applies not only to the loss of appetite in anorexia hysterica; other patients, quite unlike those in group 4, have a "diminished appetite and the conviction that that food will prove injurious." The patients here, as in the former case, are acting "in conformity to this instinctive hypothesis" (Lasègue, 1873). Lasègue gives the following sketch of the psychological manifestations of the disease.

A young girl, between 15 and 20 years of age, suffers from some emotion which she avows or conceals. Generally it relates to some real or imaginary marriage project, to a violence done to some sympathy, or to some more or less conscient desire. At other times, only conjectures can be offered concerning the occasional cause, whether that the girl has an interest in adopting the mutism so common in the hysterical, or that the primary cause really escapes her.

At first, she feels uneasiness about food, vague sensations of fullness, suffering and gastralgia post-prandium, or rather coming from the commencement of the repast. . . . The patient thinks to herself that the best remedy for this indefinite and painful uneasiness will be to diminish her food. Up to this point there is nothing remarkable in her case, for almost every sufferer from gastralgia has submitted to this temptation. . . . With the hysterical, things take another course. Gradually she reduces her food, furnishing pretexts, sometimes in a headache, sometimes in temporary distaste, and sometimes in the fear of a recurrence of pain after eating. At the end of some weeks there is no longer a supposed temporary repugnance, but a refusal of food that may be indefinitely prolonged. The disease is now declared, and so surely will it pursue its course that it becomes easy to prognosticate the future. Woe to the physician who, misunderstanding the peril, treats as a fancy without object or duration an obstinacy which he hopes to vanquish by medicines, friendly advice, or by the still more defective resource, intimidation. With hysterical subjects a first medical fault is never repairable. Ever on the watch for the judgments concerning themselves, especially such as are approved by the family, they never pardon; and considering that hostilities have been commenced against them, they attribute to themselves the right of employing these with implacable tenacity. At this initial period, the only prudent course to pursue is to observe, to keep silent, and to remember that when voluntary inanition dates from several weeks it has become a pathological condition, having a long course to run [Lasègue, 1873, pp. 145-146].

Once this stage has been reached, there are only three possible outcomes: a spontaneous recovery through some unexpected joyful or sorrowful event; a compromise (i.e., a *vita minima*) that may last for years, even life; or death from some secondary infection (according to Lasègue, usually pneumonia). It is interesting that Lasègue is also of the opinion that anorexia hysterica should be regarded as an "intellectual abnormality" (perversion). In the same sense, Gull (1873b) stated: "The want of appetite was due to a morbid mental state." He stated further, "This story, in fine, is an illustration of most of these cases, perversions of the 'ego' being the cause and determining the course of the malady. As part of the pathological history, it is curious to note . . . the persistent wish to be on the move, though the emaciation was so great and the nutritive functions at an extreme ebb" (Gull, 1888, p. 140).

As soon as the description of the symptoms was complete, the problem of classification came to the forefront—a position it still holds today. As it happened, Gull did not discuss the relationship of "nervous anorexia" to other psychiatric disorders. In fact he chose the slightly ambiguous adjective "nervous," only because he wanted to emphasize that, in his opinion, the lack of appetite was caused by a "central rather than a peripheral" disturbance, and was thus the product of psychic influences.

Among his English colleagues, Gull's psychogenetic explanations found unhesitating acceptance (Dowse, 1881; Edge, 1888; Mackenzie, 1888; Marshall, 1895; and L. Stephens, 1895). Nobody gave much thought to fitting the syndrome into any definite psychiatric category. In France, however, controversy was still raging over Lasègue's use of *hystérique* in the title of a paper (1873). But Gull took the wind out of the sails of that debate by refusing to classify anorexia nervosa as a hysteria. Indeed, he had good grounds for this. As he pointed out, anorexia nervosa could be regarded as hysterical only if there were no strict adherence to the etymological meaning of the term, and thus no expectation that anorexia nervosa patients would show the rest of the symptoms of hysteria proper. It should be remembered that, at this time, hysteria was considered to be a nosological entity, with anesthesia, paralysis, and seizures as its chief symptoms. Thus Lasègue associated anorexia nervosa with hysteria because seven of the eight patients between 18 and 30 years of age on whom he based his reports had exhibited hysterical symptoms. The case of the one patient who had no hysterical attacks was complicated by the fact that her mother had suffered from paralysis (i.e., she came from a *famille névropathique*).

Lasègue's superb description of the symptomatology and disposition of his patients almost makes us forget that, like his contemporaries, he saw hysteria as a predominantly hereditary disturbance of the central nervous system. After all, Charcot himself assumed that hysteria was a hereditary disorder of the "internal capsule," producing "stigmata" and seizures, which were engendered by and released from certain "hysterogenic" zones, particularly the ovaries. However, Gull's observation that anorexia was not necessarily accompanied by the typical symptoms of hysteria was confirmed by the French writers Deniau (1883), Sollier (1891), Girou (1905), and Ballet (1907); and again the problem of nosology came to the fore. Lasègue himself had once noted that there seemed to be a connection between hysteria and hypochondriasis, and that, during the course of hysterical anorexia, both hypochondriacal and delusional ideas might appear. However, there was no complete fasting as there was in melancholia. Though it seemed commonplace enough at the time, this diagnostic distinction did much to pave the way for the more accurate differentiation of recent years.

In view of the fact that Germany was to be the source of the confusion which nearly banished anorexia nervosa from the medical scene for almost 40 years, it is interesting to note that Soltmann (1894) wrote regretfully that Gull's and Lasègue's work had not found its way into the German textbooks; he referred to an "anorexia cerebralis and central nutrition neurosis":

The source of the illness in this form of anorexia must undoubtedly be sought in the central organ, in the brain itself. However, since we cannot ascertain what kind of metamorphoses have taken place in the brain, we must content ourselves, as with many other cerebral neuroses, with the assumption of "impalpable nutrition disturbances" of the brain. They are probably due to the functional hyperemia, anemia, and stagnation of the circulation of the blood in certain cortical areas, and their ensuing consequences. Hence also, presumably as a result of severely depressive psychic influences (which in turn were due to more or less pronounced slackening of the speed of the bloodstream, vasomotor blockages in the vascular regions of the cortex, and the consequent effects on the metabolism of the gangliar cells), this remarkable reduction in the normal sensations of hunger and thirst [Soltmann, 1894, p. 6].

Soltmann's attempts at terminological reformulation contributed little to our knowledge of the clinical picture of anorexia nervosa, but he deserves mention for being among the first pediatricians to report cases of anorexia nervosa (see also Kissel, 1896). Soltmann also described perversions of appetite (pica) as "nutritional neuroses," explaining them as cortical excitation of the taste areas under the influence of severely depressive emotional states, such as anxiety, worry, sorrow, deprivation, and homesickness.

During the long search for a suitable psychiatric category for the psychopathological and somatic facts of anorexia nervosa, the strange disturbance of the nutritional drive (the anorexia) gave rise to more speculation and clashes of opinion than any other symptom. The matter was made even more complicated by the fact that loss of appetite and refusal of food are symptoms of many other mental illnesses. However, considerable progress was made in the elaboration of Gull's and Lasègue's original observations. For instance, many of the patients vomit, complain of stomach and abdominal pain, and refuse food in order to avoid the unpleasant aftermath of eating. Others have a hearty appetite, but suppress it because they are ashamed of being fat. Huchard and his pupil (1883) used this as a basis for differentiating between two categories: *anorexie gastrique* and *anorexie mentale*. Patients whose digestive troubles lead them to refuse food were assigned to the first group; patients whose mental disturbances are the major cause, they assigned to the second. The validity of this dichotomy was doubted by Sollier (1891) who introduced the unmelodious word *Sitieirgie* (derived from σιτος = food and ειργω = to refuse), which was never widely adopted.

Other writers have coined names that reflect the frequency with which the onset of the illness coincides with puberty. For example, in 1896 Régis wrote of a "cachectic anorexia of puberty" which appeared only in the female sex, and which should be regarded as related to functional disturbance of the ovaries. According to Roch and Monnier (1941), Babinski coined the term *partheno-anorexia,* while Wissler (1941) was the first to suggest the present German word, *Pubertätsmagersucht* (puberal emaciation). The syndrome's "trial by baptism," however, is over at last. In the French literature, *anorexie mentale* has won the day; Anglo-American writers prefer the traditional "anorexia nervosa"; in Germany, *endogene Magersucht* (Falta, 1927; Stroebe, 1938) or *psychogene Magersucht* (Bergmann, 1944; Heni, 1951) are frequent, although the most favored is *Pubertätsmagersucht*.

Another eminent writer who contributed to contemporary knowledge of anorexia (and incidentally helped to complicate the problem of classification) was Janet. His report of the case of "Nadia" was published under the title "Obsessions de la honte du corps" in the 1908 edition of *Obessions et la Psychasthénie*. Unfortunately, Nadia's anorexia was due to an obsessional neurosis. The following features are taken from L. Binswanger's (1957) summary of the case: excessive dieting, from dread; no anorexia, but a suppression of appetite; occasional surreptitious breakthroughs of instinctual drives, followed by terrible pangs of conscience; hours of daydreaming about banquets, in order to participate in them in the imagination and thus trick herself into not feeling hungry. Fear of becoming fat is related to this patient's rejection of her mother. She demanded that everybody notice her thinness, and developed a "question-compulsion." She considered overweight, or even eating, to be immoral; she was ashamed of possessing a body. Nadia tried to conceal her sex and to give the impression of being masculine.

> Janet believes, however, that we should not speak of an inversion here, because Nadia would be just as ashamed of being a boy. She wants to be completely sexless, apparently even completely bodiless, because every part of her body arouses the same feeling. Her refusal of food is only a particular manifestation of this feeling. . . . But the real reason why Nadia dreads being ugly is that, according to Janet, she fears people are laughing at her, do not love her, and think she is different from others [L. Binswanger, 1957, pp. 155-157].

Nadia did not want to become a woman; she wished to remain a child.[1] In fact, she not only suspected people of laughing at her, but suffered from hypochondriacal illusions. In reality, she was pretty and slim, and yet she had managed to persuade herself that her face was puffy, red, and covered with pimples.

The relationship between hypochondriasis and hysteria had already been discussed by Lasègue, who also shrewdly observed that, although the melancholic's refusal of food was absolute, the loss of appetite in hysterical anorexia was only relative. In discussing melancholia, Freud also made an interesting comment on the same theme; in a manuscript probably written about 1895, but not published until 1950, he wrote:

> The nutritional neurosis parallel to melancholia is anorexia. The well-known *anorexia nervosa* [Freud's italics] of girls seems to me (on careful observation) to be a melancholia occurring where sexuality is undeveloped. The patient asserts that she has not eaten simply because she has no appetite and for no other reason. Loss of appetite—in sexual terms, loss of libido [Freud, 1887-1902, p. 103].

[1] Some years later, Leibbrand (1939) pointed to the dread of growing up as the chief symptom of the disease. Yet this fear is the catalyst of many illnesses, particularly for persons who become ill as the result of *"an inhibition in development* . . . as soon as they get beyond the irresponsible age of childhood"* (Freud, 1912b, p. 235). Dread of growing up as a precipitating cause of illness, or an inhibition in development, in Freud's sense, does not provide more than a preliminary foothold for our understanding. Such problems as the connection between the contents of anxieties and the form taken by the illness only begin at this point.

In the treatises of Gilles de la Tourette (1895) and Déjérine and Gauckler (1911), *anorexia mentale* is differentiated from the loss of appetite in various psychoses, and from melancholic and paranoid anorexia. Observations made by R. Dubois in 1913, however, brought this classification into question. He reported a 16-year-old girl who showed all the signs of anorexia mentalis in the early stages of dementia praecox.

The following French psychiatrists took part in a conference held to clarify the relationship between anorexia mentalis and dementia praecox: Seglas, Charpentier, Delmas, and Dupouy; they held widely differing opinions. In contrast to Charpentier, Seglas offered a bleak prospect for anorexia mentalis sufferers (excepting only hysterics), predicting a 13-15 per cent mortality. Delmas reported a case of anorexia mentalis in a girl of five. Finally, Dupouy described a seventeen-year-old girl, whose illness had also been diagnosed as anorexia mentalis, but who showed other signs of negativism besides a growing distaste for food. These were bouts of mutism, inhibition in learning, and antagonism, along with a decrease in emotivity, intelligence, and the capacity for work; all of this was accompanied by underlying delusions. Dupouy's thesis was that the root of every true anorexia nervosa was an *idée fixe* and a pathological hyperaffectivity. The position of French psychiatry on the question of anorexia mentalis was eventually summed up in a symposium led by Crémieux in 1942.

During this time, however, Simmonds' publications, which had won almost instantaneous approval, were setting all previous hypotheses to nought, so that for several decades the classification and pathogenesis of anorexia nervosa were completely obscured theories of pituitary malfunction. No sooner had Simmonds' reports made the psychiatric headlines, than anorexia nervosa was written off as a functional disturbance of pituitary origin (i.e., a hormonal-endogenous disorder). This explanation was particularly popular in Germany, but it also found friends in America (Berkman et al., 1947; Farquharson and Hyland, 1938; Richardson, 1939; Calder, 1932), in England (Sheldon, 1937;

Langdon-Brown, 1937), and in France (Bickel, 1936; Loeper and Fau, 1936).

In retrospect, especially in the light of the work of Bahner (1954) and Jores in 1955, it seems amazing that the two clinical pictures should ever have become confused. A whole chain of misidentifications must have come together to create such a tragedy of errors. Nevertheless, after the appearance of Simmonds' work, it became practically impossible for any physician to gain hearing for his unfashionable ideas, no matter how experienced he was in the treatment of this disorder or how convinced he was that at least a large number of anorexia nervosa cases must be of purely psychic origin (Löffler, 1955).

But since the anorexia nervosa syndrome was unknown, and there were no facilities for the type of psychotherapy that might have systematically unravelled its psychogenesis, it is not surprising that Simmonds' pathogenetic theories provided a ready-made explanation for the cachexia of anorexia nervosa.

As every physician knows, it is only too easy for a diagnosis to confirm one's expectations, and after Simmonds' work had taken the medical world (especially in Germany) by storm, it was "pituitary" and "endocrine" that came to the tip of the tongue when cachexia revealed itself, not "abnormality of the ego" (Lasègue, 1873). Nevertheless, there were some dissident voices even then. As early as 1926, Reye pointed out that there could be no question of cachexia in the early stages of Simmonds' disease, and that even Simmonds' first case apparently did not display any signs of cachexia until the last nine-year phase of the illness.

Fortunately, the problem of distinguishing between the two diseases is no longer a matter for debate; pituitary genesis is becoming an anachronism (Broser and Gottwald, 1955), and pituitary implantations are rarely prescribed any longer (Ewald, 1954). Yet the dust raised by the confusion continued to becloud the issue for many years—even after the attention of physicians and endocrinologists had been drawn to a multitude of anomalies.

But the matter does not end there. Even though the field is once again open, anorexia nervosa remains an extremely difficult syndrome to classify. This is particularly well illustrated in the case described by L. Binswanger (1957) under the title "The Case of Ellen West," which he and Bleuler diagnosed as schizophrenia simplex. Other cases of anorexia nervosa have been diagnosed by Kraepelin as melancholia, and by an unnamed psychiatrist as progressive psychopathic constitution. In 1948, Zutt gave the following definition of anorexia nervosa:

> The whole clinical picture . . . proves that it is essentially a hormonal disorder. . . . Anyone who has had any real experience of endogenous psychoses will soon be struck by the similarity in form between these psychotic symptoms and those of anorexia nervosa. Indeed, every experienced psychiatrist is well acquainted with the usually gradual changes in personality that set in without any apparent reason, the development of the typical syndrome and its variations, the sporadic fluctuations in health and behavior, the periodic improvements that occur either simultaneously or in connection with various attempts at therapy, the gradual convalescence, the retarded development of personality, or the years of persistent, grave illness in spite of every therapeutic aid. *This is just the kind of thing that happens in the manic-depressive psychoses, the schizophrenias, and obsessions* [my italics].

The sad fact is that the "pituitarists" left in their wake numerous publications on the differential diagnosis of anorexia nervosa and Simmonds' disease, each excellent of its kind, and each giving a lucid, graphic description of what anorexia nervosa is *not*. Naturally, modern refinements in diagnostic technique make it possible to give a far more accurate picture of the psychophysiological changes taking place in an advanced cachexia due to starvation. But the anorexia nervosa patient's stubborn refusal of food, and his eccentric attitude toward meals and milieu alike cannot be explained simply in terms of endocrine secretions, as Heni did (1951) when he diagnosed anorexia nervosa *per exclusionem* and suggested the synonym, "psychogenetic anorexia." He believed that the mental attitude was the expression of a palpable biological situation, and that every other symptom was controlled by the missing nutritional drive. According to this theory, in a large number of cases, the lack of appetite would have to be construed as the result of unfavorable environmental influences. Heni also believes that Gull's first description is still valid for post-puberal anorexia, and that no modifications of any importance have been made since. "Some of them are psychically quite inconspicuous, but all are very sensitive people" (p. 31). In order to stimulate the absent nutritional drive, Heni recommended as sole treatment "dosage with Desoxycorticosterone as an acetate" (p. 50).

Formulations like this are the inevitable outcome when diagnosticians become more concerned with ascertaining what a disturbance is not, than with plumbing the depths of the psychogenesis. This is the reason why *per exclusionem* diagnoses of anorexia nervosa are as inadmissible as they are unsatisfactory, and why they contribute nothing to the solution of the mystery of the vanishing nutritional drive, to which every other factor is subordinate, as Heni so rightly says. For it is precisely this problem which has remained unsolved. Pointing to the correspondence between the loss of appetite in depressive psychoses and in anorexia nervosa, Bergmann (1934) said, "the lack of nutritional drive demands a functional interpretation which is still to come" (p. 124).

There can be no doubt that we must pay tribute to the exemplary clinical picture provided by Gull and Lasègue. On the other hand, even they were not able to give more than a fragmentary answer to such crucial questions as why these patients do not eat, how and why their nutritional drive has vanished, and why there is no drive satisfaction. In fact, until now we have not had enough insight into the psychogenesis of the symptoms even to be able to construct a systematic psychotherapy, and, in consequence, treatments have consisted primarily of isolation and forced feeding. True, measures like these do often have a psychotherapeutic effect—in some cases they even lead to an improvement or a cure—but they have contributed little to the illumination of the psychogenesis. Not one of Lasègue's patients, as he himself confesses, was able, even after convalescence, to give a precise description of her feelings during the illness, or of the sensations that had driven her to avoid food. Each one simply repeated the typical answer, as she had done during the course of the illness, "I just could not, it was stronger than I was, and anyway I felt perfectly well" (Lasègue, 1873, p. 386). The "subjective phenomena of [these patients'] morbid psychic life" (Jaspers, 1963) remain veiled in mystery; their rejecting attitude shields them from observers glimpsing into their world of feeling, and successfully defeats any attempts at understanding the symptoms within their experiential framework.

Since the patients themselves have not altered since Lasègue's day, we are left with only two alternatives: either to make do with the usual answer, or to apply a system—psychoanalysis—which has based an entire theory on discoveries of attitudes like these. For as Freud (1914a) expressed it, "The theory of psycho-analysis is an attempt to account for two striking and unexpected facts of observation which emerge whenever an attempt is made to trace the symptoms of a neurotic back to their source in his past history: the facts of transference and of resistance" (p. 16). Bahner's extensive survey has shown only too clearly what the consequences are when these discoveries are ignored or set aside.

In effect, we are left with a Hobson's choice. Only explanations based on the fundamentally defensive nature of the anorexia nervosa patient's rejecting attitude have any constructive value in practice. This is borne out by the fact that the fruitful method of psychotherapy described in this book has resulted from the attempt to understand the symptoms as the typical form taken by a conflict, or as the way in which conflict is overcome in the realm of conscious experience.

The conclusions set down here are grounded in personal observation and a knowledge of the psychopathology, psychogenesis, and psychosomatology of anorexia nervosa, based to a large extent on the teachings of psychoanalysis. At the same time, every opportunity has been taken to make comparisons with the findings of other methods of investigation in this field, concluding with the most recent contributions, those of the existential-analytical school of analysis. Indeed, it is remarkable how faithfully the history of anorexia nervosa, right up to the present day, has mirrored the changing fashions of medicine—from Morton's isolation and fattening diets to frontal leucotomies (see Chapter 2).

Anorexia nervosa, or anorexia mentalis, has been renamed as often as it has been discussed. Since the essential contours of the syndrome have been mapped out already by Gull and Lasègue, there is no particular purpose in deviating from the names these authors thought appropriate; we would do better to devote our energies to increasing our knowledge of the pathogenesis, and hence power for healing, rather than wasting time coining new Graeco-Latinisms.

This brief historical survey will be amplified in the succeeding chapters; the following points are of particular importance.

1. The physical symptoms of anorexia nervosa were attributed by all workers, from Gull and Lasègue in 1873 to Simmonds in 1914, to the effect of undernourishment caused by an anorexia of psychic origins.

2. During this period, the disease was often described and classified, particularly by French authors. However, to date, anorexia nervosa has never been assigned any definite place in a psychiatric nosology.

3. The confounding of anorexia nervosa with Simmonds' disease has caused confusion since 1914. There are essential differences between the two illnesses.

4. Because of this confusion, the pathogenesis of the clinical picture has been sought in an altogether wrong direction; therapies have been derived from false premises. The fact is that there was no set method whereby the psychogenesis of this syndrome, as postulated by Gull and Lasègue, could be investigated. Thus there has been no knowledge of the psychic situation on which to construct an adequate psychotherapy. The contribution made by psychoanalysis will be presented in connection with my own research.

✖ 2 ✖

Definition, Incidence, Physical Symptoms, and Therapy

A. Definition

The signs which distinguish anorexia nervosa from all other illnesses that result in emaciation and loss of weight are as follows: (1) the age of onset is usually puberty or postpuberty; (2) the patients are almost all female; (3) the reduction in nutritional intake is psychically determined; (4) spontaneous or self-induced vomiting occurs, usually in secret; (5) amenorrhea usually appears either before or, more rarely, after the beginning of the weight loss; (6) constipation, sometimes an excuse for excessive consumption of laxatives, speeds up the loss of weight; (7) the physical effects of undernourishment are present. In severe cases, they can lead to death.

Thus the symptomatology of anorexia nervosa can be divided into three categories: (a) psychopathological characteristics, (b) functional disturbances which are not direct consequences of malnutrition, (c) the physiological effects of the mentally determined fasting. These closely resemble the effects of enforced starvation. It is remarkable, nevertheless, that anorexia nervosa patients rarely show starvation, edema, and avitaminosis. Even in advanced stages of marasmus, they are usually active and full of energy. Apart from this, the somatopsychic effects of anorexia nervosa and starvation are very similar, although anorexia nervosa patients will go to great lengths to conceal their condition. If we compare, for example, the reminiscences of a man starving in a prisoner-of-war camp (Schilling, 1948) with the autobiographical novel of Lore Berger (1944), an anorexia nervosa sufferer who eventually committed suicide, or the results of partial starvation reported from the Minnesota Experiment (Schiele and Brozek, 1948; Franklin et al., 1948) with psychotherapeutic observations of anorexia nervosa patients, one remarkable fact stands out: in every case, the theme of food preoccupies the subject to the exclusion of everything else. In both groups, anorectic or otherwise, illusional wish gratifications were experienced; in the case of my patients, "larder" anecdotes give vivid proof of the clandestine pleasures in which these usually ascetic personalities indulge. Indeed, they become the victims of precisely the same drive breakthroughs as people starving through no choice of their own.

The essential and most obvious hallmark of anorexia nervosa is a psychically determined refusal of food. This is sometimes a partial refusal, sometimes absolute, as in the more severe cases. For both types, it leads to cachexia, often even death. Amenorrhea—or, in some cases, dysmenorrhea and constipation—occupy a special position in the pathogenesis because they often make their appearance before any loss of weight is apparent. They are fairly constant symptoms; there are even some doubts as to whether we should diagnose anorexia nervosa in their absence. But historically, and even on occasion today, anorexia nervosa presents dilemmas of its own, many of which have incalculable importance for this comparative study of incidence, results of therapy, prognoses, and several other problems.

The historical survey in the previous chapter must have made it obvious that medical diagnosis of a typical case is no longer any great problem. But this has been so only since the reappraisal and confirmation of Gull's and Lasègue's classical diagnoses enabled us to recognize the functional defects (hypothermia, hypotonia, lowered metabolism) as side effects of malnutrition. The "severe emaciation and a certain similarity in physical appearance make these patients look so alike that they might have come from the same family" (Löffler, 1955). This constellation of psychopatho-logical symptoms has now been classified as a syndrome (Mas-serman, 1941). Any differences of opinion regarding the illness as a whole are chiefly due to the fact that certain psychiatrists favor certain nosological categories.

In the light of these considerations, anorexia nervosa will be referred to throughout as a syndrome, and the question of its re-lationship to other psychiatric nosological units will be postponed to a later chapter.[1] Obviously, the diagnosis becomes less and less certain, the more indistinct the outline of the syndrome—for in-stance, when an older girl or a woman experiences considerable loss of weight, but without menstrual disturbances or constipa-tion, or when the refusal of food appears in conjunction with a depressive or schizophrenic psychosis. In contrast to the majority of writers (e.g., Nemiah, 1958; Durand, 1955), who keep to the classical descriptions as their blueprint—anorexia,[2] loss of weight, amenorrhea, or menstrual disturbances—Bliss and Branch (1960) chose their cases according to the sole and, in my opinion, totally inadequate criterion of a "loss of 25 pounds or more . . . attribut-able to psychological causes" (p. 25). This approach resulted in neurotics and psychotics, men and women, adults and adolescents, all being lumped together in one sample. A total of 22 patients was examined, including four men and 18 women. Of the latter, 14 were married and had at least one child (pp. 29-31). The ages ranged from 15 to 54. The most common diagnoses were obsession-al neurosis, schizophrenia, and depression.

The outstanding disadvantage of this kind of all-embracing definition is that it avoids the nosological problem associated with

---

[1] Von Baeyer (1959b) speaks of a specific type of illness which is self-enclosed. According to him, the characterological deviations of anorexia nervosa do not correspond to those of the endogenous, psychotic type of reaction, the phasic fluctuations of the cyclothymic, or the schizophrenic group. Nor could it be any longer designated as a neurosis, "for the disturbance emanating from the disease pierces so deep into the structure of bodily existence that in severe cases it leads to the end of life itself."

[2] It has already been stated that these patients often merely make a show of having no appetite. For brevity's sake, the term anorexia will be used, never theless.

the difficulty of deciding whether a four-year-old child with a psychogenic anorexia (Sylvester, 1945) can be said to have anorexia nervosa any more than an eighteen-year-old patient of mine (case 29), who showed all the typical eating conflicts of anorexia nervosa, but was not constipated. Perhaps it would be misleading to proceed from the similarities among the various psychological motives that—at different stages of life, and in otherwise different psychiatric clinical pictures—impel a person to refuse to eat. In this way, we would have the advantage of being able to consider the loss of appetite in schizophrenia, depression, and anorexia nervosa all together, and our psychological lens would not be obscured from the very beginning by a nosological classification (see Chapter 7, section H). But, although Bliss and Branch have not shouldered this responsibility, sooner or later some form of differentiation must be made. We must be able to distinguish, for example, between the psychopathological processes at work in the anorexia of an "Augustus" and other types of anorexia. However much the clinical picture may vary, that kind of differentiation is indispensable. In spite of all the borderline cases, anorexia nervosa is typically an illness that appears at the onset of, or soon after puberty. In fact, a completely accurate diagnosis can be made only when the physician has been successful in gaining sufficient insight into the connections between the psychopathological and functional symptoms. As can be seen from the cases described here, there is no single unvarying psychopathological picture (Palmer et al., 1952). Loss of appetite, as might have been expected, does not belong to any one particular form of neurosis. Nevertheless, the clinical picture of anorexia nervosa, as described above, is easily recognized as a syndrome in line with Nemiah's (1958) definition of the term.

B. General Incidence

From the literature alone, the incidence of anorexia nervosa is extremely difficult to ascertain, especially since, as Sheldon (1939) pointed out, about half the published cases of anorexia nervosa have appeared under other names, such as Simmonds' disease. However, since accurate records of the frequency of Simmonds' disease exist, we can make a reasonable estimate of the relative frequency of anorexia nervosa. Escamilla and Lisser (1942) examined all the available literature for cases of Simmonds' disease. Of a total of 595 case histories, one group (A) of 101 could be verified from the pathological-anatomical aspect. A second group (B) comprised 158 cases which showed the typical clinical signs of an insufficiency of the anterior lobes of the pituitary (loss of weight, loss of sexual function, asthenia, lowering of basal metabolic rate by at least 20 per cent), while 180 putative cases made up the third group (C). The remaining 155 cases could not be classified from the scanty material provided.

Escamilla and Lisser (1942) compiled a very detailed statistical analysis in which they compared the findings from 20 accredited anorexia nervosa cases with the findings in Groups B and C. They eventually arrived at the conclusion that there were probably many anorexia nervosa cases in the latter groups. The number of unchallenged cases of Simmonds' disease is quite small as compared with the number of authenticated anorexia nervosa cases published to date. In 1942, the total roll of cases of Simmonds' disease in the literature of the entire world stood at 101. Where anorexia nervosa is concerned, it is quite a different matter. Comparatively large numbers can be discovered in many individual records, such as those of the Mayo Clinic where, between 1917 and 1929 alone, 117 cases were diagnosed. In the Maudsley Hospital (Kay and Leigh, 1954), over a period of 20 years, 38 cases of anorexia nervosa were admitted (four of whom were male), and Ryle (1936), in London, saw a total of 51 cases in his private practice, an average of four a year.

Above and beyond these figures, there is certainly a large number of very light cases which do not require hospitalization. Some do not even get as far as the doctor's waiting-room. Certainly anorexia is being diagnosed far more frequently than in previous decades, but whether this indicates a greater prevalence is hard to say.

Distribution between the Sexes

Anorexia is much more common among women than among men. Both Morton and Gull have each described a male case but, to judge from recent reports, only a small proportion of cases occurr in men (Kay, 1953; Rüegg, 1950; Ryle, 1939; Laboucarié and Barrès, 1954). Bliss and Branch (1960), after surveying the literature, estimate the distribution at 89 per cent : 11 per cent, but these figures may be too heavily weighted on the male side, since Bliss and Branch presumably also applied their own wide definition in their survey. A closer look at Ryle's (1936) study also reveals a lower percentage of male patients; one of his cases was psychotic.

Age of Onset

The illness generally begins at puberty or postpuberty. However, there can be no doubt that the anorexias of childhood are not all mere tantrums, but often resemble anorexia nervosa in their psychopathological structures. As far back as 1894, Collins described a seven-and-a-half-year-old girl who suffered from the same symptoms as many older patients. Also among the earliest publications on the subject are the studies of Kissel (1896), who cured an eleven-year-old girl, and Forchheimer (1907), who cured a boy of 12 who had been anorectic for three years. Comby's (1909, 1912) reports are also interesting in this context. He observed cases not only among girls at and before puberty, but also several among infants, and he considered infantile anorexia to be the same disease as the anorexia of adolescence. One of his patients was a nineteen-month-old girl whose hunger strike took several weeks to quell, but eventually disappeared. Milner (1944), Rank et al. (1948), Rose (1943), Sherman (1929), Sylvester (1945), and others have given detailed accounts of the psychogenesis of severe anorexias in small children. Incidences of the illness before puberty appear in the reports of Catel (1940), Lutz (1947-1948), Rüegg (1950), Trefzer (1939), Wissler (1941), and others. For adolescents and adults, Bliss and Branch (1960) have calculated an average age of onset at 21½ years. This figure has been reached on the basis of a random selection of 245 female cases of anorexia nervosa from the literature. The critical age must lie between puberty and the first half of the thirties. Older patients are rare, and the diagnoses dubious except, of course, where the anorexia nervosa symptoms begin in puberty and merely grow worse with age.

C. Physical Symptoms and Differential Clinical Diagnosis

As has been stated already, the symptomatology of anorexia nervosa corresponds largely to that of exogenous undernourishment. The brief survey below follows that of Bahner (1954).

Morton (1689) described an extreme case of anorexia nervosa in the following words (see also Chapter 1): "... like a skeleton only clad with skin." All over the bodies of these girls, the bones jut out. The creases in the skin around the mouth and lips are so deep that they look like hags. Every curve has disappeared, the stomach is hollow, the limbs like sticks. Even when the patient stands with her legs together, there is a yawning gap between her thighs.

The skin is dry and scaly, and has a greyish tinge that admits no confusion with the alabaster whiteness of the complexion of Sheehan's syndrome. While the loss of axillary and pubic hair is a *sine qua non* of pituitary insufficiency, it rarely even becomes sparse in anorexia nervosa. Occasionally, there is a slight loss of the dry, brittle hairs from the head and the secondary hair, but the body hair never disappears completely. Often the loss of weight is accompanied by an increase of lanugo hair on the chin and upper lip. Decourt (1953) traces this hypertrichosis to an increase in the androgen-estrogen ratio, and Altschule (1953) agrees with him. In actuality, in average and not yet severely cachectic cases, the same hyperactivity in the adrenal cortex can be observed as in laboratory animals during experimental starvation.

The concentration of 17-ketosteroids tends to be at a low level only in extreme cachexia, and is otherwise normal or above normal.

It is possible that the lanugo hair that appears in individual cases is only a constitutional variant. But since it frequently develops at the same time as the emaciation, and disappears with the reappearance of menstruation—i.e., at the moment when the androgen-estrogen balance has been restored—the explanations of Decourt and Altschule are probably correct for the majority of cases. Certain clinical observations confirm this. In Case 22, hypertrichosis developed side by side with the illness. This female patient was treated for amenorrhea, while still in a state of considerable inanition, by the family doctor, who gave her a course of injections. Regular repetition of this treatment was followed by the reappearance of menstruation, which stopped again when the treatment was discontinued. The hypertrichosis, however, responded to the treatment and receded.

The nails are sometimes brittle and the teeth loose. Apart from gingivitis, which points to a vitamin deficiency (see section on avitaminosis, this chapter), the carious condition of the teeth of anorexia nervosa patients seems to be due chiefly to neurotic fears of seeing a dentist, which sometimes last for years on end. In spite of their extreme loss of substance and muscular atrophy, there is a strong urge for activity. But we should not let this impressive capacity to be up and doing in spite of severe cachexia blind us to the facts; this should really be regarded as an almost hypomanic hyperactivity (Baeyer, 1959b). Every patient wants to trick herself and her investigator into thinking that she is a kind of Jack-in-the-box. Even those who have no energy do not show the sluggishness and slowness of panhypopituitarism (Bleuler, 1954).

Body temperature, heartbeat, breathing, and basal metabolism are all shifted into lower gear, just as the early authors remarked. The temperature falls to 35°C., and the rate of heartbeat to about 50 per minute; the blood pressure values are under 100 mm. Hg. Peripheral vasomotor disturbances are almost always present and take the form of acrocyanosis. There is a tendency toward chilblains, and in one case the development of gangrene necessitated the amputation of several finger joints (Kretschmer, 1958).

Only severe cases show any considerable degree of anemia; Evans' (1939) patient (erythrocytes: 1 million per cu. mm.; hemoglobin: 20 per cent) was exceptional.

As far as gastrointestinal disturbances are concerned, it is almost impossible to ascertain to what extent the subjective complaints of discomfort are based on fact and caused by stubborn constipation. This discomfort is a mixture of hypochondriacal fears and compulsive purification ceremonies, including enemas several times daily, vomiting, and rationalizations concerning abstention at mealtimes. Since the patients are aware only of the conscious motives which drive them to refuse food, they cast around for likely explanations of their "lack of appetite," and eventually locate them in the abdomen. The complaints they voice are many and varied, so that they may even succeed in leading the physician astray into the operating theater.

Constipation may very well have existed before and independently of the anorexia nervosa. However, in most cases it is a concomitant of the illness. It is caused by psychogenic factors and is exacerbated by the mechanical effects of a subnormal intake of food and drink. In my experience, the mental factors outweigh all others; in fact, I have had ample opportunity to observe how constipation decreased with improvement in the patients' psychic state—even though their intake of food and drink remained minimal and their weight did not increase (see Cases 2 and 5).

The metabolic findings in anorexia nervosa are unspecific; the lowering in the metabolic rate tallies with the general economy measures being taken by the organism. Thus the decrease in basal metabolic values should not be measured against normal rates, since extreme emaciation brings a completely different set of standards into force (Bahner, 1954, p. 1147). It has also been proven that there is no hyperthyroidism (Bliss and Branch, 1960, p. 90), for not only has no myxedema ever been observed in a case of anorexia nervosa, but there is also a normal uptake of I^{131}.

The anorexia nervosa patient's metabolism of carbohydrates has been the specific subject of studies by Evans (1939), Ross (1938), Sheldon (1937), and Small and Milhorat (1944). Different values were found for preprandial and postprandial blood sugar levels. Ross regarded slowly falling alimentary hyperglycemia—during oral or intravenous administration of glucose—as a disturbed glucose tolerance due to inanition. These investigations have as yet shed no new light on the diagnosis of anorexia nervosa. Indeed, Bahner (1954, p. 1114) feels that even routine checks of blood-sugar level, basal metabolic rate, and specific-dynamic effect are wholly superfluous.

Edema due to loss of albumen is equally rare (Berkman et al., 1947). Since there is frequently an oligodipsia, dehydration occurs, while parenteral hydration or increased intake of fluids results in water retention. The researches of Rossier et al. (1955) have also contributed valuable information to the therapist. In contrast to the acidosis of states of starvation of short duration, long-lasting malnutrition results in alkalosis and loss of potassium (the lowest recorded potassium count in one of Rossier et al.'s cases was 7.6 mg. per cent).

Menstruation

The early onset of amenorrhea proves that anorexia nervosa is not a simple matter of undernourishment. The abrupt cessation of the menses, even before loss of appetite and weight are apparent, is the rule in a large number of cases. Other cases start with irregular or scanty periods, and amenorrhea does not appear until the loss of weight is far advanced. In light cases, the disturbance usually progresses no further than irregularities (Case 8). However, there are exceptions to this rule. Bliss and Branch (1960) describe a thirty-year-old patient of long standing who was still menstruating regularly, though feebly, even after she had reduced to a weight of 45 pounds. Sometimes a dramatic event coincides with the sudden cessation of the menses (Case 27), but in the typical case nothing out of the ordinary has happened, and the amenorrhea sets in unheralded by any abnormal reaction to a life experience. Decourt et al. (1950) agree by and large with the figures given in the next chapter (see Table 7). Only three of their 32 cases had developed anorexia nervosa after menstruation had been interrupted by overwhelming emotion; the remaining 29 were menstruating normally before they fell ill. In fact, amenorrhea was the first sign of illness in 19 out of 24 cases. Only one case continued to menstruate for ten months, until cachexia developed suddenly. The reappearance of the menses was as sudden and unexpected. Nineteen of Decourt's patients began to menstruate again spontaneously. Five were treated with hormones, but only briefly and after there had been some increase in weight, so that the writer concluded that the menses would have started again just as well without hormone treatment. My own observations (see Tables 22 and 23) confirm this judgment.

Decourt was able to follow up eight of his cases. One patient went eight years without menstruating (her drop in weight was from 130 to 60 pounds); she recovered without any hormone therapy. It might almost be said that the beginning and end of the illness are signaled by the amenorrhea and the reappearance of menstruation respectively. Decourt believes that the amenorrhea of anorexia nervosa is caused by one of two processes. Abrupt cessation of the menses because of emotional shock is considered to be derived from a sudden outpouring of adrenalin in the same sense as Cannon's "emergency reaction." The more common form of amenorrhea, which does not accompany any apparent trauma, he explains as a form of psychogenic or hypothalamic amenorrhea, as described by Reifenstein (1946). Reifenstein's theories are also cited by Kelley et al. (1954) and Moulton (1942).

Kelley et al. distinguish among four types of secondary amenorrhea: hypophyseal, ovarian, endometrial, and the amenorrhea of systemic disturbances such as hyperthyroidism and Addison's disease. By this definition, the amenorrhea of anorexia nervosa would belong to the ovarian type, and indeed a lack of estrogens has been established by Papanicolaou on the basis of vaginal smears (Kelley et al., 1954; Moulton, 1942; Koller, 1954; and Case 30). Ovarian is distinguished from hypophyseal amenorrhea by the fact that the gonadotropic hormone of the anterior pituitary is produced normally, and there is therefore no anterior pituitary deficiency. Reifenstein (1946) suggests that this should be seen as a psychogenetic or hypothalamic amenorrhea. He bases this on the hypothesis that psychic influences cause a partial damming up of hypothalamic excitation, so that the correlation between the follicle-stimulating hormone (FSH) and the luteinizing hormone (LH) of the gonadotropic hormone of the anterior lobes of the hypophesis undergoes a change, to the detriment of the LH. In this way, it is possible to explain why, despite normal or only slightly lowered secretion of gonadotrophin, the change in correlation prevents maturation of the ovum. The results of Papanicolaou's vaginal smears and the atrophy of the endometrium agree closely with the analysis of the phenosteroids carried out by Decourt, for most of these cases lay in the zone which is usually characterized by the diminished function of the follicles, i.e., under 30 gamma. However, the fact that the primordial follicles remained intact prognosticates reversibility (Menze, 1947). It is interesting to note that the amensis of internees and refugees (Martius, 1946) comes about in much the same way. In concentration camps and prisoner-of-war camps (Sydenham, 1946), it has been observed that amenorrhea usually appears before loss of weight and is indubitably due to emotional influences (Kelley et al., 1954; Stieve, 1940). However, it will be unnecessary to pursue any further the psychosomatic problems that emerge from these considerations, and also the hypothesis of a hypothalamic or psychogenic amenorrhea, since these will be taken up again in Chapter 7 (section B). For the moment, we can assume that the amenorrhea of anorexia nervosa is due to ovarian insufficiency. According to Reifenstein (1946), this deficiency occurs because of changes in the gonadotropic relationship brought about by psychogenetic-hypothalamic-hypophyseal influences.

Avitaminosis

Both H. A. Palmer (1931) and Smitt (1946) have encountered symptoms of beriberi in anorexia nervosa; Aggeler et al. (1942) reported the presence of purpura; Clow (1932) observed signs of pellagra.

Intercurrent Illnesses

In spite of severe and chronic inanition, anorexia nervosa patients have a capacity for resistance that is astonishing. Nevertheless, complications are frequent. Anorexia nervosa is sometimes accompanied by tuberculosis resulting in death (Galdston, 1956; Osgood, 1938), thus refuting Boss's (1954) suggestion that the two illnesses are mutually exclusive. Stäubli-Fröhlich (1953) reports a purulent pyelonephritis and a lobar pneumonia.

D. Therapy[3]

The method of treating the starvation cachexia adapted here was to take whatever emergency steps were necessary on the spot, and to follow them up with psychotherapy as soon as possible. "Psychoanalysis should not be attempted when the speedy removal of dangerous symptoms is required as, for example, in a case of hysterical anorexia" (Freud, 1905c, p. 264). According to the investigations of Rossier et al. (1955), one of the chief dangers is a low level of potassium in the blood. But apart from the alleviation of the acute symptoms of starvation of this undoubtedly chronic illness, the organic therapy of anorexia is of little more than academic interest. It is undeniable that all sorts of medication have had favorable results in individual cases, only to fail and be abandoned in others. But it is in the nature of the illness that remedies of every kind can be understood only as having prevailed by suggestion, or accidentally. This is not a solution, but

[3] The section on pathological anatomy is omitted from the English translation, since it gives only negative findings. These have already been described very well by Bliss and Branch (1960).

rather a statement of the problem. Wherever spontaneous improvement does occur—whether because of some natural process of development or of a change in the environment that proves favorable for a particular patient at a particular time, or as the result of suggestion—in psychoanalytic terms, some change has taken place within the id-ego-superego relationship and the interpersonal relations. This is true, no matter how minute the structural shift; something must have altered to make these patients begin to eat normally. Before we can penetrate to this something, we must gently pare off the prevarications that have so successfully veiled the inner world of these patients.

It is a recognized fact that, so long as these patients are not *in extremis*, there is no actual lack of appetite. The proof of this is the attacks of frenzied gluttony which often assume unusual forms. For instance Lore Berger (1944), an anorexia nervosa sufferer whom we have already mentioned, described in her autobiographical novel the pleasure with which she ate yellow shoe polish, while being repelled by the odor of ordinary food. Wulff (1932) investigated similar oral drive breakthroughs and their connection with addiction, from a psychoanalytic point of view. It is possible that patients who have hitherto disguised their gluttony, or have discharged their inner tensions in a regressive way through hyperactivity, are able to reveal their greed after taking adrenal cortex hormones because now the blame can be put on the drug. It is no longer their own guilt-laden, drive-ridden desires breaking out, but the fault of the physician and his medicines. This may be pure speculation, but after close perusal of Heni's (1951) report it does not seem too great a flight of fancy. Heni's Percorten treatments were based on the supposition that his patients were suffering from a real lack of appetite. This approach must have strengthened their tendency to conceal their hunger until some drug made a breakthrough permissible. No wonder Heni discovered that Percorten had only a questionable effect on the less severe cases. Doubtless, these patients had not yet retreated far enough from the natural satisfaction of their hunger to need magic elixirs. In any case, the spell wears off quickly. Even in the case Heni described at length, the guilty feelings recurred, and the patient was "really upset about her increase in weight" (p. 47). Of course, this is the typical attitude of a patient who has not overcome her conflicts about eating. Success like Heni's, however obtained, must in all fairness be weighed against a whole row of uncontested failures. Broser and Gottwald (1955, p. 17), for example, report the appearance of symptomatic psychoses during the course of a "substitution treatment" (Praephyson, Percorten, Progynon, or Cortisone and ACTH in three cases of anorexia nervosa).

In other words, Percorten is no better and no worse than any other of the pharmaceuticals that have been applied in the treatment of anorexia nervosa; after a brief success, each has been challenged and then has lapsed into desuetude again. There have been innumerable nine-day wonders of this sort since the time of Gull and Lasègue. In any case, substitution treatments—whether with pituitary implantations (Kylin, 1943; Krauel, 1942), with ACTH (Musso et al., 1952), adrenal cortex hormones (Broser and Gottwald, 1955), or *thyroida sicca* (Berkman, 1943)—are based on false premises. In principle—according to an endocrinological opinion (Altschule, 1953; Perloff et al., 1954)—hormonal substances not only have absolutely no specific value in anorexia nervosa, but are even contraindicated, since the reduction in endocrine activity is an adaptive mechanism designed to conserve energy. Nevertheless, Thorn et al. (1950) reported excellent results when they administered ACTH to their patients.

Treatment with small doses of insulin is equally suspect. Since there is a tendency toward hypoglycemia, these patients are particularly sensitive to the drug. Although this sensitivity is not the same as the sensitivity in hypophyseal insufficiency, it can, in severe cases, lead to a dangerous hypoglycemic coma, albeit seldom with fatal results (Decourt, 1953; Gilbert-Dreyfus and Mamou, 1947). Of the five out of thirty patients described here, who had received small doses of insulin before commencing treatment in the hospital, one patient went into hypoglycemic coma. As for the rest, the psychological barrier that prevented them from eating was proof against stimulation by insulin. Besides, even when such patients do eat something under insulin, this success is often short-lived, since they are quick to find ways and means of reversing the deed, e.g., vomiting, laxatives, increased activity, or refusal of meals they might otherwise have accepted.

It would be well beyond the scope of this work to furnish a complete list of all the therapies that have been tried out on anorexia nervosa patients during the last hundred years. "Every variety of treatment has been given these patients, limited only by the preconceptions and ingenuity of the physician and the availability of pharmacologic agents" (Bliss and Branch, 1960, p. 106). Indeed, a full list would do more credit to the "pharmacologic agents" than to the ingenuity of the doctors and laymen who have tried to coax these patients to eat.

There are two methods of treatment which deserve further discussion: the psychiatric methods of electroshock and insulin shock, and leucotomy. Apart from isolated cases, Laboucarié and Barrès (1954) have reported the largest number of cases treated with electroconvulsive therapy—i.e., 39 out of a total of 50. In conjunction with isolation of the patients, who were mainly nonpsychotic anorexia nervosa cases, this method has resulted in occasional success. This is probably also the largest group of anorexia nervosa patients to have been given systematic courses of electroshock therapy. The purpose, as Laboucarié and Barrès put it, was to unblock the inhibition mechanism that had been set up by psychic agents. Carmody and Vibber (1952), Glazebrook et al. (1956), Moore et al. (1948), Sargant (1951), and Sifneos (1952) have all reported successful leucotomies on chronic cases. In every case, the criterion had been a gain in weight and, particularly in Sifneos's case, good social adjustment. Often, after the operation, anorexia nervosa turns into bulimia, and the problem around eating remains (Sargant, 1951). Carmody's patient became a chain smoker (60 to 80 cigarettes a day).

The ingenuity of the physicians who have been successful in achieving cures without any significant use of drugs is another matter altogether. Indeed, even laymen have had cures attributed to them. Schur and Medvei (1937), for example, quote the case of a woman who had been ill for 16 years in spite of orthodox treatment, but who regained 30 pounds in weight and began to menstruate again under the care of a nature healer who prescribed homeopathic remedies and vaginal massage. In some respects, we might even take note of a lack of ingenuity on the part of the practitioner—especially the one who advised one of my patients (Case 28) to seek salvation in marriage!

On only one aspect of treatment is agreement almost unanimous: patients must be removed from their home environment. Every other facet of the therapy provides material for endless contradictory advice. For instance, we are advised to increase caloric intake gradually, beginning with 1300 calories (Berkman, 1945), to show no particular concern about weight, vomiting, and diets (Palmer and Jones, 1938; Small and Milhorat, 1944), or to feed immediately (Hurst, 1939). On occasion, forcible feeding has been shown to have dangerous results, even to provoke attempts at suicide (Richardson, 1939; Stephens, 1895). Venables (1930) stayed by his patients at mealtimes, regardless of the time it took, and advised postponement of any discussion of psychological motives, so long as the physician did not lose patience. Ryle (1936) considered psychiatric methods undesirable. He felt that it was enough to insist in a firm but kindly way that sufficient food be consumed. In one case, the patient's sudden realization that he would die in a few days led to a cure (Odlum, 1938). Other patients remain completely indifferent to this knowledge and do die (e.g., four of the 37 cases that Ryle followed up and six of a group of 38 reported by Kay). Delay (1949) put his faith in narcoanalysis.

Obviously, there is an infinite number of contrary opinions about the nature of anorexia nervosa, and about the methods the physician should employ in order to overcome his patient's resistance. It may be that the variety of failures to do either bears witness not only to the intractability of the patients, but to a very human failing—the mistake of attributing too much importance to one's own pet theories.

✠ 3 ✠

Clinical Survey of Thirty Cases

A. General Remarks

This study is based upon the examination and treatment of 30 anorexia nervosa cases referred to the Heidelberg University Psychiatric Hospital over a period of about ten years, from April 1950 to December 1959. Actually, 41 patients were examined during this time; but unfortunately, not all of them could be included in this study, since in 11 cases the notes and case histories were incomplete.

Might these missing cases have changed the emphasis or perhaps even have invalidated the calculations and follow-up studies? The question springs naturally to mind, but this potential source of error has been fully investigated, and the findings indicate otherwise. Indeed, there seems to be every justification for asserting that, even if these cases had been included, the same conclusions would have been reached on every score, particularly in regard to the etiology, treatment, and prognosis of the disease. Admittedly, the one extreme case among the 11, who died at home of progressive marasmus, might have affected the emphasis, but that omission was fully compensated for by the favorable progress reports received concerning the other ten—some with, some without psychotherapy. Thus there is no reason to believe that the restriction of the analysis to only 30 of the patients in any way falsifies or misrepresents the situation as a whole. The diagnostic criteria which determined the choice of patients are given in Chapter 2.

The next three chapters will be devoted to case histories, divided into two groups; five patients are described at some length.

For professional reasons, all data that might have betrayed the real identity of a patient have been altered. In order to preserve the anonymity of the patients, their family backgrounds have sometimes been deliberately distorted, and occasionally even events of psychological significance—such as the death of a close relative—have had to be disguised. However, these expedients have had little or no effect on the tables of the fathers' professional and social status. All the patients have been given pseudonyms and case numbers; in this chapter they are usually referred to by the latter.

Of the five case histories presented, those of Henriette A. (1) and Sabine B. (2) are prefaced by psychogenetic reconstructions, whereas case histories 3, 4, and 5 (Chapter 6) are given in an abridged form. In many instances, essential material for a psychodynamic schema could not be obtained, but wherever deductions are presented as formulae (as is true particularly in cases 1, 2, and 5), copious circumstantial evidence is also provided, primarily because it is not always easy to understand psychoanalytic schemata and relate them to empirical observations without some frame of reference. Thus particular pains have been taken to present a balanced view of both "schema" and "evidence."

Unfortunately, it also proved impossible to express the psychic symptomatology as a curve; in several cases, the information available about the personality development before illness was not reliable enough to permit, for instance, the drawing up of a table of some of the early "oral" symptoms or individual peculiarities. Similar difficulties were experienced during the computation of the follow-up reports. In fact, when viewed as a whole (this group is probably a representative sample), anorexia nervosa patients exhibit such a hodgepodge of character traits, and the psychopathological picture has so many aspects, that it would be senseless to try to tabulate them (see Chapter 7). It is quite untrue to say, as did F. A. Dubois (1949), that all anorexia nervosa patients are obsessive, or that they are all conscientious, ambitious, and exceptionally energetic, as Rahman et al. (1939) would have us believe. Certainly, some of the patients showed symptoms of severe obsessive neuroses (2, 28), and many were hyperactive; but others were listless by contrast, and two even bedridden (2, 24). In short, it is possible to find a completely random assortment of phobic, obsessive, depressive, and hypochondriacal symptoms among them. The nonmanic fear of poisoning exhibited by two patients (2, 24) will be discussed further in the last chapter.[1]

It will also be noted that all description of the outward appearance of the patients has been omitted, and no photographs have been supplied.[2]

Table 1 gives a survey of the data for 29 female anorexia nervosa patients and one male. Nineteen patients received psychotherapy; 11 were merely examined.

Since the heights of the patients before illness could not be ascertained, the following comparisons are based on the average height at examination. At that point the average patient was 19 years old and about 5 ft. 5 in. tall. The average lowest weight was just under 79 lbs. It is interesting to note how little the patients' heights and weights before illness varied from those of normal girls who had remained healthy. For instance, their average weight at the onset of the illness (two and one-half years previously) was 112 lbs. If allowances are made for the fact that they were an average of only 16½ years old at the time, and thus probably somewhat smaller, this figure coincides exactly with the

---

[1] Although the rigid descriptive diagnostic criteria of traditional German psychiatry are not applicable from a psychodynamic point of view, I have tried to be as conservative as possible in making diagnoses, in order to exclude all other forms of anorexia.

[2] Morton, Gull, and Lasègue remarked on a trait that these patients shared —namely, the typical way in which inanition divested them of individuality and made them all look alike.

TABLE 1

General Survey

1	2	3	4	5	6	7	8	9	10
No.	Age	Height	lbs.	lbs.	lbs.	lbs.	lbs.	% weight loss	lbs.
1	19	5′ 8¾″	141	115	102	121	88b	24	121
2	26	5′ 3⅜″	127	*132*	73	88	73e	46	unknown
3	18	5′ 10⅛″	150	143	84	99	84e	42	148
4	27	5′ 8⅛″	148	143	104	114	104e	28	121
5	18	5′ 5″	130	121	83	79	64d	47	77
6	18	5′ 1⅜″	118	*132*	66	95	66e	50	95
7	42	5′ 2¼″	126	112	58	75	55d	49	unknown
8	19	5′ 3″	123	117	99	—	—	15	110
9	25	5′ 3¾″	129	121	60	88	60e	50	unknown
10	21	5′ 3¾″	126	101	54	76	53e	46	unknown
11	15	5′ 1″	106	66	53	58	46a	30	77
12	21	5′ 2⅝″	122	110	88	88	84b	24	unknown
13	14	5′ 3″	116	115	82	82	82e	28	110
14	16	5′ 1⅜″	111	99	82	79	79d	20	unknown
15	15	5′ 7¾″	135	*146*	116	118	117e	20	137
16	15	5′ 2⅝″	115	*119*	103	108	90b	24	112
17	14	5′ 5⅜″	125	110	91	93	90e	18	123
18	14	5′ 1¾″	112	104	75	87	68d	34	104
19	17	5′ 6⅛″	135	117	66	66	66d	44	130
20	13½	5′ 6½″	130	99	68	—	—	32	119
21	20	5′ 5¾″	133	126	84	—	—	33	154
22	18	5′ 10⅞″	154	143	99	—	—	68	110
23	16	5′ 6⅛″	129	*132*	75	—	—	43	123
24	14	5′ 3¾″	119	*150*	93	—	—	38	130
25	22	5′ 2⅝″	122	*128*	82	—	—	35	unknown
26	23	5′ 5¾″	136	115	95	—	—	17	unknown
27	27	5′ 7¾″	147	149	77	—	—	46	64
28	28	5′ 5¾″	139	126	82	—	—	35	unknown
29	18	5′ 11¼″	157	123	93 } 78 }	105 } 93 }	77e	38	121
30	17	5′ 7¾″	139	126	64			49	

Columns refer respectively to 1, case number; 2, age at examination; 3, height at examination; 4, normal average weight; 5, weight before illness (figures in italics = above average weight); 6, weight at beginning of therapy, or at examination; 7, weight on discharge; 8, lowest weight (corrected), b = before, d = during, a = after therapy, e = at examination; 9, per cent weight loss; 10, weight at follow-up.

norm. According to Geigy,[3] an average fifteen-year-old girl of 5 ft. 4 in. should weigh about 112 lbs. On the other hand the average healthy nineteen-year-old who is 5 ft. 5 in. tall weighs about 132 lbs.—53 lbs. more than the average patient at examination!

Seven patients were slightly overweight before onset, but only by about 3 to 14 lbs. According to these tables, then, their physical constitution scarcely deviated from the mean. The weight losses indicated refer to the weight before illness, not the normal weight. Reckoned in terms of the normal weight tables, the smallest loss of weight (15 per cent) would correspond with a decrease of 20 per cent, and the maximum loss (50 per cent) with a drop of 55 per cent. The average loss of weight calculated against the weight before illness was 34.3 per cent.

The results of these calculations, combined with the age at menarche, which also did not deviate from the norm, but appeared at the average age of 13¾ among my patients (see Table 6), lead incontestably to an all-important conclusion: *anorexia nervosa patients have normal physical constitutions before illness. There is not one shred of evidence for constitutional hypogonadism.* This verdict is borne out by the observations of several other writers. Thus we can completely dismiss the widespread fallacy that the root cause of anorexia nervosa is a constitutional anomaly, or a failure of hypophyseal or ovarian origin. In fact, Bahner (1954) has already proved that these arguments are unsound. They have arisen, it seems, from two false conclusions: the first, generalization from small samples; the second, the assumption that a symptom, such as genital atrophy, observed during a disease cachexia, must be due to a prior defect—in this case, a constitutional anomaly. (There will be some further discussion of this problem in Chapter 7.)

The family trees of the five cases reveal the following: schizophrenia (maternal great-uncle); depression (mother); suicide (grandfather); suicide (father); anorexia nervosa (maternal

---

[3] The normal weights are based upon the "Scientific Tables" of J. R. Geigy. These tables have been issued by the Life Extension Institute of New York.

TABLE 2

History of Mental Illness in Family

	Number of Patients	Per Cent
present	5	17
not present	25	83
	30	100

aunt). It is not possible to predict whether the family histories of anorexia nervosa patients would reveal a significant number of deviants, even if apparent eccentricities were taken into account. Kay and Leigh (1954) have rejected the hypothesis that anorexia nervosa has a genealogical relationship to cyclothymic states, even though among the 76 parents of their 38 patients, 26 had characteristics which set them apart from the norm, and there was one case of an affective psychosis. It is interesting that two of my cases (3, 7) had sisters who suffered from anorexia nervosa. Dührssen (1950-1951) also reported a pair of twins who fell ill of the disease, and Souques (1925) told of two sisters who both died of it.

TABLE 3

Professional Status of Father

	Number of Patients	Per Cent
unskilled manual worker	1	3
skilled manual worker	4	13
tradesman	3	10
shop manager	1	3
clerical worker	6	20
executive	1	3
small-scale, self-employed businessman	2	7
large-scale, self-employed businessman	3	10
salaried professional	4	13
self-employed professional	5	18
	30	100

Table 3 shows that the anorexia nervosa patients stemmed mostly from middle-class families.

As far as the familial environment is concerned, it is worth noting that all the patients were born in wedlock except one. The parents of more than half of them are still living. It is also interesting that six patients lost their fathers in infancy and that only one widowed mother remarried. In the other five cases the mothers remained single, except for one who is living with a man. All these last cases were particularly severe (1, 5, 6, 19, 22, 24). The one illegitimate girl eventually acquired a stepfather, but only after infancy. Another patient was born in wedlock, but her parents divorced soon afterward, and the mother remarried while her daughter was still small. In all the rest of the cases, the families seemed perfectly average, at least on the surface. It is also worthy of note that none of the mothers had died while the patients were children.

TABLE 4

Siblings

	Number of Patients	Per Cent
only children	5	17
1st of two children	5	17
1st of three children	1	3
2nd of 2 children	6	20
2nd of 3 children	4	14
2nd of 4 children	2	7
2nd of 6 children	1	3
3rd of 3 children	2	7
3rd of 4 children	1	3
3rd of 4 children and stepchildren	1	3
3rd of 5 children	1	3
3rd of 15 children	1	3
	30	100

This table shows that the patients mostly grew up in families with 2 or 3 children.

TABLE 5

Age at Onset of Illness

	Number of Patients	Per Cent
13 years	2	7
13½ years	3	10
14 years	5	17
15 years	2	7
16 years	6	20
17 years	3	10
18 years	3	10
20 years	2	7
21 years	1	3
23 years	1	3
24 years	1	3
25 years	1	3
	30	100

The average age at the beginning of the illness was 16½. From this table we can see that the age groups 13–15 and 16–18 are the most strongly represented.

Tables 6, 7, and 8 show the pattern of the menstrual changes. The menarche occurred at an average age of 13¾. Two patients, 14 and 15 years old respectively, had still not menstruated. In the majority of cases, the cycle was regular until the beginning of the loss of weight. In four cases, the amenorrhea preceded the rest of the symptoms. It must be emphasized, however, that the time of menarche corresponds throughout with the norm. The usual age in Central Europe in 1948 was calculated to be between 13 and 14 years (H. A. Müller), and more recent Anglo-American studies have confirmed this (see Israel, 1959). The two patients of 14 and 15 who had never menstruated had fallen ill at 13 and 14 respectively. Since it is the fact of menarche which enables us to make claims about the functional capacities of these patients, my figures (which do not vary from the mean) completely disprove any theories which presuppose a constitutional endocrine insufficiency before illness.

TABLE 6
Menarche

	Number of Patients	Per Cent
not yet appeared	2	7
at 12 years	5	17
at 13 years	7	22
at 13½ years	2	7
at 14 years	6	20
at 15 years	2	7
at 15½ years	2	7
at 16½ years	2	7
not known	1	3
not applicable (male)	1	3
	30	100

TABLE 7
Menstrual Cycle before Illness

	Number of Patients	Per Cent
regular	18	60
irregular	4	13
regular, heavy, painful	2	7
irregular, painful, heavy, scanty	3	10
none	3	10
	30	100

TABLE 8
Onset of the Amenorrhea

	Number of Patients	Per Cent
before loss of weight	4	13
with loss of weight	18	60
after loss of weight	4	13
irregular periods	1	4
none	3	10
	30	100

TABLE 9

Gastro-enteric Symptoms

	Number of Patients	Per Cent
present	28	93
not present	2	7
	30	100

Almost every patient complained of *constipation,* with or without stomach trouble. The scanty intake of food was often explained by feelings of fullness or all sorts of hypochondriacal ailments. Attacks of *emesis* could not be expressed in statistical form, since the patients who were merely examined, or treated for a short while, and who denied having this symptom, may have been vomiting in secret.

Tables 10, 11, and 12 show that most cases had already been diagnosed as anorexia nervosa during previous hospitalizations. But to assume that this diagnosis involved a predominantly psychogenetic etiology would be far from the truth. The patients were sent to this unit after an average of two and one-half years of illness. In most instances, their condition had become static, both objectively and subjectively. The number of abortive attempts at therapy were legion.

TABLE 10

Previous Hospitalizations

	Number of Patients	Per Cent
none	7	23
one	15	50
two	5	17
four	2	7
six	1	3
	30	100

TABLE 11

Diagnosis at Previous Hospitalizations

	Number of Patients
anorexia nervosa	18
Simmonds' disease	3
hypophyseal insufficiency	1
cyclothymic depressive phase	2
psychogenic reaction	1
disturbance of hypophyseal diencephalic regulation	1
no diagnosis	1

TABLE 12

Previous Therapies

	Number of Patients	Per Cent
general supportive treatment	5	18
hormones	2	7
gen. supp. and psychotherapy	1	
gen. supp., hormones, and pituitary implantation	3	10
gen. supp. and insulin	3	10
gen. supp., hormones, and insulin	3	10
hormones, insulin, and pituitary implantation	1	3
gen. supp., hormones, and psychotherapy	1	3
gen. supp., hormones, psychotherapy, insulin, and insulin shock	1	3
no previous therapy	5	17
	25	100

Precise indications of the type of hormone treatment have been omitted; the commonest was a combined dosage of adrenocortical, anterior pituitary, and ovarian hormones. Three patients had undergone attempts at psychotherapy. In the case of Paula T. (20) this was of short duration; Lore D. (28) was treated for a long time as an outpatient; Erna V. (21) spent about two months in the hospital. In none of the 25 cases who were given treatment of some kind did any improvement ensue.

B. *Results of Follow-up Reports*

The follow-up reports were obtained in Autumn 1959, by either examination or questionnaire. In five cases, the family doctors concerned furnished the information about the progress of the illness. In order to give the reader a clearer picture of the periods of time involved, the data have been listed under eight headings (Table 13). Column 7 gives the time since examination or since therapy was terminated. "Total Time" (Column 8) indicates the span of time from the beginning of each individual illness, regardless of the course it took.

Follow-ups were available in 18 cases. Seven patients did not answer the questionnaire; one patient had died; in the four remaining cases, therapy had either not been terminated, or not for a sufficient length of time. The figures in Column 8 are important because they indicate, in each individual case, the total time since the beginning of the illness. The length of psychotherapy, if there was any, can be calculated from the difference between the figure given in Column 8 and sum of Columns 4 ("Length of Illness before Examination") and 7 ("Follow-up"). For example, Case 1, Henriette A., had been ill for three years when therapy began. There is no follow-up, since therapy had not yet been terminated at the date of inquiry. Column 5 shows that she was treated for about two years. In Case 2, Sabine B., the follow-up covers a period of four years; she had been ill for five years when therapy was commenced. Thus the difference between the sum of these two periods (nine years) and the figure in Column 8 (12)—three years—is the duration of psychotherapy in her case.

Several remarks can be made about the seven cases where no follow-up reports were obtained. Four of these cases (7, 25, 26, 28) had histories of 24, 7, 5, and 11 years of illness, respectively, when they came here. This circumstance makes it possible to take these cases into consideration even without a completed questionnaire. The course of Case 9 had already been under observation during about a year of psychotherapy, and the prognosis did not bode well. Neither of the remaining two cases (12 and 14) was under treatment very long, and the relatively brief duration of

TABLE 13

General Survey

1	2	3	4	5	6	7	8
No.	yrs.	yrs.	yrs.	mos.	hrs.	yrs.	yrs.
1	16	19	3	24	289	—	5
2	21	26	5	30	304	4	12
3	16	18	2	3	46	7	9
4	24	27	3	1½	35	7	10
5	16	18	2	24	440	—	4
6	14	18	4	18	282	—	5½
7	18	42	24	2	35	0	24
8	18	19	1	—	—	½	1½
9	23	25	2	8	259	0	3
10	20	21	1	2	28	—	1
11	14	15	1	2	40	1½	2½
12	20	21	1	½	11	0	1
13	13½	14	½	1	14	2½	3
14	14	16	2	1	28	0	2
15	14	15	1	3	53	5	6
16	14	15	1	2	53	5	6
17	13½	14	½	3	72	3	3½
18	13	14	1	9	72	3	4
19	16	17	1	3	30	5	6
20	13	13½	½	—	—	4	4½
21	16	20	4	—	—	1	5
22	17	18	1	—	—	1	2
23	15	16	1	—	—	6	7
24	13½	14	½	—	—	5	5½
25	15	22	7	—	—	0	7
26	18	23	5	—	—	0	5
27	25	27	2	—	—	½	2½
28	17	28	11	—	—	0	11
29	17½	18	½	6	120	2	3½
30	16	17	1	—	—	—	1

0 = no answer
— = not applicable

Key to table:
Column 1 = case number
Column 2 = age at onset
Column 3 = age at examination
Column 4 = length of illness at examination
Column 5 = length of psychotherapy
Column 6 = number of hours of therapy
Column 7 = follow-up report
Column 8 = total time since onset of illness

their illness did not permit any predictions. Thus five of the cases omitted from my follow-up report came from the category of particularly severe illness, and all the statistical averages would change for the worse if these cases were to be included. It should be noted that it was not possible to estimate in every instance the direction of the change that would take place in each table if these seven cases had been incorporated.

TABLE 14
Course of Illness

	(a)	*(b)*	*(c)*	*(d)*	*Total*
cured	4	1			5
improved	13	2	2		17
unchanged		1	2		3
worse	1				1
died				1	1
excluded (only examined and without follow-up)				3	3
	18	4	4	4	30

(a) patients from whom a follow-up was obtained
(b) patients still under treatment, or who have just completed treatment
(c) patients treated in this hospital, but who did not return the questionnaire; the "course" refers to their condition at the end of treatment.
(d) patients who were examined but did not return the questionnaire; also, one female patient who died shortly after examination

The progress of the illness was judged on the basis of the changes in the chief symptoms of the syndrome. For purely practical reasons, the concept of cure has been measured against clinical rather than psychotherapeutic or psychoanalytic yardsticks. It was impossible to do otherwise, since a satisfactory psychoanalytic and diagnostic evaluation of the degree of improvement or cure demands a depth of knowledge that cannot be gathered from a follow-up interview and questionnaire alone.

Cured: From a psychotherapeutic point of view, of these five patients (1, 3, 4, 17, and 24), three also recovered satisfactorily (1, 3, and 4). The length of illness—up to the disappearance of even the mildest symptoms—was four (1) and five (3 and 4) years. Cases 17 and 24 recovered spontaneously, after one and two years, respectively—psychotherapy was of no avail in these cases.

Improved: Four of the 13 cases in column (a)—8, 13, 15, and 18—showed extensive improvement after one (8 and 13), one and one-half (15), and two (18) years of illness, but there were some residual disturbances in social contact and appetite, or some constipation. Of the nine remaining cases, five (16, 20, 21, 23, and 29) still have marked symptoms; in cases 2, 11, 19, and 22 these are still severe. Their condition has certainly improved, but after an average of five and a half years of illness, they are still ill, or at least extremely disturbed, and the prognosis is unlikely to be anything but bleak.

Of the two patients in column (b), Case 6 has improved remarkably after five and a half years of illness, and her prospects are decidedly hopeful. Case 10, after one year of illness, has achieved only a good increase in weight.

Both of the cases in column (c) put on weight, one (7) after 24 years of illness, the other (9) after two years. It seems unlikely that either will improve to any satisfactory degree now.

Unchanged: Case 5 has remained unchanged despite intensive psychotherapy, and the prognosis remains unencouraging after three years of illness.

There was no alteration in the condition of the cases in column (c)—12 and 14—after one and two years illness, respectively; but in both instances psychotherapy was terminated after only a short while.

Worse: Case 27—merely examined in this hospital—had been ill for two years; she has since undergone treatment in two other hospitals, and has lost even more weight.

Died: Case 30.

Excluded: When Cases 25, 26, and 28 arrived for examination, they had already been ill for seven, five, and eleven years, respectively. These cases have had consistently grave symptoms for a long time, and the prognosis is correspondingly unpromising.

On the basis of this breakdown it can be said that, of these 30 anorexia nervosa patients, five have been clinically cured, after an average of two and a half years of illness. In a further group of five cases, a far-reaching improvement could be observed and, at the time of the follow-up, the illness was taking a more or less encouraging course.

Of the remaining 20 cases, two cases (12 and 14) had had too short a period of illness and therapy for assessment. One case ended in death. Seventeen cases continued to exhibit symptoms, some superficial, some grave; some have taken a turn for the better, some for the worse. The only patient who has deteriorated to any degree (Case 29) has been treated in two other hospitals during the six months between examination here and the follow-up investigation. She has also decreased in weight from 77 to 64 pounds.

The following tables give a survey of developments in the social lives and symptomatology of these patients, as far as this can be expressed statistically. The body weights shown on the follow-ups are given in Table 1 for easier comparison. (In these tables 100 per cent = 22 patients, since seven did not return the questionnaire and one died.)

TABLE 15

Marital Status

	Number of Patients	Per Cent
married in the meantime	1	5
unchanged	21	95
	22	100

TABLE 16

Children

	Number of Patients	Per Cent
given birth in the meanwhile	2	9
no children	20	91
	22	100

TABLE 17
Interpersonal Relationships

	Number of Patients	Per Cent
good	5	23
satisfactory	4	18
bad	13	59
	22	100

TABLE 18
Professional Adaptation

	Number of Patients	Per Cent
good	10	45
satisfactory	3	14
bad	9	41
	22	100

TABLE 19
Eating Disturbances

	Number of Patients	Per Cent
removed	9	41
improved	7	32
unchanged	2	9
worse	1	5
bulimia	3	13
	22	100

TABLE 20
Gastro-enteric Symptomatology

	Number of Patients	Per Cent
removed	6	27
improved	6	27
unchanged	2	9
constipation still present	6	27
never present	2	10
	22	100

It is obvious that tables 15 to 20 give only a rough outline of the development revealed by the follow-up reports. In addition, it should be mentioned that four patients have been treated unsuccessfully in other hospitals since: three patients (19, 26, and 27) twice each because of the basic illness, Sabine B. (2) for attacks of hysteria (hyperventilation tetany). Severe secondary illnesses did not appear, and none of the patients who improved to any extent, or were cured, has suffered from any serious illnesses in the meantime, except for angina and the common cold.

Since most of these patients were about 21 years old at the time of the follow-up, the fact that 21 are still unmarried is hardly significant. However, it is probable that almost all have some residual difficulties in personal relationships. Judging by more stringent standards, only Agnes C. (3) and Gertrude D. (4) can be said to have overcome completely the subtler characterological side- and after-effects of the disorder on mind and body. Both of these girls underwent successful psychotherapy.

TABLE 21
Length of Amenorrhea

	Number of Patients	Per Cent
3 months	1	5
6 months	1	5
12 months	1	5
18 months	2	9
24 months	2	9
3 years	1	5
4 years	1	5
5 years	3	13
menstruating only with hormones	3	13
still amenorrheic	6	27
not applicable	1	4
	22	100

Four of the six cases who still have no menstruation had a secondary amensis which had already lasted for at least two, and up to a maximum of twelve years (Cases 2, 5, 10, and 27). In two cases (11 and 18) aged 16½ and 17 respectively, primary amenorrhea was still present, although all the other symptoms had been allayed.

In the seven cases from whom no subsequent reports were obtained, the amenorrhea had lasted once for one year, twice for two years, and once each for seven, eleven, and twenty-four years before examination; in the last instance, there were severe irregularities.

It is particularly interesting to note that ten patients recommenced menstruating spontaneously—in three cases, after five years without a period. In order for this to happen, the body weight must have returned to, or at least be approaching normal, and there must have been adequate mental reorientation. Apparently, the degree of mental adjustment determines whether the weight increase, brought about by the retreat of the psychically conditioned refusal of food, causes the menses to reappear. A closer examination of the three groups—"menstruation after hormone treatment," "only after hormones," and "still amenorrheic"—proves the point. The course of illness in Cases 8 and 24 makes it very unlikely that a short, oral hormone treatment could have had any significant influence on the return of the menses. Kathe X. (24) was already convalescing on her own, and has had a normal confinement since then. Rosa H. (8) was the mildest case examined; she had not ceased menstruating, but was slightly irregular. It is impossible for a hormone treatment to arrest severe illness. Hormone treatments are useless unless the necessary biological and psychic conditions for the return of the menses are present—and then they are superfluous. In fact, there is widespread agreement on this point among most modern writers (see Chapter 2, "Menstruation"). Lore C. (28), for example, remained amenorrheic during the entire 11 years of her illness, in spite of continual hormone therapy of every kind.

The most intriguing of all are the three patients who could not menstruate without some form of cyclic treatment. Beate V. (22) was still well underweight at the time of the follow-up (110 lbs.

with a height of 5 ft. 11 in.). In contrast, Therese P. (16) had returned to her normal weight three years previously, but still remained without menstruation except for isolated bleedings produced by hormone treatments. Lena S. (19) became overweight after an anorectic phase which lasted several years. She is now dieting in order to keep down to a weight of about 154 lbs. Without regular hormone treatments she immediately stops menstruating. In both these last cases, the illness has lasted for six years; they provide excellent illustrations of the fact that *mens sana* comes before *corpore sano*. In both cases, we are probably encountering some form of "somatic compliance" (S. Freud, 1905a, p. 40), although no one yet knows its nature. The same factor is undoubtedly active in those cases who, for example, also undergo a phase of overweight, and who are neurotically disturbed to a considerable extent, but who menstruate perfectly normally.

C. *Results of Psychotherapy*

The task of evaluating the therapeutic effect of medicinal or mental treatment on the progress of chronic illness must always be approached with great care. Martini's methodology (1953) gives a good idea of the multiplicity of aspects that must be considered. It is not enough to ascertain that improvement has been achieved during, and by means of, psychotherapy. Research carried out at the Menninger Clinic has shown how much importance must be attached to questions of the method and purpose in this type of treatment (see Wallerstein et al., 1956). Indeed, the history of the organotherapy of anorexia nervosa makes it abundantly clear that this is a problem which cannot be neglected. In view of the preeminently psychogenetic etiology of anorexia nervosa, we can assume that the successes of purely physiological treatments—apart from removal of the acute effects of starvation, such as a lack of potassium in the blood and starvation edema—should be explained in terms of unconscious transference, processes in the patient-doctor relationship, and hence "suggestion."

Of course, it would be impossible to compare psychotherapy with other methods which have a psychotherapeutic-suggestive purpose, since no one can solve an equation consisting exclusively of unknowns.

The first question in every individual case must be: what has helped here; why is the patient eating now, and why did she refuse to eat before? In examining the literature as a whole, one is astonished to see how many writers—except those proceeding on psychoanalytic and psychodynamic principles—are reluctant to face these questions squarely. Fundamentally, it is essential that the therapy be determined by the diagnosis, and not be subject to the physician's whim (see Chapter 2, "Therapy"). But whether a more enlightened understanding of the genesis of symptom formation can be turned immediately to profit is quite another matter. Freud (1916-1917) once remarked, referring to the therapeutic value of knowledge, that:

> The Doctor's knowledge is not the same as the patient's and cannot produce the same effects. All we have to add is that the knowledge must rest on an internal change in the patient such as can only be brought about by a piece of psychical work with a particular aim [p. 281].

Of course, the problem of making the physician's knowledge fruitful for the patient is no easy task, nor is it one that should be undertaken lightly. Nevertheless, there can be no doubt that knowledge of the psychogenetic relationships is an essential prerequisite for all therapeutic measures; in this area there is much interaction.

> The basic fact remains that, through psychotherapeutic intervention and the experience of effect and countereffect in relation to the patient, perceptions become possible which can never be gained through *mere observation, without the venture of therapeutic experimentation.* . . . They [the perceptions] are, it is true, limited by the practical horizon, but, to the extent they contribute experience, they introduce something essential for the completeness of *psychopathological theory* [Jaspers, 1948, p. 791; *my italics*].

Except in fields of research that have been enriched by psychoanalysis, too many writers have shied away from the "venture of [psycho]therapeutic experimentation" in anorexia nervosa as well as in many other illnesses. It is no wonder that so little progress has been made beyond those facts which can be gleaned by mere observation, and which have been familiar to every physician since the days of Gull and Lasègue.

Of course there are anorexia nervosa patients with whom psychotherapy cannot even be initiated, and who might well benefit from hypnosis, for example, although in von Eiff's case the relief was temporary (1957). On the other hand, anorexia nervosa patients, especially very simple and pseudo-imbecilic cases like Sabine B. (2), often present the therapist with a Herculean task. It is a strong temptation—as any analyst with experience in hypnosis will understand—to give preference to a nicely controlled hypnosis, conducted with flawless correctness in both the initial observation period and the therapeutic examination.

As it turns out, both the initial observation time and therapeutic examination demanded by Martini (1953) are superfluous. As far as it is possible, without an "individual diagnosis" (Siebeck, 1949)—which can only be obtained by therapeutic methods in anorexia nervosa cases—to make predictions about the spontaneous course of the illness (i.e., "individual prognosis"), we can assume an average "initial observation period" of two and a half years. As we have seen, the average length of illness before examination of the patients described here was two and a half years, and the most varied attempts at treatment had been of no avail. We cannot rule out the possibility that in many cases the self-curative tendencies were becoming stronger, and that the analyst started from an advantageous position. But these intrapsychic processes do not necessarily have any influence on the symptoms themselves, so that even a constant body weight during a long period of "preliminary observation" is not of itself a reliable criterion. For, despite this seeming stagnation, some change may have taken place; some adolescent conflict may have lost its sting over the years, and analysis can now begin under more favorable circumstances.

These considerations must be taken into account whenever any claims about the success of psychotherapy are made. Certainly, some courses of psychoanalysis have lasted for many months, or years, and we would be wrong to overlook the part played by time and the *vis medicatrix naturae*. As Freud (1916-1917) put it, "We must not forget that the patient's illness, which we have undertaken to analyze, is not something which has been rounded off and become rigid but that is still growing and developing like a living organism" (p. 444). On the other hand, it would be equally mistaken to ignore the fact that in many cases there is very little room left for the forces of nature, and that often living functions have indeed become frozen into rigid structures. To understand and correct this part of nature—or perhaps it is anti-nature —and bring it into motion again, is a task of almost superhuman dimensions, as the more detailed case histories illustrate. To appeal to the *vis medicatrix naturae,* particularly in the realm of mental disturbances, is often just the simplest and most comfortable way to soothe a troubled conscience when the problems of handling resistance and transference have been avoided. In every other circumstance great pains are taken to support nature in every way. We do not count the hours we devote to some of our patients, since we believe that the firsthand experience gained from *difficult* patients and *long-term* treatment will guide us eventually to the best techniques. Indeed, every scientific attempt to reach a better knowledge of the psychogenesis of this clinical picture can only improve our technique.

Table 13 indicates the number of hours of treatment and the length of the psychotherapy. Apart from one case, all the patients were treated first in the hospital, seven cases continuing after release. The only break in therapy was a period of ten months in Case 29. The patients were treated for five hours a week while hospitalized, three to five hours a week after discharge.

In Table 22, group (a) includes only those cases where there is no doubt whatever that the improvement was due to psychotherapy. The criteria are not merely those of clinical or psychopathological improvement; in these cases, indications can be given with certainty, or at least with a high degree of probability, of the way in which the psychotherapy had its effect.

TABLE 22

Course of Illness and Therapy

	Number of Patients
(a) improved with therapy	8
(b) improvement largely spontaneous	9
(c) psychotherapy fruitless, no improvement	2
	19

The eight cases in group (a)—1, 2, 3, 4, 6, 9, 10, and 29—were all seriously ill. Cases 2 and 9 had undergone hospital treatment, respectively two and four times apiece, and all of them equally futile. Cases 1, 3, 4, and 6 were clinically cured; the results of treatment are, on the whole, satisfactory from a psychotherapeutic point of view. In cases 3 and 4, a long period elapsed before the follow-up, while the treatment of the other two cases has only recently been terminated. Two cases (2 and 29) have retained marked traces of the illness. Patient 9 did not return the questionnaire, but the severity of the clinical picture, and the fact that she did not provide the information, after nine months of treatment in the hospital, point to a relapse. Thea J. (10) has just terminated her treatment and the prospects seem bleak.

All the cases in group (b)—7, 11, 12, 13, 15, 16, 17, 18, 19—were treated for only a short time, an average of 42 hours each. In seven cases, there was hardly any weight gain by the end of the treatment; although two patients (17 and 18) did put on 18 and 11 pounds respectively, these increases cannot be attributed to successful analysis. Follow-up reports were available for seven of this group (11, 13, 15, 16, 17, 18, 19). One of these cases belongs to the "cured" group, three show a marked improvement, and three have become chronically ill. Psychotherapy could do nothing for Marthe E. (5) and Regine N. (14), the two cases in group (c). In the first instance there was some minor psychopathological, but no clinical, improvement; the second case, Regine N., did not return the questionnaire.

As mentioned above, in spite of the most careful descriptions of the proposed method of treatment, only 19 of the patients could be persuaded to give it a trial, and even these often agreed with many reservations. Out of the remaining 11 cases, 9 refused treatment. In one instance, improvement began soon after a brief treatment, which almost coincided in length with the examination stage. This patient, Rosa H. (8), was the mildest case, and provided ample proof that, under favorable circumstances, many anorexia nervosa patients are accessible to even short-term psychotherapy. Brunhilde A. (27) was referred, after examination, to a hospital near her home. Full information about the rest of the cases (20, 21, 22, 23, 24, 25, 26, 28, and 30) is given in the tables. On the basis of the follow-up report and without closer examination, there seems to be every justification for classifying case 24 as cured. Every other case still exhibits more or less severe symptoms; some even show signs of chronic illness. There can be no doubt that those who received psychotherapy have by far the best prospects for recovery.

In Chapter 2, in the "Therapy" section, there is a description of the way in which extraordinarily optimistic, almost impassioned reports of improvements and recoveries are punctuated with diffident, even despairing portents and predictions. This striking anomaly is doubtless due to differences in the severity of the cases in question. For instance, Hurst (1939) claims not to have had one single failure in a group of 56 cases in which he used his "persuasion" methods. Venables (1930) reports equally successful results in nine cases, eight of which were later followed up for periods from 18 months to nine years (seven cures, one "neurasthenic" case). Even if we assume that all these cases are comparable in other respects, many of the reports do not give a fair picture, since so few describe the course taken by a *large number* of cases over a *long period* (Beck and Brøchner-Mortensen, 1954; Nemiah, 1950; McCullagh and Tupper, 1940). Beck and Brøchner-Mortensen, who followed up cases discharged from a hospital for internal medicine in Copenhagen (25 cases: 20 cures, 4 chronically ill, 1 death), attribute this high proportion of success to the fact that only the lighter cases were admitted to this type of hospital—lighter, that is, in comparison to the severely ill girls who are sent to psychiatric hospitals. In any case, the measurement of weight loss is at all times an unreliable standard for judging *long-term* prognoses. It is rather the severity of the psychopathological symptoms which determines the course of the illness.

The cases seen by Kay (1953) at the Maudsley Hospital, London, provide the best comparisons with my group. Their degree of illness matches that of my patients; the difference is that his patients did not respond to psychotherapy. The following synopsis gives the key figures from the studies of Kay, and of Kay and Leigh (1954); the corresponding figures from my own study are put in parentheses.

Total patients: 38 (30); 34 women (29), 4 men (1).

Married: 6 (2).

Most frequent age at onset: 16-20 years old—five less than 16, three over 35— (16½).

Length of illness at examination: about 50 per cent, two years or more; 20 per cent, five years or longer (2½ and 3½ years).

Treated in hospital previously: 50 per cent (77 per cent).

Menarche: between 11 and 15, in 30 cases; delayed by 1-4 years in 4 cases (13¾).

Average lowest weight: 96 lbs. (79 lbs.). [When the three patients of Kay and Leigh who were over 35 years old (1), and 4 (1) male patients are also taken into consideration, the loss of weight in my study seems even more remarkable.]

Follow-up: 30 cases (23).

Period of time under survey from the beginning of illness: 25 cases, five years and over—of these, 16 had fallen ill ten years or more before the follow-up examination; in five cases the onset was of recent date. (My survey covered an average of five years after the illness began.)

The psychopathological symptoms of my patients and those of the Maudsley Hospital's group are very similar. The Maudsley cases also had no definite forms of neurosis, but showed, as did my patients, a whole mosaic of structures. Some individuals were more obsessive; others exhibited chiefly depressive or phobic characteristics; schizophrenia was diagnosed in one case. It is interesting that five of the Maudsley patients attempted suicide. As a general rule, anorexia nervosa patients do not have this tendency, and in my group there were no psychoses, nor did any patient seriously try to take her own life. At Maudsley, the immediate results of treatment were unsatisfactory. Only one quarter of the patients gained 11 pounds or more, during an average stay of three months in the hospital. The treatment consisted of controlled diets and insulin in 60 per cent of the cases, hormones in 30 per cent, nine patients received electro- or insulin shocks and three of these were leucotomized. There was improvement in 2 cases. The writers are skeptical about the future prospects of the leucotomized patients, since both still show personality difficulties. Eight patients were given psychotherapy, seven to no avail; three patients died in the hospital. In eight of my cases (29 per cent) the considerable improvement or cure that was achieved could only have been obtained with psychotherapy.

Of the original 38 patients from Maudsley, eight had died by the time of the follow-up—six in connection with and two independent of the anorexia nervosa; three died in the hospital, three after discharge. There were two deaths of tuberculosis, and one each of collapse, bronchial pneumonia, suicide, and heart failure during appendectomy in a cachectic condition.

Since three of the remaining cases provided no follow-up, only 27 remain. Four of these are cured, a group of 12 patients have adapted themselves, although they still show neurotic symptoms, and 11 patients are chronically ill (see Table 14). This comparison shows a definite advantage for systematic psychotherapy based on psychoanalytic research. The almost total failure of psychotherapy in Kay's (1953) cases presumably is due to some misapplication of psychoanalytic technique and theory. In fact, his methods seem to have been inadequate, or at least inappropriate, in other ways as well. For instance, Richardson (1939) and Stephens (1941) have both reported attempts at suicide by anorexia nervosa patients who were being tube-fed. We must at least wonder whether the remarkable frequency of attempted suicide among these patients at the Maudsley Hospital was not due to the way in which diet control was enforced.

In practice, it is extremely difficult to express the course of psychotherapy in figures. However, it was striking that the technical problems of treatment were most marked among the younger patients. There seems to be a direct relationship between age and success or failure. The following table illustrates this point.

TABLE 23

Correlation between Age at Examination or Beginning of Treatment and the Results of Psychotherapy

| Age at Examination | Results of Psychotherapy | | | |
	Improvement by Psychotherapy	Spontaneous Improvement	No Improvement	Total
14 years		3		3
15 years		3		3
16 years			1	1
17 years		1		1
18 years	3		1	4
19 years	1			1
21 years	1	1		2
25 years	1			1
26 years	1			1
27 years	1			1
42 years			1	1
	8	8	3	19

The technical complications[4] which make the path of therapy particularly difficult with younger patients, really only reflect the

[4] It is possible that the sex, age, or personality of the analyst may have had some influence, particularly on the 13 to 17 year old group; but as these younger patients were treated to no avail by various female and a male physician, it seems unlikely that such factors seriously affected the outcome.

inner turmoil of these girls. Play therapy is rarely a useful tool; it is often flatly refused by the patients. Nor are they in any condition to communicate verbally, and often they decline to give the remotest clue that might help the analyst toward insight and influence. Briefly their situation is this: On the one hand, they refuse to be children, and view the invitation to play, consciously, as an insult and, unconsciously, as a temptation to regress. Still they do not feel capable of, or permitted, adulthood. This leads us to the theme of the following chapters.

❧ 4 ❧

Case 1: Henriette A.

Synopsis

Henriette A., a nineteen-year-old secondary-school girl, was admitted to the hospital in the winter of 1958. She had originally fallen ill three years previously, at the age of 16. Her weight before the illness had been 110-114 lbs., but she had since reduced to as little as 88 lbs. At the beginning of psychoanalysis, in 1958, she weighed 102 lbs. and her height was 5 ft. 7¼ in. She had had amenorrhea and constipation since the onset of the disorder.

During a course of analysis which consisted of 289 sessions spread over about two years, the patient's weight increased to 120 lbs. After an interval of almost four years, her periods returned spontaneously and the constipation improved. A brief description of the precipitating situation, which is closely allied to what Anna Freud (1946a) terms "asceticism at puberty," will provide some immediate insight into the most important psychodynamic processes at work in this case.

Henriette A. suddenly began blushing when boys looked at her, or when any theme connected with love was brought up at school. The fear of blushing which developed was a torment to her. Until then, the patient had felt that she was "master of [her] house" (Freud, 1916-1917); now something was happening over which she had no control. Eventually, she discovered that she could quiet her fear of blushing by fasting in the mornings. As she began to lose weight, the blushing did in fact disappear. During the course of psychoanalysis, this process was reversed. When the blushing reappeared, the old conflicts which had been responsible for the asceticism could be recognized and, for the most part, overcome.

It soon became evident that Henriette A. was blushing because she was ashamed of being looked upon as a "girl." The anxiety accompanying this involuntary show of feeling, and the corresponding defense strategies employed by the ego will form the focus of this chapter. The choice of emphasis was determined by the material itself, since the themes mentioned are closely bound up with the patient's experience, and help us to understand the motives behind her symptoms. The crucial question is: why was the anxiety generated by a superficially harmless onset of blushing so intense that it could lead to years of deliberate abstemiousness and a general rejection of all impulses and drives, coupled with the isolation that was the unhappy outcome? The following brief psychodynamic outline is an attempt to answer this question.

1. The observation that this patient had, until the blushing started, considered herself to be "master of her house" indicates, in topical dynamic terms, an unusual ego ideal for a girl. The fact is that Henriette A. wanted to be a boy, and not be counted among the girls. This desire to be male was particularly strongly rooted in her because of certain influences in her past life. She had grown up without a father and had lived, an only child, alone with her mother. The widowed mother, who supported herself, projected the image of her dead husband onto the girl, seeking and finding in her both helpmate and counselor. In general terms, the patient was pushed into assuming a "masculine" role. There was no opportunity for the normal oedipal conflicts to develop within a mother-father-child triangle. Instead, the identification was exclusively masculine. Characteristics such as independence, sternness, and decisiveness—which are not "masculine" or "feminine" as such but which, in our society, tend to be attached to the male sex—were reinforced by her family circumstances. She "wore the pants" and was used to having her mother at her beck and call. This situation was partly responsible for the way the patient clung to the belief in the omnipotence of thoughts. Thus it came as a bitterly harsh blow when she was severely punished for petty misdemeanors—such as taking something without asking,

when she was with relatives—and suddenly treated like a naughty child.

Even in her long friendship with another girl, the patient always took the active part. As long as she could play a boyish role un-hindered and never needed to put herself out—she was a first-class sportswoman and scholar, without having to try—her ego ideal remained intact. Nothing occurred to upset her inner equilibrium until the advent of puberty.

2. Torn between her inability to be a boy and her dislike of being a girl (based on the ego ideal which had meanwhile be-come firmly anchored in her unconscious), she bolstered up her confidence with a new ideal—asexuality. In this way, that indis-criminate and primitive hostility of which Anna Freud (1946a, p. 172) speaks in connection with asceticism at puberty sprang up between ego and drive. The results of this sweeping rejection of drives could be recognized in the changes of attitude that took place at the time, particularly in the eating difficulties. By deny-ing "dangerous" aspects of the outside world and by repressing her drives, the patient eventually attained a state of the ego that was free from anxiety.

3. In the patient's experience, hunger stood for drive-impelled behavior; asceticism served to overcome her fear of the strength of her drives.

4. On closer examination, fear of the strength of a drive can be divided into several drive components. Repression disturbs and inhibits both thinking and doing. As a result, there are (a) a reduction in the patient's ability to enter into interpersonal re-lationships, (b) disturbance of her powers of concentration, and (c) functional disorders. These symptoms are the last traces of the doomed affective and ideational representatives of the drive impulses, although the repressions themselves were buoyed up by countercathexes and changes in the ego. This could be deduced from her attitude and behavior.

5. In the anorexia itself, the following psychogenetic processes are discernible: (a) avoidance of realistic drive satisfaction; the drive is withdrawn from the object, and wish satisfactions appear in the imagination, e.g., daydreams of food. There is already an

attempt here to avoid the risks inherent in uninhibited drive satisfaction. (b) It is obvious that the rather amazonlike behavior of the patient, as well as the anorexia, are consequences of the fending off of receptivity ("something comes into me"), because the unconscious is linking nourishment with impregnation. Revulsion and vomiting are related to the sexual defense. (c) Oral satisfaction is connected, unconsciously, with destruction and killing. Therefore, eating is restricted, or it is fraught with guilt.

6. The psychogenesis of some of the symptoms begins to emerge: (a) Isolation; relationships must be avoided because danger threatens from within and without. (b) Feelings of inferiority and guilt because of unconscious aggression. (c) Disturbances in concentration and work; thoughts may not be thought to completion because—and this is only one aspect of the question—they might come true (omnipotence of thoughts). The fear of the strength of the instincts contains, above all, the threat of the ego being overwhelmed and losing its capacity to discriminate between fantasy and reality.

7. The fear that controls might be broken indicates a yearning for a relationship that would encompass or supersede all contradictory elements. Since Henriette A. was afraid of her ambivalence and of her destructive, all-devouring oral demands, this yearning became repressed and could be satisfied only in a regressive way. From the economic point of view, tensions generated by the blocked hunger drive were discharged into an excessive urge for motor activity (strenuous walks). Seen topographically, there is also regressive cathexis of processes which, though remote from consciousness, lead to pleasure which the ego need not reject as instinctual (gratification). On the contrary, the urge for movement and for other activities simultaneously served the function of "purification" and the purposes of the defense.

Family History

Henriette A.'s father had been a post-office official. He died of a sepsis at the age of 40, two and a half years after marriage. Mrs.

A.—now in her fifties—was 28 years old when she married. The patient is an only child. There is no history of mental illness in the family.

Biography

The patient grew up in a small east-coast town in Germany, in the house of her maternal grandmother. She never knew her maternal grandfather. The grandmother had died only recently, at a very advanced age. She had been in need of constant care for some time, and, in the end, was hospitalized because of her senile condition, the result of cerebral sclerosis. The grandparents kept a general store, which the mother helped to run until her brother returned from the armed forces. Then Mrs. A. opened a general store of her own near the little town, in order to support herself and the patient.

Henriette A.'s mother provided the following information about her daughter's early childhood. The birth was normal, but since the baby was lazy about sucking at the breast, complementary feedings were given while mother and baby were still in the hospital. The breast milk had to be pumped off, since the baby would just suck a little and then fall asleep. During her early years, the patient had eating difficulties, but this improved when she was eight years old and, indeed, changed into its opposite. The mother suffered from stomach trouble during pregnancy, as well as from periods of depression, which she feared she had transmitted to her daughter. When Henriette A. was one year old, her father died and her mother returned to her parents' home. When the patient was six, her uncle came back from the war, and her mother moved into a separate house. Henriette A. slept in a twin bed beside her mother until she was 12, at which time she was given a room of her own. She was a happy, vivacious child, and preferred being out of doors to playing with her dolls.

Henriette A. was very fond of her uncle and, in some respects, he took over the paternal role; being a soldier, however, he appeared only when on leave. After the war, he married and then became fully occupied with managing the shop and bringing up a family. The mother, a kind but simple woman, lived only for her child and the running of the shop.

At home, Henriette A., who was rather spoiled, was difficult to manage; she showed a very early and quite clear inclination to have her own way. However, she is said to have seemed extremely well brought up in company, over-retiring rather than the opposite. The mother's somewhat matter-of-fact manner made it difficult for her to make any easy show of affection. However, during the child's frequent attacks of *pavor nocturnus,* the mother did take her into bed to comfort her. It was no light task to cope with Henriette A.'s rebelliousness, and Mrs. A. often threatened that her daughter's misbehavior would send her "to the grave."

Henriette A. was a child with a fertile mind and a lively imagination. From early childhood, she had shared everything with her bosom friend Gerda, the daughter of a master butcher. It was almost certainly Henriette A. who called the tune from the beginning. With her energy and ingenuity, she swept her mentally and physically less precocious friend along with her. In the well-to-do butcher's house, Henriette A. was welcomed as one of the family, although the standards of living were very different from those in her own home. At first, the income from Mrs. A.'s little shop was small and, even when it was supplemented by her widow's pension, strict economies were necessary. Henriette A. became miserly; later on, she would not permit herself to spend her pocket money during excursions so that she could revel in dreams of all the things she would do with the money she had saved. At that time, the fleshpots were not far away. At the butcher's, the girls ate with such good appetite that they are even alleged to have outeaten the apprentices.

The Henriette A.-Gerda partnership afforded limitless scope for make-believe, in which Henriette A. was not only the most inventive of the two, but usually assumed the active, "masculine" part.

She made the transition from primary to secondary school without difficulty. The school was situated in the nearby town and could be reached by foot. Gerda accompanied her. Even in the coeducational secondary school, Henriette A. took the lead almost at once. Everything she touched turned to gold. She was an excellent athlete and a talented pianist. She had a natural flair for her own and foreign languages. Mathematics was her only weak subject, and she would have had to work many additional hours even to keep up with the class. But she was unwilling to take the trouble, and compensated for her low marks in mathematics with outstanding performance in other subjects. In the classroom, she was always a ringleader, and contributed as much as any to the rough-and-tumble atmosphere. Her friendship with Gerda fulfilled her and sheltered her from any need to come into close contact with the other children in her grade; in practice, she encountered them almost exclusively in rivalry on the playground. She clung feverishly to this state of affairs; she resented her periods which put her out of the running for days on end.

Onset of Illness

With the changes that puberty wrought in her and her classmates, Henriette A. gradually began to be ousted from her position as leader. Her behavior changed: she became quiet and moody, and lost her sense of fun. Although she had once enjoyed meals with Gerda, she now began to diet and, occasionally, to vomit. Her success at games fell off, and she was unable to compete at the same level. At about 16, she had to move to another school further away, which involved traveling instead of walking. She also had to separate from Gerda, who had decided not to continue with her schooling because of her poor grades, and who was now helping in the family business. Henriette A. spent two years in the new school before beginning treatment at the hospital. During that time, the illness, which had begun to manifest itself both physically and psychopathologically, progressed little. However, her weight fell from 110-114 pounds to 88 pounds. Her menses ceased, although they had hitherto been regular since their onset at the age of 14.

During the summer holidays of 1955, the patient went for an extensive bicycle trip and arrived home exhausted and half-starved. In August of the same year, she underwent her first detailed clinical examination; the diagnosis was anorexia nervosa.

Previous Illnesses

In her twelfth year, Henriette A. had an appendectomy. As a child, she had a tendency to stutter, and her voice would crack because she spoke so rapidly.

Clinical Findings on Physical Examination

The mother reported that the patient tired easily and had lost her usual vivacity. She ate less, and her menses had ceased. On admission, the patient proved to be in a considerably reduced nutritional state. The fat deposits on the trunk were at a minimum, the collarbones and pelvis jutted out, the intercostal spaces were sunken, the stomach was caved in.

No important pathological defects were found. The heart and lungs were examined and X-rayed and found to be in the normal range. Blood pressure was hypotonic at 95/50, and there was a marked brachycardia with a resting frequency of 42/min. Blood count and urine were normal. The basal metabolic rate, taken on two separate occasions, was -22 per cent and -21 per cent respectively. Thus, the loss of weight cannot be attributed to hyperthyroidism. The Staub-Traugott test on sugar metabolism was carried out and also gave no indication of any disability. The stomach X-ray showed no signs of gastric or duodenal ulcer, although there were traces of a slight gastroduodenitis. After a test drink of caffeine, the gastric juices were somewhat subacid with maximum values of $+20/+38$. Finally, X-ray photographs of the skull taken along two axes, with extra shots of the *sella turcica*, gave no grounds for assuming changes in the hypophyseal area.

On the basis of the history and the clinical finding, the diagnosis was anorexia nervosa. The absence of the menses, slow heart rate, and lowered metabolic rate thus fell into place, especially since our investigations gave no reason to conclude any disturbance in glandular function. The grounds for this disorder, so often due to psychological disturbances, could not be established in spite of repeated interviews.

During her week under observation, the patient gained three pounds (from 92 to 95 lbs.). In the meantime, Henriette A. was also examined at another University Hospital and, again, the diagnosis was anorexia nervosa. Accordingly, her family physician recommended that she consult a psychotherapist some distance from the small town where she lived. Since the length of the journey alone would have precluded outpatient treatment, the therapist referred her to this unit as an inpatient.

When she was admitted to the hospital, early in 1958, the laboratory investigations were not repeated, since there could be no doubt, both from the history and previous findings, that the first diagnosis was correct. On arrival, the nineteen-year-old girl was 5 ft. 7¾ in. tall and weighed 102 lbs. In spite of considerable emaciation, she appeared to be quite fit. Her skin was cool, but not dry or flaky; her extremities were strongly discolored with chilblains around the toes of both feet. Of the remaining data, only a bradycardia of 44/min. and hypertonia at 95/55 are worth noting. The secondary hair had remained and the distribution was feminine in type.

First Test[1]

This patient is of above average intelligence, quick on the uptake, with good general comprehension and a distinct streak of imagination. Basically a lively and active person, she seems to be in a state of crisis, in which she vacillates between hypermotility and introversive reticence, to the detriment of her ability to learn and work, as well as of her social life. Feelings of inferiority and a tendency to melancholic mood swings are further signs of the way in which she has lost her grip.

---

[1] The psychological tests in this case and the interpretation in the case of Martha E. (see Chapter 6) were carried out by Dr. Vogel, to whom I am deeply indebted. In the case of Henriette A., he knew only the diagnosis; in the case of Martha E., he had become acquainted with the patient through discussions in our seminar.

This crisis is due, undoubtedly, to a problem of maturation which has appeared in connection with the physical onset of puberty. It is easy to recognize that the patient is afraid of growing up, chiefly because it means committing herself to womanhood, which she rejects as inferior, constricted, a state of passive dependency. Her defense against the implications of adulthood appears to express itself in several ways: the patient attempts to overcome her fear of passivity and violation by assuming an active and aggressive role herself, a type of defense suggested by her physical energy, and possibly conditioned in part by her constitution. In this case, it is not improbable that narcissistic, kinesthetic eroticism, such as latent homosexual leanings, contribute their part. The identification, however, is not exaggeratedly masculine; it would be better to say that a narcissistic, sexless existence is seen as providing a refuge from feminine, genital sexuality.

Since she feels threatened by reality, this narcissistic image spurs increasingly regressive fantasy activity, in which every attempt is made to prolong the "safety" of childhood. Thus, interpersonal relationships are restricted, and there is a growing reliance on the magical, anthropomorphic world of animals and nature. A strong, unconscious tie to the mother probably plays a focal role in the patient's life; traits indicating oral ambivalence and the disavowal of infantile desires for contact cannot be overlooked. The patient should respond to therapy because of her intelligence and imaginative powers which, although infantile, give promise of good development. The prospects for recovery would seem to be favorable.

Course of Therapy

Stage 1. Hours 1-28 (inpatient, five sessions per week)

The first clues to the salient psychodynamic interrelationships of the symptom formation were gained while the physical examination was in progress. During the introductory stages of therapy, the basic conflicts and their pathological solutions came to the surface. By the time analysis was begun, after three years of illness, Henriette A. had regained the inner equilibrium which had been so shaken by her fear of blushing. She was a boyishly slim, intelligent, and self-confident girl, who obviously had no intention of acknowledging any conflicts at all. But the parting from Gerda had deprived her of her best and only friend. In the new school, she had been unable to make any new friendships, especially since her classmates were interested chiefly in other things, e.g., boy friends. Thus her denial of conflicts involved considerable isolation. Although her field of perception and experience had contracted, she still felt herself to be living on "another [asexual] plane," and her old faith in herself returned.

Henriette A. was anything but eager to submit to treatment, and tried, if not to escape it altogether, at least to curtail her stay in the hospital, lest she lose her personal freedom or fall into a state of dangerous dependency on the therapist. She was apprehensive not only of her demands for totality, but also of having to part from the therapist some day (hour 25).

She did not know in which direction to develop. She could not decide—and in this sense recognized her basic conflict as early as the eighth hour—whether to be a boy or a girl. All her inclinations protested against her feminine anatomy. This dualism showed itself, for example, whenever she needed clothes or shoes: in her uncertainty she always ended up choosing men's shoes. She wanted her body to be angular, hard, and boyish, not soft and curved like that of a girl. She wanted to feel free, and had a marked urge for motor activity, which she channeled into taking long walks, rowing, and swimming. Not satisfied with walking for several hours every afternoon, she would follow her hike with a visit to the swimming pool and, if possible, spend the evening in a gymnasium. This pleasure in movement provided Henriette A. with a gratification which was far removed from consciousness and thus could provoke neither anxiety nor guilt. The explanation she herself offered was that this excessive urge for exercise acted as a sort of "purifying" process, urgently necessary because the missing periods had to be replaced with some form of cleansing. These activities also provided her with an ever-present excuse for avoiding transference and a "dangerous closeness" to some other person. At home, she was accompanied on her walks by her dog, Hasso. It was easier for her to imagine exchanging tokens of love with an animal than kissing a young man on the cheek (hour 10).

Henriette A. could never make up her mind whether to arrive late for an appointment—as she frequently did—or to give up going swimming. This very conflict was verbalized in her first report of a dream: "A lake was covered with slowly melting ice; I wanted to go swimming, but had an appointment at the same time with the hospital doctor. I let the doctor wait."

Henriette A. was rarely punctual, occasionally arriving up to a quarter of an hour late. Once she simply skipped the appointment and, instead, traveled to Lake Constance for a long week end with a girl who used to work in her mother's shop. Gestures like this were intended to show the analyst how independent she was, and to ward off those fears whose contents were becoming manifest in the transference situation. Her behavior was interpreted to her along these lines, although it was not yet possible to point to specific anxiety contents or to their instinctual sources. During this time, the analyst was collecting more and more important information about the patient's early life. Her friendship with Gerda, for instance, almost deserves a chapter to itself. It provided the patient with unlimited opportunity for role playing as the two girls sat in the bathtub together, often for hours on end. In fact, the friendship was both a direct and an indirect answer to Henriette A.'s need for tenderness which, as often as not, was refused by her mother (hour 10): "We have never shown much affection." It was plain that Gerda usually had to acquiesce to the patient's demands, since the latter went into a rage whenever anyone crossed her, or when any wish was frustrated (hour 21).

It was already evident that resistance and transference would be governed *inter alia* by fears of persecution which derived, on the one hand, from her fear of being raped and, on the other hand, from the projection of her own aggression. Both aspects appeared in dreams.

Dream 10[2]: We were playing cops and robbers. Two boys followed me on bicycles. By braking suddenly, I was able to escape being taken prisoner. The boys shot past me and missed me. They were the same boys that Gerda and I used to sit opposite to, and whose glances made me blush.

Dream 23: A woman was following me. She was a murderess, but was accusing me of having committed murder. She almost got me arrested. Later, we caught her after all, although the police did not come to help.

The first dream (Dream 10) paved the way for sexual anxiety to enter the field of conscious experience. After the murder dream (Dream 23), her anger against her mother and anxiety with regard to her could be verbalized, even though the time was not yet ripe for any clarification of the connection between dream, conscious experience, and symptom formation.

Several anxiety components emerged at this time. Henriette A. was worried about her voice. She spoke very fast, and was afraid it would crack. She had had dreams of being chased ever since she was a child. She believed that, on the whole, the fear was the same whether her pursuer was a man or a woman.

In the hospital, she behaved like an overnight guest. She went for long walks with one of the other anorexia nervosa patients, but would have preferred having no social obligations, even to the extent of taking her meals alone. She also objected to having to eat with the family with whom she was to live during her stay in the hospital. She tried to persuade her mother and the analyst to give instructions to this effect, but in vain. Keeping to her diet was not easy for her; to still her hunger pangs, she bought chewing gum or nibbled licorice sticks. At mealtimes, she still ate very little.

Her spare time was spent mainly in window-shopping. She would sometimes tour the nearby department stores several times

---

[2] In all the case histories, the number refers to the hour in which the dream was reported. In this, as in the other case reports presented in this volume, an attempt has been made to quote patients verbatim by writing down the material immediately after the sessions.

a day, devouring with her eyes all the things she wished to buy or eat. Anticipation seemed to give her more pleasure than realization. Her avarice was an important factor here, because when she did finally buy something, such as a piece of cake, she did not eat it all at once, but saved half for later.

She went to school every day from the hospital, having enrolled as a temporary pupil in the local secondary school. During the past few years, she had fallen far behind in her schoolwork, especially since she suffered from poor concentration. She did particularly badly in mathematics, physics, and chemistry. Sudden changes of mood would make her want to leave school at a moment's notice, saying that she was too stupid to pass her matriculation examination. The problem of school and career pervaded every stage of the therapy, and it was often necessary to restrain the patient from overhasty decisions. Since there was no doubt that Henriette A. was of at least average intelligence, her learning problems were interpreted as follows:

1. The poor concentration was understood as the result of inner disturbances due to repressed drive impulses and hyperglycemia.

2. Her laziness was considered along with the narcissistic injury, which also played an essential part in other aspects of the pathogenesis. Until she started blushing, everything had gone smoothly for her. Up to that juncture, she had scarcely ever had to prepare her lessons; now she could not endure having to work in order to obtain a passing grade.

3. The tensions engendered by the conflict between coddling and independence were analyzed. ("Everything will be all right somehow without my having to work for school.") Later it emerged that her schoolwork had grown progressively worse, over a period of years, since she had been harshly reprimanded by a teacher for competing with another girl for first place. This had evoked strong guilt feelings in the patient, and her performance suffered as a result.

At the end of four weeks in the hospital (after hour 28), the patient's persistent pleas were granted, and she began treatment as an outpatient. Immediately following her discharge, many other difficulties presented themselves, which influenced the transference. The analyst was obliged, at times, to telephone the various foster families.

Stage 2. Hours 29-41 (outpatient, four sessions a week)

In the 29th hour, Henriette A. announced that she felt very unhappy with her foster family because her security was being menaced. The landlady, a war widow, was living with a man, and turned a blind eye to any little irregularities in the house. She allowed her daughters and her female lodgers considerable latitude. Furthermore, she did not bother much about meals, and Henriette A. was bitterly resentful at being neglected, and furious when one of the girls in the house unconcernedly ate the fruit she had set aside for herself. This incident provided an excellent opportunity to draw her attention to her gluttony and greed, and also to her aggressive, self-destructive reactions as exemplified in the patient's statement: "If I don't get the rent back, which I paid in advance, I won't let another bite pass my lips."

Frustration in the oral sphere was accompanied by unremitting sexual temptation. The schoolgirls who lodged in the house apparently had little else on their minds than boy friends, cosmetics, and clothes. Henriette A. was shocked and started to scour the town for new accommodations at once. She soon found a room in the home of one of her schoolmates.

Henriette A. quickly made friends with the girl, Angelika, who was the daughter of a schoolteacher. The family was vegetarian, and strictly patriarchal. At last, the patient began to take a more optimistic view of the future. However, any attempts to persuade her to work through her conflicts in the analysis rather than to take flight were nipped in the bud by accusations that the analyst was siding with the previous landlady.

Gradually, she began to criticize the analyst more harshly, directing her anger mainly at trivial things, such as the time of her appointment. Everything had to be done her way. She wanted to dovetail the sessions into her own timetable, so that she could walk for hours beforehand and still depart in time for rowing, the gymnastics classes, or some other athletic pastime. In a dream (hour 40), she "could not find the door of the consultation-room at once," and she took a hot and a cold shower "which the analyst found to be highly significant." Although she was poking fun at the analyst and his interpretations, she was also enjoying the relaxed atmosphere of the therapy sessions, for in the same hour (40), she spoke of the analyst as being "neutral," and "therefore ideal."

Little by little, her dread of the consequences of "thawing" and venturing down from her ivory tower became clearer. In a dream (hour 37), she pictured herself as Snow White, standing, radiantly beautiful, on a stage. She was full of indignation when she reported this dream, and refused to discuss it or the content of the fairy tale itself any further.

In school, Henriette A. was beginning to make friends, but only on a superficial level. Gradually, however, she noticed that, although she could always have sufficient company if she wanted it, she still remained an outsider. Fear of her all-encompassing demands, and dread of yet another parting made her prefer isolation as a way of avoiding any new disappointments. She had not yet gotten over the fact that Gerda had recently fallen in love and was now behaving like all the other girls.

Stage 3. Hours 42-82

The patient spent the Easter holidays with her mother in the Black Forest. Coincidentally, a conference about natural diets was taking place in the small health resort where they were staying. Henriette A. found the whole business unnatural[3] rather

---

[3] Although the patient had never read the theories of Katz (1932) on the subject, she recognized the essentially magical character of the vegetarian food reform cult. There can be no doubt that the unconscious motives of this widespread movement may be sought in apotropaic magic and in the yearning for mystical alliance with the healing forces of earth and sun, and for eternal health. The separation of the world into "good" and "bad" foods corresponds, at the level of identification and group formation, to this idea: "I/we, who only eat good foods are good; everyone else is bad and inferior." Ludwig Feuerbach meant much the same thing when he wrote: "Der Mensch ist was er isst [Man is

than otherwise. She became disappointed with her mother when she realized that the latter was not infallible. The woman was, in fact, awkward, slow, and unstimulating as a conversationalist. Henriette A. began by criticizing the limited intellectual capacity of her mother; later, she gave a detailed description of her anxiety about her. She felt superior to her mother, but at the same time feared the omnipotence of her own thoughts and her ability to "influence God" (hour 76). She wanted to dominate her mother but also longed for dependency and pampering.

In the new lodgings, everything went wrong from the first day on. Henriette A. inaugurated the next treatment hour with an attempt at blackmail: she refused to go on for another day unless she could live in a room of her own. Fortunately, it proved possible to arrange this prior to the next session and to use the interim to confront the patient with the facts. In order to conceal her neurotic rivalry with Angelika, she used all her ingenuity to play up her vegetarian hosts' idiosyncrasies in "justified criticism." She was treated as a guest, and felt most uncomfortable at having to limit her freedom to suit someone else. Henriette A. also complained about the analyst's professional manner. She said she could not be frank with him unless she were treated in a less impersonal way. At the same time, she took shelter behind her positive transference relationship. After being accosted once or twice on her walks, she developed fears of violation which she tried to overcome by means of identification with the aggressor.[4]

> *Dream:* My mother was strangled by a man. There was an altogether completely crazy atmosphere in this dream, because I also saw another man, an ice-cream man, who was having a fit. In my fear, I shouted for help, for you, and then found you in the corridor.

---

what he eats]" in his essay, "The Secret Sacrifice, or Man Is what He Eats." Feuerbach continued: "Surely the Jews were also scorned and hated by the heathens because they despised the foods the heathens loved. . . . And at the root of this hatred is there not the thought: 'the man who does not *eat* what we eat cannot *be* as we are'?" (Cf. Büchmann, 1942).

[4] Cf. A. Freud (1936): "Moreover there are many children's games in which through the metamorphosis of the subject into a dreaded object anxiety is converted into pleasurable security" (p. 119).

In hour 61, the fear of blushing, of which she had once rid herself by starvation and denial, reappeared. Henriette A. berated
the analyst, accusing him of being responsible for the return of
the symptom after three years of freedom from it. It was pointed
out to her that she had merely replaced one demon with another,
and that now she was in the thick of the very same conflicts from
which she had sought to escape previously. She feared becoming
fatter because, for her, this meant being at the mercy of her instinctual drives. She was also infuriated at being courted by a
male student, that is, being treated as a girl; having to walk on
the inside, for instance, made all her fears of being violated rush
to the surface again. On the one hand, she was quite taken aback
when she remembered how she used to try to pitch her voice
lower. She also now favored the idea of parthenogenesis, which
was interpreted to her as a triumph for feminine "emancipation":
men were simply no longer necessary.

Henriette A. made friends with a girl some nine years older,
who was in treatment with the same analyst. The soft-hearted
Miss N. allowed herself to be exploited to the full by Henriette
A. and, owing to her own positive transference, and in order to
please the analyst, Miss N. took endless pains with her. Henriette
A. was also able to benefit from Miss N.'s positive transference,
and it gave her more courage.

Although Henriette A. had, in the meantime, given up some of
her activities, too little time was left to find a room before school
closed. She went off for the holidays, full of confidence that her
friend would arrange this for her.

Stage 4. Hours 83-134

The patient spent the summer holidays (six weeks) at home.
For a few weeks, one of her classmates from the Heidelberg school
stayed with her. Henriette A. was not able to make close contact
with the girl, and preferred to go on solitary walks with Hasso,
the dog. She insisted that her friend treat the A. home as her own,
but was horrified to find that the girl did not hesitate to go into
the tiny shop to eat whatever caught her fancy. Henriette A.

hardly touched her schoolwork, and took great pleasure in being pampered by her mother, which, incidentally, also increased her weight. She spent much of the time trying to recapture her past life, only to make the painful discovery that she could no longer attain the feeling of merging with nature, as in the past. As far as Gerda was concerned, she did her best to re-establish the old "bosom friendship," and the feeling of being "wrapped up in each other." In fact, she tried her best to persuade Gerda to move to Heidelberg, but in vain. In her disappointment, Hasso was her only comfort.

The return to Heidelberg brought problems that Henriette A. found unbearable. Miss N. had taken great trouble to secure a room for her; but now the landlord objected to subletting, and Henriette A. was forced to move again. After days of hunting, she and her friend found another room, but this time Henriette A. complained that the street noises were so annoying that she could not stay. Within a few days, she took flight again and settled down, at last, in a garret which caught her fancy.

In bursts of despairing fury, she admitted to her helplessness, although she still preferred to ascribe her own transference wishes to her friend. One day, she said that Miss N. had suggested, in fun, that they should ask the analyst to help them with all their moves, since he had a car. In reality, the patient had herself given voice to this thought.

It became evident that it was not only the noise that had driven Henriette A. to take refuge in an attic. The landlady of the second room had a son whom Henriette A. found attractive, and she was afraid of falling in love with him. She dreamed (hour 89) about a young man whom she kissed and wanted to be alone with. She also had innumerable fear-cathected dreams of rape. In these dreams, either the patient herself or other girls would be tortured, mutilated, or raped on the battlefield by the Russians, after being dragged into a feudal mansion where large-scale training for various sports was taking place. The Russians were allowed to choose any girl who appealed to them. Even in these dreams, Henriette A. felt inadequate, and realized that since her illness she was good for nothing, a failure in every field—including "sports." The struggle against eating had exhausted her. She said that she was "neuter, wanting to keep to a golden middle path, thus neither boy nor girl." She felt inferior and complained about the imperfections of her figure.

As the defense structures began to crumble, it became evident that Henriette A.'s feeling of inferiority was due to unconscious penis envy. For instance, as already noted, she did not want to walk on the inside of the pavement like a girl, nor to be treated with customary courtesy; she pitched her voice low and bought men's clothes; she found it easier to imagine being a man and seeking out a wife than being wooed herself; she wanted her body to be angular and hard, not curved, soft, and feminine. As a child, Henriette A. remembered creeping into her mother's bed during episodes of *pavor nocturnus,* although later on she was disgusted by her mother's sweat, particularly during the latter's menses. Her identification with the aggressor—she wanted to purchase a pistol to protect herself from assault—has already been mentioned above.

At about this time, the patient dreamed about a girl whose fingers and toes were chopped off. She then related how, before puberty, she used to imagine having an operation performed to change her sex. No details of this daydream were forthcoming, however. Henriette A. claimed that she could not remember anything more concrete about its content, and there is no telling whether she had really forgotten or whether, as is more likely, the defense processes had obstructed the psychic act and prevented the idea from being thought out in full. Wrestling with the problem of Henriette A.'s faulty identification occupied a large part of many treatment hours. The accent, however, was on interpreting the patient's dread of surrender, and the mastery that a masculine identification provided.

Memories of childhood flooded back, and the patient remarked that, although she had taken mutual exchanges of affection with Gerda for granted until then, at the age of about eight, she began to feel occasional twinges of uneasiness about their sleeping together, bathing together for hours on end, playing "father and mother," going to the toilet together. This was exemplified in a dream (115) wherein Gerda and Henriette A. were standing naked in an outsize pipe and the Russians were forcing their way into the pipe. Henriette A. recollected that, when she was eight, a rather precocious little girl from the city had come to visit, and they had played "doctor" with her. Afterwards, Henriette A. and Gerda had imitated the sexual act in bed (dressed in pajamas), taking turns at being the man. At this time, they were already avoiding direct skin contact or caresses, and Henriette A. was behaving as coldly as possible in order to keep her friend at a safe distance. The "pipe dream" was interpreted in terms of both its homosexual and its heterosexual overtones.

In the first part of this stage of treatment, the transference was mildly positive: Henriette A. thought of the analyst as a protector, different from the brutal pursuers of her dreams, and indeed a refuge from them. If ever fear overcame her in the daytime, she used to comfort herself by seeking protection and help from him in her mind. This idyllic state did not last, however. The increasing frequency of her blushes and her growing uncertainty now made the patient storm and rage at him. At the same time, more aggression was being directed at her mother. The latter sent her food parcels with, among other things, cans of ready-cooked food. If anything was missing from the packages which she wanted urgently, Henriette A. would fly into a rage and send off indignant cards and letters to her mother. She also persisted in regarding a hunger strike as revenge, however much this was interpreted to her as pure self-punishment.

Just before hour 99, Henriette A. learned that Hasso had been run over and killed. Her mother wrote that, after such a tragedy, she was not going to buy another dog. Henriette A. was filled with fury and despair. In her grief, she suffered from mild feelings of depersonalization, so that everything seemed strange and meaningless. She wrote to her mother that, if there was no dog there, she would never come home again.

Now, at last, the true depths of her many-layered affection for her dog could be sounded.[5] In hour 104, she dreamed that Hasso had changed into a sweet three-year-old boy, whom she kissed passionately. The question of object cathexes and identification was broached in therapy, and her yearning for unity and her fears of her passions and aggressions were discussed.

In an "injection dream" (106), Henriette A. yielded to her fate and did not flee from the injection as she had in a previous dream. She dreamed that she was seriously ill and finally gave in when her mother remarked that it was senseless to keep on rebelling: "So I said, well, I don't care; the doctor might as well give me the injection." To her unconscious, the acceptance of help signified being raped. The patient then suggested, of her own accord, a whole series of symptoms that might be linked with the defense and the horror of sexuality, e.g., her vomiting, and her horror of jellyfish which spoiled her enjoyment of sea-bathing and caused her to scrub and disinfect herself after swimming.

Her schoolwork was erratic. In her grandiose way, she made many careless mistakes which caused her to obtain poor grades. She still tended to make crucial decisions at the drop of a hat; one day, she suggested dropping out of school in order to enter an athletic training college. The possibility was considered that she stay in Heidelberg to take her final examinations rather than return to her old school as originally planned. The status of guest-pupil accorded her all too many unnecessary privileges which she always turned to her best advantage.

From the point of view of the therapy as well, it seemed preferable for her not to be tied down to any definite dates. The patient not only resented advice to this effect as unwarranted interference with her right of self-determination, but also as being dangerously seductive. "Next, you will be wanting to marry me in Heidelberg," was her reaction, although in the same treatment hour she claimed that psychoanalysts ought to be celibate. This challenge was interpreted as a device to keep the analyst neuter like herself,

[5] Cf. Heimann (1956).

and at a distance, and thus attain a fear-free position of sexual indifference. The interpretation cost the therapist his post as ideal guardian and the patient now began to associate him with her fears. "Since you destroyed my ideal, I am afraid of you too," she remarked about a dream (hour 111) in which she saw the analyst lying covered with a cloth and felt sure that a terrible deed had been committed. When she reported (hour 132) that she had dreamed of seeing the analyst in bed with one of the girls in her class, she also revealed that it was not only in the dream that this thought had occurred to her. At last, she could no longer ignore the way in which her sexual desires and fears were coloring her transference and resistance.

The patient had not managed to lure her friend Gerda to Heidelberg, and she was thrown off balance when Gerda accepted a position in another town. However, there was a substitute at hand, Miss N.—although the latter had to keep a firm grip on herself in order to avoid becoming a slave to the patient's whims. At the same time, Henriette A. was made aware of her overwhelming greed and of her desire to find a prop in every friendship. The two girls went on many outings together, often visiting the sauna baths, where Henriette A. could indulge in athleticism and asceticism under the pretext of cleansing herself. Well supplied by her mother, but half against her will, she began to put on weight.

Stage 5. Hours 135-171

The patient spent the Christmas holidays at home, where her disillusionments were as great as her joys. Gerda was also at home for a few days, but she was completely taken up with her boy friend and hardly had a moment for her old companion. Henriette A. was also being courted, as she had been for some time previously, by an old schoolfellow. He invited her to a New Year's ball, but Henriette A. was unable to make up her mind. She wanted her mother to decide for her and became furious when the latter refused to take a stand. The patient was now consciously aware of her aggressive feelings, and she hung around the house in order to worry her mother.

Henriette A. was pleasurably surprised when she found that her mother had filled Hasso's place with a German sheepdog. Senta, a bitch, seemed "like a lady who bears the destiny of being female with dignity, in contrast to myself." The important part played by Senta in the patient's experience became apparent when treatment was resumed after the holidays. Reluctantly, she reported a dream which seemed ridiculous to her: "I had a baby which was just barely full-time, almost an embryo still. This baby sucked at my genitals while Senta licked my breast, before or after."

After some hesitation, the patient began to grasp the dream on the subject-object level: she suckles, permits herself to be licked, and is also a baby. She was reminded of a childhood pregnancy and birth fantasy with urethral content—begetting a child by urinating. She thought that she might at some time have tried to urinate like a boy. Licking, sucking, and particularly biting played a conspicuous part in the patient's sensual life. In tantrums, as a child, she had occasionally bitten the bed. Her identification with Senta was demonstrated by her predilection for blood sausages made especially for dogs and by the way she gnawed at bones.

In her deliberations about whether to continue treatment or return home at Easter, Senta was the prime consideration. In view of the number of potential relationships and identifications that Senta provided, it was hardly surprising that the dog also took the place of her mother, and that she thought of Senta whenever her mind turned to her home. Her need for regression was interpreted in that light. The following night, she dreamed that she was romping with Senta. Upon returning home, she was greeted by her mother with the news that it had been decided to marry her to a farmer. She accepted this decision. In the dream, she knew that the dog was going to have puppies and she thought that, if Senta was to have puppies, why should she not also have children one day.

During the preceding stage of treatment, in a dream, Henriette A. had a sensation in the lower abdominal region as if she were about to menstruate. Now, she sometimes had drawing pains during the daytime, but menstruation remained absent. Over Christmas, she had gained more weight, so that she now weighed 128 lbs. Although she actually wished to lose weight now, because the girls in her class were commenting on her round cheeks, she could no longer curb her appetite. With the patient's active participation, the following constructions were framed. While she controlled her eating, Henriette A. not only kept herself at a distance from other people, but was a stranger to herself. While she was fruitlessly trying to lose weight once again, she said, "When one does not eat, everything is different. In those days, I was unhappy and blunted; now, I cannot imagine how I ever managed it."

As repressions are undermined and emotional relationships are resumed, we can predict, with considerable assurance, that the fears which forced the drive to retreat from the object will reappear. This is what happened in the case of Henriette A. The partial withdrawal of object cathexes was accompanied by typical changes in ego structure, i.e., by secondary narcissism. This is well illustrated by the patient's question, "Can't one live without another person? I used to be able to," and by some of her characteristic attitudes toward life. For instance, she would demonstrate her arrogant independence by frequently arriving late for her appointment, and she still expected to be at the top of her class without any hard work. It is true that she also had feelings of inferiority and doubted that she would ever pass her examinations, but this does not weaken the case or invalidate the omnipotence of thoughts hypothesis.

During the anorectic phase, hardly anything could touch her emotionally; now that it was a thing of the past, she became alarmed by the fantasied omnipotence of her thoughts: " 'Thoughts are almost deeds,' our Scripture teacher says." She once experimented with telepathy, trying to will a boy to turn toward her or speak to her; at the same time, she felt terrified that the barrier between thinking and doing might be breached. Fear of what the force of her love and aggression might wreak haunted her day and night during this stage.

There were other occasions when the patient's narcissistic self-sufficiency and amazonlike autarchy were evident. For instance, when she had been reading an article on artificial insemination, her preoccupation with parthenogenesis was reintroduced, although in disguised form. This time it was expressed as a fear of hypodermic needles and syringes. Looking back she came to think that her early apprehensions about such things were well formed. She then suggested, spontaneously, that artificial insemination meant having something injected into the thigh. She realized the significance of this displacement only after the analyst had put a few leading questions to her.

It now became easier to understand her former unwillingness to permit herself to be injected prior to her appendectomy. The patient argued that she must be on guard against artificial insemination, if there were such a thing, since her mistrust of injections would then be fully justified. This rationalization, however, did not stand up to her further associations. She described details of childhood games mentioned in a previous hour, games which involved the use of syringes to bring liquids near the genitals. Infantile ideas about impregnation were associated with these experiences, and Henriette A. was correct, in her way, when she interpreted her fear of hypodermic needles as fear of artificial insemination. She drew parallels between this apprehension and her disinclination to allow other people to penetrate into her inner world. Her unwillingness to enter into abstract, intellectual communion with another person could therefore be traced back to an unconscious defense against concrete, bodily contact.

Henriette A. continued to pursue the subject of artificial insemination, concluding that it made man no better than a vegetable. Then, apparently changing her mind, she suggested that artificial insemination was a sign of self-sufficency, and that it was probably practiced by women who were repelled by any sort of physical capitulation. She spoke of her own sexual fears and, on the same occasion, remarked that tablets could be substituted for meals.

The analyst then pointed out that man not only descended to the level of a vegetable by practicing artificial insemination, but that he also became an all-powerful deity. The deeper significance of the idea of parthenogenesis emerges when we realize that Henriette A. was growing increasingly reconciled to the idea that she might marry some day, but not to "just anyone." In artificial insemination, the donor of semen, the father, is anonymous, and thus exempt from human frailties. He may be seen as "perfect"—an ideal object for identification. In actuality, Henriette A. was fascinated by the idea of how many children a donor might father.

During the consideration of this question, the transference relationship became colored in a typical way. Also, the patient's primitive feelings and fears toward her mother were reawakened. Henriette A. began to endow the therapist with magical powers. She yielded to the wish-fulfillment fantasy that he would do everything for her—in particular, that he would supply doctor's certificates of illness to help her escape the consequences of her poor grades.

The nonfulfillment of her wishes disappointed Henriette A. and made her realize that it was fear of her own rage (provoked by frustration) that had led her to withdraw from her environment. She turned to her mother when she felt misunderstood by the analyst, and vice versa. When neither would grant her wishes, she took action. In this connection, Freud pointed out in the "Studies on Hysteria" (1895, p. 91) that some motor symptoms can be explained in terms of the Darwinian principle of overflow of excitation. Some of the patient's symptoms can be said to have had similar symptomatic properties: for instance, she was probably attempting to discharge excess excitation in exercise and, instead of becoming aware of her motives and aims, she channeled them into sports and hobbies that did not impinge upon the ego. Since eating and motor activity are closely connected on the neurophysiological level (Brügger, 1943), it is likely that the patient was exhibiting a kind of displacement activity (Tinbergen, 1952). Henriette A.'s displacement activities took several forms, the

essential feature of each enactment being the prevention or replacement of conscious awareness. Thus it became easier, for
example, to guess what Henriette A. was seeking in the sauna
baths, apart from purification. The next time her mother came
on a visit, the patient took her along. She then became aware of
sensations and perceptions which, although primarily defensive
in nature—i.e., disgust with her own and her mother's bodies—
later gave way to positive homosexual feelings.

For a long time, the patient had recurrent dreams about water
where she found herself "in her element" (hour 33). The skin
sensations in these dreams were as pleasurable to her as the feelings of warmth and well-being she used to experience when she
would snuggle in her mother's bed during attacks of night terror.
The meaning of water and of dreams of the sea may be interpreted as aspects of what Ferenczi termed the "thalassal regressive trend" (1924). Here, as in her urge for motor activity, the
patient probably experienced physical pleasure. From the point
of view of the act itself, swimming is, of course, not only a form of
resistance; it also represents an attempt on the part of the patient
to experience sensual enjoyment without having to admit to it
or to remember its genetic associations.

In line with the psychoanalytic belief that thinking and doing
are closely allied, it is to be expected that remembering and realizing, thinking and behaving would be closely interwoven in the
course of therapy; in the ideal case, they advance side by side.
This means, for example, that memory and insight can be supplemented, even corrected, by meaningful behavior. Unfortunately,
such harmony exists only in the ideal case. More commonly, there
is a split between affect and representation which Freud has described as an important precondition for neurosis formation.
Thus, both in and out of analysis, people frequently act solely on
the basis of affect while remaining blind to the corresponding representation, or they may remember the representation, but devoid of its affective content. Henriette A., while repressing the
representational contents, showed a tendency to act out; naturally,
this had a considerable influence on the nature of her resistance.

Henriette A. reported a dream wherein she made a girl friend lick a biology book which had been soaked in urine. That evening she had seen the tragedy *Hinkemann*, and she drew a parallel between herself and the hero. He, castrated by an injury, was no real man; she, amenorrheic, was neither man nor woman. It was also part of the Hinkemann story that he tried to earn his living and compensate for his sexual impotence by doing a one-man show in which he killed rats and mice by biting their throats. These associations pointed up the theme of oral aggression. Other day residue material which appeared in the dream had to do with the fact that Henriette A. had been reviewing the maturation processes of the ovum, in a biology book. In its entirety, the dream content (licking-urine-biology book) describes the patient's early notions about impregnation (by urine) mixed with oral instinctual drive components displaced upward.

The patient had a peculiar habit: she almost always saved part of her meal. Even when she was invited out, or when she ate pastry in a coffeeshop, she would leave something and smuggle it into her handbag to be enjoyed at home. In this way, she doubled her pleasure by having something to nibble on later, she exercised a certain amount of control, and at the same time managed to stave off her fear of starvation.

The treatment was interrupted at this point. The patient went away for the Easter holidays without reaching a decision as to where she would finish her schooling. However, she was scheduled to take an examination two days before the beginning of the following term to determine whether the Heidelberg school would accept her as a regular pupil.

Stage 6. Hours 172-189

On the pretext that she had been waiting for the school to let her know the date of her examination, Henriette A. delayed her return until the first day of the term. In reality, she had been hoping that her belated arrival would disqualify her, and that the school authorities would send her home. When she was called

up for her lack of punctuality, she assumed an air of injured in-
nocence, protesting that she had been anxiously awaiting a letter
which never came. Fortunately, the school was lenient, and she
was forced to take the test after all. Her disillusionment grew
apace. In fact, she had started feeling resentful as soon as she dis-
mounted from the train and found neither the analyst nor her
friend waiting on the platform, but she had quickly suppressed
this feeling and filled its place with rancour and thoughts of revenge ("I shall go straight home again").

New accusations were added to the old reproach that the analyst had made her blushing symptom return. During the holidays,
two events had caught her off guard: a sudden interest in boys,
and the reappearance of her periods after a four-year absence.
The analyst was blamed for both these changes.

> *Dream 174:* Gerda and I had to sleep with dwarfs. It was utterly
> revolting. I threw one of them out of the window, and then escaped
> myself by jumping. The dwarf was smashed on the ground. I set
> Senta on to him and she took up the dwarf in her jaws.

The dream that followed directly after this made it obvious
that the dwarf stood for the analyst and his penis. She dreamed:
"Dr. T. is dead." This interpretation was confirmed by observation of Henriette A.'s actual behavior and by her associations.
She complained that the consulting room was too small and
frightened her. Thus, her claustrophobia was introduced into
the transference. She stated: "I always have to sit on the aisle so
that I can get out into the open immediately." She was constantly
on guard against situations in which she might be in danger of
having to comply or compromise her liberty. She also remarked
that the dwarf reminded her of a man who had danced with her;
as time went on, this association became attached to the analyst.
Her identification with the dog Senta was interpreted as an unconscious wish to bite the analyst to death. This interpretation
led her to think of the analyst's death and how terrible it would
be, and at the same time of her own death, to which she claimed

to be indifferent. She became depressed and comforted herself by switching suddenly to the subject of her father: "Of course, he is dead too. If I were dead, I could be joined to him." She was also of the opinion that people could have (as she imagined after the death of her paternal grandfather) complete possession of someone who was dead.

In retrospect, although this was not discussed at the time, there was probably also a dream thought of sleeping with the analyst which was being warded off here, and it was breaking through in the combination: death, oral (castrative) incorporation of the dwarf-phallus. This discovery reveals one of the motive forces of the anorexia and, at the same time, supports the hypothesis that an underlying mechanism—i.e., the fending off of sexual and aggressive impulses—resulted in an intrapsychic displacement and symbol formation. The clinical symptom corresponds to this, for the oral-castrative tendencies made the rejection of intimate contact logical.

At this stage, one of Henriette A.'s fundamental difficulties was coping with her need for "all-or-nothing." *If I take the beloved object into myself* (Senta biting the dwarf), *then for all practical purposes I shall have lost it and I shall be bereft and forlorn.* As long as the cat is playing with the mouse, its fate still hangs in the balance. It is likely that Henriette A. felt she had to save something from every meal in order to keep its fate "in the balance."

Henriette A. passed her examination and was enrolled as a regular student. However, she still had not made up her mind to stay, and she went on trying to play the guest. By now, she was on a good footing with the girls in her class, but she still did not want to submerge herself in the crowd. For days she argued back and forth about joining her class on a school expedition during the Whitsun holidays. In the end, she went with them after all, and gave up a trip home on that account. In day-to-day life, she still felt less certain of herself than during the anorectic phase, and she suggested that: "It would have been far better to stay thin for good; then I would have had everything under control." As time went on, however, she blamed the analyst less and experienced some feeling of gratitude. She showed an additional sign of recovery: she began to perspire on the playing field when she became hot and out of breath, just as she had before she fell ill.

Stage 7. Hours 190-214

Henriette A. came back from several days' excursion with her class in the best of spirits. She was less preoccupied with herself and more concerned with the thoughts and feelings of other people. The outing had also given her an opportunity to get to know her teachers. Furthermore, she had stopped feeling that analysis makes people egocentric—a fear as common as it is mistaken. On the contrary, she was delighted to find that the dissolution of her repressions had made her more receptive to the world around her and had increased her interest in other people. New sensations led to an upsurge of fresh and unconquered anxieties, but the patient had come to the point of a "complete reversal of values" and had begun to feel "human" again. Up until then, she had always been an outsider. She once remarked that anorexia nervosa was "the nicest illness anyone could have" because, when she was anorectic, she had never really been a participant, but had been able to live, so to speak, outside of herself.

Stimulated by the conversation course she was taking in school, she wondered whether there could ever be such candor and trust between human beings as between man and animal. She was still searching for an understanding without words, although she fought shy of the intimacy involved in such a relationship, and was afraid of it. She had once looked on while a school friend and the latter's boy friend shared the same slice of bread, and had regarded this as a vulgar display of affection—one that she could only have indulged in with her dog. The receptive function of eating then became the focus of her associations for a whole analytic hour. She associated: "bottle-fed baby, disgusted when I think of one; injection, the idea that something is flowing into me—horrible! just as bad as thinking of being in mommy's stomach. *Integer, integra, integrum* comes to mind. Untouched. A man is more untouched than a woman. He is inviolate; he does not have to be pregnant. A man remains himself, does not have to assimilate, renounce; only women have to do that." Henriette A. thus linked oral receptivity with conception. Her rejection of the female role was evidenced by her association for *integer,* the superior role attributed to men, and other ideas described below.

Both "an understanding without words" between man and beast and a "marriage of true minds" are comparatively unalarming forms of communion. Henriette A. dreamed of being spiritually united with the analyst. Further dreams showed that this fantasy served to stave off her anxiety, i.e., to consummate her yearning for her father in a "pure" way. In fact, she was idealizing both herself and the analyst. That month, her period was late—which pleased her, at first. The delay was connected with a renewed effort to escape full awareness of her sexuality. At the same time, a tormenting symptom appeared: she began to dread that her hands might do something terrible. It soon became apparent that she was trying to banish the expressive content of her hand gestures in the same way as she had tried to reject it earlier by constant movement. As soon as she was made to understand that, for her, hand gestures meant aggressive as well as tender, sexual impulses and that she was trying to shut these out, the symptom subsided.

The circumstances of the appearance of this symptom are also extremely enlightening. Henriette A. felt lonely. Hints in her letters ("I'll try to get my mother to come for a visit") eventually persuaded her mother to come to Heidelberg. The realization that her mother was not exactly quick-minded or a kindred spirit provided material for the rationalization of deep-seated resentment: "Mother is not giving me what I am looking for." During a walk, Henriette A. was astonished by the terrible idea of grabbing her mother by the throat and strangling her to death. It is hardly surprising that, with this idea lurking in her unconscious, the patient had developed a habit of stopping to stare down at her hands. When the idea eventually emerged, she was shattered; later, she learned to integrate her aggression, as well as to free herself from the symptom. Nevertheless, the fear of what her hands might do did not disappear until she became aware, on a conscious level, that the symptom was linked with tender, sexual impulses: "I might behave like a maniac. I might touch a boy whose skin I liked the look of, or pick up feces and eat them." Although the patient was temporarily shattered by the contents of her associations, she soon realized that it was senseless, psychoanalytically speaking, to repudiate desires and obtain symptoms in exchange. She resolved to give up "trying to find new methods of avoiding contact, as I used to manage to do by being good at games and dieting."

The transference is well illustrated by an excerpt from a novel on which the patient dwelled. Two girl friends were living on a lonely farm. One fell in love with the old, married village doctor. She experienced her love as if it was attached to the doctor and to her friend, as if both were united in one person. Homosexual and heterosexual elements were combined in this love. Henriette A. was reminded of herself in the transference situation, particularly in view of her friendship with Gerda. Like the patient, the girl in the novel wanted "to have a baby without a man." This same theme was expanded further after a dream in which the patient came for her appointment only to meet her mother, who was then replaced by the analyst.

Stage 8. *Hours 215-254*

A Rorschach test, administered about 18 months after the initial test, gave a vivid picture of the patient's state of mind. The following summary of the tests will help to reveal the extent of change.

> The patient's basic psychic structure shows signs of change; there are distinct shifts in the mental economy. Both the introversive-remote aloofness and the tendency toward hypermotility have receded. The personality leans less toward extreme mood swings and has become better balanced, as a whole. The patient's emotional responses seem better adapted. Since both hyperactivity and introversion must

be understood as defensive behavior, it is understood that loosening of these defenses will lead to increased emotional instability, free-floating anxiety, and strong feelings of unpleasure and disinterest. The patient is in a transitional phase. Although pathological anxiety has been, at least partially, laid bare by the analysis, there has not yet been sufficient opportunity for a new orientation to develop or to become stabilized. In her interpretation, "an icicle with a puddle underneath; perhaps it is thawing," she probably expresses her feelings about herself. Her fear of being violated and her ambivalent need for tenderness seem to have become less active. While she has not yet accepted all of the implications of the adult female role, it is obvious that she has begun to move in that direction.

While at home, Henriette A. felt uneasy because of the loss of her self-confidence; for instance, she began to fear that she would tire and drown while swimming. The uneasiness was interpreted as a dread of surrender, in the sense of a phobic displacement. Henriette A. blamed the analyst for her loss of confidence. She tried in vain to idealize the analyst once again in order to free herself of anxiety-provoking ambivalence and to insulate herself in feelingless neutrality. A particularly difficult problem in the analysis was due to the fact that the patient was at an age when, normally, infantile ties are dissolved. In Henriette A.'s case, infantile object relationships had to be revived in order to permit resolution and integration of conflicts that had been improperly solved before. Thus, on the one hand the patient was striving toward a sense of independence normal for her age and, on the other hand, she tried to achieve independence by total neurotic rejection of all dependency. It would seem that the patient had been cast in the role of adult at one moment, and then, abruptly, in the role of helpless child. She described her mother's treatment of her in this way. Thus it may be assumed that the patient's enormous self-sufficiency contrasted with a constant search for support can be attributed to the mother's own insecurity. Henriette A. was now seeking protection from her own ambivalence in the transference. Presumably, the mother's slightly depressive attitude toward life, aggravated by stomach ailments and by the strain of her husband's sudden death only a year after the patient's birth cast a shadow over Henriette A.'s childhood. Certainly, this atmosphere of gloom may well have rendered more acute the conflicts which arose as a result of the patient's ambivalent feelings. There are two main reasons for such a hypothesis: (1) Henriette A. was fatherless. Thus, she was forced to repudiate the hostile aspect of her ambivalent feelings because losing her mother meant total loss of love. (2) The mother had not yet sufficiently worked out her own ambivalent strivings, so that she viewed every sign of ambivalence in her daughter as threatening; the mother's fear reflected and heightened that of the child.   Henriette A. began to realize that she had always been afraid of what she might do, and was alarmed by the idea that she might lose control. During the holidays, her mother had to bear the brunt of this fear, but afterward it was transferred to the analyst. An episode that took place during the holidays gives a good illustration of Henriette A.'s insecurity. When a guest—a school friend—arrived for a visit, the latter was suddenly stricken with severe stomach pains and had to be put to bed. Henriette A. was seized by an onslaught of envy and jealousy. However, she was able to recognize that what she wanted was to keep her mother all to herself, something which—being fatherless and an only child—she had always been able to do. At the same time, she was conscience-stricken because her mother did so much for her. There had always been someone to take the work off her hands—a form of pampering which was to have unpleasant consequences later on. Soon afterward, Henriette A. related a daydream, incidentally providing the analyst with added insight into her transference feelings:

> A duck was pining away in its nest on dry land. It was discovered by a wild gander who carried it, nestling on its back, over wide tracts of land to the sea. The gander and the duck were in their element and disported themselves in the water. At last the frightening question of what to do next arose. The duck could not abide the thought of having to return to her humdrum existence with the drake. She considered all the solutions, and eventually decided to fling herself to her death on the return journey.

The gander symbolizes, on the one hand, a confidence-inspiring superiority, a longed-for relationship, and, on the other hand, an ideal of perfection. The patient was really yearning for an all-knowing, all-powerful father whom she sought in the analyst, in the transference. The fantasied relationship between the gander and the duck thus contains both a narcissistic and an anaclitic object choice.

> A person may love:—
>   (1) According to the narcissistic type:
>   (*a*) what he himself is (i.e. himself),
>   (*b*) what he himself was,
>   (*c*) what he himself would like to be,
>   (*d*) someone who was once part of himself.
>   (2) According to the anaclitic (attachment) type:
>   (*a*) the woman who feeds him,
>   (*b*) the man who protects him ... [Freud, 1914b, p. 90].

In transference, Henriette A. was also seeking a projected masculine ideal, because she was one of those women who, according to Freud, "Before puberty ... feel masculine and develop some way along masculine lines; after this trend has been cut short on their reaching female maturity, they still retain the capacity of longing for a masculine ideal—an ideal which is in fact a survival of the boyish nature that they themselves once possessed" (Freud, 1914b, p. 90). Henriette A. was unable to picture herself marrying a run-of-the-mill "drake" for the very same reason. However, the alternative, an anaclitic object choice—a mother transference —would have presented too many problems because of her fear of regressing into infantile dependency and of the ambivalence that such regression would entail.

During the last stage of the analysis, the subject of the idealized gander and of the inferior drake cropped up again. Miss N., whom Henriette A. seldom saw anymore now that her role as subsidiary transference figure was no longer necessary, became engaged to be married. Henriette A. was introduced to the fiancé and found him very ordinary. She fell into a strange and, to her,

inexplicable state of excitement which grew throughout a treatment hour and finally exploded in violent remonstrations against
the analyst who "should have forbidden" such an unfortunate
match. Obviously, Henriette A. was identifying with Miss N.; she
was indignant not only because the analysis was being terminated,
but because the analyst had failed to provide an equally power-
ful substitute and had lost her to an "ordinary" man instead of
marrying her himself.

The fatal plunge in the daydream was interpreted as the symbolic representation of a union (love-death), and it was pointed
out to the patient that this was a way of delivering herself up to
nature in order to satisfy her yearning. During the night that followed this hour, the patient dreamed of being raped by her uncle.
In the dream, she just let it happen because it was a "law of nature." Since the previous interpretation had indicated that the
plunge was the consummation of a union, it was deduced that
she was blaming everything on nature in order to keep the episode as far as possible from her ego. It is noteworthy that the
uncle in the dream is the same one who had been the little
girl's ideal, who had taken the place of her father, and who
thus provided the prototype for the transference fantasy of the
gander.

Reacting against her erotic desires, Henriette A. considered
becoming a nun, and tried to give herself added protection
against temptation by claiming that psychotherapists should
not marry. In a dream mentioned some time later, she was sitting
in a monastery watching the monks having their heads sound-
lessly lopped off, but the material was never worked over. However, the dream and its latent dream thought do seem to throw
more light on a particularly important aspect of Henriette A.'s demand that psychoanalysts ought to lead lives of monastic asceticism, for this call for celibacy also had a reactive-aggressive component (killing the monks), and thus might be translated in the
following way: "If my analyst does not love me, he must go into
a monastery." The thought behind the manifest content (behead-
ing) is probably a castration wish, as the preceding dream would

seem to confirm; before this is discussed, however, a brief outline of the circumstances will be necessary.

Before this dream, any brief encounters (in the street) between the patient and the analyst with his wife or family had passed without repercussions. At yet another encounter, during the evening, Henriette A. took a closer glance at the analyst's wife and found her to be better-looking than she had expected. She was surprised by this, since she had heard from another patient that Mrs. T. was ugly and probably no more than a high-class housekeeper. During the next hour, Henriette A. announced that she was planning to arouse Miss N.'s jealousy, should they meet again, by telling her that Mrs. T. was pretty after all. However, it was not long before she conceded that she was trying to project her own guilt onto Miss N., in order to avoid the pain of her shame.

In fact, Henriette A. had erected a barrier of pride to shield herself from ever being deceived by a man, or from having to experience the humiliation of competing for a man's favors. She could see that this was a method for escaping every potential disappointment and, incidentally, every potential conquest. Within the analysis, disappointment plays a dominant part, because not only do *old* wishes, now *transferred,* remain unfulfilled, but within the analyst-patient relationship *new* aspirations concerning the physician as a person cannot be realized either. However natural the attempt to avoid new hurtful experiences, there is no way for the patient to evade the revival of old ones, because all neurotic problems have their origins in an incorrect assimilation of earlier conflicts. It was also important that Henriette A. should be made aware of the way in which she held herself aloof from life in order to spare herself any discomfiture. It is in the light of these conjectures that the dream evoked by the evening encounter should be considered; it shows particularly clearly her profound disappointment at not being loved best.

> *Dream:* I wanted to go in the evening to my treatment hour and found my analyst lying on a couch outside in a street. In the dream, however, Dr. T. was a fat eunuch, and I rolled about on top of him and finally, with indifference, lay down beside him.

It is easy to see how the residues of the previous evening have been woven into the fabric of the dream. The fact that the patient had made her analyst into a eunuch was interpreted as a reaction against her resentment at not being loved. At the same time, this castration calmed her jealousy. "He can but may not love any other woman." The unconscious wish that the analyst should at last prove himself to be a man (hence the provocation of his demotion to a eunuch) probably also enters in here. Be that as it may, these were the interpretations given, and they seem to have been well-founded in that they throw light, in retrospect, on the "execution" and "dwarf" dreams.

One day, when Henriette A. was browsing in a bookshop, she happened on the essay, "The Nature and Critique of Psychotherapy," a reprint of two sections from Karl Jaspers' book, *General Psychopathology*. Here she read those final sentences which deal with the therapist's duty to combine "personal function" with "impassable distance," the need for the "preservation of Objectivity," and the risks that accrue when this aloofness is not maintained. The passage goes on: "Once an element of desire ... enters into the ordinary respect for the person who carries out psychic counsel and cure ... psychotherapy would have become little else than skillful seduction. The historical study of the gnostic sects reveals the unending metamorphoses which the role of the therapist can assume in the guise of physician, savior or friend" (Jaspers, 1948, p. 822). While she was still reading, it struck Henriette A. that the analyst had obviously persisted in drawing her attention to this idolization in order to make her conscious of her own wish for a "miracle worker," and thus to prepare the way for a more reasonable mode of behavior.

However, she was very pleased to read about the need for an "impassable distance." Adopting Jaspers' position, she eagerly criticized interpretations of the transference given hitherto, since they had stressed the libidinal object cathexes in the transference. In fact, the call for distance is nothing more than Freud's rule of abstinence, which certain patients often use to buttress the resistance. Such patients, although their symptomatology may differ widely, have one trait in common: the reality-testing function of the ego is so labile that they cannot differentiate adequately between thinking and acting. Consequently, they attempt to suppress all personal feelings for the analyst, especially drive-wishes. They are fearful that their drive-wishes might break through, and thus they barricade themselves behind precepts such as "the need for objectivity" and "keeping at a distance." This type of patient is similar to the anorexia nervosa patient in many ways, particularly in youthfulness. The reason for this is as follows. In the psychoanalytic sense of the word, the ego is the agency for reality-testing. At puberty, more than at any other time, the ego is exposed to structural changes and unexpected onslaughts of instinctual drive activity. Thus, it is easy to see why there are so many teenagers among those patients who are apprehensive of the "omnipotence of their thoughts" and who seek, therefore, to keep everyone and everything at a distance (Eissler, 1958; A. Freud, 1936, 1958).

Experience of this form of resistance engenders interpretations that soon lighten the patient's burden, however. Even the assurance that speaking about sex and aggression need not lead to uncontrolled behavior has a liberating effect. Thus Jaspers' remark (1963, p. 822): "Once an element of desire or mutual private attachment enters into the ordinary respect for the person who carries out psychic counsel and cure, in principle the situation is ruined . . . ," is true only in so far as it refers to a *mutual* private attachment. As soon as Henriette A. began to understand the web of connections between reverence and desire, she realized that she had taken up Jaspers' position only out of anxiety lest her erotic and aggressive thoughts turn into deeds.

Since it had become possible to alleviate her anxiety by means of relevant interpretations, the analyst's ability to help her had also become the measure of his perfection. Thus the patient began to wait eagerly for him to say the "right word." The unconscious alignment of word and object came to be expressed as, "My analyst understands me and, in tone and content, always knows how to say the right word." The word became a present, a token of love. If the patient felt misunderstood—i.e., if nothing were given to her—she began to lose faith. Once, in such a crisis, she dreamed of meeting a stupid, unattractive, physically malformed man. The interpretation made was that she feared the aggression stimulated by her resentment.

With mixed feelings of uneasiness and pleasure, Henriette A. remarked that the increase in her weight during the past several months had brought with it new physical sensations, including a softening of her muscles. She complained of a feeling of pressure in the stomach when she wore a tight skirt or belt. She also reported other physical sensations which could not be explained satisfactorily, but which highlighted the closeness of the relationship between function and form—the disturbance of the nutrition function and of the body schema. One of the most astonishing things about anorexia nervosa patients is the way in which they manage to hold their weight constant, with only minor fluctuations, for years on end. Presumably, the intake of food, in some cases, is automatically regulated by cues from physical sensations such as these.

Henriette A. was as perturbed by the restlessness which drove her to eat as by the awareness of the new contours of her body. During moments of anxiety, she was terrified of being overpowered by unknown dangers, both from within and without. The encounter of inner and outer that occurs during the acts of eating and making love was the theme of several dreams.

In the first dream, related in treatment hour 237, Henriette A. started by seeking shelter with her mother and ended up lying on the analyst's bed. A wrestling match followed, with injuries and bleeding. The most significant detail of the dream was that she was suffocated by thick beams from the ceiling which, in the dream, were Bahlsen biscuits.[6]

In the next dreams (hour 240), the feeling of being suffocated returned, and also (in the dream) she had her period. Finally, in hour 245, she reported having dreamed of having a period which

[6] *Translator's note:* Bahlsen is the name of a well-known brand of German biscuits, and is pronounced like balzen ("to pair," like game birds).

was flecked with white. In the dream, the menstrual blood (including the white parts) was mixed with food which she ate. During the next part of the dream, she was lying under a particularly beautiful girl, having intercourse with her. She did not perceive any penis, however, but just felt the girl's beautiful body and saw the latter's well-formed breasts in front of her.

The words Henriette A. once used to describe her predicament, "being wedded to food," took on a new meaning. In the dream about menstrual blood flecked with white particles and mingled with food, an event took place which contained the elements of parthenogenesis (oral self-impregnation) and of autophagy. Accordingly, the dream was interpreted at both levels. In brief, the white particles were associated with sperm in one case and with milk in the other. It was now easier to understand an earlier dream in which a baby was sucking at the patient's genitals; this form of excretion was unconsciously aligned with food. Besides the interpretation of the content, reference was made to the narcissistic enclosedness of the dream: "I am autarkic and can do everything, begetting and living on my own substance."

The closed circuit of the dream points to a fear of loss and death (nothing must be wasted), and also presents an attempt to surmount this fear. When such a process takes place not only at dream level, but governing active behavior, the result is one of those paradoxes that are typical of many anorexias. So long as the ego's defense strategies are enforcing a strict state of emergency, no changes can take place within the psyche; however much the patient may be hovering between life and death, he clings irrationally to his belief in immortality. The fatal decline of many anorexia nervosa patients can easily be understood when the theory of ego psychology is applied. The paradox might be formulated somewhat like this: "I am living on my own inexhaustible substance[7] and am no longer subject to the dangers of exchange which end in death. I am independent of everything,

---

[7] There is an unconscious confusion here between the substance of the self and that of the mother.

even death." This sweeping disavowal frees the patient from any
fear of death.

Fortunately, Henriette A. was not living in such a state of
autarky, so that other dreams of hers made it possible to understand why she was reverting to narcissism. She had to ward off
dangerous object relationships—oral violation by Bahlsen biscuits
(displacement from below upwards) and homosexual relationships and the attendant drive impulses. The displacement in the
dream—the suffocation by Bahlsen biscuits—also came up in the
course of her associations in the form of a physical sensation. She
said she felt as though her tongue were swelling, and she re-en-
acted the sensation of being suffocated in the dream. The swelling
of the tongue was a displacement of excitation. It caused the
patient worry that she would not be able to speak normally and
would have to stammer. This fear ceased abruptly as soon as she
understood how the mouth could be an organ for the articula-
tion of dammed up libidinal strivings. The homosexual dream
was also mentioned in this context. Henriette A. remarked that
she had just stopped consulting a lady doctor because she could
not have endured discussing her need for affection with a woman.

It was very encouraging to observe Henriette A.'s capacity to
accept interpretations and to assimilate seemingly unmotivated
anxiety states into the framework of her life in an integrated
form. In particular, she was plagued by aggressions directed
against her mother, which were partly due to the fending off of
her longing for support and partly the results of frustration. Occasionally, her feelings of guilt would make her behave carelessly.
For instance, she took great pride in her skill and agility on a
bicycle, which she would ride in heavy traffic, swerving across
streets inches ahead of a car.

To her great surprise, her schoolwork improved, even though
she worked far too little in comparison with her classmates.
Choosing a career presented problems. She not only wanted to
put off her decision until the very last moment; she also wanted
to seek out a career that would serve in lieu of marriage, a family,
and everything else. The school guidance counselor told her that

she was a good "jack-of-all-trades," somewhat above average, and that her intelligence compensated for her lack of concentration. She had already considered the possibility of becoming an interpreter and, as time went on, this field of studies seemed to choose itself.

Stage 9. Hours 255-289

Henriette A. had intended to study during the Christmas holidays before her final examinations, but this did not happen. Instead, she gave a party with her friend Gerda, and for the first time enjoyed every minute of it. She was composed, on good terms with herself, and did not feel the need for constant self-control. She was also a social success, admired by the boys and courted in a friendly way. Murderous impulses no longer beset her, although she had begun to be afraid of taking long lonely walks, and had occasional choking sensations.

Her relationship toward her mother had changed, and she regretted the development of a greater feeling of inner detachment toward her home. It was obvious that she was still fighting off strong anaclitic wishes, and this had a strange effect on her attitude toward children. Certainly she enjoyed playing with her young niece and nephews, but she still had the impression that she was not inwardly relaxed and free, or able to make any real contact with them. "Now that I don't feel anything for my mother," she said, "I ought to be able to feel something for children." It seemed natural enough to her to want to have a love affair, but unthinkable to have to bear, feed, and rear children. It was pointed out to her that this lack of feeling was probably due to the fact that she was identifying herself with the children, and such an identification would only emphasize her feelings of infantile dependence. The dream of sucking and licking was also reconsidered in the light of this interpretation. However, the fundamental problem behind the patient's words and the interpretation is concealed in the intricate web of relationships between subject and object, the unraveling of which presents no easy problem for the analyst.

During the last months of analysis, Henriette A. once dreamed that she had strangled the analyst during her sleep. Somehow the topics of love and greed also entered into the dream. Henriette A. was reminded of a fable about a devil who ambushed his victims in order to devour them. It also occurred to her that, while she had been playing with her nephew who was about four years old, he had whispered (she did not know why) into her ear: "I am going to say something especially nice to you: I want to kill you." The destructive force of her desire for love was making her fend off her wishes for dependence, for in that condition she would be defenseless, at the mercy of her own impulses. It is also interesting that hours 258 and 259 were separated by a weekend in which Henriette A. went dancing and fell in love for the first time. One of her school friends said, with a grin, "Thank heavens, you're getting normal at last." On the following evening, the day before she dreamed of throttling Dr. T, a mild *angina tonsillaris* developed—the first illness Henriette. A. had had during the whole analysis, apart from minor foot troubles.

As it happens, the psychosomatic implications of *angina tonsillaris* are interesting enough in their own right. The patient had heard from someone else about the "flight into illness," and she now applied this phrase to herself, suggesting that she might have fallen ill so as to avoid her new boy friend. From the psychosomatic point of view, of course, the pathogenesis cannot be so simply deduced from the so-called epinosic gain. However, Henriette A. had feared the consequences of such a relationship since well before the angina, and her fear had already expressed itself in her unwillingness to be kissed. After the illness, she put up no more resistance. Indeed, there can be no doubt that Henriette A. was "at the turning point of a complete reorientation of her inner development," as V. von Weizsäcker phrased it, when the tonsillitis appeared, very much as in the *angina tonsillaris* patients he observed during research conducted at Heidelberg Hospital in collaboration with Bilz, Cohen-Booth, Plügge, Vogel, and others. Indeed, the analogies (von Weizsäcker, 1946, p. 25) are striking in other ways, including the number of questions that defied every attempt at solution.

In all cases, the crisis is a formal one, which can only be characterized as containing some sexual temptation. But, as von Weizsäcker (1946) pointed out, it would be too trivial to conclude that the "psychogenetic origin of the angina is frustrated or badly conducted sexual activity," or that "tonsillitis cannot substitute for the genital process as such because it does not arise out of the frustration itself, but out of the particular form that frustration of this process has taken" (p. 23). This "particular form" is "nothing more or less than an injury to the erotic relationship." This and subsequent definitions prove that von Weizsäcker was attributing special importance, in psychoanalytic terms, to the form of defense, the "form of frustration." As he put it: "The psycho-physical excitation does not flow toward the oral pole of the axis because the outlets there are similar to those at the genital pole, but because *something is hindering its progress to the latter*" (von Weizsäcker, 1946, p. 24; *my italics*). In fact, there is a "displacement of excitation" here, in the psychoanalytic sense of the words. Von Weizsächer toys with the notion that, by analogy with the formation of symptoms in hysteria, the concept of conversion[8] might also be applied to the pathogenesis of tonsillitis. True, the comparison suggests itself. As is clear from the definition given below, the concept of conversion implies both the displacement of excitation and the avoidance of any conscious working through. Although these implications are both part of the concept of conversion, he eventually discarded the idea.

Mysterious though it may seem, the leap from the mental to the physical mentioned by Freud with reference to conversion (1916-1917) can be retraced in the realm of the manifest symptoms of hysteria. In these symptoms, the psychic content is retained, and the only leaps to be made are between different levels of a "similar functional niveau." It is therefore possible, in principle, to see

---

[8] Freud gave the following definition: ". . . hysterical symptoms originate through the energy of a mental process being withheld from conscious influence and being diverted into bodily innervation (*'conversion'*)" (1926b, p. 263).

Anorexia Nervosa

a "sense" in a conversion symptom of a conversion hysteria, if "sense" is interpreted, as Freud would have it, in terms of its " 'meaning,' 'intention,' 'purpose' and 'position' in a continuous psychical context" (1916-1917, p. 61). It would be a methodological error to attempt to interpret psychologically an organic symptom which is the end result of an intermediary chain of organic processes, instead of trying to understand those vegetative nervous impulses in their relation to psychological factors which introduce a chain of organic events resulting in an organic disturbance[9] (Alexander, 1935).

Unlikely as it may seem, even such a slight visitation of *angina tonsillaris* as this, which affected the patient's normal good health for only a few days and subsided without aftereffects, can pose a most difficult problem for psychosomatic medicine to resolve. Indeed, it seems as if all efforts to track the mysterious leap from psyche to soma are doomed to failure. For there is no quick way to pierce the obscurity that sunders the "crisis" and the "displacement" from the disease, the tonsillitis; simply to cancel out the discrepancies and interpret the local inflammation as the direct equivalent of a crisis is a convenient solution which leads nowhere. When Kütemeyer (1959) claims that, in malignant diseases, "madness has become a structural part of matter," he is probably basing his argument on speculative comments culled from the later works of von Weizsäcker. In practice, there do not seem to be any grounds for believing that the principle of equivalence of the *Gestalt Kreis*[10] can be applied to the relationship between part and whole, organ and subject, so that the degeneration of body cells might be construed as an act of repression, a kind of substitute for conscious actions.

It is easy to recognize here—just as in the apparent solving of psychosomatic problems by Boss and the existential school of analysis—nothing more than interpretations of symbols of physical

---

[9] Freud (1910c) had already mentioned, in principle, the difference between those functional disturbances that could be symbolically interpreted and others.

[10] von Weizsäcker's definition: "Principle of equivalence (principle of substitution): for the *Gestalt Kreis,* the equivalence is not that of a quantity of energy, but a substitution in the establishment of the classification of a biological organism in the environment. In this classification, a perception can stand for a movement and vice versa" (1950, p. 201).

events wrapped up in anthropological or existential psychologizing. But, if we do not permit ourselves to become fascinated with their eloquent language, it becomes obvious that both parties are committing the error of transferring the psychoanalytic concept of defense, to which conversion is subordinate, to pathogenesis and pathology. For Kütemeyer, it is the cell that is possessed by madness instead of the patient; for Boss, it is the extent of suppression of any life possibility (1954, p. 91) that decides whether an organic-neurotic or hysterical type of neurosis takes the stage. When von Weizsäcker (1950) says that, "As a rule, it is not the similarity or causality of the psychic and physical series which obtrudes, but rather the opposite: interruption, disruption and incoherence" (p. 35), he is describing aspects of the defense processes. The field of phenomena encompassed by all the better-known psychosomatic theories corresponds almost exactly to the range recognized by psychoanalysts as purely defensive maneuvers.

To return to the patient, Henriette A., it might have been possible, in the light of this knowledge, to trace the mysterious leap whereby the sensations aroused by the neurotic oral conversion and linked to the course of the excitation were diverted into physical innervations with psychic contents. Such an interpretation might have initiated conscious working-through. Not that this interpretation would have done anything to clarify the process Freud was referring to (1916-1917, p. 258) when he was discussing why the mysterious leap takes place in hysteria and not in the compulsive neuroses (cf. Thomä, 1962). Organic symptoms, even acute inflammations, are far too complicated for that, and the "intermediary process," to use Alexander's phrase, is not open to view. Indeed, our categories of thought seem to be limited here by bounds that cannot be crossed from either direction—either from the psychological or the physiological side—without infringement. This is why, for example, phrases like "couvade angina" (Bilz, 1936) although vague, are useful to us. They describe a total situation—in this case, a woman's lying-in, which is proving conflictful for her husband. Unfortunately, we are not yet qualified to reduce psychogeneses and somatic pathogeneses to a single common denominator.

It is also likely that, at the moment of "crisis," Henriette A. was more susceptible to a physiopsychical reorientation and that there may have been a predisposition arising out of neurotic conversion processes. The vantage point of the "crisis" enables us to see through a momentary break in the clouds that surround the psychosomatic entity. But if we are to advance beyond inconclusive and unconstructive generalizations, we must make some effort to distinguish form and content in the critical reorientation and, inevitably, to dissect and examine it in order to classify all the levels at which such an upheaval reverberates. In summary, there is no advantage to be gained from attempting to psychologize inflammation processes; hitherto, all efforts to embrace psychology and physiology in one analytic Esperanto have been remarkably unimpressive. They seem instead to lead to a mutual compromise of those special discoveries that are best described in their own languages, pathophysiology and psychoanalysis.

As has been pointed out before, the tonsillitis subsided without treatment after a few days. In contrast to Sabine B. (Case 2), whose anorexia nervosa was prefaced by diphtheria, this illness marked a turn for the better. Henriette A. took her examination without undue anxiety, while still letting slip no opportunity of participating in the pre-Lenten celebrations. Her first violent love affair was swiftly replaced by another. One evening, during Carnival week, she fell in love with a young "existentialist," who was in many ways her opposite. They sat up until the small hours discussing good and evil, and denying the existence of either. They also both resolved to follow high-minded, ascetic ideals, declaring that all dependence on the body was base and unworthy of humanity. However, these lofty ideals did not prevent them from exchanging passionate caresses. During the short sleep that followed this episode, Henriette A. dreamed about being in bed with a young man and hiding him under the bedclothes when her mother came in. After waking, she had some difficulty in getting to sleep again, partly because of the sexual excitement experienced during the previous evening. She now remembered being sexually stimulated before, although she had never admitted to it.

The happenings during Carnival week evoked a dream which exposed one of the roots of her feelings of inferiority as a woman. She dreamed that an army of black beetles was coming out of her taut, distended breasts. The dream was motivated by her having noticed her partner's sexual excitement while dancing; the equation breast=penis represented this sensation in autoplastic form. The black beetles symbolized sperm—depreciating it to something disgusting. Henriette A. arrived at this interpretation almost by herself; it showed her that she felt incapable of fulfilling the function of a mother, because her breasts ought to beget and not suckle.

During the last days of the analysis, the patient had a disabling bout of insomnia. As a child, she had had a quick and effective hypnagogic fantasy which no longer worked: she used to imagine that she was falling down a deep well. It emerged that the difficulty in getting to sleep could be understood in the following way: falling asleep signified both violation and a regression into longed-for security. It was characteristic that the patient began to be afraid of falling asleep during the interview. She found this thought particularly unpleasant because she was very much aware of the fact that she wanted to stay with the analyst, although she was also eager to part from him, even in the realm of thought. The extent to which her fear of letting herself fall was still complicated by the unconscious overtones of aggression and danger that surrender had for her was shown by a dream in which she was wounded by a man with a poison-pistol and fell over. Interpretative work improved this symptom considerably.

Henriette A. did well on her examinations. She could now be discharged in a good all-around state of health: her periods had been regular for months, she weighed 121 pounds, and her constipation was much improved. In sum, there was every indication that she would make excellent progress. As far as the symptomatology is concerned, the patient did not yet feel free to eat to her heart's desire, but preferred to put the last mouthful aside so that her stomach would not stick out too much. The decisive change, however, is that the defense processes have far less influence over her thoughts and behavior, and the relationships between id, ego, and environment are far less rigid.

It thus seemed justifiable to let the *vix medicatrix naturae* take its course, and to terminate the analysis. The patient wished to pursue her studies elsewhere, but it was arranged that she would return for a subsequent course of treatment during her holidays. Accordingly, she arrived, several months later, for a series of fifteen hours. The patient's development had made promising progress in every direction.

❦ 5 ❦

Case 2 : Sabine B.

Synopsis

Sabine B., an unemployed, single woman of 26, was treated for a total of 304 psychoanalytic sessions after five years of illness. On admission, she was 5 ft. 3 in. tall and weighed 73 lbs. The hysterical, obsessive, depressive, and paranoid symptoms of her anorexia nervosa had confined her to her room for the previous few years, where she had been tended by her family, especially after she became completely bedridden. During the course of the analysis, she became capable of working, and it was possible for her to achieve some social adjustment.

Sabine B. was the third child of an agricultural worker. She had been breastfed up to the age of three months. When weaned to the bottle, she had had an attack of vomiting and diarrhea which, according to her mother, left her dangerously weak. The births of the younger sisters released in her a hate and jealousy which throughout her life continued to poison the relationships to her siblings, without the rest of the family being aware of it. On the contrary, she was considered a model child, giving trouble only at mealtimes, when she often fussed over her food and occasionally vomited. Sabine B.'s grandmother A. played a dominant role in her childhood.

The little girl's resentment at having to share her mother with the others, particularly the younger sisters, suffused her with vindictive jealousy which she experienced as absolute evil. She was not able to tolerate her feelings because of a "basic trust" (Erikson, 1961) in her mother and grandmother; instead, these feelings were repressed. Thus she felt secure in her grandmother's love only when she was being a good girl. Under the old woman's influence, her ideal of perfection became a doll "which does not eat or defecate." Any bodily functions which clashed with this ideal were given a negative value. She was not allowed to behave like a normal child and, since she was afraid of losing her grandmother's love by playing "dirty games with the other children," she retreated deeper and deeper into a world of her own. Throughout the analysis, this case afforded a renewed confirmation of Freud's observation that ". . . the instinctual representative [ideations and affects] develops with less interference and more profusely if it is withdrawn by repression from conscious influence. It proliferates in the dark, as it were, and takes on extreme forms of expression . . ." (1915c, p. 149). The result was a vicious circle in which every new phase of development recharged these unconscious fantasies and affects, sparked off new anxieties and feelings of guilt, and set in motion a chain of defense processes; all of this led to a development disturbance.

The following reconstruction gives a rough schematic outline of the most important root causes of the symptom formation. The scheme begins with the early stages of development, which did not appear in the illness itself in a "pure" form, but which first became visible through a regression, and thus were seen in a form adulterated by later modes of experience.

It should be remembered that, even today, the exact timing of the various stages of development is still a matter for doubt and debate, although many gaps have been filled by direct observation and the experience of child analysis since 1936, when Anna Freud pointed to the discrepancies in our chronology of the defense mechanisms.

In this case, however, the patient was already adult, and it must be emphasized that in our formulations we must always take the factor of regression into consideration. As Freud put it, "My formula needed only to hold good where there was a higher degree of differentiation in the psychical apparatus" (1927, p. 156). To take paragraph 1 below as an example: there is no implication here that any feelings of guilt actually arose during the stage of oral ambivalence. Such feelings must always be preceded by a definite ego development and a higher stage of differentiation. The same applies to the reaction formations of revulsion and disgust described in paragraph 2.

1. Sabine B.'s relationships with people and things were essentially governed by a primitive ambivalence, which she often expressed as "devouring out of hate and love." "Now, I think, we can at last grasp two things perfectly clearly: the part played by love in the origin of conscience, and the *fatal inevitability of the sense of guilt*" (Freud, 1930, p. 132; my italics).

We do not yet know all the reasons why the experience of ambivalence should set pathogenic defense mechanisms in motion. Possibly a constitutional component in the sense of an unfavorable relationship between the strength of the instincts and the modification of the ego, as described by Freud (1937)—had made the patient particularly vulnerable to her grandmother's methods of education. Be that as it may, there can be no doubt that in this case, fears and feelings of guilt in regard to natural bodily functions were overcome by pathogenic defense mechanisms.

2. Reaction formations of disgust and revulsion spread from breast and milk to food, and eventually to matter of every sort. Food also remained unconsciously linked with cannibalism; this repressed association made it impossible for her to eat normally. As she grew older, she began to shut herself off from social contact, and the conflicts that had originated in the oral relationship between mother and child were generalized to family mealtimes. Since an oral identification was disrupted by feelings of guilt, the patient actually sought her mother all of her life.

3. The unconscious oral-aggressive instinctual drives gave the world—via projection—a terrifying aspect. Sabine B. was afraid of being poisoned. She managed to rid herself of guilt feelings through this projection of her incompatible drive impulses: "It is not I who am bad and poisonous; poison is given to me by other people."

4. By absenting herself from the family table and expecting her mother to cook specially for her, she was repeating her exorbitant demands; these were insatiable since food (which was

equated with mother) had to be avoided because of guilty feelings. Later on Sabine B.'s emotional and intellectual needs for company fell victim to her grandmother's veto.

5. A static ideal of beauty caused repression of anality and all interest in physical functions. Eventually she discovered that stubbornness—even as a small child, she had no recourse to open, direct aggression—provided her with an indirect means of controlling and punishing her family.

6. She developed a taboo against touching. An excessive compulsion to wash and cleanse satisfied her ideals of purity and at the same time allowed repressed material to reappear. In addition, her obsessive behavior helped her to fend off pent up aggressions, which dissociation had made appear even more gruesome.

7. In an exact and detailed repetition, the patient was now duplicating her relationship to her grandmother with a niece, Gitta, who as a small child was already becoming her aunt's twin likeness.

8. The patient's nutritional disturbance was overdetermined at the oedipal level. At the beginning of treatment, oral and anal fantasies of reproduction still had not been corrected.

9. The development of her breasts and the menarche had come upon the patient without explanation or expectation, and merely reinforced her disgust with all bodily functions. Her ideals of beauty and purity were shattered by these physical changes. She did not want to become like other women; she wanted to be a boy. This unconscious identification expressed itself in her unconventional behavior and the nickname Franz, a boy's name which stuck with her for years. Her imitative behavior was related to penis envy, and can be formulated: "I am what I want to have" (see Freud, 1921, p. 105).

10. There are few incidents of interest in her "superficial" life history. Apart from a short trial period as a domestic, which failed because of her overwhelming homesickness, she remained at home. During the winter she attended needlework classes.

When she was 21 years old, Sabine B. met a young man, Karl; at that point her reality testing became more impaired, and she began to misinterpret the facts—that is, she denied the difference between the sexes. This denial of perception (in the sense of an unconscious defense mechanism) was accompanied by repression of her wishes for a sexual relationship, and a regression to the oral stage of development. Thus, she was abandoning "acting out" as a method of surmounting anxiety through identification, and as an expression of penis envy; and regressively, oral strivings were being recathected. As a result, sexual wishes and penis envy, for example, underwent a transformation. One of the earliest symptoms is an illustration. One day when her boy friend offered her something to eat, she was suddenly striken with a fear of being poisoned, and never again accepted anything from him. Along with the "denial," the projection mechanism determined the psychopathological picture. Oral-aggressive (see p. 121, no. 3) and sadistic-sexual *substance* took on the *form,* through projection, of a fear of poisoning or violation. Sabine B. also experienced many other thoughts of her own as though they belonged to the outside world. For example, she heard "the voice of conscience" speaking as her grandmother. In spite of its appearance, this was not a schizophrenic disturbance.

11. The persistence of her boy friend in sexual matters intensified her fears. A few days after Karl had tried to kiss her for the second time—under the influence of alcohol, they had once gotten as far as fondling—she contracted diphtheria. With this acute illness, her previous conflict resolutions collapsed, and she fell into the condition described above. Later, the patient described her situation in these words, "I wanted to be as small as a baby; time stood still."

Follow-up Report
(four years after analysis was terminated)

Since the termination of analysis, Sabine B. has been working as a domestic helper in a private hospital in a south German town. She has proved well able to cope with life, although she is still a retiring, obsessive, and timid girl. She is now 33 years old, and lives in a dependent relationship to the matron. Her job is mainly to look after the doctors and run their canteen, giving her ample opportunity for transference. She is still amenorrheic and underweight. Later, the hyperventilation tetany reappeared, and she was treated in the hospital for a short time.

Family History

The following family tree gives a survey of ages and, as far as possible, the causes of death of the grandparents. Sabine B. was born into a rural working-class family. As is usual in that part of the country, her parents tend a small plot of land in addition to their regular work.

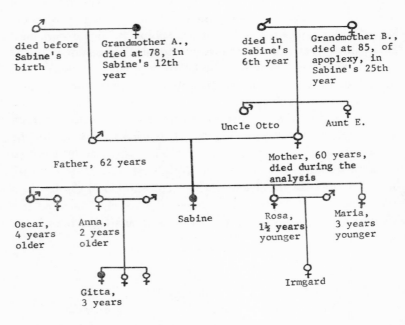

There is no hereditary indication of mental or endocrine disturbances in the family. The relatives marked with black circles played a particularly important part in Sabine B.'s life. Her beloved grandmother A. probably suffered from osteo-arthritis; she died at the age of 78. Gitta, the niece, was Sabine B.'s pet. On the whole, the patient felt that her other relatives rejected her—particularly Uncle Otto and the "wicked" grandmother B., who preferred her younger sister Maria. She was always fearful that her father had repudiated her because she had been such a bad eater as a child.

Biography

Sabine B.'s earliest childhood recollections revolve around her adored grandmother A. and the birth of her younger sisters. The two sisters are one and a half and three years younger than she, and the births are probably telescoped in her memory. She believed that she could remember being unable to endure seeing her little sister feeding at the breast; apparently she wanted to push the rival away and drink herself. Later on, she would not allow her sister to sit on the mother's lap. Sabine B.'s feeding disturbances during childhood were punished by the parents, without success. Her mother threatened that she would sell her to the gypsies if she would not "be good and eat." There is no means of telling when Sabine B. repressed her desire to suck milk from the breast. Milk became something disgusting to her, and she is supposed to have said that she would cut off her breasts when she grew up.

Seemingly, apart from her stubbornness at mealtimes, Sabine B. was a paragon of goodness and cleanliness. As far as can be ascertained from her mother, no one even guessed how much she loathed her siblings.

She was always unsure of her mother's love; the threat of being sold to the gypsies convinced her that she would not really be missed. In addition, grandmother A. is alleged to have said that it would have been better if Sabine B. had died in infancy of her bilious attack, since the mother did not really like the child.

From her earliest days, Sabine B. was the favorite of her grandmother, who was very much attached to her. However she felt secure in grandmother A.'s love only as long as she did as she was told. She was particularly praised and held up to the others as an example when she did not play with the rest of the children and get dirty. Grandmother A. considered everything natural and childlike to be ugly, sinful, and expliable only through hell-fire. Suffice it to say that Sabine B. came to think that anything that did not match her ideals of purity and beauty was wicked—just as her grandmother had taught her.

Sabine B. was a particularly inquisitive child, but her questions were answered with evasions or with the adage, "children should be seen and not heard." Consequently she suppressed her curiosity in order not to lose her grandmother's love. Even when she was still quite small, she cared for the sick old woman and ran errands for her. Her obsession with cleanliness began to show itself in the way she cleaned shoes, even the soles, polishing them until she could see her face. She earned her grandmother's special approval by never playing in the sandbox with the others. Instead, she stayed indoors with the old woman.

During her whole childhood, she had neither friend nor playmate. Her sisters were perfectly normal children, but she was something special, especially pretty, especially good, and her grandmother's favorite. Sabine B. could not remember ever having wanted to do the same things as other children, such as going to the playground or smashing something to see what was inside. She always kept everything tidy and did not even play with her dolls, so that they would stay new and beautiful—which always pleased her grandmother very much. Boys were especially alien to her. She also always felt a certain fear of her father, which she later expressed as the belief that he, like all men, could kill women.

Sabine B. was an average scholar. She had no schoolfriends; in the years just before puberty, she had gone through a phase of being a tomboy and playing all sorts of pranks, which had won her the nickname Franz. Nevertheless, she was a great help at home in the kitchen, doing her best not to let her younger sisters help, so that she might win all the praise and stay close to her mother. In her twelfth year, her idolized grandmother A. died. At first Sabine B. wanted to die too, but she eventually contented herself with moving into the vacant room which the grandmother had occupied during her illness.

After she left school, she was supposed to attend trade school, but since her sisters were not able to go with her, she wept so long that the project was finally abandoned. Following a brief employment in a household where she suffered from homesickness, she returned home. Now at last she felt like an only child, because all her siblings were either married or working. Sabine B., having made up her mind to stay with her mother forever, learned sewing and embroidery which she worked at with great enthusiasm.

The menarche came upon her in almost complete ignorance, between her fifteenth and sixteenth years. She reacted with disgust, the feeling she had toward all physical functions.

At the end of the war, the situation in Germany gave Sabine B. new substance for her fantasies of murder and rape. Until she was 21, her life was very uneventful. She lived at home, knitting and embroidering from morning to night.

Apart from a stubborn boil, when she was about 20 years old, she had no serious illnesses.

Notes on the Previous Medical History

Five years earlier, in 1947, the patient had fallen ill with an attack of diphtheria, which she attributed to a chill. A few days before the attack, she had been to the movies with a young man. While saying good night, they had stood on the doorstep for a long time; it was very cold, and she thought she had caught the chill there. The young man tried to kiss her, but was sternly refused. A few days later, there was a purulent discharge on her tonsils. At first a mild angina was diagnosed, but soon afterward she was inoculated for suspected diphtheria which bacteriological tests confirmed. Sabine B. entered the hospital for treatment of postdiphtheritic polyneuritis—paralysis of the soft palate, and paresis of the arms, and later of the legs. The polyneuritis responded satisfactorily, eventually receding completely. However, some pain in the left leg remained, and a psychogenetic dysbasia developed which did not improve even after further treatment. At first, the patient was up for several hours during the day; during the last few years, she became almost completely bedridden. Devoid of all interest in life, she lay in a darkened room, eating practically nothing. Her weight sank from 132 lbs. to about 73 lbs., probably at times to even lower. At one point she was so cachectic that the village priest was called to administer the last rites.

Sabine B. had been amenorrheic since 1948, but her menses were irregular even before that. Hormone treatments produced a solitary show of blood, one year before the analysis began. The menarche occured between the ages of 15 and 16; it came regularly every 28 days, lasting for three to four days, with some pain. She had severe constipation and, according to her report, went for weeks without a bowel movement. She also complained of spasmodic pains in her body and an ache in her left leg.

The illness intensified her already existing obsession for washing and cleaning. As long as she still had enough strength to do things for herself, she spent all day washing her body and scrubbing her room. Later, when weakness confined her to bed, her family, especially her sister Maria, had to polish the floor for hours every day and bathe her, although the latter could be done only after great precautions had been taken. A bowl of disinfectant was set out, and the community nurse and family had to cleanse their hands thoroughly before touching her.

Sabine B. was always afraid that her food might be poisoned; occasionally, she vomited. She showed many other symptoms of severe anxiety, insisting that all the doors be kept locked. Her fear grew stronger when she began to hear whispering in the room, although no one was there. She usually could not understand what the voices said. But she did recognize her dead grandmother A., who gave her directions, in the form of commands and prohibitions: "You are not permitted to do that; this is good; that is wicked," and so on. At times she searched the room for the speaker although she really knew that she was imagining it all.

Four years before treatment in this hospital, she had her first attack of tetany. She had a total of ten attacks, due to hyperventilation. Mrs. B. hardly dared to leave the house, and the patient herself refused to see any of the other villagers. The only people she could endure around her were Gitta, her four-year-old niece, and a female friend who suffered from severe polyarthritis. Her mother and sister Maria had a difficult job in nursing her, because Sabine B. had to have everything cooked specially for her, and she would often decline even the most carefully prepared food. She could not eat any meat at all, because she vomited it up immediately. Warm food disgusted her and was usually sent back untouched. She lost all her appetite and drank little, except soda water, or a little fruit juice after much coaxing. She had gone back to using her baby silverware and a miniature plate and cup, and she watched anxiously to see that nobody else used them, lest they be "poisonous."

Although she made inordinate demands on her mother and sisters, she never expressed her desires, her disappointments, or her hostility. Instead she bottled everything up inside her and would often cry the whole day long. Everything was disgusting and threatening. Animals, except for birds and goldfish—she had some in an aquarium in her room—revolted her. She destroyed all the photographs from her childhood. Over her bed hung a painting of a woman lying on a bed of roses, surrounded by angels. By her bedside stood a photograph, a particularly bad snapshot of herself.

Two years before this, the patient had been admitted to a neurological hospital for examination and treatment; the diagnosis was "anorexia nervosa following diphtheria." There were no more traces of the postdiphtheritic polyneuritis. The patient's mobility disturbance, especially in the strength and trophism of the left leg, was attributed to her lack of exercise. The neurological findings were otherwise normal. Apart from the reduction of weight (she was then 88 lbs.), the amenorrhea, constipation, and functional dysbasis, a general psychic adynamia was observed. The internal examination disclosed no primary organic changes, such as occur in Simmonds' disease. The psychic symptoms were particularly noticeable: the patient seemed depressive, with a childish affect, no will to recover, and a rejecting attitude toward life.

Following this hospital examination, the patient was put under the care of her family doctor. During the last two years, her general condition deteriorated, and her weight dropped to around 73 lbs.

Findings at the Beginning of Treatment

Height: 5 ft. 3 in.; weight: 73 lbs. At first examination there was no edema, although this appeared at a later date. The extremities showed acrocyanosis; the skin felt dry and cool. At the beginning of the treatment, the patient had a complete physical examination. Neurologically, there was an obvious disturbance of the mobility of the left leg, particularly in regard to its strength and trophism. No organic explanation could be found for this disturbance (no impairment of sensitivity or abnormality of the reflexes). There was, however, a slight hypotonia of the muscles.

Other important features of the findings are as follows: Extreme emaciation; marked curvature of the spine with slight scoliosis, which corrects itself, however, when the patient is sitting. Teeth in need of dental treatment. Thorax and lungs normal; heart of normal size with regular rhythm. BP 100/85, in a recumbent position, hypotonic. ECG: Normal tracing. Epigastric tenderness; meteorism; murmuring sounds. ESR 6/20. Blood count and urine, normal. BMR: + 9.1%. Glucose tolerance test (100 gm glucose), fasting, 88 mg%; 15 minutes after glucose, 78 mg%; after one hour, 64 mg%; after one and a half hours, 94 mg%; after two hours, 78 mg%; after two and a half hours, 56 mg%; after three hours, 60 mg%; after three and a half hours, 78 mg%. This is a pathological and hypoglycaemic curve.

Since the patient was no longer a member of any health insurance plan, and the diagnosis had already been clinically determined, no further tests were made.

Notes on the Diagnosis

The physiological and psychopathological findings indicated that Sabine B. had been suffering from a psychogenetic anorexia for five years, which had developed after diphtheria. The constellation of symptoms was typical for anorexia nervosa: extreme emaciation, loss of appetite, sporadic vomiting, spasmodic epigastric pains, severe constipation, and amenorrhea.

This syndrome was accompanied by noteworthy psychopathological phenomena. Sabine B. lived in complete seclusion, isolated even from the family, and during the last few years had not even shared their meals. Her mother had to cook specially for her, but even the daintiest of morsels—and Sabine B.'s thoughts rotated chiefly around the theme of food—was spurned with loathing, and usually, silence. Her relatives were permitted no access to the isolated patient, who stubbornly refused all consolation. She merely existed from day to day, without any interests or aims. As long as she had been strong enough, she had embroidered and knitted for hours on end, occupying the rest of her time with her excessive compulsion to wash and to cleanse. By the end, even this had to be done for her.

It is particularly interesting that Sabine B. not only avoided family meals, but also shrank from any contact with healthy people. Indeed her fears of poisoning and her auditory delusions might have led to a diagnosis of schizophrenia, were it not that the "voices" spoke only when she was alone. And Sabine B. was never so affected by these exhortations that she allowed them to govern her behavior. In view of the fact that she had heard these voices for years and still showed no disturbance of the ego, no automatic obedience, this symptom alone is clearly not sufficient grounds for diagnosing her as a schizophrenic.

The patient's fear of poisoning fits in with the general pattern of mistrust and diffuse anxiety symptoms; "My food might be poisoned," was the phrase she used herself. Still, the anxiety never took on the form of a delusion. Somehow, she managed to retain a sufficient grip on reality to be able to question these fears herself. Thus neither the dread of poisoning nor the hearing of voices provides satisfactory evidence for paranoid schizophrenia, even of a *simplex* form. This conclusion was confirmed during the course of the analysis.

In fact, food was merely drawn into the revulsion against all natural things; in this case, the obsessive-neurotic symptoms were particularly marked.

It is also noteworthy that Sabine B. had been a backward girl even before she became ill, that she had not kept up with her age level in any area of life. Although her school work was up to standard, she had not managed to study for a career. She also had such large gaps in her general knowledge that a tentative suggestion of mental retardation was made; the results of the analysis showed, however, that here it was a case of pseudo imbecility.

Preface to the Description of Analysis

However far-reaching the following report may seem, it is only a selection of a few of the observations and conclusions that were made during the 304 treatment hours. The leading themes are the experiences of transference and resistance. Much space is given to accounts of dreams. This particular method of presentation has been chosen because the patient's often undisguised infantile dream-wishes and her way of dealing with them afford a good idea of the form the analysis took. Every attempt was made to elucidate the relationship between day residues, dream thoughts, childhood development, and symptom formation, and to give as accurate a picture as possible.

At the time, I probably concentrated too strongly on following Freud's precept that, "as a rule we put off telling him [the patient] of a construction or explanation till he himself has so nearly arrived at it that only a single step remains to be taken, though that step is in fact the decisive synthesis" (1940, p. 178).

Today, about seven years after beginning this analysis, and nearly four years after drafting this monograph, I can see that lack of confidence made me hesitate to offer any interpretations except those of the resistance. I was also anxious to bring the patient's experiences into view untampered with, as intact as possible. On the whole, this patient's dream series provides an impressive view of the "royal road" that leads to the unconscious. But it is equally remarkable that Sabine B. found it easier to understand pictorial language (*Bildersprache*) than the language of thought (*Denksprache*). Since her I. Q. was only 79, Sabine B.'s capacity for psychoanalytic working-through was limited and did not go beyond the social level.

The following brief notes will give some idea of the main themes that were discussed during the 16 stages of the analysis. The fluctuations in the patient's weight have been indicated.

Synopsis of the Analysis

Stage 1. Hours 1-23

Despite mistrust and anxiety (fear of rape), it was possible to start analysis. The hysterical oedipal anxiety contents are clear, and appear in the initial dream, which also marks a positive transference. It is remarkable that the patient's infantile ideas of rape (= being killed with a knife) remain unchanged until the fourteenth stage of analysis, and that a far-reaching denial of reality is dominant. (73 lbs.)

Stage 2. Hours 24-41

(After an interim of two months, since the insurance company's ratification had to be obtained.) Her physical condition has deteriorated: damage due to lack of albumen. It is possible to see the decisive influence of grandmother A. on the patient's obsessive symptoms, and their development in the anal phase. In her repetition compulsion, Sabine B. influences her niece in the same way. Oral revulsion as a defense against oral impregnation. (73 lbs.)

Stage 3. Hours 42-51

Therapist: Dr. M-N (took over treatment in the treating
analyst's absence). Even women (Dr M-N is a woman) are
menacing, fear-provoking. The female body is rejected as revolting. Mother and youngest sister must fulfil her enormous demands. Autism and eating disturbances serve to punish her family. (71 lbs.)

Stage 4. Hours 52-90

Analysis of the share of the grandmother in her superego and
beauty ideal. In dreams, libidinal and aggressive themes from different phases of development appear, and can only be handled in
the face of strong resistance. (77 lbs.)

Stage 5. Hours 91-100

For external reasons, analysis under Dr. T. is terminated. Substitution of Dr. M-N is unsuccessful because of a negative mother transference. Institutional care is arranged in F., where Dr. T.
can continue the treatment. (78 lbs.)

Stage 6. Hours 101-133

Hate of her brother and sisters. Repetition of her relationship
to siblings in her friendship with her niece Gitta, who assumes
every possible role (Gitta is her child, her husband, her mother,
her brother and sisters). (80 lbs.)

Stage 7. Hours 134-156

Sabine B. works as an aide in an institution. Hate of her siblings
enters transference. Sexual curiosity. Oral pregnancy fantasies.
(82 lbs.)

Stage 8. Hours 157-182

She now earns pocket money and is asked to pay something for
each session. Great stubbornness; refuses for three weeks to tell

about a dream. Anality; constipation. The patient's parents do not want to contribute to help pay for her treatment. Sabine B. feels rejected and has to learn to stand on her own feet. (84 lbs.)

Stage 9. Hours 183-199

Cloaca theory and other fantasies of procreation and birth. Oral sadism in transference. For the first time, a friendly relationship—with a fourteen-year-old boy. (84 lbs.)

Stage 10. Hours 200-214

The sister had a baby. Fantasied ideas about reproduction run through every phase of development. Discussion of relationship between parthenogenesis, denial of sexual differentiation, and penis envy. Compulsive washing and cleansing (the libidinal aspect becomes clear); introjection and identification and their connections with the eating disturbances are considered. (100 lbs.)

Stage 11. Hours 215-231

Her regression. The "voices" as a superego projection (the voice of conscience). The situation that precipitated the illness—friendship with a young man—is related to her regression and made the focal point of the therapy. Renewed regression can now be intercepted. (96 lbs.)

Stage 12. Hours 232-249

Insuperable resistance against working out the conflict that brought on the illness. Threats to end the treatment and regress. (c. 77 lbs.)

Stage 13. Hours 250-267

Work on the precipitating (oedipal) conflict enabled the patient little by little to relinquish her denial of reality. (86 lbs.)

Stage 14. Hours 268-280

Fear of violation and murder. Denial of the difference between the sexes is relatively resolved (as regards the oedipal phase): "The penis isn't a sharp knife, after all." (88 lbs.)

Stage 15. Hours 281-294

Temporary excessive maturbation. Friendship with girls. Significance of imitation. (88 lbs.)

Stage 16. Hours 295-304

Death of the mother. Important regressive dream (returning into the belly of a fish and having to bite her way out.) Capable of overcoming the death of her mother. Analysis terminated by the analyst. (88 lbs.)

The Course of the Analysis

Stage 1 (during examination). Hours 1-23 (inpatient, daily sessions).

Sabine B. was brought to the hospital by her sister Maria, a lively, vigorous girl, who addressed the patient as Franz—her tomboy nickname.

Years of keeping to her bed and lack of food had made the patient so weak that sitting was difficult for her; from the first day, treatment was conducted lying down. The analyst began by sitting beside the couch, but later moved behind it.

Sabine B. had to be assisted to the interview by the ward nurse. Atrophy of the leg muscles and general frailty made her unable to walk without help. I learned as much of her life history as was possible, in view of her distrust of all doctors, especially psychotherapists (during a previous stay in the hospital, she had apparently been thoroughly questioned and reprimanded for her lack of will to recover). Sabine B. wept with complete despair in almost every treatment hour, sobbing that she had been like this since she was small and could not change now; that she should not have her family's care taken away from her, since it was the only thing she had left in the world. "People die, when they have everything done to them that they hate most." She felt it was her right to make enormous demands. She expected her relatives to know what she wanted at every moment without her even uttering a word. There is no doubt that she did realize that the person who could fulfill all these wishes did not exist. This realization was stifled, however, by the complaint that she had not gotten anything out of life, and so nobody should begrudge her a few little pleasures. For example, it was not expecting too much of her youngest sister to demand that she polish her bedroom floor every day.

She described the earlier treatment she had undergone during the third hour, stimulated by the initial dream.

> *Dream:* An old doctor came to me; he wanted to help me. I did not really believe him. He stroked my legs and arms, everything became quite easy, even when I awoke.

The psychotherapy was compared to a "magnetopathic treatment" which she had not believed in. The advice of a priest to go to Lourdes or Fatima had aroused similar doubts and misgivings, and she had not gone. The doctor's stroking reminded her of being washed and brushed down by her mother, a sensation she particularly liked, since it gave her such a feeling of well-being.

Of central importance in this phase of analysis were the anxiety symptoms, particularly the patient's fear of attack, which also was applied to the analyst.

> *Dream 12:* Black beetles came to my bed. They had horrible faces, just like the pictures I had to look at recently [Szondi test].

> *Dream 16:* Lots of snakes with human heads and evil, sinister faces met me wherever I went.

Sabine B. was afraid of being hypnotized because "someone might stick a feeding-tube into my mouth," or "a man with a knife might rape me." Just as she had done at home, she tormented herself with daydreams of being attacked, although at the same time she wanted to hear nothing about such "dreadful things." Sabine B. often used the word "rape," when she meant murder or killing. When asked what "attack" meant, she answered, among other suggestions, "A man murders his wife."

In addition to the patient's rejection of sex, she also had a horror of milk. "As soon as I smell milk, I have to leave the kitchen. Breast-feeding is a filthy process; people should bring up babies on powdered milk." She herself drank only dried milk.

The patient felt that her own beauty could only be compared with birds flying far above the earth, or fish swimming in pure, clear water.

> *Dream 22:* An angelic figure lay, clothed, on a bed of roses. Then I saw a bird in the sky.

She saw herself in her dream: "I wanted to be beautiful forever. I am not a being of the future. Maria lives in the future, not me." When some of the reaction formations were explained to her, she acknowledged that she sometimes made herself vomit, and that she was the only person responsible when she did not practice walking. The fact is that regular remedial treatment was improving her mobility, although all the other symptoms persisted unchanged.

After this trial period, psychoanalytic treatment on a long-term basis was recommended. This decision was considerably facilitated by the cooperation of the insurance company, which agreed to bear the cost of a long treatment in spite of the unfavorable outlook.

Stage 2. Treatment Hours 24-41 (inpatient, daily sessions).

After a two-month interval, Sabine B. was readmitted. In the meantime, her mother had had a stroke with partial paralysis of one side; her condition had improved, however. Sabine B. had moved into her mother's bed.

She planned to die before her mother did, and had a white robe made for her "like a wedding dress," so as to be beautiful even in death.

Once at home, she had stopped trying to walk. Her chronic undernourishment had led to edema from lack of albumen, and several injections were given.

In this segment of the analysis we dealt with the influence of grandmother A. and Sabine's wish to repeat this influence on her niece. The patient had adopted Gitta when she was still an infant. Now she took care of her niece's "beauty," making her eat properly even when she was still a baby and training her in every respect. In contrast to her little sisters, Gitta was growing into a strange unnatural girl, just like her aunt, and was also troubled with an eating disturbance.[1] Sabine B. was determined to make her niece into the image of herself, and to bind the little girl to herself forever, not without the idea of having a prop for her old age.

The demands she made upon her family—especially her mother and her younger sister Maria—and her fury at being neglected were described in several dreams.

> *Dream 28:* In the dream I was outraged. Maria had taken a pillow I had been given by Aunt E. as a present, and filled it with grey down instead of white.

Her family thought that her sheer rancor would eventually consume her. If even one wish did not materialize, she relapsed into stony silence and went on a hunger strike or vomited—a highly successful method of getting her own way. The purposeful vomiting mechanism, which she had developed when she was still small, was a complicated piece of machinery. If she were to keep food down, certain ceremonials had to be observed during its preparation. The kitchen had to be kept spotlessly clean in order to prevent impurities from contaminating the food; even then she

---

[1] When the patient was given a follow-up examination, it was learned that Gitta had retained her disturbance.

might feel disgusted and vomit, "because it is not only when you eat eggs that something could grow in your stomach"—a chicken, for example—but also when other foods were eaten. She used to gaze out of the window at mealtimes to take her mind off the food; otherwise, she was invaded by horrifying fantasies. Anything reminiscent of milk called to mind cow and udder, and repelled her; if she ate it, she vomited. She was quite surprised to find that she was able to use the common eating utensils in the hospital. At home she had made terrible scenes when she was not given her childhood set (she used a place setting in miniature). The knives and forks her family used were poisonous. Everything about people was revolting, particularly ears, nose, mouth, and buttocks. He grandmother had strictly forbidden her to touch the ugly parts of her body.

Sabine B. had trained herself to be good and neat even when she was asleep. In the morning her bed looked fresh and unrumpled, and she hoped the nurses would praise her for it.

Previously, she had always used her illness to excuse her behavior—"no one could begrudge me a little pleasure"—and it became of vital importance that she should realize how angry she was with everybody, particularly when she refused to speak and went to bed, never to get up again.

At the end of this stage of the treatment, this compulsion had abated enough for the patient to be able to follow the analyst's advice and do some pastels and model with plasticine. She took up the plasticine and pastel crayons only after a great struggle, but she finally brought herself to use even the colors she had rejected at first, red and black. Left to herself, she drew flowers, houses, birds, and children playing; with a little encouragement, she drew "revolting" and "wicked" things: chimney sweeps, witches, and a sinister man with a big knife.

The patient progressed enough to be able to walk from the ward to the consulting room without help; yet her weight remained at 73 lbs. and the rest of the symptoms were unchanged. Analysis was an exhausting undertaking. For hour after hour she would speak hardly a word; she wept or talked about her distrust.

Stage 3. Treatment Hours 42-51 (inpatient, daily sessions).

During the therapist's absence, the case was taken over by Dr. M-N. Sabine was still beset by fears. At night, especially, she felt that shadowy forms were threatening and persecuting her. It emerged that the analyst was also drawn into these fears, in transference. She confided in her new (female) analyst that she suspected that her previous doctor had not kept everything secret, and had discussed her with the ward nurse. Sabine B.'s sister Maria had also gone to their mother behind her back, she believed, and told her everything. While Dr. T. was away, they would certainly come and rig up a microphone in her room, in order to eavesdrop on her thoughts. But she also added that the doctor had always been so good to her—quite unlike her father, who was always angry and wanted to force her to eat. She could still not conceive of ever getting better: "Then I would have to be like the others, and that is impossible." She thought that, when she was able to go home again, everything would be as before, the lying in bed, the hours of combing her hair, the obsession with cleanliness.

Sabine B. felt that the ward nurses treated her as badly as her family and the rest of the world. But she did not press to be discharged, as she had done in earlier stages when her homesickness was still intense. Best of all she would have liked to go to the relatives who had no children—"I'd be the only one"—or to a strict penitential order, where she could be cared for by the novices. Her dreams were mainly concerned with the theme about which she talked most—disappointment.

> *Dream 42:* Maria got married, but I was not pleased. She had such a pretty dress on, but I just had to cry. Mother said, "You should have gotten used to the idea a long time ago. Be pleased that she is happy; she is so nice to you." I said, "But she can be horrid, too."

Maria was indeed intending to get married, and Sabine B. wanted to prevent the ceremony. "There will be no one then to look after me." She was completely dependent on the outside

world. The threat to her existence was the fact that all her defiance and anger was so suppressed and guilt-laden that it could
appear only in a cryptic form—in silence, crying, eating disturbances, flight into bed. These were her most effective weapons
against her family; even though she had brought herself to
death's door, she would still have believed that *they* were to
blame.

Her deep disgust of milk was brought up. She was also horrified
by the thought of plumpness and putting on weight. The only
exception was her sister Rosa, "the dumpling," whom she enjoyed touching; otherwise, beautiful = slim, fat = ugly.

In a dream, all of Sabine B.'s teeth fell out, and this made her
sad, both in the dream and in her associations; for the first time,
she talked about the pleasure that biting gave her. After she had
stopped sucking her thumb, she sucked her younger sister's ear
(they slept together). Now she slept with her baby pillow held
in her arms, so that she could chew at the corner.

Since Dr. M-N.'s office was a short five-minute walk away
from the hospital, the patient had used her legs a little. Sometimes she even went into town, but found it very frightening. The
symptoms did not improve in any other respect. If anything, the
patient ate less; she lost two pounds. (71 lbs.)

Stage 4. Treatment Hours 52-90 (inpatient, daily sessions).

Dr. T. resumed the analysis.

Sabine B. behaved like a small, defiant child who could not exist without her mother's ceaseless care. The vicious circle—exorbitant demands, disappointment, rage, and punishment of her family—persisted. She was indifferent to the possibility of destroying
herself in the process. At last a new clue to the pathogenesis appeared.

She had not always rejected breasts; on the contrary, when her
little sister was born (Sabine B. was one and a half years old),
she had tried to push the infant away from her mother's breast.
She was apparently told this by her grandmother, and in fantasy
she had a vivid picture of the scene. Actually, the births of the

two younger sisters are probably confused in her memory. She also did not want the baby to be put into the carriage, and persuaded her mother to put her in, instead. Even after she had reached school age, she used to get into her mother's bed to play with her. However, as soon as they had emerged, her mother-breast fantasies were again swallowed up in revulsion. She remembered another fantasy from her childhood: "If I get breasts like mother's, I shall cut them off." At this point she began to voice her jealousy of the sister she was supposed to love so much —the "baby," her mother's favorite.

The idolized grandmother A. appeared in a new light. Apparently she used to tell that Sabine B. had nearly died when her younger sister was born, because Mrs. B. had had no time to attend to the toddler, who refused the bottle. "If I hadn't had my grandmother, I probably would have died." She felt that her grandmother's love was conditional to her remaining "clean, good, and beautiful." "But only dolls are beautiful, because they do not eat or defecate, and I believe that I wanted to be beautiful when I was little, and that is why I hated breasts. I became like grandmother, who always lay ill in bed. I have the tastes of a great grandmother. Best of all I should like to dress in black." While she was ill, she often used to dress like her grandmother and lie in bed.

Dream 53: I saw a lovely apple, but it was all rotten inside.

Her associations: "Yes, that's just how it is; everything's rotten inside because I only want beauty. When I wanted to eat the apples, they had gone bad. You couldn't eat them, they were only good to look at. Things always happen to me like that. Things only have to be appetizing and beautiful, they do not have to be good. The inside of the apple was like feces. When I see meat on my plate, I am reminded of the pig and all that muck."

Dream 79: When I was with Mrs. F. or R., I saw a box with a wonderful doll, beautiful eyes, hair and clothes, as if it were alive. I would have liked to take the doll out, but I wasn't allowed to touch it.

"When I was little, Aunt E. always said to me, 'You ought to be put in a glass case, where everyone can see you and not touch you.' It was just the same with the doll in the dream. I forbid Gitta to touch the things that particularly interest her—just as Grandmother forbade me. I was not allowed to burn, prick, cut, or dirty myself." That is why she ate for such a long time with a teaspoon, rather than a fork or knife; since becoming ill, she had returned to that practice. After all, forks and knives prick and slice. "I just can't watch Gitta eating with a knife or fork. She might spear her tongue," and so on. "Even now, cleaning the knives frightens me."

> *Dream 90:* I was dead, but yet alive, and had my prettiest dress on, a silk one. I was not sad when mother cried a lot.

"When I was so dreadfully ill and hardly able to speak, the thing I most wanted to say was that they should lay me out in my best dress if I died. I am glad mother was crying in my dream, because now I know she loves me." If Sabine were to go home now she would polish the floor for 14 days, and then allow nobody to go into her room. "I could soak my hands and feet in water for hours on end, although I'd still be frightened that there was something in the water—worms and small fishes that could get into your stomach and grow there. When Gitta once asked me why Auntie had such a big stomach, I said to her, 'Because she has eaten so much.' During her illness, Sabine B. destroyed all her old photographs. She never wanted to look so healthy and fat again.

Grandmother A. had the strongest influence on the formation of her ideals of beauty, cleanliness, and purity. Curiosity of any kind, childish questioning, touching her own body, playing in the open air, and so on, were forbidden. Even more effective was the suspicion and the eventual certainty that "Grandmother loves me only when I am like that." In the education of her niece, Sabine

B. followed in her grandmother's footsteps with diligence, "Gitta may not play with other children. She must stay with me and not ask questions." The repressed material broke through into her dreams more and more often, and was as vigorously beaten off.

Dream 59: Aunt E. wanted to take me and her son to the zoo. But I said, "You won't get me over the water to those animals." She replied that the animals there were dressed like humans and lived like them too. There were a lot of people in the zoo, but children were not allowed to see the monkeys. The monkeys lived like humans, loving and kissing, and sleeping together, but children were not allowed to go in. We went to see the rabbits, which also performed like humans. I said, "But how can people stand going there, where the animals act in such an awful way?"

Dream 78: I was in the slaughter house with my younger sister Maria, and saw slaughtered animals—cows and sheep. The entrails of these animals were like I imagine human insides to be. Maria was disgusted by it all, but I was so interested I could not tear myself away from the building.

Associations: "In real life, I would feel disgusted now, but when I was little, it was different. Then slaughtering interested me. I always wanted to watch, imagining that piglets would come out or, when hens were killed, hoping to see the eggs. Granny said I mustn't." Concerning her grandmother, "I used to be afraid she might eat me. When I touched something I wasn't allowed to, she always said my hands would rot away, or they would be cut off."

Dream 80: I was in a shop with Maria. They made men's shirts there, but I was only interested in brassieres and corsets.

"I did not want to see dresses and suits. My attempts to look carefully at the brassieres and so forth were unsuccessful. They stocked particularly beautiful styles there—how odd that I was so especially interested in these things." At home, she had always insisted that her parents' bedroom door remain open, explaining that she was so very fond of the green carpet on the floor. Now she admitted having other reasons. She wanted to know exactly what went on in her parents' bedroom, what her father and mother were doing together. She was afraid her father might eat her mother.

> *Dream 88:* I was sitting in a circus, pretty near the front, and I was afraid the others might see how interested I was in the performance. The performers were dancing in the nude. I saw the breasts and the buttocks.

Associations: "I regarded all of that as a sin, probably because Granny forbade it above everything else, and threatened me with purgatory." She wondered if she would go to heaven when she died.

Sabine B. had hitherto regarded her unexpressed feelings of hatred as fully justified. Now at last her excessive dislike of her siblings could be interpreted. The fact was that her own behavior provoked her family into giving her just cause for her hate, and thus a reprieve from remorse. Her mother's worrying put her into a good mood; she saw it as evidence that her mother loved her. Thus her mother should come up to the sickroom even a hundred times a day, and stay with her all of the time. The mother's tears in Dream 90 were the ultimate proof of her devotion. During the analysis, Sabine B. was afraid that one of the woman doctors in the hospital, or the analyst, might get annoyed with her one day; at the same time, she did everything she could to provoke trouble, in order to have confirmation of their lack of love. She also treated the female house doctor, Dr. S., with the greatest caution. On one occasion, when she was given tonic beer to drink, she vomited it up immediately. "Dr. S. might have poisoned me; everything might be poisoned." Sabine B. had once given the "witch," the bad grandmother B., sleeping tablets, "because she was afraid to take them herself, and also so that the old witch should never wake up again, and mother could spend her time caring for me, and not have to fuss with that old woman."

One afternoon, when she was sitting with her aunt on a park bench, "A man stared at me so, I thought he would chase me." Aunt E. inquired, "Would it be so awful, then, to be kissed by a man?" "It would be quite horrible." During the following night, Sabine B. dreamed of an "attack" by the analyst, and the theme of her fears of rape came to the surface again.

Dream 70: I was attacked by the analyst [no details given].

Dream 75: I was sitting downstairs on a bench. A snake had coiled itself around my legs. It did not go away, and then there were people around me, including Dr. S., who told me to take hold of the snake. At first I tried to do this with a stick, but that did not help. Then I grasped the snake with my hand, and it became very friendly and went away.

Dream 82a: Dr. S. said to me, "Decide whether you want to stay ill or get well. A blood transfusion must be made." I said, "I cannot bear the sight of blood, and I don't want it." It was a curious blood transfusion: a tube was put into my buttocks, and Dr. S. said, "Do you see how fat you are getting? You'll put on weight quickly this way."

Dream 82b: Dr. T. lay on the couch and looked so peculiar, as though he were drunk. I was to lie down with him. Then we cuddled up, just as I do with Gitta or Maria. We were very affectionate.

Sabine B. disregarded these dreams and it was impossible to coax her into producing associations about her ideas of pregnancy and procreation.

Referring to Dream 75: "The oddest thing was that the snake had your [the analyst's] face. Why do I dream about you? Do I have to handle the snake because I did not touch anything with my hands before? Is that what the dream is saying? I also do not like painting and modelling. But that's because I feel everything too clearly. When I dream about worms, I feel them too." She wondered if the analyst would be angry with her if she dreamed such things, or if she said something (critical), as she had just done. "I knew the blood donor was a man, without seeing him. I was afraid that it might be a convict or someone from the psychiatric hospital. I would take a transfusion from Maria or mother."

The analyst asked what she meant by getting fat. She simply pushed it away, and had nothing to say. When she was younger, she used to dream that she had a baby, but always it had already been born. It gave her no pleasure; babies could fall to pieces in your hands, like chocolate figures, and that is why she did not handle them. "I don't like chocolate, because it's brown like feces." Concerning Dream 82b, she suggested, "All men ought to be like the analyst in the dream; then I wouldn't be frightened of being murdered any more."

The above sequence of dreams shows how the patient's anxieties were beginning to diminish. She had learned to "touch the snake (penis)," which then assumed a friendlier aspect. During her illness she had reached a point where she would touch practically nothing, but armed herself with a stick so that she could push everything away. At the end of this series of dreams, Sabine B. was astonished to find herself suddenly wishing for a visit from her father, although the idea had never occurred to her before. She was equally amazed by the following dream.

> *Dream 89:* Dr. S. took me into her room. In the closet hung a row of clothes hangers with plaques. Dr. S. said, "The clothes hangers represent the souls of patients." There were hearts on them, and on the hearts were spots. R.'s soul had only a few spots (R. also suffered from anorexia nervosa). My soul was still quite tarnished. And then I saw the soul of the analyst, which was beautiful and almost completely unspotted. It made me think, "He talks about such ugly dreams, but his soul is quite pure, while mine is covered with spots."

Sabine was still straining with all her might to stave off the "ugly and the common," but her dream taught her that it was possible to discuss such things without damaging the soul, and that she herself had a particularly ugly and dirty soul, because she had kept everything inside her: "Good on the outside, bad on the inside."

In hour 90, the inpatient treatment was terminated. As long as one of her relatives could bring her, Sabine B. was now well enough to come as an outpatient. Her weight was 77 lbs., but there was no other noticeable improvement of her symptoms.

Interval of four weeks.

Stage 5. Treatment Hours 91-100 (outpatient, over a period of three months).

Since Dr. T. was moving to another town, treatment was continued under Dr. M-N.

While she was at home, Sabine B.'s condition deteriorated. In the meantime, her younger sister had married, and now had less time to attend to the patient. Furious and despairing, Sabine B. took to her bed again. "I covered myself up completely, just as I used to; I even put a handkerchief over my face." She had frequent bouts of vomiting and, after meals, feared that something might take root and grow in her stomach, a giant or an animal. Although she realized that she was tyrannizing the whole household, she believed that she could not exist if her mother left the house, even for a short time. Now she was the only one and entitled to her mother's undivided attention.

Sabine B. was despairing about the change of analysts and said she would never get well now. Best of all she would have liked to have taken Dr. T. home with her so that he could nurse her as her mother did, or perhaps even better, since the patient did not think that her mother's love was inexhaustive enough. Another complication was that Dr. T. had spoken the same dialect as the patient, and thus she felt better understood by him than by her new doctor. Also, during treatment hours Sabine B. was not able to communicate her rejection of Dr. M-N. in the mother role. Instead she acted this out with her real mother. ("I torture mother, so that she will think of me all the time.") Only the distant Dr. T. was excluded from her mistrust of all mankind; he was all-powerful, only he could make her well.

> *Dream 92a:* Dr. T. is dead. I had to get used to the idea, or so I was told. But I cried and cried. Mother said, "Why are you crying

so much? He is a complete stranger to you." Then I looked at him; he had a girlish, beautiful face, not a bit like he really is.

From her associations: With her niece Gitta, she played "Dr. T." The niece had to be the analyst and kiss and love her, and give her the bottle of tea. "Dr. T. had the face of such a beautiful girl; he looked like you [Dr. M.-N.], only much more beautiful. In the dream he had such pretty, curly hair, just like I used to have. I always used to say to my sister Maria that if I died, I must look beautiful. She must give me red cheeks and red lips, and have my hair beautifully curled. Even today, I think this is very important. . . . I often look in the mirror to see whether my mouth is red, because if it isn't red I won't live much longer. I don't want to die, and yet I am afraid of getting well. I always think that I am not good for anything, and that I couldn't manage by myself."

In another dream the beloved dead grandmother A. appeared to her and said that she wanted to stay with her forever. In reality, Sabine B. had only her niece Gitta, her hot-water bottle, her canary, and the corner of her pillow. But she was afraid of the canary, for fear it would suddenly begin to talk; and she felt that even the chairs in the room might start conversing.

Finally she became so weak that she could no longer undertake the journey to the hospital. Therefore, accommodation was arranged for her in an institution. This was a better arrangement for several reasons: her family's acquiescent behavior was only aggravating the regression, and Sabine B.'s influence on Gitta had to be halted at all costs. (78 lbs.)

Interval of four weeks.

Stage 6. Treatment Hours 101-133 (outpatient, three sessions a week).

The patient was lodged in an institution in F. Dr. T. resumed treatment. The patient's weight was 78 lbs. at the beginning of this stage. She still limped slightly with her left leg, making a big step with the right leg and then dragging the left after it.

In the home, Sabine B. was expected to do light chores. Her expenses were paid by the insurance company. Surprisingly enough, she did not feel a qualm of homesickness, but this was understandable in view of the transference. "You are now every-thing to me, my mother." She sought her mother everywhere. "I would like to talk to the bird I just saw, and take it home with me; it has a motherly face." In the very first hour, she explained why she had not been able to endure Dr. M-N.; it was because of her breasts. She could not have said that to her, of course. One could not be as rude as that, and then Dr. M-N. might have stopped liking her. Sabine B. wanted to be the sole patient and have the analyst all to herself.

As has already been mentioned, the patient had an eating dis-turbance in childhood, marked by vomiting. When her younger sisters were being fed, Sabine B. wanted—as an assurance of ma-ternal love—to be treated in the same way, to sit on her mother's lap and be fed like a baby. Unfortunately, the mother responded to this with threats, and Grandmother A. increased the child's in-security and terror even more by inventing infernal punishments. "Even today I am afraid of a snake or worm crawling into my be-hind. Granny said, 'When you do your business in the yard, a snake or worm will crawl in.'" During this phase of the analysis, the inexhaustible fund of the patient's hatred for her siblings was a fruitful source of discussion.

> *Dream 115:* I went on the lake in a small boat with my brother, my sister-in-law and my niece (my brother's daughter). There was a hole in the boat and it slowly filled with water. The others did not notice, but I jumped into the water in the nick of time. It was of no consequence to me what happened to them.

Associations: "I am not interested in the others. I was pleased to let them drown." Her niece was associated in her mind with her younger sister. But she also said that this niece was as skinny as she, and that the mother did not care about the child or pity her.

>   *Dream 125:* I was at home, and my mother brought a washbasket
>   in. In the basket lay pieces of flesh, head, feet, arms, and so on. They
>   were Maria's. Mother had a black dress on.

She often occupied herself with imagining how it would be if
anything happened to her "beloved" sister. Perhaps she would
get Maria's fur coat. Sabine B. had always been such a "model
child," as her mother put it; the children had never quarreled
among themselves. It now emerged that Sabine B. was anything
but good; in fact, she had incited the other children to tease the
youngest two, especially the baby. For instance, Maria would be
shut up in the pigsty so that she might be eaten by the pigs, or
die of starvation. Or, when she was still an infant, Sabine B. used
to put her in the sun, "to burn her up." Or else she would take
away her shoes, and make her run barefoot, imagining that her
little sister would "run her feet off." She also used to tear her
younger sister's pinafores and dresses, or dirty them, "so that I
would have the cleanest one and would be praised by mother,
while Maria got smacked." When the baby was being bathed, she
used to wish that the water would freeze over so quickly that her
sister would be turned to ice; she wanted to be able to keep a close
watch on the process through the ice.

She showed this raging hatred toward even her "adored" little
niece Gitta—not to mention the other children, whom she liked
to punish as severely as possible. Dirty hands, uncleanliness, and
noise were all incitement for her anger. Actually, she was punishing her own unconscious anal needs by projecting them onto the
unfortunate youngsters. Sabine B. had a predilection for smack-
ing her sleeping niece on the buttocks and pinching or biting her
chest and toes.

As a child, Sabine B. had had to wash her grandmother, even
her breasts. "I was so interested in them and wondered what they
could be. The fanny [buttocks] too, I had to wash that too, but I
was not allowed to look there." Now Gitta had to do the same for
her. "With her little hands she has to touch my hole" (*orificium
urethrae;* this is the patient's word for the genitals). Although

Sabine B. was imitating her grandmother, at the same time she was pretending to be a baby. "Gitta had to treat me like a baby, powder me, give me a bottle—but only with tea, not that revolting milk. But sometimes I was Gitta's husband, when I had forbidden her to play with the boys." Then the patient would play the man's part.

At the same time as she was playing these games with her little niece, the patient contracted a generalized *pruritus*, originating in a *pruritus ani*. Before the itching started—which made the patient wash even more—she brought up the subject of her hobby, embroidery (hour 115). She had always pursued this with exaggerated zeal, but now it was getting worse, and Sabine B. could hardly tear herself away from her needle. She felt compelled to embroider for hours on end.

> *Dream:* I sat at the sewing machine, making a dress for my niece. The machine stitched so quickly I could not stop it any more and the needle broke. But the machine sped on and on.

Sabine B. produced these associations, "I am afraid of needles, but I like pricking myself." A doctor had once lost a cannula in her bed and, finding it herself, she had pushed the needle into her thigh until the blood came. "But it did not hurt at all." Ordinarily, she was afraid of blood; she had her first attack of tetany when one of the nurses accidentally cut her finger. Flies, bees, and wasps had to be driven out of her bedroom. Once she said to her sister Rosa, "Have you got any flies in your room? Are you afraid of being stung too?" But her sister just laughed and said, "I've got a different sort of fly to sting me." "Did she mean her husband? But he doesn't sting, does he?"

She also wanted to know how flowers are pollinated, and what part bees and insects take in the process. Some time later she dreamed that a bee lighted on her hand, and she let herself be stung, completely fearlessly.

The itching persisted until hour 123, when she reported the following dream.

Dream: I had lice on my head.

Associations: "I always wanted to feel about my body, but it is forbidden to touch some parts. Gitta always wants to do this too, to play around with her genitals and her bottom. But that is just what grandmother always forbade me to do, and so I slap Gitta's fingers." At length she began to understand that healthy children do have autoerotic needs, and the itching subsided.

Although Sabine B. did not put on much weight in this period, she began to be able to eat meat occasionally without vomiting. It became more and more obvious that biting had erotic overtones for her, as well as aggressive (carving her little sister into pieces) and self-destructive ones ("I think that I was enraged in my dreams last night and bit my own arm, because I could still see the teeth marks this morning"). As the patient expressed it herself, she was "eating for love," a phrase in her native dialect.

Her behavior outside the doctor's office was also changing. She still had frequent fits of weeping, but in hour 111 she remarked for the first time that she was enjoying the fine weather. The nurses in the institution agreed that she was gradually improving, although in the analytic hour she complained that people had stopped treating her like a child, which she so longed for them to do. Several times she even visited an indoor swimming pool, but called the women bathing there "dirty pigs." She now regretted having destroyed all her old photographs, for she wanted to know what she had looked like before she became ill. Staying in bed all day was something she could no longer envision; she could not "lie that still any longer." She considered giving her mother something she had made herself, but eventually decided against it, because her mother might interpret the gift as a sign that she was well, and "my mother would not love me any more."

Between hours 128 and 129 an important incident occurred. In silent rage against her roommate, who had taken on a mother role for her, she decided to urinate in her glass, and was caught in the act. The nurses were extremely understanding about the whole affair, but the roommate hinted that Sabine B. might have stolen some of her things. The patient herself wanted to pack her bags and disappear as soon as possible, continuing treatment only after a holiday, and from a different institution (both of these changes had already been considered). Sabine B. arrived for treatment already determined to flee, but was made to choose between the alternatives of sticking it out or of terminating analysis. She eventually elected to stay. The working through of this incident uncovered a whole series of childishly defiant reactions, and also convinced her that the analyst's firmness was a good thing, and that her mother had been too lenient with her. (80 lbs.)

Interval of two weeks.

Stage 7. Treatment Hours 134-156 (outpatient, three sessions a week).

In the new home, Sabine B. was treated just like the rest of the domestic staff, and no longer enjoyed the privileges of an invalid guest. During the two-week interval, she had been at home, and had felt like romping with the children the whole day long. Her family was delighted with the change. In the evenings, she enjoyed staying up, although she occasionally felt the urge to go to bed and be cared for by her mother. She kissed and cuddled passionately, without being completely free from disgust. The excessive hate of her siblings appeared again. "When people asked me how many brothers and sisters I had, I used to say I was an only child. My mother had no right to have any other children." When her mother was nursing one of the babies, Sabine felt like tearing her clothes with rage.

> *Dream 139:* I sat by a fishpond with Gitta. The fish came to the surface of the water, but when they opened their mouths I hit them. Then my niece Irmgard floated to the top. I hit just as hard, so that she would go under.

Sabine B. associated her younger sisters with the floating niece. "I could have chopped their fingers off. I should have loved to

put Maria into a matchbox so that she would suffocate. Right now,
I could shut you (Dr. T.) into the cupboard." The blows on the
fish's mouths reminded her of her childhood, when she particularly liked to hit animals on the jaws so that they would have
to starve. Animals had to be burnt or starved to death in the
place of her sisters. "One mustn't be spiteful to one's sisters, so
I had to take my revenge on animals." All of this took place in
secret, so that grandmother and mother would not find out.

Other examples of dreams:

> *Dream 135:* Rosa was so fat, particularly in the stomach. I asked
> her how she had done this. I would have loved to peep into her
> stomach.

> *Dream 141:* Gitta had a baby; she drove nails into it—all the way
> through.

> *Dream 143:* An old woman with a fat stomach came to us
> and begged for a plate of soup. We were having our meal, but I
> said there was none left. My mother protested that the woman had
> a fat stomach. But I did not care, and I was more enraged than ever
> when mother gave her a worn out piece of clothing of mine.

The last dream reveals not only Sabine B.'s lifelong unwillingness to give anything away, but also a fantasy about pregnancy
which she reenacted in her games with Gitta: "Gitta had to open
her mouth wide; I looked down it to see the baby inside and
where it came out of the rectum." We are already acquainted with
her fear that eating could make something grow in her stomach;
"I don't think I would have a baby, but rather an animal, a wolf."
Sabine B. was particularly fond of describing wolves in her fairytale games with Gitta, and she used to frighten the little girl by
making the wolves savage biters. When she was a child herself,
she had once chewed the heads off the crib figures, taking particular care to bite the parts around the mouths, "so that they
couldn't eat any more, and would have to starve" (cf. her love of
hitting animals on the mouth).

She now began to take a special delight in watching the family
dog while he ate, and reported that, in fantasy, she was completely

preoccupied with the thought of meat. "I could gaze at raw meat for hours on end." At the same time she felt a strong desire, mingled with slight revulsion, to drink milk.

Two further dreams were described, on the theme of squashing.

Dream 134: A cock sat on a hen and did dreadful things to her.

Dream 154: In the woods, men were sawing up a tree, which was hollow inside. A bird flew out to the hollow and pecked another smaller bird to death. I was eager to see how the bird was pecked to pieces.

Sabine B. had admitted earlier that the cock and other animals had to serve to placate her anger. But in these later dreams and the related associations, the cock appeared somewhat differently; the curiosity and pleasure with which she watched the two scenes could be directly linked with childhood experiences. When she was little, she was afraid that her father might squash her mother. "When I hid in father's bed to flee from the Moroccans, I had the same fear of him as of the approaching armies."

Referring to Dream 154: "The tree was beautiful, but hollow inside. I also wanted to be beautiful forever." She associated the smaller bird with the little sisters she had tormented so cruelly, and with her enjoyment at watching a cat teasing a mouse to death. "It had to happen slowly, so that I could see everything— especially how the cat ate the mouse."

During this period, the transference relationship changed. In hour 151, Sabine B. brought a bunch of pussywillows with her, probably the first present she had ever given in her life. Although she still regarded the analyst as her private property—whom she wanted to completely incorporate and bite to pieces, from love and hate—there were signs that a maturer relationship was developing.

New changes could be seen in her behavior outside the analysis. She had gained 7 lbs.; by the end of this stage of the therapy, she weighed 85 lbs. Her washing compulsion was less noticeable, and she now often went to bed without a bath. During the winter, she had enjoyed sleighing expeditions with the other girls. "I want to be like other girls, not something special." She had lost her fear of going into town, even after dark. Now she felt like being as silly as the other girls, but she still did not dare to, for fear of losing the matron's good opinion. She had an urge to drink milk.

In spite of all of these improvements, however, it was doubtful whether Sabine B. really did want to be like the other girls. In fact, she thought up all sorts of mischievous tricks which were disruptive to the functioning of the institution. For instance, she would try to dupe the other girls by offering to make their beds; then she would just toss their bedclothes together, and tuck her own in neatly, so that she would earn the recognition and love of the staff. Thus she re-experienced her sibling rivalry and prevented herself from making friends.

Stage 8. Treatment Hours 157-182 (outpatient, three sessions a week).

Sabine B. was now being paid pocket money for her work in the home, about $2.50 a month. She was reminded of the agreement made at the beginning of the treatment that, if she ever began to earn money herself she should contribute—the sum of ten cents per hour was suggested—toward her fees; but she pretended she had forgotten all about it. Then she said that she was going to be really difficult and refuse to pay a thing for her analysis.

In hour 159 she arrived in tears because the matron had scolded her. "I was really cross—when I cry and am unhappy, I get angry too—and at lunchtime I vomited." When she was weighed (hour 162), her weight had dropped again to 75 lbs.

She still felt completely revolted by her dreams.

> *Dream 160:* I stood by a stove and kindled a big fire; I kept on throwing more into it.

Sabine B. always used to burn anything she did not want to keep: nobody was going to have it after her. Once she even tried to cram the cat into the stove. "If I was upset with Maria or my uncle, I used to burn something, in place of them."

There was an interval of a week between hours 163 and 164 because Mrs. B. and Gitta had come to stay. The patient had looked forward to kissing and cuddling little Gitta, but somehow things were not quite as they used to be. Gitta was very surprised to find that she was allowed to touch everything in her aunt's room and even to break things.

Sabine's warning, that she would really begin to be difficult now that she had to pay, was soon fulfilled. In hour 163 she refused to disclose a dream, and the resulting struggle with her defiance lasted for three trying weeks. She imagined that, by remaining silent, she was maintaining control over the analyst; the dream itself was of secondary importance. The analyst's persistence was countered with the remark, "If you aren't interested in me except for this dream, I shan't say another word, and it will be your fault if I never get well." Gradually, her silent resentment began to erupt in violent aggressive outbursts, interspersed with moments of self-condemnation. "Not just now; like at home: not until Maria and mother have worried themselves to death. My fury is growing and growing; I could kill you and then bite you to bits, because I like you so much." All the time her fear of being bitten or devoured herself was increasing. ("The cover on the couch might bite me.") "When I won't, I won't," she had once remarked about her habit of sitting on the toilet for hours, holding back her feces. Eventually the analyst abandoned the struggle, letting the patient know that her obstinacy was too much for him. At last she showed some compassion. After hour 169, Sabine B. paid the first bill for $1.50, and tried to give the analyst $1.00 extra, but this was refused. In hour 170, she related the disputed dream, prefacing it with the remark, "If you had not wanted to hear it now, then things would have been really bad."

> *Dream 170:* Dr. T. visited me in the home. He was brought into my room. It looked very untidy there. Dr. T. sat on a chair and spoke to the matron. I was to sit on his lap.

The analyst's lap was to be hers alone, not shared with any other patients. Her mother was to be there only for her in the same way, and was to take only Sabine onto her lap. The latent genital-sexual thoughts of the dream were of no interest to Sabine B.; in fact, she would have liked to stop sleeping altogether, in order to be free of the sinful, wicked, ugly things she was dreaming.

> *Dream 176a:* I was given a book as a present. There were beautiful religious pictures on the first pages. Pictures of men and women came afterward.

> *Dream 176b:* There was a conveyor belt in the therapist's room. It had parts of people and animals on it. The finished creatures came out of the back. But I did not look there.

Sabine B. wanted to read like other girls, but she still found herself curbing her curiosity, both in dream and reality. She wanted to examine everything, but did not dare to, for fear of going to Hell. Even eating was sinful. "My illness did not quite reach the point where I did not need to eat any more, although I was already getting to the stage where I was angry if I sometimes kept a meal down. But finally I could not speak any more, and I did not want to lose that."

Further facets of her oral aggression emerged. When she was a child, she often used to put her toes into her mouth. They were Mommy, Daddy, and Maria—the last toe suffered particular biting and maltreatment. Once one of her toes was crushed by a watering can. "It would have been all the same to me if these 'Mommy-Daddy-Maria' toes had fallen off."

> *Dream 174:* A shepherd with a flock of sheep. The shepherd wanted to give me an old sheep at first, but I did not like it. When I complained, he gave me a small one. I took it into bed with me and dressed it. "Is it a girl or a boy? Is it housebroken?" one of the nurses in the home asked. I got angry, "It is just as housebroken as your parrot." [The nurse actually had a parrot, which Sabine B. looked after, and which apparently kept saying "You silly ape" to her. "Do parrots have minds?"] When the nurse said the lamb was female and would have children in due course, I became angry and chucked it out.

Once again her beauty ideal and her principles of upbringing were the subject of discussion. Gitta had to be toilet-trained very quickly, and when she was once found playing with her feces, Sabine B. tied her up in a sack. In her dream, Sabine B. was indignant at the nurse who objected to the lamb's dirtiness; but when she was told that it was a female and would have lambs of its own, that was more than she could bear.

Sabine B.'s appearance was changing, too: she now wore pretty clothes in bright colors. Red, a color she had abhorred for so long, had become one of her favorites, although she did not yet dare to wear a "fire engine" red apron.

> *Dream 181:* Mr. L., a close friend of the family, was painting our house. On the wall of my room he painted the picture of a woman. At first I was not pleased, but the woman was so lifelike, in bright colors, that I began to like her.

We have already heard of Sabine B.'s picture of her ideal woman hanging above her bed. "The woman is like a corpse, like a ghost. That is what I used to look like." These developments in her life and dreams brought other changes. In hour 171, the patient began to feel homesick for her niece Ruth, a normal, natural child, whom she had not been able to endure before. She had now lost all interest in Gitta.

Hour 177 brought a troublesome circumstance. Some time before this, the analyst had suggested to the insurance company that the patient's family ought to be paying something toward her fees. It seemed best to share the costs in this way, if only to prevent the family from evading all the financial responsibility. However, the B. family, although financially in a position to do so, refused to contribute. Fortunately, the insurance company consented to continue to subsidize the therapy, and Sabine B. was treated, as before, for ten cents an hour, the most she herself could afford.

Not surprisingly, Sabine B. felt that her parents were rejecting her. She stopped writing to her mother, and left the latter's letters to her unopened. "Let her suffer." "It was never as bad as this; I'm so angry I just don't know what to do." Her anxiety increased again. There were some pansies on the table—"I am afraid they might eat me. Each one has a face. I could part with everything, give it away. I do not want to talk or eat any more."

Dream 180: I wanted to take a good look at beavers in the pond. There was a nest under the water. The littlest one, a particularly beautiful animal, could not find the way back and cried pitifully. The horrid old mother beaver searched for the little one, but could not find it.

Sabine B. wept for days at the thought that her mother did not care for her any more. She remembered that she had once wandered off in the wood and had lost her mother, who later found her, she was told, next to a horsecart. Sabine B. was having to buy her independence dearly at the price of disillusionment, despair, and rage.

For the first time in her life she made a friend, a fourteen-year-old boy named Fritz. She was often afraid of him ("He might do something to me") and wanted him to keep himself very beautiful. On bad days, she hated him. Fritz became a playmate and the recipient of her generosity. "I like him much more than any girl." She also found a girlfriend, but could not decide whether to yield to the temptation of going for walks with her friend or other girls, or to stay in the home. Superego anxieties were still active. (84 lbs.)

Stage 9. Treatment Hours 183-199 (outpatient, three sessions a week).

During a week's holiday, Sabine B. went on a trip with several other girls. She was beginning to identify herself with them, and cried when one of them was reprimanded by the matron. Previously, she had always been glad to see someone punished. It is not surprising that her behavior was still subject to huge vacillations, but at least she was now showing some interest in her future. However, under no circumstances did she want to become a wife like her sister Maria, who was expecting a child. Her father came on a visit, and thought her nearly well, but he agreed that the treatment should be continued. Again she wept for hours, "because I shall soon be well, and no one will be interested in me any more."

> *Dream 184:* I was standing in front of a rock in which I saw a small hole. Above it was a notice: "Whoever gets through here is in another world." I was already nearly through.

Sabine B. had a peculiar fear of all holes. At home, she stuffed up all the crevices, for fear something could slip out. Only the cracks in her parent's bedroom door remained and she would not hear of a sound new door being put in. On the other hand, she herself wanted to stay thin enough to slip through everywhere. Curiosity and fear of the "hole" stood side by side; Sabine resumed the theme in a later dream.

> *Dream 192:* I came to Dr. T. There were a lot of children in the room who belonged to him. In one corner of the room lay some stones. Dr. T. went away and told me to mother the smaller children, which did not suit me at all: the children ought to have been looking after me. They had bits of babies, which they stuck together. Then we took away the stones from the corner. Before he left, Dr. T. had told us that they must not be moved. But I was inquisitive and took a beam away as well; then I saw a dark hole, completely red inside. I put the stones back again so that Dr. T. would not know that I had disobeyed his orders.

Up to the present day, Sabine B. has not yet properly discovered her vagina. She thinks that the menstrual blood flows from the anus. When her older sister started menstruating, Sabine B. asked whether she too would ever have such a filthy thing. Although her interest in sex was now growing, she was considerably restricted by her anxiety and revulsion. She thought that children were born through the anus. "Or does the stomach burst? Does a child eat nothing in the stomach? If Maria [her pregnant sister] eats a lot of tomatoes, will her child be half tomato? If you swallow fruit pits, will a tree grow in your stomach? Were all my sisters and brother in my mother's stomach, and did she let the children out when she wanted them? Can my sister Maria let out three more children? Can I have a baby too?" Sabine B. knew little about procreation and birth, and this was a good opportunity

to find out why she was concealing her curiosity and her knowledge about the "red hole" and putting on such an innocent face.
Oral drive impulses were determining the transference.

> *Dream 184a:* Dr. T. sat at his desk. He was crying. "Why are you
> crying?" I asked. He: "Because you have bitten me. I could see all
> your teeth." I said to him, "If you don't keep still, I shall bite you
> much harder, so that it hurts you even more." I was very angry.

The previous evening, Sabine B. had taken a stuffed toy to bed
with her; the next day it was found to be mauled and chewed.

> *Dream 196:* A cow lay on a big table. Beside it stood a butcher in
> a white apron. The meat of the cow was almost all cut away. I said,
> "There's nothing left of it; I wanted the whole cow." The butcher
> said, "Come, surely you could manage another piece." Other peo-
> ple stood further away, eating the raw meat. I ate at once too, but
> kept apart, away from the others. I did not like it; when I woke up,
> I was sick. Then I went to the butcher and said to him, "Tomorrow
> I shall be here first and get a piece I like."

This dream paints a vivid picture of the patient's aloofness and
solitude, and her desire to have for herself the best piece of the
cow (as a mother symbol). She preferred to eat apart from the
others because they might have disputed her right to absolute possession. Hence also her insistence that her mother cook separately
for her, so that the mother should be hers alone, through the specially prepared food.

Deliberate isolation, solitary eating, and the desire for sole possession are themes that have provided material for several important theories. They also afford particularly good illustrations of
the difference in methods of approach between psychoanalysis
and other, particularly the anthropological, schools of psychiatry.
Scheler (1957), for instance, interprets this behavior quite simply
as fear of the greed and rivalry of one's fellows. Zutt (1946) gives
an anthropological interpretation, in which he stresses the affinity
between isolation and loss of appetite, and traces them back to a

hypothetical pituitary deficiency. He also emphasizes the categorical similarity between anorexia nervosa and the endogenous psychoses. Psychoanalysis, on the other hand, prefers to concentrate on investigating the motivation behind such behavior, considering it a vital clue to the intrinsic nature of a particular patient's urge for solitude. Although there is no space here for a detailed investigation of the connections between the "essential nature" of the isolation and its origins (cf. Kunz, 1951-1952, pp. 247-249), I shall say that the schools of psychiatry which overlook the psychological significance of the symptoms they observe are ignoring a mine of information—to the detriment of all concerned. For it is scarcely convincing to claim to have reached a superior, more comprehensive "anthropological" vantage point, and therefore to have access to sources of information more reliable and pertinent to mankind, if this position can be neither defined nor demonstrated. Von Gebsattel once commented that "since Max Scheler's ambitious attempt [to construct a "theory of the essential nature of man"], anthropologies have been mushrooming overnight" (1947, p. 66). Indeed, anthropologies that have not incorporated the essential anthropological facts revealed by psychoanalytical methods are by no means rare among these "mushrooms." But to exclude these methods is to restrict one's view of such psychopathological phenomena as isolation, and to make it impossible to see totality. In practice, Zutt's rejection of the psychogenesis of anorexia nervosa is connected with a therapeutic nihilism (see 1946, p. 22).

Sabine B.'s friendship with Fritz grew stronger. Now she worked frequently in the garden of the home. With childlike affection, they often used to feed one another, and it even happened that Sabine B. accepted an unwashed carrot from him. She still had frequent moments of being frightened of Fritz and occasionally a still deeper anxiety that she might be poisoned after all, perhaps by a peach stone.

> *Dream 194:* On a hot day, Fritz fetched me to go bathing. He already had his bathing suit on, and I got mine. On the way to the

swimming place, Fritz said, "What would you buy if you found a whole lot of money, brassieres or corsets?" I shook my head and said I would build a house with the money. When I countered by asking him what he would do with the money if he found it, he said, "I would marry you." We then came to a pond where lots of children were splashing around.

She showered Fritz with presents, saying that she had never liked anyone so much. She often felt like giving everything away, to atone for her past selfishness. Sabine B. had now grown into an esteemed and particularly reliable member of the staff, and was often entrusted with missions which had to be carried out in the town. On the analyst's recommendation, she was given more work to do in the garden, since household chores might tend to foster her cleansing compulsion. (84 lbs.)

Stage 10. Treatment Hours 200-214 (outpatient, three sessions weekly).

Sabine B. spent a week at home. Her sister Maria had just given birth to a baby, and the event stimulated her imagination. When she questioned her sister about the actual birth, she was told that the baby came out where it went in. This answer prompted her to invent all kinds of theories that she did not want to talk about at first. During the previous stage of treatment, the analyst had once sketched a rough diagram of the womb and the fetus, which proved to be a great mistake. The patient had since been very upset about her ignorance, and refused to draw or expose her fantasies about pregnancy, except to say, "It isn't right to talk to men about these things, but you are like a mommy without a dress. Do only women have children, or can men with fat stomachs also have them?"

When she arrived for hour 205, however, she brought a drawing depicting her friend Fritz, and Gitta, and her sister Rosa with her husband. The only difference between men and women was that the women had bigger breasts and buttocks. She could not imagine the male genitals, and although she had seen her nephew naked, she thought that such a sight was sinful and ought to be confessed to a priest. All the same, she was interested enough to ask whether boys' genitals grew as they got older. Gradually her idea of parthenogenesis faded, and she began to accept the male genitals as part of her thoughts. At a later session, she even brought a drawing of Fritz in the nude, complete with genitals. Her previous denial of the difference between the sexes had originated in her need to overcome her castration complex; this misinterpretation of reality served to protect her ego against the unconscious penis envy. Before puberty, when Sabine B. had not yet begun deception and regression, she had expressed her wish to be a boy by behaving like a tomboy and earning herself a masculine name. When the pressures of reality forced her to progress from imitation ("I am like a boy") to a relationship ("I have a boy friend"), she took flight in regression, repressing her penis envy and twisting the facts to match. She thus managed to avoid the realization that boys have something she had not, and her envy shifted itself almost exclusively to orally directed objects: *my mother has given me too little, the others have gotten more than I have.* Many of the essential elements of this accusation were repressed, since her covetous desire for possession would otherwise have led to destruction of the beloved object.

Thus she once dreamed of a man and woman who were completely transparent. The woman was lacking a breast and several toes, and her heart was missing. The man had no sexual parts, no teeth, ony three fingers and one lung. The missing breast reminded the patient of just one thing: "When I was small, I decided that if I got breasts later on, I should cut them off." This "turning against her own person" was the consequence of the wish, which acted as the motivating force for the dream-thought, to take oral possession of breast and penis.

Her childish affection for Fritz remained. "He likes me so much; even if he gave me a pear that was rotten all through, I believe I would eat it." She was now attracted by the idea of living with a family with plenty of children and being "one of the crowd."

Dream 287b: I was with other children in a wading pool, and splashed and stamped with all my might.

There could no longer be any doubt that the patient's compulsion to wash and cleanse was not only a ritual that protected her from dirt and feces, but that washing, brushing, and rubbing were all autoerotic activities. Sexual needs, unrecognized as such, which could not be realized socially, were released on her own body. The conceptual representation of the drive impulse was repressed and its object displaced from the genitals to the rest of the body.[2]

The patient's relationship with Gitta, and the games she played with her, were predominantly narcissistic in character; in Gitta she saw herself, forming the child in her own image. It is interesting that Sabine B.'s *pruritus* reappeared about this time, and that she recognized her scratching as a self-destructive transposition of her repressed aggressive impulses ("I could have scratched Maria to death").

During the same period her fetishes, her pillow and hot-water bottle, began to lose some of their importance. As her instinctual drives, which were cathected with anxiety and guilt, came to the surface in analysis, she began to make friends, and her fetishes became unnecessary. Nevertheless, her feelings toward other people were still determined by her absolute claim on her mother, and she was still subject to a law of "all-or-nothing." "If I can't possess mother completely, I don't want her at all, and I shall die."

The following dreams are interesting in this connection.

Dream 207: I come to Dr. T.'s room and knock at the door. Hearing a clear "Come in," I go into the room, but see no one. Soon afterwards I knock again, and again there is a loud "Come in." But Dr. T. is nowhere to be found; I search the whole room for him,

[2] Cf. Freud (1926a): "If we ask ourselves why the avoidance of touching, contact or contagion should play such a large part in this neurosis and should become the subject-matter of complicated systems, the answer is that touching and physical contact are the immediate aim of the aggressive as well as the loving object-cathexes. Eros desires contact because it strives to make the ego and the loved object one, to abolish all spatial barriers between them" (pp. 121-122).

open the closet, peer behind the desk, and so on, without finding him. Finally, it occurs to me: I have swallowed Dr. T.; he has spoken from my stomach.

Sabine B. presumably wishes to incorporate the analyst, who has a mother role, and unite herself with him (her) in order to possess him (her) forever. In the same way, a girl of about four who was being treated for an eating disturbance by Rank et al., said to the therapist, shortly before an impending break in analysis: "I am going to swallow you and keep you in my stomach; then I will have you to talk to." Sabine B. had to reject her own unconscious longing to unite with another being, with "mother-food," because of her oral ambivalence (love-devour-destroy), but she expressed it indirectly in her behavior toward her mother by alternately seeking her passionately and then ruthlessly repulsing her. An unresolved oral ambivalence has fatal effects on a person's capacity to relate to others.

> *Dream 213:* The matron sent me to a publishing house, where I was to deliver something to the editorial staff. I stood in front of a huge building and was rather frightened of going in. I could not find the editor's office anywhere, until I came to the last room, which had double doors. In the room there were monks, naked and with long beards. One monk looked like Dr. T. A fire was burning in the middle of the room, and there were some men sitting there on the ground, the way Fritz always sits [cross-legged]. I pitied the monks and gave them some of my clothes, but I did not undress completely. The monks asked me whether I did not want to stay with them. I remained, on the condition that they would tell me everything I wanted to know. They promised me this. I then set to work and cooked for the monks over the open fire. The monks had collected the food, including human flesh. I cooked a meal, and then we all ate out of one dish.

Although this dream was particularly rich in symbolism, the patient's associations could account for very little. At first she merely commented that her grandmother had always taught her that poor old men with beards were monks, a clue to one of the least significant features. She found the communal meal the most striking part, and she was reminded of earlier dreams (184 and 196, and especially dream 207 in which she had swallowed the analyst). As was often the case, she was completely involved in the pictorial content of the dream, and could not go beyond it, possibly because of a disturbance of the synthetic function of the ego. This would explain her limited ability to raise conflicts from the dream level to a higher psychic plane, where they might be worked through in full consciousness.

The context of the dream, however, provided several useful clues. In hour 213, Sabine had arrived with the sketch of a naked youth which, unlike previous drawings, included the genitals; in her dream she also saw naked men. The fact that Sabine B. could now envision the naked male body in dreams and reality was undoubtedly a good sign. At the very least, this dream was a sign of an unconscious transformation which should not be underestimated. Sabine B. not only found herself in the company of naked men, but also shared her clothes with them and pitied them. But the main theme of the dream was the communal meal, eaten out of one pot, and consisting, among other ingredients, of human flesh.

About this time, Sabine B. expressed the desire, for the first time, to eat her meals with the other girls. This advance was probably due to the interpretation of her oral aggressions and the recognition of the guilt feelings associated with them, which were connected with the refusal of food. In addition, her previous isolation and the secret devouring of the best pieces of the cow in dream 196, as well as the incorporation dream 207, were motivated by the desire to have mother-nourishment all to herself, without sharing with siblings or table companions.

Dream 213 also contains a primal event (cannibalism) and Christian figures (monks). An initiation ceremony takes place: she remains and prepares the meal on the condition that she will learn everything from the monks. Up to this point, Sabine B. had lived outside a (table) community, and now, at the dream level, intimate communication is achieved at a communal meal—an act of incorporation, representing a primitive type of identification.

The whole question of identification has far-reaching implications, which are particularly well illustrated by this dream. For instance, Freud has commented that identification "may even be created by a meal eaten in common" (1921, p. 110). Concerning the juxtaposition of images from the primal and Christian worlds, he wrote (1923): "An interesting parallel to the replacement of object-choice by identification is to be found in the belief of primitive peoples, and in the prohibitions based upon it, that the attributes of animals which are incorporated as nourishment persist as part of the character of those who eat them. As is well known, this belief is one of the roots of cannibalism and its effects have continued through the series of usages of the totem meal down to Holy Communion" (p. 29).

Even earlier, Freud had been spurred by Frazer's theories to investigate the bonds between guilt, penance, and identification at totem meals, animal sacrifices, and the Holy Eucharist. Volhard's comprehensive ethnological work on cannibalism (1939) leaves no doubt about the significance of identification in patrophagy; and his researches have led him to the conclusion that identification with the plant world is a crucial experience for cannibalistic tribes. In fact, Volhard regards all anthropophagy, whether in the ritual and magical rites of a cult, the commemoration of the dead, patrophagy, or victory feasts, as the consummation of a feeling of communion with nature, which is thought to assure immortality.

Oral incorporation, as a primitive identification, is connected with anxieties and fears that can be traced back to an oral ambivalence. "Eating is loving and killing," as Sabine B. might have said. Abraham (1924) had used these words: " . . . in cases of melancholia, where the patient absolutely declines to take nourishment . . . his refusal represents a self-punishment for his cannibalistic impulses" (p. 448). This formula can be expanded today as follows: " . . . *the fatal inevitability of the sense of guilt*" (Freud, 1930, p. 132; my italics) is the consequence of equivocal feelings, which in the dream example, was directed toward the mother (eating, loving, killing). However, eating as such is a process that takes place outside the realm of good and evil—

Abraham spoke of a pre-ambivalent oral phase—and it can be experienced as ambivalent only secondarily and in connection with the development of the ego. Before the innate ambivalence conflict can begin to have a psychological effect—in guilt feeling and the need for punishment—the ego must have reached a certain degree of development, even if this is only the vaguest capacity to differentiate between no and yes (in the sense used in Spitz's investigations).

For the psychoanalyst, instinctual drive and ego development are interwoven in a highly intricate manner. Where there is an oral object-cathexis and drive-satisfaction, there is also an identification. Therefore, the sternness of the conscience (superego), taken over by identification, depends on the ambivalent strivings directed at the parents. However, we are not concerned with the chronology of superego development here, and Freud's (1930) minute differentiation between the awareness of guilt that is due to the fear of internal authority and that which is evoked by external authority (p. 128) will have to be disregarded for the moment. So long as we can accept the part played by love in the origin of conscience (Freud, 1930, p. 132), it will be easy to understand how a love as destructive as that depicted in the dream could develop into an especially harsh superego. Thus, anxiety and guilt feelings have prevented the satisfaction of an unconsciously destructive drive directed against the mother (= anorexia).

In view of its complexity, it is hardly surprising that the patient was able to contribute so little to the understanding of her dream; she was given only as much of these interpretations as could be supported by earlier associations.

On the whole, Sabine B. made good progress during this period. It is significant that she even occasionally put into action her desire to eat with the other girls. She gained 16 lbs. (100 lbs.)

Stage 11. Treatment Hours 215-231 (outpatient, three sessions weekly).

During this stage of treatment, one of Sabine B.'s most curious characteristics came to light. In some areas she, now nearly 30 years old, knew as little as a child. It seems fantastic that she should have spent four years in a secondary school without assimilating even the most rudimentary knowledge of the facts of life. Actually, the explanation is simple: Sabine B. skipped all her biology classes. Alarmed that she might be confronted with the forbidden and the sinister, she always made some excuse and missed the lesson. Her sisters had to write her biology papers for her. Of course, other factors played a part. The capacity to learn is not just a matter of intellectual ability; it is also dependent, to a great extent, on the individual's emotional affective powers. An affective inhibition can mean that a child sees and hears without taking anything in.[3] There was thus little purpose in enlightening Sabine B. In addition to skipping some of her lessons, she had also been in a state of regression for five years, during which time she not only shrank from anything new, but "forgot" much that she had already learned, using all her strength to repress such knowledge further and to avoid all external stimuli that might have pushed the repressed facts into consciousness. The patient herself produced an excellent description of the implications of the phenomenon of "regression."

> *Dream 225:* Some dwarfs were sitting on a bench outside the doctor's office. Dr. T. stood nearby and I asked him whether I could buy a dwarf. But I only wanted a dwarf with sperm. I also wanted to know what could be done with dwarfs. Dr. T. answered only, "You'll be surprised at all the things you can do with dwarfs." I immediately began examining one of the dwarfs. I cut his stomach open, cut off his arms (in the dream I knew the dwarfs would grow together again), but I couldn't find the sperm anywhere. I grew very angry.

Sabine B. supplied associations that rotated mainly around the dwarfs. "I like small people. Dwarfs don't grow, but they can still have babies. While I was ill, I ate hardly anything and had

---

[3] Cf. the work of Schilder and Wechsler (1935) and the investigations of Michel-Hutmacher (1955). The latter concludes, "Children's knowledge about the inside of the body is usually strongly affect-laden, and their apparent disinterest is more the result of repression than true indifference" (p. 25).

no appetite at all. I had a stupid idea: if I am this thin, I shall become a little baby. I did not get smaller, but at least I got thinner; as long as I could still feel some flesh on me, I ate even less."

This reversal of maturation, of growth, was accompanied by a singular change in the patient's attitude toward time. She had all the clocks taken out of her sickroom, saying that their ticking irritated her. The fact is that she could not bear to have clocks remind her that time was not standing still. "I just could not listen to time passing; I did not want the time to pass, nor anything to change." She also had her room darkened. Here one could speak of a specific elaboration of the disturbance of temporal growth, in the sense of von Gebsattel (1947). What he said of depressives applies in a literal sense to Sabine B.: "Time was not the medium for his opening up, his growth, his proliferation, and his increase, as for healthy people, but rather the opposite: the medium for his diminution and dwindling" (p. 141). Nevertheless there was not a single "fundamental disturbance" (as von Gebsattel describes it) at the root of this behavior, any more than there was one single disturbance at the root of Sabine B.'s compulsive actions. Certainly the patient's banishment of all clocks created a "basic growth inhibition," but the disturbance of the basic process itself is hardly an occurrence so far removed from psychological categories that only its side effects can be grasped and understood. We can understand this disturbance psychoanalytically as a defense against "drive-impelled strivings," which bring on the "nuclear experience of temporality," according to Scheler (quoted from von Gebsattel, 1947, p. 129).

Although we cannot go into the complex and hazy connections of "chronological event" and "chronological experience" and "lived" and "experienced" time, it should be remembered that even von Gebsattel had traced his "basic development inhibition" back to unconscious defense processes, at least in essence. For example (1954): "We maintain not that the symptoms of melancholia, such as inhibition, compulsion, mania, consist of a change in time awareness, but rather that they are signs of a change in the fundamental processes of a maturing personality.... Disturbances in the subphysical happenings of life, which, in accordance with their position, never come into consciousness, should not be denied merely because their concealment requires methods of discovery other than the so-called 'empirical' information furnished by the patients themselves" (p. 137).

Sabine B. was not so much stimulated by her recollections of the days when "time stood still," as by her curiosity, which manifested itself in her frantic search for sperm in the dwarf. She wanted to see with her own eyes how babies are conceived, grow, and are born.

> *Dream 218:* I arrived for the interview. But Dr. T. was not in his room. The doorman told me that Dr. T. had been run over by a car and was dead. I went to the scene of the accident. There I heard that Dr. T. was squashed flat and that there was nothing left of him. I searched for myself and eventually found a small piece of flesh, which revolted me at first. Then I took it with me after all, thinking, "Perhaps a new human being will grow out of it." It occurred to me at home that Dr. T. had once told me that babies in their mothers' stomachs are nourished by blood. I thought to myself, "I can also nourish the piece of meat with blood; I only need to have a good nosebleed—which then actually happened. [The patient had occasional nosebleeds.] I caught the blood in a bowl and put the piece of meat in it. Now I could see exactly how the arms and legs grew, and I thought, "Later on there'll be a head as well."

Sabine B. was satisfied that in reality she could not watch how a baby is born; in this externalized pregnancy she could observe the growth. "I always used to think that when a bone from a rabbit was buried in the ground, another baby rabbit would grow. Do you have to swallow male sperm to get a baby? Now I know why I could not eat or drink. I was afraid that sperms might be in my food. So I shall have to eat, or no babies will grow." It is amazing that Sabine B. was still pursuing her fantasies of oral pregnancy, even though she had already been told all about conception and birth

Dream 221: I saw my sister's behind in front of me.

Associations: "Behinds are disgusting. Yesterday I had a pear in my hand. I could not eat it; it looked like Mommy, like Fritz, like something from Mommy. At first I thought of the breast, then of something even more disgusting." And she refused to pursue the matter any further during this hour. It was not until the next session that she divulged the more revolting "something": the pear she had been about to eat reminded her of feces.

The resistance that kept obstructing her development, both inside and outside the consulting room, was now chiefly expressed by her "voices." Whenever she wanted to do or say certain things, she heard the voice of her grandmother commanding her, "No, you are not to eat that. You may not go to the movies. The therapy is bad, you will go to Hell if you tell Dr. T. your dreams and share your thoughts." These fragmentary and externally imposed aspects of her personality gave ample proof of connection with the superego, particularly since the "superego voices" lost some of their power during the course of the analysis. There can also be no doubt that Sabine B. was actually hearing these voices. She went so far, on occasion, as to search for the speaker, even though she knew all the time that it would be impossible for her grandmother to speak from the dead. Nevertheless, she often abided by her grandmother's admonitions, even against her own will.

Sabine became more and more preoccupied with the future. Although still tied fast to mother's apron strings, she was considering the idea of becoming independent of her family, and later earning her own living. The analyst was pleased with these fantasies and encouraged her. Not so her family. They believed that Sabine B. was now quite well enough to help in the house and that, since it was obvious that she would never lead an entirely normal life, home was the best place for her. Her sister Maria was particularly insistent that, since she had had to wait on the patient for so long, she was entitled to some help in return. Her plan was that Sabine B. should come home and run the household, so that she could get out and take a job. Understandably, Sabine B. suffered from a conflict. At first she felt that she had to bow to her parent's wishes in order to assuage her sense of guilt through gratefulness and sacrifice. Then she realized that such childish obedience was only a pretext for her desire to stay at her mother's knee. She saw the danger of another relapse, and decided to continue the treatment.

The situation gives a good picture of the many factors which affect the success of analysis. Since the psychoanalyst is permitted to exercise his influence only through the medium of interpretative understanding, and since this weapon is almost useless in a dispute of parties, it is often very tempting to give way to countertransference, especially when the resistant patient is at best only half open for interpretations. On a later occasion, the analyst found himself compelled to intervene on the patient's behalf, and to bring his professional authority to bear on the family; but interventions of this kind should always be rigorously examined from the standpoint of transference-countertransference. This time, however, interference was superfluous, since the patient had made up her own mind not to go home.

Sabine B.'s friendship with Fritz was changing. Their childlike games continued as before, but she had begun to hold herself aloof from him. He seemed sinister: "Sperm might fly away from him." Only one dream hinted at a close bond: hugging one another tightly she and Fritz rolled down a steep slope together. Sabine B. often wondered about the difference between liking and loving: "I am fond of Gitta and Mommy. But what is love? Is my sister Maria loved by her husband? And Mommy and Daddy? I am too stupid to understand it all." She regretted having no friends of her own age.

Dream 229: I was with a dressmaker who was making me a dress. I had a fat stomach and the dressmaker said that I would give birth in a few weeks. Then she wanted to know if I had a boy friend. I shook my head and was sad; I wished that the child could be born immediately.

Associations: "Can only girls who have a boy friend give birth to children? Is there no other kind of semen in the body? As I have no menses, is that a sign that I do not have semen in my body? Now I begin to wish I were like other girls—have menses and breasts." Her loneliness oppressed her more frequently. "I have a longing to touch and be touched." Whenever such wishes emerged the compulsive washing returned.

> *Dream 227:* Gitta showed me a picture book. On the title page there was a picture of a tall girl. There were little doors in the picture, just as there are in an Advent Calendar, and I opened them all. I saw everything that was inside, hidden behind the doors. Only one door was closed fast. I knew that there was something special behind it, but I was not allowed to open the door.

Sabine B. thought that it was probably something that people were not allowed to see or mention. Since the door was barring entry to the tall girl's abdomen, it would be logical to assume that the special thing that was hidden behind it was the reproductive organs. This is confirmed by the way in which Sabine B. enlarged upon her fantasies of procreation and pregnancy. But: "I prefer to think it, rather than say it. Once said, it's gone. If I keep quiet about it, it stays in my head, and I do not have to give it up." It was not possible to discover what the patient was withholding, even in view of the next dream.

> *Dream 230:* Dr. T. had cut open my stomach and peered around in it with a lighted candle. He said, "Something must be concealed." I said to him, "You can look as long as you like, you won't find anything. I know exactly what you are looking for, but I shan't help you."

This dream reveals, in symbolic guise, what is supposed to stay hidden: Sabine B.'s desires for cohabitation. "Of course what I am concealing has something to do with the stomach, otherwise I wouldn't be dreaming that it had to be searched for in my stomach. I am much cleverer than you, but I am just not going to tell you everything."

She hinted that her secret had something to do with the relationship to her boy friend, preceding her diphtheria and anorexia nervosa. "I already had a good idea about what men do with women. If I had been completely in the dark, I wouldn't have gotten so ill."

It was not until hour 231 that Sabine B. told, for the first time, of her experiences directly before the illness. As was quite obvious from the dream of the previous hour, she had succeeded in suppressing much essential material, but her resistance was not to be overcome at that point. However, Sabine B. at last found herself face to face with those problems which she had been unable to solve on her own, and her past was brought up in the analysis. During this period, the transference resulted in a crisis which will be described in the following stage of the analysis.

Stage 12. Treatment Hours 232-249 (outpatient, three sessions a week).

The very next day, Sabine B. retired to bed, and the doctor was called. She found a slight temperature and diagnosed *pleuritis sicca.* Two days later, the patient was admitted to the F. University Neurological Hospital. She greeted the analyst with a distant air, but divulged a short dream.

> *Dream 232:* A man beat up a woman and screamed in a terrible way.

She was reminded that she was concealing something, but merely replied that it was impossible for her to give everything away. Suddenly she refused categorically to participate in any more analysis, accusing the analyst of not knowing her properly yet. At heart she was still unchanged, she went on, and Dr. T. simply had no idea how wicked she was. Though fully aware that she was harming only herself, she declared that she wanted to break off the treatment and return to bed. Clinical examination and X-rays disclosed nothing that could have caused the temperature, and it finally emerged that Sabine B. had secretly heated her thermometer in order to trick the home into letting her go to bed.

She had now become completely unapproachable, and was waiting for the therapist to make the next move. Her stubborn negation—"Just now I say no, all the time, to everything"—put the countertransference to a difficult test. What had happened to make Sabine B. decide so unexpectedly to cancel the analysis and regress once more? Undoubtedly, the main responsibility lay with the reemergence, in the last two analytic hours, of the problem which had coincided with the onset of her illness. Again Sabine B. was running away from the task of developing her ideas about sexual relationships and conquering her oedipal conflicts. This new regression gave, by repetition, a good view of the history of the illness. Now she was retreating through anal defiance. "I won't tell you what I think about men, nor even about my wickedness. Now at last you're finding out what I am like. My silence, my negation of everything was what annoyed Mommy most. My wickedness has not reached its climax yet, but I may not and shall not be like this. I would have to reproach myself severely." Sabine B. hoped that the analyst would take the initiative and also the responsibility.

Underneath her show of defiance, she was really saying, *"If Dr. T. loves me, he will continue the analysis; if he rejects me, he will break it off. But I must not admit to my oedipal infatuation."*

Sabine B. had fallen into a pitiable state. She ate almost nothing, and was losing weight rapidly. Her constipation, which had improved, was as serious as it had been before. She hardly uttered a word and could not be prevailed upon to tell about her oedipal desires and anxieties.

It seemed that she had lost all interest in the theme of sex, and her stubbornness was very strong. Occasionally, direct anger flared up: "As soon as I see your face, I lose my temper," and so on. But she usually bottled up everything inside her.

> *Dream 241:* I was at home; there was a mountain in my room. The matron said, "What's that mountain you have got there?" I

had piled up everything I could find and hidden it under a blanket: baby clothes and shoes, things to eat, toys, and so on. The mountain kept falling down. In vain I tried to build it up again in the old way. All my efforts were useless.

Associations: "I always hoarded everything and kept it for myself. Everything had to last for a hundred thousand years; everything had to stay as it was. All the other children enjoyed breaking things. I would have liked to do that too, but I never went through with it."

This dream shows clearly enough how hard the patient was trying to restore her old situation and retreat into anal defiance to avoid the oedipal conflict. In the home, she shut herself off again and did her work like an automaton. Not until she had vented some of her wrath on the analyst, toward the end of this stage of treatment, was she more accessible to the outside world. Her physical condition was now considerably diminished and, since she refused to be weighed in the hospital, her weight had to be estimated. (77 lbs.)

Stage 13. Treatment Hours 250-267.

At Christmastime, Sabine B. was at home during a two-week interval. After the holiday, she found herself a job in a home where she would have to do only light work and would earn a little pocket money. The move was necessitated by Dr. T.'s return to that town. Although the holiday had been free of problems, the first hours of this stage of treatment were dominated by resistance against breaking her silence and working on her problems.

The analysis gradually threatened to become a trial of strength, and the patient took every chance of tormenting the analyst with her silence and the deterioration of her health. Interpretations of the motivation behind her resistance were of no use. Dr. T. fell more and more into a state of negative countertransference, until he had to warn the patient that her self-destructive behavior could no longer be tolerated. The following night, this piece of information, which had been given during the course of an hour, stimulated a dream.

Dream 257: Dr. T. lay on the couch and cried and cried. I felt pity for him and I asked why he was crying. He said, "All the flowers, the tulip and hyacinth bulbs, have not been watered for far too long; they have almost dried up." Perhaps it was not too late to save them; with Dr. T.'s permission, I watered the flowers.

Interpretation of her behavior as unbearable and tormenting to the therapist made the patient feel compassion in the dream. After all, she did not really want to lose the analyst, and so she made a show of her love and kindness. In reality, she was offering up the secret of the love she felt for her father—boy friend—Dr. T. as her associations to the following dream show.

Dream 258: I was being watched by seductive men's eyes.

Associations: "Why do I keep thinking that my father might seduce me, or my uncle? Now I can't see enough of my brother."[4]

Dream 260: I was with mother in the kitchen, quarrelled with her, and finally sent her away, so that I could be alone with father.

Associations: "Why do I want to be alone with father in my dream, all of a sudden? I always used to be so afraid of him. As a child, I often asked father whether he loved me. But he said, "Nobody loves a naughty little girl." Sabine B. had begun to en-joy reading detective stories, but she liked love stories even more. "I've got such a long way to catch up. Most of all, I would like to go to school again. I want to experiment with everything, with being a boy and doing everything that boys do with girls."

At long last, she gave an account of her friendship with her boy friend Karl, revealing a little bit more in each of the following sessions. Her mother had not known anything about the affair. "I did not really have a mother, only a grandmother. Mother always said, 'You don't need me, you've got your Granny.'" Ap-parently Karl had mothered her; the illness actually began long

---

[4] It is interesting that the "rejected" brother, who was referred to only in the family history, was now spoken of as a desired person to relate to.

before the diphtheria, when Karl offered her something to eat, and she felt a sudden dread that there might be poison in it. During a birthday celebration, Sabine B. had gotten a little drunk, and was in high spirits. Karl kissed her and touched her genitals ("Is that the reason why my periods have stopped?"). This experience, her drunkenness and its consequences, was the secret Sabine B. had hoarded so long.

In the home, she made friends with an eighteen-year-old girl who had a boy friend. She felt that she was worthless, a feeling that she had had from time to time before, but which was intensified now by her awareness of the discrepancy between her age and her maturity. Eager to become a woman as soon as possible, to have breasts and menstruation, she grew jealous of her sister Maria, who had a husband. "I take my teddy bear to bed with me, but then I put him aside after all. A teddy bear is not quite the right thing. Will I find a husband some day?" She often thought about the future and deliberated whether to complete her training as a dressmaker. But, as often, she threw her plans out of the window with the excuse: "After all, I have a mother and father; they will look after me." (86 lbs.)

There was an interval of two weeks, while the analyst was on vacation.

Stage 14. Treatment Hours 268-280.

Sabine B. had a way of withholding important associations until the end of the hour, and then producing them at the last moment, while walking out the door. But little by little she was learning to disclose her ideas at once and not store them up, "as I used to store everything up. Perhaps that is why I always had a stomach-ache, because huge mounds of feces were inside."

> *Dream 277:* The analyst sat at home by the coffee table. I then showed him around the house so that I could shut him in, because he had annoyed me so much and must make up for it. I shut him in and ran away. After a few days, mother said, "But Dr. T. will starve if we don't let him out."

Day by day she found it easier to give vent to her aggression in a far more direct form: "I could just beat you up, particularly on the bottom." Any remark from the analyst would suffice to infuriate her. At the same time, she was anxious to keep the analyst forever, locked up in her house, and in the dream she united this wish with retribution for the analyst's disappointing aspects.

In hour 276, Sabine B. was informed that the analyst would have to turn over the treatment to Dr. S. in about three months, since he was going abroad for some time. "I shall be unhappy, but not so much as I would have been a few months ago; then it would have been terrible for me." However, she felt that her relatives should not be told, "since then they would take me home at once." Under no circumstances did she want her family to have any communication with the analyst or the superintendent of the home. "They—my family—must not find out that I am working now and earning as much as other girls, because I would have to go home at once and lose everything I have gotten so far." During a weekend spent at home, Sabine B. acted this part. She ate very badly, "so that mother had to cook specially for me. The family then said that Dr. T. would never teach me to eat properly in a hundred years. My sister Maria, the silly goose, also said that I was trying to get from Dr. T. the same thing she gets from her husband. She is partly right, but that is not the whole story. She is right, and again, she is quite wrong."

In hour 279, Sabine reluctantly related a dream which made her earlier fears of rape and murder more understandable.

> *Dream 279:* I was with my sister and wanted to see her little boy and girl. And she showed them both to me. First, I compared the girl with myself, and saw no difference. Then I looked at the little boy and was absolutely astonished to see that his penis did not look like a sharp knife. My sister asked me, "Well, what did you think the penis looked like, a sharp knife?"

Sabine B. was beginning to understand some of her anxieties: "I was always afraid that men murdered women with a knife. So

I must have been seeing the penis as a knife with which father could kill mother." It can be surmised that Sabine B.'s aggressive fantasies had transformed reality and caused the penis to become a knife; indeed, fear of the strength of her own drive impulses appeared to her as fears of external reality.

In the night following this treatment hour, she noticed that she was no longer disturbed by the snoring of the man in the next room. "I stopped being afraid, and wondered whether he would come in, so that I could at last have a look at the thing that used to terrify me so much."

She was very much saddened by the feeling that she had slept her life away, and that now, slowly awakening, she found herself childish and left behind. "I want my friend to be my sister and my brother; she should belong to my mother too. I have tried on all her clothes. I enjoy eating with her; when I'm alone, I am sad. I let her touch and look at all my things; before this, I never let anyone look at anything. I hid everything, because the others might have stared it away."

She had occasional problems with the matron of the home. Hypersensitive as she was, she found it difficult to take reprimands. From the standpoint of the analysis, it was unfortunate that the matron and nurses expected Sabine B. to set a good example for the younger girls, and forbade her on religious grounds to read the cheap love stories she had just begun to find interesting. (88 lbs.)

Stage 15. Treatment Hours 281-294 (outpatient, three sessions a week).

Sabine B. was very happy that some younger girls, just out of school, entered the home. She soon made friends with Anna, an energetic, normal girl of fourteen. Sabine B.'s interest in her eighteen-year-old friend was waning and, in maturity, she felt more akin to Anna than to the older girl who already had a boy friend. "I should like to be at the age when girls become women, develop breasts and start their periods." This is probably the reason why she had attached herself to a girl who was at puberty age.

Sometimes she fantasied that Anna, who had short hair and behaved rather brusquely, was a boy. "Anna might change into a
boy." This idea often filled the patient with anxiety, but imagining the strangeness and "otherness" of the male in her own sex, in
her friend, allayed her fears.

Gradually her desire to be physically close to another human
being, "to abolish all spatial barriers" (Freud, 1926a), grew into
a yearning; in hour 285, she reported that her body had begun
to feel different. Sabine B. was masturbating. "It used to feel
dead before, like withered flesh." Right away she experienced
feelings of guilt. "Grandmother said that I wasn't to touch myself,
since that was disgusting and forbidden, but if I keep all that
back now, it will only get much worse." For some time, the patient had a violent compulsion to masturbate.

She rebuked herself more and more often as "good-for-noth-
ing." Her desire to be like other girls as soon as possible led her
to copy their appearance.

> *Dream 286:* Fritz came to visit. I stuffed modelling clay under my
> clothes and molded clay breasts, to look fat and normal. But after
> only a short while, everything fell off me.

> *Dream 288:* I was playing a game with dice with my eighteen-
> year-old friend and her boy friend. I beat everybody, but I had
> skipped some important squares which were marked on the board
> with red dots. I wanted to avoid these points.

These two dreams, especially the first, helped Sabine B. to understand that she was struggling "to do everything like the other
girls, but I am only like them on the outside." As in the dream,
Sabine B. was trying to sidestep the hazards of life in order
to reach her goal as fast as she could. She was putting up a façade
to deceive herself into believing that she did not have to wait for
her development to proceed naturally from within. Outwardly,
she wanted to have the attributes of a woman, but without re-
linquishing the ideal image that her grandmother had given her.

Of course, imitation has a positive side, but in Sabine B.'s case, it became a center of resistance. "But is there no other way? Must I, if I want to get well, be as natural as the other girls? Isn't it enough to work the same way they do? Will my breasts grow only when I eat as much as Anna does?" This was the negative aspect of her mimicry; she really wanted to have only the outward semblance of conformity.

Sabine B. was sorry that she could not be with her family for the coming Mothers' Day, because the home would not be able to spare her. In the last hour before the holiday, she related the following dream.

> *Dream 292:* I was at home and felt very thirsty. Mother handed me a glass which I first sniffed at. Then I drank down one glass after another; my thirst seemed unquenchable.

The patient described how she ate with her new friend; they exchanged plates and pushed food into one another's mouths. "There must have been milk in that glass. It used to turn my stomach, and yet in the dream I just couldn't stop drinking it. But Sabine B. was still too disturbed to realize the wishes expressed in the dream. She was thus advised to think of this or similar dream-images at meal time, for the analyst hoped to make it easier for her to break through the automatic aspect of her refusal of food. With the same goal in mind, when she paid her monthly bill of $1.10, ten cents was returned to her with the request that she go and buy herself something to eat, and think about the dream while she was eating it. But she did not comply; instead she said, in the next hour, "I did not want to eat alone; it would have made me unhappy. As soon as Anna is free, we will go and drink a glass of milk together."

Although she had moments of sadness about the approaching end of the analysis, she also skipped a session for the first time, preferring to help her companions move into a new home. At the next interview, she anxiously asked if the analyst were angry with her for not having come. (88 lbs.)

Stage 16. Treatment Hours 295-304 (outpatient, three hours a week).

Between hours 294 and 295, Sabine B.'s mother died suddenly of a stroke. The patient was called home immediately by her sister Maria. Among themselves the family had decided that Sabine B. should now come home and keep house for her father. This put the patient into a terrible position: she was the one who was most deeply affected by her mother's death, and now she was being expected to return home, where she would be reminded of her mother at every turn.

A few days after the funeral, Sabine B. arrived with her father to discuss the matter. It is understandable that her married sisters, her father, and indeed the whole village, assumed that she would be returning home. At least, this seemed the obvious solution to everybody, except Sabine B. herself. Admittedly, she was prepared to acquiesce, but with such great internal resistance that the plan seemed doomed. It was explained to Mr. B. that, from the medical point of view, Sabine B. was not fit for such a homecoming, and that the family would be taking on an enormous responsibility if they chose the simplest solution. Sabine B. was eventually given her father's permission to stay in the home, and it emerged that even the sisters had become apprehensive, after a few days, that she might have a relapse and be on their hands again. A week later, Sabine B. came to one treatment hour from home, and then returned to her job.

She was in a miserable frame of mind. She had hardly been able to eat anything at home, slept less, and found everything strange. Luckily she did not shut herself away from her companions this time, and her friendship with Anna was a great source of comfort to her.

In hour 298 she reported her first dream since the death of her mother.

> *Dream 298:* I went for a walk with one of the nurses from the home along the river Neckar. We met a fisherman who had already caught some fish. I was very interested in what he was doing, sat down beside him, and after a while, felt a bite. I tugged at the line

and had to make a big effort. The fisherman said that a big fish must have bitten and helped me to land it. It turned out to be an enormous fish, much bigger than a man. The fisherman cut the fish's belly open. I was very intrigued and peered in, and then said that I wanted to be laid inside the fish's stomach. The fisherman agreed, laid me inside, sewed up the belly of the fish, and threw the fish back into the water. I was very disappointed to find how dark it was inside the fish. I could not see a thing, although I had thought that the stomach of the fish would be so arranged that one could live in it. My disappointment was very great, and I realized that there was nothing else to do except to find a way out. I started to bite my way through the fat belly of the fish. But the belly was incredibly thick, and biting so much tired me out; I did not manage to get through the stomach wall.

Without a pause, Sabine B. went straight on to talk about her mother's stomach. "I always used to ask her why she had such a fat tummy." "Because all of you [the children] have been inside it; that's why it is so fat," she used to reply. For a long time Sabine B. wondered about herself biting through the stomach wall, and the exhaustion that sometimes overcame her at mealtimes.

This final stage in the analysis was automatically dominated by the death of the mother and the coming termination. Sabine B. skirted these problems by attending her appointments irregularly and by spending more and more time with the other girls in the home.

> *Dream 303:* I bring Dr. T. an empty vase. Sadly he comments that something essential that belonged in the vase is not there.

There could be no more realistic description of the situation than this dream. Sabine B. has made good progress; she has cut her infantile ties and is capable of regular paid employment. But, as the dream reveals, she could sense the analyst's unspoken regret that the flower vase had remained empty, that something essential was missing; i.e., complete, sexual maturity. Sabine B. was still amenhorreic and, as the follow-up report showed, had remained an "empty vase." (88 lbs.)

❧ 6 ❧

Cases Three to Five

Case History 3: Agnes C.

Age: 18
Height: 5 ft. 10 in.
Weight: 84 lbs.
Weight before illness: 121 lbs.
Age at onset of illness: 16
Length of illness before examination: 2 years

Family History and Biography

A great-uncle on the maternal side (mother's mother's brother) was schizophrenic. The father is a scholar, who, in spite of a secure position, has always had a marked fear of life. Although the academic attainments of the children left little to be desired, he never felt that they would amount to anything. The mother is less complicated and better able to cope with life. During the early years of the marriage, she worked as an interpreter, and later assisted the husband with his literary work. She had feelings of inferiority because of her obesity. By her own admission, she found it difficult to express affection and felt that she had never succeeded in achieving a proper relationship with her children. In spite of a somewhat bitter atmosphere, the parents actually did the best they could.

The patient was breastfed for about three to four months; she learned to walk early, but was a late talker. She sucked her thumb until she was five, and bit her nails until she was 11. She was a friendly vivacious child. During their early years, she and her siblings were cared for almost exclusively by a nursemaid, whom they both loved and feared. When the patient was seven, the father was transferred to another town and the family followed. At first, the patient found it very hard to adjust. She had to have extra classes to help her keep up in her school work, and felt inferior to her sister, who was a year younger but much quicker. She had plenty of friends at school, and was always popular, although she changed her best friends so often that she never had a chance to make lasting contact with anyone. In fact, her closest friend was always her sister, even though outbursts of jealousy and rivalry clouded the relationship from time to time. Her brother, who was several years older, stuttered. The youngest child, a girl, seems to have been the least complicated of the children.

The rivalry between the patient and her younger sister grew more bitter after the war, when it looked as though they would have to be in the same class. However, the patient fought against it, terrified that her sister would overtake her, and they were sent to separate secondary schools. When she was about 15, the sister fell ill with anorexia nervosa; she remained ill for about a year. Agnes C. was perfectly well at the time her sister began to show the first symptoms, but her jealousy was soon aroused when she saw that the sister had become the center of attention in the family and had attracted the special concern of the father. She began to long for someone with whom she could discuss her problems; although she admired both her parents, she had no ready contact with them. A young teacher was the first adult with whom she felt she could talk about personal matters. When she was about 16, she made friends with a boy a few years older. She went through a religious crisis and left the church. Her friendship with the boy remained intact in spite of the illness.

Previous Illnesses

The patient had apparently never been seriously ill before.

Present Illness

In her sixteenth year, she became amenorrheic (menarche at 13, menses regular, no pain). About the same time, the first eating difficulties appeared. Agnes C. had to go for long walks before she permitted herself to eat any dessert. This habit became more and more engrained as she substituted her urge to eat with the urge to be active. For a year, she would accept only food that her mother had prepared specially for her; if she were forced to eat with the family, she either concealed the food and later threw it away, or else she vomited. Constipation set in. A pituitary implantation carried out by a relative and several series of hormone injections were tried, with no success. Her condition grew steadily worse. Her school work was neglected, and she lost her ability to concentrate. Actually, her main talents were artistic, but in the end she gave up even these interests.

When Agnes C. was admitted to this clinic in 1952, she exhibited starvation edema and extreme emaciation. Her body hair had remained, and she had marked acrocyanosis. The following findings are noteworthy: serum protein 5.8% (Alb. 3.2%, Glob. 2.6%), Hb 70%. RBC 3,450,000, marked anisocytosis and microcytosis, ESR 6/13, serum iron 154%. Basal metabolism -25%, BP 95 mm. Hg. Serum potassium normal (5.3 meq = 20.6 mg%).

Psychotherapy and Psychodynamics (46 Treatment Hours)

At the beginning, the patient's ambivalence toward food was the main subject of discussion. Although she could never stop thinking about food, an inner voice kept forbidding her to eat. She felt that she had to earn the right to eat by going for long walks and doing exercises. An urge to be on the go all day, and sometimes all night, was supposed to keep her from putting on weight while replacing the desire for food. She had stopped sucking her thumb and biting her nails, but now she pulled at her pubic hair or picked her cuticles. In the years before she fell ill, she had masturbated for a while during which she had been tormented by such stereotyped daydreams as lying in a harem and being raped by naked men. She also fantasied flogging scenes. Now she became exaggeratedly conscientious and developed an ideal image of herself as pure and without aggression. She tried to transform herself into a Madonna, and indeed, considered that she had achieved this state by fasting, at the same time putting an end to her masturbation and sexual fantasies, and curbing her aggression toward her brother and sisters. In reality, all she felt at this time was an inner void. Her illness was preceded by a dream which deeply shook her.

> *Dream:* I was in the Underworld with a lot of skeletons. I myself was a skeleton, but in contrast to the others I was wearing a hooded cape which I tossed aside. I had a distinct feeling that a new life was about to start.

After this dream, the patient felt that she had undergone a transformation. Death seemed like something beautiful. She felt relieved that it was now up to her to choose whether to live or die.

Her relationship with her brother and her younger sister was discussed in the beginning hours. She had always wanted to be a boy, so that she could stand up to the stronger elder brother whom she admired. When she was little, she often had nightmares about fighting with her brother. The fact that her younger sister usually took the brother's side occasionally strained relations between them; the envy and jealousy she felt sprang to life again when her sister contracted anorexia nervosa, and thus enjoyed extra care and affection from the father. At that point Agnes C. became aware of how attached she was to her father. But when his attention was focused on her during her own illness, she could not find the right means of contact and was unable to discuss her problems with either of her parents.

Her sexual anxiety can be traced to her infancy. As a child she had imagined that there were devils behind the doors, who could cut off her arms or prick her heels with their tiny spears. In the evenings, she had to jump into bed very quickly, for fear that her leg might be bitten by a crocodile living under her bed. Later on, her fears were redoubled by her mother's warning that masturbation would show its consequences on the children later. After hearing that, the patient had felt very anxious and also developed guilt feelings. When her menses stopped two years previously, she thought she was pregnant. She imagined that fertilization took place through the throat, this belief coming from her observation of animals: the tomcat biting the cat's neck, the cock pecking the hens, and so on. She was not quite certain through which orifice babies emerged at birth, but assumed that it was the anus.

During the first ten sessions, while Agnes C. was discussing the material given above, she talked eagerly, sometimes almost bubbling over; she was consistently polite and enthusiastic about the therapist. But in hour 11 her tone changed; she cried frequently, demanded to be sent home to her mother at once, and began to criticize everything. Right up to the end of her treatment, she was subject to violent changes of mood, at one moment impudent and rejecting, criticizing everything, the next moment smiling, polite or apathetic, as though in a world of her own.

The problem of money became important. She wanted to have everything, if possible, without paying for it. She began to steal small quantities of fruit from the shops and picked up things in the hospital kitchen when no one was around. Often she persuaded other patients to buy her large bags of fruit, and then did not pay them back, or offered them half-rotten, half-eaten fruit from her hoard. In hour 18 she began a phase when she frequently was silent, tossed to and fro on the couch, occasionally uttering hissing or groaning sounds and criticizing every aspect of the analysis, or rather the analyst. When she was little she had displayed this kind of behavior toward her brother and her mother. On one occasion, when she had been spanked and sent to bed, she went straight up to the second floor and stood on the window sill, pretending she was going to jump out. Sometimes in a rage she refused to eat.

She could recognize her old stubbornness in her present refusal of food, but was not able to shake herself loose from it. She felt that she was inwardly divided. One part of her wanted to get well and grow up, the other wanted to shirk responsibility and avoid life by remaining ill and being treated like a baby.

In hour 21 she played with the sceno-box, and staged a large family celebration. At first everyone was unnaturally affectionate toward one another; soon, however, quarrelling and hatred broke out. Agnes C. was completely involved in this game and even imitated the children's talk; the baby of the family was her favorite role. She also modeled statuettes frequently, alternately making angels and horribly distorted devils. She was especially relieved after molding the devils; lending physical form to her anxieties helped her learn how to handle and eventually to master them.

From about hour 10 onwards, Agnes C. put on weight steadily, gaining about two to four pounds a week. She ate quite inconsistently, sometimes nothing, then ravenously in great amounts. She began to recognize her ambivalence in all her feelings, wishes, and remarks. Gradually the future, and particularly a career, began to take up an important part of her thoughts. She wanted definitely to take her final examinations for graduation, and her school phobia slowly subsided.

Phases of silence, criticism, and stubbornness alternated with one another. As the negative side of her ambivalent feelings for her mother became clearer in the transference, the patient remembered a similar situation in the past. When she was in the junior year, she had a teacher who resembled her mother in many ways. Her feelings toward this teacher were never quite straightened out; she had felt simultaneously attracted and repelled. The vomiting had started at about this time.

During the last few hours of the analysis, Agnes C. seemed chiefly concerned with her future. Her fear of sex had decreased, and she began to look forward to marrying one day. But she was equally interested in having a worthwhile career, particularly because of the independence it would give her. She was still undecided whether to go on to the university or study commercial art.

The eating problems had largely improved and she was rapidly regaining weight. She now weighed about 90 lbs. and the starvation edema had entirely disappeared. She was mentally more alert, could concentrate better and was no longer entangled in a network of oral and sexual daydreams.

Follow-up

Continued improvement of the anorexia and constipation. By 1955, three years after the analysis had been brought to a close, her eating difficulties and constipation had vanished, and she had reached a weight of 148 lbs., about the same as at present. Her menstruation returned without hormone treatments. Agnes herself feels that a general loosening up, through artistic work and frequent bathing, has brought back her menstruation. Having decided to study commercial art, she passed her final examinations with no difficulty. Her relationships to other people have developed in a very promising way, and she attributes this success for the most part to psychotherapy. Her sister, who also had suffered from anorexia nervosa, could not detach herself from her parents and has found no contact among her contemporaries.

Case History 4: Gertrude D.

Age: 27
Height: 5 ft. 8 in.
Weight: 104 lbs.
Weight before illness: 143 lbs.
Age at onset of illness: 24
Length of illness before examination: 3 years

Family History and Biography

No history of mental illness in the family. The father was manager of an estate. Gertrude D. was the third of 15 children; the eldest child, a girl, was adopted by relatives and raised away from home. She returned only on visits. The second, a boy one year older than Gertrude D., was killed in the war. There had been an especially close relationship between him and the patient. Since she was the eldest girl at home, Gertrude D. had to assume responsibilities early in life and help with the younger children. The family lived on an estate in West Germany which belonged to an industrialist, Mr. C.

The patient was probably breastfed for about a year, until the mother's next pregnancy, and developed normally. She was a willful child, and extremely jealous of her older brother, although this did not affect the feeling between them.

When she began school, the headstrong, energetic child suddenly turned into a weepy, sensitive, and submissive little girl. She cried bitterly when she discovered that she was not going to be allowed to be in the same class as her brother. The others called her "crybaby," and she remained shy and solitary. She never had any real friends at school, and afterwards only briefly. She was very ambitious, and though she was almost at the head of the class, she cried when anyone wrote a better essay than she. She was a very poor loser. She normally ate well, but whenever her mother had to go into the hospital for one of her many pregnancies, Gertrude lost her appetite.

Although she had previously been very proud of her father, after the age of nine or ten, she began to be ashamed of her mother's many pregnancies, and became angry with her father when she saw her mother crying. When she was ten, one of the grooms tried to seduce her. Her mother had never told her the facts of life, and she was disgusted when her menstruation began. Shortly before puberty, she lost her delicacy; she became tough and tomboyish and longed to be a boy.

Mrs. D. found her large family a terrible burden, both mentally and physically. The midwife told Gertrude D. to speak to her father about it, but she never challenged him openly. Gertrude D. was very sympathetic toward her mother, but also resentful and angry at having to stay home and help. Unlike her elder sister, she could not go on to high school, and even had to

leave grade school early in order to help care for another new
baby. Sex was repulsive to her. When she was fifteen, a young
man gave her a kiss, and she was not sure whether or not that
could make her pregnant. Mrs. D. cried a great deal, and Gertrude felt guilty when she spent vacations away from home with
relatives or in town with the family of Mr. C., the industrialist.
Sometimes she even had to be sent home, because she was so
miserable with homesickness that she could not eat.

When she was 18, she began to learn cooking and serving at
a large country hotel nearby, where she stayed for four years. At
22, she took a job as maid in Mr. C.'s townhouse. It was there
that the anorexia nervosa first made its appearance.

Previous Illnesses ·

Measles at ten years; scarlet fever at 14. Since 14, psoriasis on
knees and elbows, particularly severe in spring. At 19, a corneal
infection; at 23, an abscess on the tonsils. During the last few
years, frequent tonsillitis; tonsillectomy had been avoided, however, because of her poor general health.

Present Illness

Life in the C. household brought with it a whole series of problems. When she was little, Gertrude D. had always been treated
as one of the family; even today, the generous and good-hearted
Mr. C. signs his letters to her "Papa." But in her role as maid, she
was expected to keep her place, and to address her employers as
"Sir" and "Madam." Although once on an intimate basis with the
entire family, she now ate with the cook, the gardener, and the
chauffeur. Her childhood friendship with the youngest daughter
of the house had also changed. Inwardly and outwardly, the two
girls had grown far apart. The patient had always idealized and
envied her friend for her pretty figure; now when she came to
town, she discovered that the friend kept to a strict diet in order
to stay slim. In contrast, Gertrude D.'s figure left much to be desired. This impression was made even stronger because a young
man she had met in the hotel used to tease her about her round

cheeks. In fact, she was quite fond of this young man; whenever she went home for a few days, she visited him, and even allowed him to caress her. But there was no question of a sexual relationship: the patient wanted to remain a child and was afraid of growing up. She would have liked to have children of her own, but marriage, conception, and birth seemed insuperable obstacles. Her former friend's slim figure and the boy friend's teasing provided enough excuse for the gradual cutting down of food. Furthermore, she had a terrifying example before her: the corpulent cook, who embodied almost every imaginable negative characteristic. Since the cook had been in the C. household for a long time, Gertrude knew her well and, at first, got along well with her. But gradually she began to resent having to work under her and complained about her slowness. At the same time the cook, who hated men, began to ridicule her whenever Gertrude went out with any of the menservants. It was the final blow when Gertrude D. was told that she would soon reach the cook's generous proportions.

At much the same time, a doctor advised the patient to go on a raw-food diet in order to clear her psoriasis; she began to limit her diet and, during the last few years she ate almost nothing except bread and fruit. Her menstruation became irregular and finally—a year before treatment began—she became amenorrheic (menarche at 16½; previously, normal cycles).

Apart from frequent attacks of tonsillitis, she was also plagued, from the beginning of her dieting, with facial boils and severe acrocyanosis. Just before therapy began, she had an operation for a tumor on the hand, and the wound took an extremely long time to heal. After an unsuccessful attempt at outpatient psychotherapy, the patient arrived at our clinic with the diagnosis of anorexia nervosa.

Psychotherapy and Psychodynamics (35 Treatment Hours)

After a few preliminary difficulties, Gertrude D. was able to extend her conversation beyond a mere recital of her life history. She began to talk about her fear of the future, by which she really meant her fear of marriage. "Love can exist only between parents and brothers and sisters," she said. Until now, she had always been in a constant conflict with men, because they always wanted to have the upper hand, and she found the thought of being subordinate very frightening. But it was easier for her to imagine marrying an older man, because older men made her think of Mr. C., who had always been so kind to her. He was even contributing toward the cost of treatment. But her picture of a gentle, fatherly man had another aspect, as is shown by two dreams she had during the early stages of treatment. In both cases she was raped by an older man, and in one of the dreams she stabbed his genitals with a long needle. Her associations referred to Mr. C. and her father. During the treatment hours, she continued this theme of struggle from her dreams, with complaints about men whose only thought was to beget children and subjugate their wives. She insisted that she had never experienced any sexual feelings herself.

The future seemed hopelessly black to her. Her only real relationship was with her mother; if she died, there would be no one. She felt she simply could not cope with her feelings. She could not even manage to eat because an inner voice objected and scolded her when she did take any food. However, it turned out that there were drive breakthroughs which fooled her "superego" voice, when Gertrude D. could take pleasure in eating things like cookies, which were usually forbidden. The voice of her conscience also regulated a strict daily timetable and enforced pedantic order and cleanliness.

Once she dreamed about a deformed baby whose genitals were not properly developed, so that she could not tell if it was a boy or a girl. She interpreted this dream as a sign of her own insecurity. "I am afraid of being a woman, but I am not a boy either." She was afraid that she might give birth to a monster later.

In hour 11, she produced a dream in which she married the chauffeur, despite the objections and scorn of the cook. This led to the question of her relationship with the cook; she became very upset when she described the hate she felt for this woman, and recognized its intensity. She felt that she might have taken over from her the rejection of men and sex. Every time she wanted to do something, she had to ask herself first what the cook would say. Through exaggerated activity she tried to rid herself of this inner pressure. The cook probably represented the negative aspect of the mother-image. During these hours, Gertrude D. frequently wept in helpless distress.

In hour 16, Gertrude D. had her first dream accompanied by sexual excitement. She dreamed that a doctor came to her in bed. "It was such an extraordinary feeling of happiness and freedom, as if I were floating." In another dream, in which she fled to Mr. C., her substitute father, for protection against other men, it became possible for her to talk about her rivalry toward the younger C. daughter, who was now married and expecting a child. Gertrude D. saw herself as a poor girl, who had to struggle to earn her own dowry, and she envied the daughter of rich parents. It emerged that with her attempts to emulate her slim figure, Gertrude was punishing herself for the envy and jealousy which she felt for this girl.

She began to think about her childhood friend's pregnancy and dreamed that she herself was holding a child in her arms—but such a small, skinny, neglected baby that his legs hung down, thin and weak. She saw herself in this child; although she would have liked to become a mother, she was at the same time afraid that she would never be able to manage. She compared the enlargement of a pregnant woman to a full stomach after a meal. "When I eat something, I feel so full. I am much freer when I eat nothing. I would be even more weighed down by a child. Eating is as burdensome for me as bearing children is for other women."

Gertrude D. took particular pleasure in thinking of the "dangers of overeating"—as long as she felt safe from them. She took special delight in imagining the fat cook, eating more and more, and eventually being destroyed. These thoughts were connected with a dream in which a meal was being prepared. The procedure was very much complicated by the fact that, after three hours of cooking, the chicken was not yet done; in fact, it was still alive and had to be killed over again. When the patient served the meal to Mr. C., the chicken changed into a goose and then into a fish. The woman who killed the chicken in the dream was well known for her cruelty to animals, whereas the patient herself could not bear to look when a chicken was being killed in the farmyard. She then saw herself as the goose, who floated about for three years, stayed "raw," and did not know what she was: fish or fowl, child, man, or woman. This dream also showed the danger of eating, in two aspects: killing and being killed, devouring and being devoured.

For a short time, she was very much worried by the extent of her ambivalence, and she had thoughts of suicide. But eventually she gained a greater feeling of inner security and was relieved to find that she was not punished for her aggressive hatred of the cook, who played the role of "bad" mother for her, and her criticism of the analyst.

During the six weeks of treatment, Gertrude D. gained ten pounds. The treatment then had to be terminated for external reasons, and she returned to the C. family. At the beginning and again at the end of the analysis, she had a scanty menstruation.

Follow-up (after 7 years)

The patient reported that her six weeks of treatment had given her a completely different attitude toward life, and that she had gained in courage and interest. The appetite disturbance gradually improved; two years later it was gone. Her digestion has been normal since. Two years after treatment she married, and in 1956 she gave birth to a healthy child. Since then, her menses have been regular. The marriage is harmonious and successful, and except for an attack of tonsillitis in 1955, she has remained in good health. (Weight: 121 lbs.)

Case History 5: Martha E.

Age: 18
Height: 5 ft. 5 in.
Weight: 83 lbs.

Weight before illness: 121 lbs.

Age at onset of illness: 16

Length of illness at examination: 2 years

Family History and Biography

Martha E.'s mother was the youngest child of a wealthy East Prussian family. The maternal grandfather had been a playboy who committed suicide. The grandmother died while fleeing in 1945. An older brother of Mrs. E. was killed in the Second World War. Mrs. E. also had a sister, Aunt Erna, several years older than herself, whose influence she never seemed to be able to throw off. Martha E.'s father died when she was three.

In spite of the grandfather's extravagance, the family was never in need, and their standard of living remained at a comfortable, upper-middle-class level. Martha E.'s mother was brought up as a lady; after finishing school she went abroad to study languages, her natural talent. After a few years, she returned home to her mother. She rejected all her suitors until she met an architect 25 years older than herself, who fell violently in love with the shy girl and eventually persuaded her to marry him. Mrs. E. was not well received by her husband's well-to-do family.

At first Mr. E. did not want any children and Mrs. E. dutifully used a contraceptive. However, by a deceptive maneuver, she did conceive; again in obedience to her husband's wishes, she made several attempts at abortion. These were unsuccessful, the pregnancy lasted its full term, and a normal baby girl, Martha E., was born. Her parents were very pleased.

The mother's notes give a good picture of Martha E.'s early childhood. She was not breastfed, but, being a good eater, she had no feeding problems. Another diary entry reads: "You are such a crying little baby, and I am afraid that we are not giving you enough to eat. Your very kind physician, Dr. F., thinks that we ought to keep you on a strict diet." At 21 months, Martha E. was toilet-trained. When she was two years old, her mother wrote the following notes: "Now I am afraid I must also record that Martha is not obedient; she is good only when it suits her. She always wants to do everything for herself. Often she is such a willful little thing. Whenever anyone wants to stroke her head, she pushes them away. She won't let other children play with her toys. She won't hold Mommy's hand when we go for walks, and she is bad about eating up her food." The emphasis on willfulness and bashfulness is particularly significant.

Because of the heavy bombing of the North German town where Mrs. E. lived after she was married, the patient and her mother spent the last years of the war in central Germany. After the armistice, Aunt Erna (Mrs. E.'s older sister) arrived with her son and immediately began to take control over her sister, as she had always done. Martha E. herself had no recollection of this period.

A few months later, Mrs. E. went alone to the city to try to bring her family together again. It was not until then that she discovered her husband had died a short time previously, probably of heart failure. Her husband's family was unwilling to give her financial help, and she lived through a difficult period. However, she soon was able to take advantage of her linguistic abilities, and as an interpreter for the occupation forces, she earned enough to live comfortably. During this period, Martha E. was put into a children's home, and a few years later, she started attending an anthroposophical school.

Martha E. was always a very shy girl, and somewhat coy; she was held up to the others as a good example by the nurses in the home. She could remember having been embarrassed by her plumpness when she was still only six, and thought that this was probably the time when she started hunching herself over to conceal her breasts, which were fatter than those of the boys. In any case, there can be no doubt that long before puberty she began to have round shoulders, and wanted to be a boy.

She was especially pampered when she stayed with her mother, who was employed as interpreter in a hotel which had been requisitioned by the occupation forces. Her one recollection of her father had probably become confused with these visits: "I am sitting at father's side, and he is feeding me caviar."

Mrs. E.'s honesty and reserve earned her a special place in the management's trust; she remained at the hotel for a long time, and even after the end of the requisition period her dismissal was postponed many times. She had no interest in a second marriage.

Bad management had brought her former husband's small contracting firm into debt. Through her frugality, she was able to give financial assistance and to prevent the manager from usurping complete control of the business. She was also fortunate enough to find a good accountant, who protected her against the manager, and kept the books. Mrs. E. herself knew little about her financial affairs. She received a varying amount of money from her husband's estate, which covered their living expenses. She relied on the generosity of her fellow men, and indeed she always found someone ready to give her impartial advice. However, this trait also caused her to be very easily influenced, and she often made decisions that were not in her own interest or in that of her daughter. This was due in part to the fact that she was dependent on Aunt Erna.

In accordance with Aunt Erna's wishes, they built a house in a village in central Germany. Mrs. E. provided the money, but somehow Aunt Erna managed to have her name entered on the deed. Mrs. E. could really have had no possible reason for wanting to move into this village; the whole plan was actually for the benefit of the sister, who needed somewhere to live with her son, and preferred to be in the same village as her future husband, who was obtaining a divorce. Since Aunt Erna also wanted to keep the fees which would otherwise have been paid to the children's home every month, in 1952 Martha E. went to live with her. After the move, Martha E. went to the high school in a nearby town. By the time treatment started, she had reached the junior year, and was said to be one of the most conscientious, hardworking, and intelligent girls in the class.

However, the transition from town to village was difficult; it was not easy for the patient to adjust to an ordinary secondary school, after spending so many of her school years in the relatively free atmosphere of a Waldorf school, with its emphasis on arts and handicrafts.

In order to enhance the intelligence and charm of her own son, and thus her own importance, Aunt Erna took advantage of every opportunity to belittle her niece. Everything that Martha E. could do well she counted as a credit to herself and her methods of upbringing. She felt that no one else could possibly have done anything with Martha E. The patient's description of her aunt has been substantiated by several outside accounts, and she is probably giving a very fair picture of the facts; there can be no doubt that Aunt Erna systematically developed an inferiority complex in Martha. The girl was told that she was ugly, stupid, impertinent, conceited, and unsightly. The result of this treatment was that Martha E. withdrew completely into a world of her own and revenged herself with visions of committing suicide, for example, by poisoning herself.

Previous Illnesses

The patient has never been known to have been seriously ill before.

Present Illness

In 1955 Mrs. E. was dismissed from her job. She retired to the small house she had built for Aunt Erna, so that she could take over the education of her daughter. Although Aunt Erna had now married and no longer needed the house, it still remained her property. Mrs. E. was unable to gain any influence over her daughter; on the contrary, she was ruled by Martha, who assumed control over her pliant, indecisive mother. In fact, life with her mother merely strengthened the patient's previous ideal formation, and her snobbish, precocious rejection of everything her schoolmates were thinking and doing. "One must not go out with boys; one must not read popular magazines; one must not go to sentimental films." Martha E. made a virtue of necessity, and her classmates thought of her as a conceited outsider.

It is important to note the changes in her life which were brought about by the arrival of her mother. Since rebellion a-gainst Aunt Erna's regime was doomed to failure, Martha E. withdrew from this "bad" mother image. The relationship be-tween niece and aunt was quite straightforward: inexorable stern-ness on one side and suppressed hatred on the other. It was not until her mother arrived that Martha E. became torn between at-tachment and aversion, and the mother, with her insecure man-ner, was practically never emotionally consistent. In any case, Martha E. dated the beginning of her illness from this difficult time. Soon after her mother came, the patient found a way of ex-pressing her ambivalence. She began to tickle her mother, and in-sisted on doing so several times a day. The patient also annoyed her mother in other ways, but she always ended by torturing her-self with self-reproaches and self-imposed punishments, such as slapping her own face, scratching herself, or begging her mother's forgiveness with earnest soulful resolutions.

At first the patient still enjoyed nibbling, and both mother and aunt teased her about her fatness. Then she began by herself to diet, compensating by forcing her mother into a fattening cam-paign. Martha E. had always enjoyed housework, especially cook-ing, and now she took over these duties, tormenting her mother by pressing food on her. The patient herself scarcely ate anything, and her demands dwindled from day to day. She used to watch the forced eating of her mother, thus satisfying herself vicariously. "Now I don't need to eat anything myself at all," she used to say. But this did not prevent her from hiding tidbits and eating them in secret, which only reaffirmed her sense of guilt and kept the vicious circle in operation.

Before the illness, the patient, who was 5 ft. 5 in. tall, weighed 121 lbs.; during its course she lost weight until, at the time of her admission to the hospital in March 1958, she weighed only 83 lbs. Although her menstruation had been perfectly regular (men-arche at 14 years) Martha became amenorrheic after Christmas 1956, and the menses have not returned since. The patient would have welcomed the absence of menstruation if she had not been afraid that she was pregnant (nothing her mother could say would dissuade her from this fear). At Christmas 1956, she had been skiing in Switzerland with a party of young people; there she had met a French student, who was very attentive to her, and with whom she still corresponds. They spent the night in a communal dormitory, and although Martha E. remained fully dressed and apparently did not even exchange caresses with the boy, after her menses ceased she lived in the irrational fear that she had somehow been impregnated during the night. She confided her fears to her mother, who tried in vain to calm her. Only after nine months had passed did she relinquish the idea that she had been raped in her sleep. During the illness her isolation in school became more acute. At the same time, her constipation, which had been troublesome before, grew worse, and acrocyanosis appeared, increasing as the cachexia advanced.

Before admission to the hospital the patient had been treated by two general practitioners; among other things, hormone injections had been administered, but had had no effect on the amenorrhea. A pituitary implantation had been considered, but on the advice of her teacher, the patient was referred to us first.

Clinical findings: Height: 5 ft. 5 in. Weight: 83 lbs. General emaciation in relation to the reduced weight, mild acrocyanosis, dry, scaly skin, and cutis marmorata on the inside of both thighs. No jaundice, no edema. Body hair retained, the hair on the head dry and falling. Scaphoid abdomen; small scar from omphalocele operation in infancy. Hypotonic blood pressure; bradycardia.

Laboratory findings: Anemia (Hb 11.4, RBC 3,200,000). Hypopotassemia: 3.2 mq (12.5 mg%) and 2.4 mq (9.3 mg%).

Medical treatment: Until the findings returned to normal, potassium and iron preparations were administered. Because of the drop in weight (during the first weeks of treatment, it dropped to as low as 64 lbs.), tube feeding was tried without success since the patient vomited immediately afterward. For several days, she refused food and drink; continuous intravenous drop infusions prevented the severest manifestations of inanition. During the entire treatment she was administered vitamins, aids to digestion, and laxatives and enemas, according to need.

Summary of the Results of Tests (Hawie, Rorschach, and Color Pyramid Tests)

These tests were given at the beginning of treatment.

The patient is above average in intelligence, but able to use her talents for constructive thought and action only at a relatively low level, since her impulses and emotions are considerably disturbed, and her motivations will not permit a true inclination toward human and material reality. The freezing of her relationship to the environment into empty, fantasy relationships, and almost mechanical behavior routines is obviously due to an intellectualized approach to life, adjusted for the most effective and "refined" achievement of her narcissistic and egocentric needs. It also serves to help construct and uphold a sterile world of fantasy, which has no connection with reality. Thus her performance falls far below her ability, and her present capacity to learn is strongly hindered by her avoidance of any contact with, or experience of, the outside world.

The patient's basic conduct is extremely introverted and governed almost completely by subjective needs and fantasies. Her attitude is also extraordinarily rigid, indicating an intensive need for protective defenses. To a great extent, the patient is unaffected by social stimuli. Occasionally she responds at a superficial level and may even show a spark of sudden enthusiasm, but her reactions are markedly egocentric in character, thereby preventing any real contact. Her social adaptation is correspondingly disturbed. She can make use of mechanical behavior routines and has adequate intellectual sensitivity and an astonishing capacity for swift opportunistic changes from one rigid role to another; but she is nonetheless incapable of entering into or sustaining a mutual attachment, or of feeling affection for any other person.

In spite of her introversion, the patient possesses almost no insight into her motivation. Her mind is preoccupied with strong conflicting need-fantasies, which distort and befog her perception of herself and of the world around her. Two opposing forces seem to predominate; the first is an extreme narcissism, which involves an overvaluation of her own person and a cold irresponsible disregard for others, demanding their subordination; the opposing tendency is her self-destructiveness, her feelings of guilt and inferiority, and her merciless self-criticism. The marked emphasis on oral traits indicates that the center of conflict is in this area which has sadomasochistic characteristics. The patient is partially identified with both of these contradictory tendencies, and the gratification of one very often reactivates the other, just as frustration of one may satisfy the other. Her identification with the female sex has not progressed beyond the infantile-narcissistic stage. In defense against her hostile impulses, the patient envisions herself as a gentle, refined, and guileless person to whom all base impulses are alien, and who is threatened by a common, brutal, and greedy world. The adult female role is both despised and feared.

This patient apparently is suffering from a severe character neurosis, with preponderantly depressive-sadomasochistic traits. The prognosis looks, on the whole, unfavorable.

Psychotherapy and Psychodynamics (440 Treatment Hours in Two Years)

During the first few weeks of treatment, the patient's weight dwindled from 83 to 64 lbs. Since nourishment administered by stomach tube was vomited up again, infusions were given to prevent the severest symptoms of inanition. A private nurse was engaged from treatment hour 74 to 104, to ensure that the patient kept strictly to her bed, to control the amount of nutriment actually assimilated, and to serve her small and frequent meals.

For the first few months, the patient had analytic hours six times a week; later on, four times weekly. Treatment was never interrupted for more than five days at a time. During the six weeks when she was being tended and intensively fed by a private nurse, Martha E. gained 22 lbs., but this was partly due to edematous water retention. As soon as she was allowed more freedom of movement, she lost weight again. For months afterward, she fluctuated between 68 and 77 lbs. Innumerable attempts to influence her condition by external means failed completely. For example, when she was given the foods she chose, she would refuse them because she was unworthy of such privileges, share the food with the other patients, furtively throw it away, or vomit it up. When she was strictly confined to bed, she either did not stay there or retaliated by losing weight again. The only exception was during the time when the private nurse was caring for her during the daytime; however, closer examination of her behavior during these weeks, and the probable causes for her weight gain, reveals many reasons why the improvement was so ephemeral.

During the first two weeks of this time (from session 74 to 85), Martha E. showed only her best side, managing to deceive the nurse and making an ally of her. As before, she used her ingenuity to make foods disappear into thin air while pretending to eat them with great gusto. She also succeeded in persuading her nurse, Cecilia, to help her rebel against the psychotherapy. Martha E. promised that if the nurse would speak out against the infusions and put an end to the analysis, she would return the favor by eating normally. Since Cecilia (as was later learned) already disapproved of psychotherapy on religious grounds, she was not hard to convince.

When the patient realized that her deception had been discovered, she began to eat. She made one last attempt, supported by Cecilia, to discontinue the psychotherapy and the infusions. She then became willing to admit her regressive needs: "Perhaps I really have to become like a baby." But the subsequent course of the illness exposed this as a transitory symptomatic improvement for the purpose of resistance. As soon as she had gained a little weight (86 lbs.), she began with renewed vigor to deny the need for any treatment and, as she declined visibly, she petitioned for release.

It might be objected that this temporary gain was not merely a symptomatic improvement for the purpose of resistance, but rather a result of Cecilia's motherly care, and that it might have been lasting if Martha E. had remained under her care. However, there is good reason to believe that Cecilia's continued presence would not have been of any lasting value. The patient soon refused her "motherly care." As Martha E. found that she was unsuccessful, even with the nurse's help, she changed her tactics, and betrayed the nurse's unprofessional, almost unbalanced, behavior. In many ways, Martha E. could see an image of herself in Cecelia and, though this could have been useful for the psychotherapy, it was hardly an ideal state of affairs in any other sense. There can be no doubt that Cecilia was an abnormal personality. (She was not yet fully qualified and had been engaged only in an emergency, since the shortage of nurses left no other choice.) From both the objective and subjective points of view, it seemed preferable to entrust Martha E. to the supervision of the hospital staff, who had always taken special pains with her. Furthermore, since the initial urgency of the need for strict control was past, a private nurse was now no longer essential.

Despite much effort on all sides to make her meals appetizing, refusal of food remained the main symptom of Martha's illness. We must focus our attention on this symptom and try to understand the other symptoms in relation to the main problem. The following description of Martha E.'s attitude and behavior, as manifested in resistance and transference, will give an idea of the organization of the symptoms. As far as possible, the psychodynamic context will also be described.

The patient's remark in hour 84, "I want to eat now, but not to tell everything," provides an excellent point of departure for describing her behavior and resistance. Naturally, it could be proposed that, if the patient had not been forced to "tell everything" —that is, if she had been allowed to break off the analysis—perhaps her resolution would have been carried out. There are anorexia nervosa patients who fear such measures as tube-feeding, infusions, shock treatments, or psychoanalysis more than having to eat and, in the anticipation of anxiety, choose the lesser evil (food) in order to escape the greater one (treatment). But we could not depend on such a reaction, especially in view of previous bad experience with this patient, who was very fond of making "bargains." We had to regard the resistance and symptom formation, in the silence and secrecy and in the anorexia, as two aspects of a basic disturbance. In fact, her secrecy, as was revealed only after many treatment hours, was applied primarily, and on a conscious level, to food. In the meantime, she was not simply silent, but spent her treatment hours in monotonous self-reproaches: "I am inferior, wicked, stupid, ugly, conceited, miserly, egoistic. I am not worth the bother of treatment. I am too demanding; nobody loves me. I am just wasting your time. Why don't you let me die in peace?" She perpetually demanded punishment, and, in the ward, as well as during analysis, she did her best to attract hatred and contempt, or to give her fellow patients a bad conscience. With either pressure or wheedling persuasion, she forced her food on fellow patients, at the same time secretly nibbling from their plates, or more often, participating mentally in their meals. As her mother had done at home, her fellow patients now had to eat for her, while she herself scarcely took anything. She absolutely refused to be hungry, although she once admitted that she thought of nothing all day long but cooking and eating. In hour 139 she made the first mention of her pointless thefts from the storerooms and never took anything again. Further idiosyncrasies, such as her numerous schemes for disposing of food and vomitus, were either observed by the nurses or acknowledged during treatment.

One of her most carefully guarded secrets involved ruminating and regurgitating, and an appetite for the garbage pail. Surreptitiously "chewing the cud," she made use of a rumination reflex to prolong her meals without anybody noticing, taking no more than a few bites which she could spit out later. Scraps from the garbage pail were often used for her rumination. On the other hand, she did everything she could to prevent odds and ends of food from being discarded or destroyed. This behavior was in strong contrast to her extravagant desires for delicacies—which she often left untouched.

Even during the phase of especially severe inanition, when she could hardly stand on her feet, she would still not admit to being ill. Not until she had had more than 300 hours of analysis did she stop denying her cachectic appearance, and begin to be aware of the disturbance that her emaciation was creating. Direct open and verbal communication with the outside world had ceased, and she was capable of making known only symptoms or actions whose communicative content was so remote from consciousness that she could deny it completely. Love and hate, vanity and envy, to mention only two examples, were bound up in compromise-formations and either had become unrecognizable or expressed themselves in symptom formations. She did not hate; she was tormented by her appearance. She seemed to have lost every vestige of natural vanity, every desire to please. Once, when she was left alone for a moment, she struggled over to a window seat on the second floor, and sat there half naked, even though she was so weak that she could hardly hold herself upright. It was painful to see how pitifully wasted she was. Again, during a particularly bad phase, when her mother came to see her, she presented herself without a word, completely naked. But she remained totally unable to accept any suggestion that she might be trying to make preverbal communications, that she desired love, pity, and friendship, or wanted to hurt someone. Such emotions were displaced through acting out. The only thing which she explicitly wanted was punishment.

It is scarcely surprising that Martha E. remained isolated in the ward and made friends with none of the young girls who came and went during her long stay. For a long time, she merely foisted upon her fellow patients the roles that corresponded to her own inner situation, and treated them as means to an end. Once, during a phase when she was still particularly affected by her hatred, she became especially friendly toward her roommate, only to eat raw liver just in order to annoy her. When this girl left the hospital, for reasons entirely unrelated to Martha E.'s behavior, the patient burst out in terrible self-accusations: "I have driven her away; I am at fault." She repeated her self-reproaches for so long that the others, tired of having to listen, finally agreed with her.

On another occasion she displayed a form of altruism that Anna Freud (1936) has described. A young girl was discharged uncured. Although Martha E. had repeatedly denied any need for treatment herself, and wished for her own discharge, she was indignantly angry to see the other girl sent away. Interceding for someone else gave her the opportunity to demand something she had refused for herself. At the same time she sent pleading–threatening letters to her mother, asking her to take this girl into her own home. As usual, she added the promise that she would get well, that is, she would eat normally. It would be a great mistake to consider this and similar activities on Martha's part as blackmail, without inquiring into the underlying motivation. If one considers that the patient was acting on the strength of an unconscious identification, then both the intensity of her demands and her promises to get well (if her wishes were fulfilled) become understandable. The best example of this process was Martha's identificatory way of quieting her own hunger by feeding her mother. One of the chief obstacles to improvement was the obstinate denial of her wish for identification (with mother or fellow patients); even after this denial had given way somewhat, she still avoided doing her own eating, loving, and hating. To adapt Anna Freud's description: Martha E. ate along with other people, without eating anything herself. In this way the patient became greatly independent of the drive-object, food. She had limited her ties with the outside world and directed her striving toward her own ego. S. Freud (1921) called this process a regression from object choice to identification. It was expressed figuratively in the following dream:

> *Dream:* I was with a girl friend, skiing. We approached one another and finally became one person [Identification Dream].

This "uniting" at an unconscious level replaced a real relationship, in the same way that the rumination brought with it an illusionary gratification and an extensive "autarchy." In order to sustain her secondary narcissism, the patient made a particular point of rejecting everything that was at all reminiscent of an "object relationship." Unmistakable dream-wishes were pushed away by her conscious ego in order to disrupt reestablishment of a relationship prematurely, before it got beyond the stage of ideational and affective representation. She would not even allow herself to wish for what she was seeking, and certainly not to experience an actual relationship.

This statement may seem to contradict the observation that the patient did not hold back her wishes. On closer examination, however, it becomes evident that she had displaced her wants onto nonessential objects, which held no real meaning for her. Inordinate demands on her mother, for example, betrayed the dreamwish to be beside her in bed. Consciously, she repudiated all such wishes, declaring that they were not hers; thus, it is understandable that the delicacies she demanded left her empty, because the object they represented—the kind, loving mother—was unconsciously but strongly being rejected. Noninvolvement with her environment was the inevitable consequence of the secondary narcissism into which she had fallen.

Secondary narcissism was, however, only one aspect of the withdrawal from reality. In addition, there was the patient's abandonment of aggressive cathexes and the way in which she had turned them against herself in self-hate and depressive–masochistic complaints. The patient's need for punishment and her so-called "negative therapeutic reaction" both hinge upon this process, which will be described more fully later. In brief, if we assume that self-love (secondary narcissism) and self-hate (masochism) have replaced libidinous and aggressive object-relationships, then we can understand the intensity of the resistance against a return to the former state. We spent much time in dealing with a characteristic form of transference, which Anna Freud had termed "transference of defense." Thus, libidinous and aggressive strivings no longer emerged directly in the transference, but were connected with changes in the ego—the secondary narcissism and depressive–masochistic structure.

The scene of action had shifted, metaphorically speaking, from the interpersonal to the intrapsychic level; any attempt to reverse this process was regarded as a menace to the patient's equilibrium and was repulsed. For the inducement to transference, which is inherent in analysis, would have brought out those unconscious conflicts which, having led to the symptom formation, had at least insured freedom from anxiety. Here lay the inner nosological gain to which the secondary nosological gain had allied itself.

The patient found many methods of preserving the status quo. She denied being at all ill or in need of assistance, for fear of being brought into contact with other human beings. She behaved toward other people in much the same way as she behaved toward food: at a distance, and in anticipation, she could not have enough of them, but she avoided any actual give and take. Because of her constant hunger, she was always disagreeable, out of temper, and irritable. Since for a long time she had also denied being hungry, or appeased the desire by ruminating, she displaced her complaining to other, highly impersonal, themes.

In sum, we might say that the "transference of defense," apart from the individual mechanisms, was distinguished by one predominant characteristic: as long as the patient permitted practically nothing to enter her or depart from her, she could remain in a state of independence from her environment, which enabled her to master and manipulate it. To use a metaphor coined during the analysis, it was as if she had shut herself in a mountain fortress, cut off from all normal communication with the outside world. Only occasionally could messages be exchanged and supplies brought up the precipitous, winding pathways. Inside the castle, love feasts and hate orgies were being celebrated, to maintain the illusion of drive satisfaction. Since the patient viewed the present through the spectacles of the past, the fears which caused her to withdraw during childhood were still as effective as ever. The castle was besieged by the two-year-old danger of "impregnation during sleep," and the five-year-old "aggression leads to loss of love," and so on.

This metaphor is not perfect, but at least it does give some picture of the most important psychodynamic processes. In actuality, the patient communicated copiously with the outside world, sometimes writing twenty-page letters to her mother. However,

since most of these letters dealt with her concern about controlling her fellow human beings, they hindered rather than helped
the development of a meaningful relationship.

Why was the patient unable to experience a meaningful human relationship or quiet her hunger in a satisfactory way? Why
did she conceal data (such as her petty thefts, her ruminating,
vomiting, drive breakthroughs at the garbage pail, and masturbation) for such a long time? For, even when she did bring herself
to disclose a long-guarded secret, it was done in a detached report,
which might have had no reference to her at all. She did not want
to utter a word about the most important part—about her feelings
while she was ruminating or indulging in any other of her
pleasures. From her hints it could be guessed that at least some
pleasure was being found, and that rumination had taken the
place of masturbation. A dissociation of image and affect made it
possible for the patient to keep both painful and pleasurable feelings far from consciousness, and also to deprive them of any
warmth as interpretations. She would not allow "words" to go
to her "heart." Thus it is hardly surprising that she could not
produce "free associations," for it was not only her habits that
she was anxious to protect, but above all, the "secrets of her
heart"; she had to stay on her guard to prevent any uncontrolled
thought from slipping out.

The patient had several remarkable dreams which should help
us to understand the psychogenesis of the symptom formation
and her eccentric behavior, although in the early stages of treatment she was not ready to acknowledge the manifest dream
content (see the "Identification Dream" given above).

Dream 235: I was with Clara [a former patient, who had since
accepted a domestic post] on a visit. There was a donkey in the garden. I talked to him and we got along very well. We played together and were good friends. But there was another daughter in
the house who beat the donkey and tormented him in all sorts of
different ways. Then I left the house. The donkey became ill with
grief and died from longing for me [Donkey Dream].

The patient supplied the analyst with an interpretation: "I know," she said, "that you are thinking I have represented you with the donkey." She was not prepared to say any more. But the analyst already knew that Martha E.'s mother had tried to persuade her to eat by repeating: "If you die, life will have no more meaning for me, and I shall try to die too." The words of the mother, "If you leave me, I shall die," had been transferred to the analyst in the dream. There is also a very clear division of the ambivalence into two persons: there is a "good" girl who loves the donkey, and a "bad" girl who torments him. Martha E.'s dilemma was that these two strivings, loving and tormenting, were united in her. According to the influence to which she was ready to yield, she wanted her donkey to be communicative and personal, or superhumanly strict and indestructible. She longed for a relationship so close and a love so deep that the donkey could not live without her, or she without the donkey. But, at the same time, she could not avoid a terrible sense of guilt for her torture and her responsibility for his, and her, death. This aspect of the dream emphasizes one of the conditions that must be fulfilled, according to Freud, if the neurotic need for punishment is to be relieved: the "former object-cathexis behind the unconscious sense of guilt" must be unmasked (1923, p. 50). The complaints are revealed as accusations, and self-destruction as aggression directed toward a person who is loved at the same time. It is for this reason—that is, because of the ambivalence—that so strong a resistance is put up against a renewed "object-cathexis," against a transference neurosis.

Just as the "Donkey Dream" demonstrated the dilemma of an ambivalent object cathexis and the resultant withdrawal and self-punishment, the following dreams, taken from the last stages of treatment, highlight the difficulty of uniting contradictory internal images and functions.

> *Dream:* I was at a ceremony where a doll was going to be brought to life. A masklike woman handed the baby doll a bottle, and soon afterwards the doll began to show signs of life [Doll Dream].

Dream: I was the king and had a huge retinue. Then I was alone with the queen who had to excrete very thin feces. The scene changed and I stood by a bed in which an elephant lay, partially covered. It moved under the bedclothes and everything seemed very weird to me [King Dream].

Martha E. saw herself as both the doll and the masklike woman. The dream released the following day-residues: she had been looking at a doll in a shop window and had thought how nice it would be to have it. She remembered her own dolls and how much more gently she had treated them than other children had. The analyst stressed her two-fold yearning—as baby and as woman—to be brought to life; he made this the center of the interpretive work. Her negativistic refusal of every relationship was construed as fear of a "complete emotional surrender" (A. Freud, 1952, p. 265). Of course, becoming aware of the dream-wish would not necessarily mean complete dependence on another person, but since thinking is "an experimental kind of acting" (Freud, 1911, p. 221), there is a natural tendency to put thoughts and wishes into action. Furthermore, we must keep in mind that we are dealing with the *psychic* reality, that is the meaning content which has precedence in the experience of a patient.

It is very interesting that an oral satisfaction was depicted on the dream level, when in reality there existed an extreme dependence caused by her illness. At an unconscious level, her urges were apparently being satisfied, and defensive processes prevented an awareness for fear of emotional bondage. For a long time, the intensity of her defenses equalled the strength of her yearning: she avoided every thought that might have led her from the total wish fulfillment of her dreams to the partial satisfaction in reality. Although she denied it in a delusionary way, the patient's illness made her heavily dependent upon others; in spite of her protestations, she was forced to rely on care which, unconsciously, she enjoyed as the wish fulfillment of her dreams.

The "King Dream" revealed an ego ideal which excluded primitive oral, as well as feminine–sexual and other, impulses.

The patient protected herself against dependence and surrender through an exalted masculine identification and a rejection of the feminine aspect and the ordinary human needs. The latter were represented in the dream by the defecating queen and the elephant heaving about in the bed.

Some years before, Martha E. had read an article in an illustrated magazine about sex-change operations, and she began to fantasy about being turned into a boy. This wish, which is indicative of a castration complex, had faded into unconsciousness in the meantime, but it was reactivated by a day-residue and brought to expression in the elephant. At first, Martha E. said that she did not want "to have anything to do with the bed." After a long pause she associated to elephant, "thick skin." She paused again and then, instead of going on to the elephant's characteristic trunk, related a joke she had heard the day before, but had not understood: "Mrs. Longnose got a separation from her husband." In the joke, a displacement and a reversal of roles have taken place. There is a displacement from the lower part of the body to the upper (penis—nose), and reversal of the sexes, since the woman is called "Longnose." The "joke" lies in these two changes which may be translated as follows: "Mr. Longnose had intercourse with his wife." It is interesting to note how this day residue, through the dreamwork, was transformed into an elephant with its trunk (Longnose=penis) and its movements in bed (cohabitation). For fear of a sexual surrender the patient made herself into an all-powerful king. The "King Dream" also illuminated some of the reaction-formations in her behavior in and out of the treatment hour: her feelings of self-sufficiency and self-aggrandizement, which made it impossible for her to show any gratitude.

Even after hundreds of treatment hours, when she felt better and when the psychopathological picture had improved somewhat, she still ascribed every success to herself. The analyst belonged to the retinue of the king as a sort of "ass's head," and from the patient's viewpoint there was no reason for gratitude toward him. In her role as "King" she had to keep her distance and avoid having to accept anything gratefully, for accepting would involve entering into a relationship, and also admitting the desire for something—which would be the same as making her deficiencies known. She had made herself independent of boys and penis-envy, and had substituted an imaginary "being" for "having."

This circumstance could hardly do otherwise than leave insufficient capacity for transference. In describing the behavior of narcissistic neurotics, Freud (1916-1917) said, "They reject the doctor, not with hostility but with indifference. For that reason they cannot be influenced by him either; what he says leaves them cold, makes no impression on them; consequently the mechanism of cure which we carry through with other people—the revival of the pathogenic conflict and the overcoming of the resistance due to repression—cannot be operated with them" (p. 447). Thus everything hinges, from a therapeutic point of view, on the revivification of the pathogenetic conflict, or else—and here decisive advances have been made since 1917—above all the better understanding of pathological forms of conflict resolutions and the resulting forms of resistance. For instance, the statement above about "having" and "being" derives from the chapter "Identification," in *Group Psychology and the Analysis of the Ego,* in which Freud has written, "It is easy to state in a formula the distinction between an identification with the father and the choice of the father as an object. In the first case one's father is what one would like to *be,* and in the second he is what one would like to *have*" (1921, p. 106; *Freud's italics*). In this instance, the reference is to a particular *content* (father) of the previously mentioned regression in form from object-choice to identification. An alternative content of this form-giving mechanism—introjection of the hated "object" (e.g., Aunt Erna = "bad" mother)— was mentioned when we sketched the psychodynamics of the patient's depressive–masochistic structure elements.

With this insight it is easier to understand the way in which superego resistance, narcissistic inaccessibility, and refusal of food interact. At various levels, object relationships of love and hatred have been abandoned and replaced through structural changes.

Martha E. "is" king, and no longer needs love; she "is" the wicked aunt, and has withdrawn her expression of hatred more and more from the environment and replaced its "object" with her own ego. Hatred against Aunt Erna ("bad" mother) was transformed into self-destructive actions (hitting), suicide fantasies directed against Aunt Erna, and refusal of food to destroy the Aunt Erna ("bad" mother) within her.

Therefore, the hunger and its satisfaction would lead back from the "being" to an object-relationship, and thus inevitably to the conflicts which were relieved by the described "ego changes" —especially the way in which hunger could be satisfied in an illusionary way through rumination. In brief, all defense attempts are concentrated on avoiding an actual satisfaction, on preventing real loving and hating or, more precisely, on mastering an intolerable ambivalence of oral origin.

In connection with the "Donkey Dream" we pointed out the patient's general ambivalence and tried to show why she was so incapable of having a relationship. The "Doll Dream" and "King Dream" extended our knowledge of the form and content of the symptoms. A fourth dream, the "Magpie Dream," points to an ambivalence of oral origin and to problems which derived from the unconscious confusion of oral "taking" with penis-envy.

Dream: A Volkswagen drove into a garage situated in the basement of a house which had a terrace on the roof. In the process, a magpie was run over and injured (in the legs or the wings, probably the wings), so that it could not fly any more, and instead perched sadly on a wall. It wondered how it would be able to go on living now. Since it could not fly any more it would not be able to catch flies to eat. It then caught sight of a mouse, which was snapping skillfully at flies, and began to peck at the mouse furiously. It especially injured the mouse's tail, which began to bleed. Then the bird realized that the mouse really meant well, and the mouse let the magpie know that, from then on, it would help to catch flies. Magpie and mouse became the best of friends and grew inseparable. One day a male magpie joined them, and wanted to take the magpie away. But it preferred to stay with the mouse, and the two animals, magpie and mouse, disappeared together [Magpie Dream].

It is particularly interesting to note how sucessfully the patient has kept the dream events at a distance: she was only a spectator and not a participant in them.

Some interpretations from previous treatment hours are important here for understanding. The patient had described how she sometimes cleaned out her stools with her finger. During the latest stage of treatment she was given no enemas, only laxatives; although she had often complained about her constipation and dreams of defecation, she had concealed the earlier use of digital evacuation. Also, at the end of the hour that immediately preceded the "Magpie Dream," she had shown disappointment in the slowness of her progress, saying, "In this hour we did not get much further with probing into my problems, but that is probably my fault." This remark stimulated the following interpretation: She wanted the analyst to help her, to probe into her, yet at the same time she resisted the idea. In order to relieve her constipation, she wanted an enema, or a digital evacuation.

As usual, Martha E. could do nothing with her dream, but her associations were as follows:

First Association: Recently she had seen a blackbird drinking the water flowing out of the mouth of the statue of a boy on a fountain. Martha E. described this scene with much wit and feeling.

Second Association: The analyst's car is a Volkswagen. Then a pause. "I wanted to ask you for a long time what kind of a funny bumper you have on the front." In answer to an inquiry about where she herself was in the dream: "Why I must be the magpie, the thieving magpie, who loves to steal anything shiny." [Analyst: she had indeed been a thieving magpie!] The patient made particular mention of the good friendship between two such different animals, after the magpie had first taken a peck at the mouse.[1]

---

[1] This dream also explains the origin of the "symbolic theft." It concerns compromise-formations, which were built up similarly to the dream. The drive–wish is displaced to another object and, lacking a normal release, presses toward a "blind" satisfaction in the storeroom or at the garbage pail.

This emphasis on "difference" was picked up by the analyst with the question of what was the primary difference between herself and him. "You are a man; I am a woman; that is probably the chief difference. There is a difference in age, too; but that is probably not the main one." Now the patient's association "bumper" could be drawn in and tied up with the day-residue: if the bumper = penis penetrates, the little magpie will be hurt. Again her sexual anxiety, her fear of being hurt, was pointed out. At this point the thievish magpie's pecking and hostility and the friendship between the two animals could be reintroduced. The patient did not know that many women are afraid of mice, and she was also ignorant of the popular euphemism "tail" = penis, so she said. She herself thought mice were sweet, and she talked about fluffy, toy mice, whose rubber tails she used to enjoy pulling. Rats, on the other hand, were disgusting—especially their naked tails.

The next subject to be discussed was her desire to be a boy. "It is so much handier to have male genitals; it makes urinating so much less embarrassing." After this, her penis-envy was interpreted, and her aggressiveness toward the mouse's tail exposed as an expression of the envy.

The "Magpie Dream," the associations, and the interpretations are all part of the following psychodynamic picture; the "thieving magpie" is, after an injury which indicates a castration complex, dependent on another creature for something it lacks: a penis. It also cannot exist on its own, but is dependent upon another creature for food. Thus the dream expressed need and dependency in two primary zones, the nutritive and the sexual, and also suggested why these dream-wishes could not rise into consciousness. In the latent dream-thought, there was confusion of oral-nutritive with oral-phallic elements and food-envy with penis-envy.

There was a further association in this connection: the magpie drinking from the fountain reminded her of the "Mannekin-Pis."[2] From the fairytale completeness of the recalled dream we

[2] Statue of a small boy, urinating.

can see the strength of the censor who succeeded in disguising the dream-wishes in such a way. Also, even while dreaming, Martha looked on as an uninvolved observer—a further sign of defense against instinctual needs. This censorship represents her resistance against a recognition of her undisguised wishes and her functional disturbance. In the dream there was enacted a symbolic wish-satisfaction, in reality an illusionary one (rumination).

We can now pursue further the question of why her hunger could not be satisfied normally. Oral drive-impulses had to be fended off because: (a) the object would be destroyed by them, and (b) the unconscious equation of oral-nutritive and oral-phallic processes (nourishment- and penis-envy) was intolerable for the conscious–unconscious ego; because of this equation the repression prevented satisfaction of the oral as well as the sexual drive. Finally, (c) oral drive-impulses were repulsed because the processes described above under (a) mobilized anxiety against every object-relation. A reaction-formation against these anxiety-causing drive-impulses and the maze of guilt created by them, was the patient's self-glorification: *I need no one, nobody can help me.* The "fatal inevitability of the sense of guilt" (Freud, 1930, p. 132), which was due to her ambivalence, can be recognized partly in her self-reproaches, partly in her futile attempts to become pure, ascetic, and innocent. In narcissism and self-destruction the ambivalence directs itself against the self.

The drive-anxiety described above was probably responsible for the patient's secret retraction, even in the dream, of her confession of being injured, helpless, and dependent; for she described the magpie as "a particularly beautiful bird because of its black and white feathers and its long tail." Thus she attributed narcissistic phallic properties to the bird. Her narcissistic overestimation of herself is revealed in the fact that she represented her helper as a mouse—thus belittling and discrediting the analyst, as she had done previously in the "Donkey Dream." When the conversation returned to her dream-ideal of being an absolute monarch, relevant elements in the "Magpie Dream" were drawn into the analysis. At this time, an amnesia lifted and it occurred to the patient that male genitals were referred to as "little tails" in the children's home. But it remained a mere remembrance and did not progress into therapeutically-effected knowledge: the patient immediately isolated this thought again and refused to have any wish whatsoever in transference.

Martha E. felt her isolation, but was still unwilling to relinquish her independence, and she attempted, with varying success, to manipulate her fellow human beings, including the analyst, and to keep them at a safe distance. This rigid behavior pattern naturally had been determined by many factors, although it probably had an important source in the uncertainty and lack of independence of the mother. Mrs. E. had not been able to satisfy her daughter's infantile dependence wishes; on the contrary, it was she who leaned on her daughter. Martha E. was the leader, and it is probable that Mrs. E. projected the image of her dead husband onto her daughter. In any event, we can safely say that a fatherless childhood had given a particularly firm anchorage to the patient's identification with an unreal father image.

Although Martha E. was becoming somewhat more open, she remained inaccessible in regard to orality, where her emotional life was rooted. In this sphere, there was established a strict automatism, which regulated her intake of food and output of calories, so that, during an entire year, her weight varied by only two pounds on either side of 75. The patient herself blamed this stagnation on external causes, particularly her enforced stay in the hospital and her idleness. Over and over again she promised that, if only she had some work to do, if only she could be let out of this hospital and so on ... of course she would gain weight. However, when she was permitted to enroll for some domestic science courses, she immediately fell into restless activity-compulsion, and within a few days had gone down to 71 lbs. The patient showed no insight at all and denied any deterioration. In the end we had to face the question of whether to take stricter measures and confine Martha E. to the hospital against her will. Since the incident had given rise to endless and futile altercation, we decided to interrupt, or possibly to terminate, the treatment. The patient's negativistic attitude had eventually discouraged the treating analyst, and it was left to the patient to decide, while she was at home, whether or not to continue the psychotherapy of her own accord and, in a sense, to start over again. Previously, Martha E. had repeatedly been able to point up that it was not she but her mother or the analyst who had decided on this course of therapy. In addition to everything else, with this, the patient had actually hit upon a weak spot in the countertransference; because of the nature of her illness, she had placed her doctor under much the same control as her mother, and indeed, in more respects. By this time, the monograph on anorexia nervosa had already been planned, and thus a successful outcome was particularly desirable. Undoubtedly, Martha E. could sense that her case had particular importance for Dr. T. She was also told repeatedly that the therapist would deeply regret having to abandon it. As is natural when a case has such a special urgency for the analyst, the countertransference became somewhat overcharged. The kind and friendly "evenly-suspended attention" (Freud, 1912a, p. 111) became impaired and it was difficult to overcome the anxiety and aggression which was provoked by the behavior of a masochistic and, at times, seriously ill patient.

Since the analytic work on the resistance had been almost entirely fruitless, there was no other choice but to break off the treatment for the time being, and to give the patient the responsibility for resuming it. A new psychological examination, carried out by Dr. Vogel, yielded the following results:

> The personality picture shows essentially the same characteristics as in the initial tests. There are, however, some recognizable changes, which are not merely behavior variations of an unchanged basic structure, but rather apparent indications of a true and, according to every indication, therapeutically-reached, change in the personality development. The most general distinguishing characteristic of this change is a relaxation of the previously extremely strong defensive behavior and introverted isolation. The patient's responsiveness to environmental stimuli has clearly improved, and there is a greater readiness for true emotional expression, even though

the affective reactions are egocentric and highly labile, and presumably vacillate between anger and tearful, helpless passivity. The narcissistic and sadomasochistic tendencies are still present, as before, but one has the impression that the destructive urges are not directed inwardly to the same degree as before, that the aggressions come closer to consciousness, and that the patient confusedly mobilizes herself against the weakening of her defense tactics—stubbornness, evasiveness, passivity and indolence, childish wheedling, etc.—but at the same time she feels distinct unsureness and ambivalence.

An "improvement" of the patient, in the sense of improved inner and outer adaptation and better ability to cope with tasks and with varying human contact, has surely been achieved to only a very limited degree. But the relaxation of her pathological defense structures and the increased mobility of her personality dynamics, including the greater responsiveness to environmental stimuli, must be viewed as a positive development, in view of the depth of her disturbance. The further prognosis is somewhat more favorable.

Martha E. had scarcely arrived at home before her mother had to go into the hospital some distance away to be operated on for a malignant tumor. The patient stayed at home alone. She was informed about the uncertain outcome of the operation and the general suffering of her mother, but this did not affect her behavior. She invited an aquaintance to lunch, without eating anything herself. Later, when her mother was released from the hospital, Martha cared for her in a touching fashion: however, she upset her at the same time by not putting on any weight herself. After two and a half months she asked that the treatment be continued, on the condition that she be allowed to live outside the hospital. On readmission she weighed 75 lbs.; she had not fulfilled the prophesy of improvement upon being discharged from the hospital.

No new insights into the psychogenesis of the symptomatology were gained during the last 40-hour stage of treatment. Somehow the patient tried to make the impossible possible, that is, to persist in her condition and to change at the same time (or as the saying goes, "to have her cake and eat it too"). Her attitude in transference was analogous. She complained that Dr. T.'s interest in her was only that of a doctor for his patient; at the same time, she denied wanting Dr. T. in any personal way whatsoever. Martha was not disturbed by the obvious contradiction between this denial and her thinking and behavior; or rather, she used the contradiction to protect herself from "being made fat" (Martha's words) by Dr. T. Since she had learned to satisfy herself through merely imagining "cake," it was all the easier to disavow her wishes (as expressed in the "Doll Dream") to be awakened to life as child and woman, to become fat. The psychotherapy could not make headway against the timelessness of the "cake hallucination"—I *have* the cake only as long as I do *not* eat it—because the patient behaved toward her doctor in a similar fashion.

In view of this technical treatment difficulty, it ought to be considered whether perhaps the psychoanalytic situation, which as such allows no actual satisfaction of needs, was not conducive to leaving everything in suspension. In other words, was it the fault of the abstinence rule that Martha E. did not eat the "cake," because it was not offered to her in a loving enough way by the analyst? Actually, the patient had skillfully stored away the so-called abstinence rule in her resistance. She had heard of the general sense of this rule from an outside source—psychotherapists must not have any private relationships with their patients. On the one hand she complained over and over again about this rule, which, on the other hand, she welcomed in order to justify the denial of any emotional tie. Interpretation did not help to change this mixture of apparent indifference and a curiosity for "purely objective things"—the books in the office, etc. Martha E. asked "incidental" questions and became outraged when she was asked about her motives. For example, "since she happened to be passing by," Martha E. made a visit to the home of the doctor, whom she thought might be home. She stayed for a short time, spoke with the doctor's wife, greeted the older child and admired the newborn infant. The countertransference was not disturbed by the visit as such—after all it was a question here of a type of behavior which occurred in every analytic hour, in one form or another—but by the fact that the patient denied all the decisive motives for her behavior, and sought to fulfill her wishes through action, without admitting what she was really looking for in the home of the doctor. She stated that the reason for her visit was that she had forgotten the time of the next treatment hour. She could not be dissuaded from the belief that this motive was the essential one; such a defense leads to behavior which differs markedly from deliberate action because of a preponderance of unconscious motives which are converted directly into deeds. Such behavior is useful primarily as resistance, since the open confession of wishes can be avoided and satisfaction can be found at the same time. It is only through the acceptance of infiltrated isolation mechanisms—Eissler has given a comprehensive review of this defense method (1959)—that we can understand the patient's behavior when, for example, she occasionally expressed the wish to have Dr. T. as her guardian since the illness of her mother, and yet at other times she treated him like a nobody, in whom she had not the slightest interest. Thus if Martha E. incorporated the abstinence rule into her resistance, she did it, among other reasons, in order to escape the conscious experience of her yearning for dependence—to be accepted by her doctor as a child, and to be awakened into life as a woman by him; for this reason, expressions of feeling were immediately isolated again.

Just as it is oppressing to be helpless, it is naïve to believe that one can arrest the regression of object-cathexis—which causes the uncomfortable feeling of being a nobody for the therapist with all severely disturbed, narcissistic patients—through wish fulfillment. This seems to us to be a good rule: As long as wishes are defended against in a variety of ways, there remains an emptiness in the patient, in spite of any loving wish fulfillment. But if there has been an analytic working-through of anxieties and guilt feelings which have made a satisfactory fulfillment of vital needs impossible, and now wish fulfillments are being sought, it is other people, and not the doctor, who are the suitable partners (see Freud, 1915b).[3]

The treatment of Martha E. was not successful, in our opinion, because we were not able to counteract the defense processes of isolation, among other things. Thus it was possible for Martha to find satisfaction without experiencing her wishes. One can understand such a paradox only with the help of the assumption of unconscious defense mechanisms, which were also the reason that nothing appeared to affect Martha E. deeply.

The transference was repeatedly explained through a comparison: She had drawn her doctor into the rumination, and thus was in a position to find fictional satisfaction; in reality, however, it left her essentially empty and unrelated. In regard to the rumination, Freud's (1916-1917) observation seems to be especially relevant: "A symptom, like a dream, represents something as fulfilled: a satisfaction in the infantile manner. But by means of extreme condensation that satisfaction can be compressed into a single sensation or innervation and by means of extreme displacement it can be restricted to one small detail of the entire libidinal complex" (p. 366).

---

[3] We were encouraged by a meaningful work of Searles (1955) in our conviction to follow the psychoanalytic method in regard to wish fulfillment, even with severe anorexia nervosa cases. In an extremely convincing manner, this author employed the experiences gained in the psychotherapy of schizophrenics during the last decades in the Chestnut Lodge clinic, especially in regard to the technical treatment handling of dependency needs. An important point of this, which we cannot quote in its entirety, begins with the sentence: "In intensive psychotherapy with schizophrenics, as in analysis with neurotics, the most consistently useful therapeutic approach with respect to the patient's dependency needs is one of neither gratification nor rejection but rather investigation" (p. 151). Especially with unsuccessful cases it is important to deliberate in addition to objective considerations, whether and in what way an unsatisfactory countertransference contributed to the failure. We simply want to describe the following circumstance: It is difficult to endure an almost completely negative transference over a period of months or years. If the affective strain on the analyst is especially great, we believe that there is always a tendency to place the form over the spirit—to allow technical rules to become rigid protecting walls. For this reason we must ask ourselves whether we use the technical treatment rules as our protection, to put a brake on affective reaction, or as a sublime way to punish the patient through impersonal treatment.

Since the patient avoided a *normal* satisfaction, she lost weight again. Now it seemed justifiable to us to demand a visible test of her cooperation. We set as a condition for renewal of treatment that she increase her weight to 88 lbs. within six weeks. Without wishing to go into general problems of termination in analysis (Eissler, 1959, p. 53), it can be said that it seemed to be necessary to take this step in this case. Martha increased her weight to 79 lbs., but two weeks before the appointed date she terminated treatment of her own accord. Even with her words of thanks she included the remark that she could not bear to be made fat by Dr. T.; she wanted to do it by herself. She could not make up her mind to leave. However, several weeks later her mother's condition worsened and she was summoned home.

❧ 7 ❧

Psychogenesis and Psychosomatics of
Anorexia Nervosa

A. General Aspects

The syndrome of anorexia nervosa has a *consistent* nucleus—
abstinence from food, with concomitant emaciation, amenorrhea,
and constipation—but it *varies* in its general psychopathology. It
may be accompanied by hysterical, phobic, obsessional, or depressive symptoms, a fear of poisoning, or it may appear in connection with an "asceticism at puberty" (A. Freud). Several of our
patients manifested apparently tireless activity, in spite of severe
inanition.

Puberty is an important factor in the clinical picture. This description by Anna Freud could be applied to anorexia nervosa
patients: "Whether such an adolescent individual impresses us,
then, as obsessional, phobic, hysterical, ascetic, schizoid, paranoid,
suicidal, etc., will depend on the one hand on the quality and
quantity of the id contents which beset the ego, on the other hand
on the selection of defense mechanisms which the latter employs.
Since, in adolescence, impulses from all pregenital phases rise
to the surface and defense mechanisms from all levels of crudity
or complexity come into use, the pathological results—although
identical in structure—are more varied and less stabilized than
at other times of life" (1958, pp. 267-268). Variability of the total
characterological or psychopathological picture is not necessarily
incompatible with uniformity of the syndrome. We have here
many more aspects before us which reveal themselves as our viewpoint changes. For example, J. O. Palmer et al. (1952) came to

the conclusion, after psychological test examinations of five cases, that anorexia nervosa patients have only one psychological characteristic in common: an intellectualized aloofness from their environment. In the opinion of these authors, the uniform syndrome does not originate from the same emotional problems. This view is consistent with psychoanalytic experience, which shows that the symptoms are multiply determined. It is for this reason that we did not attempt to give a list of personality traits of our patients in Chapter 3. The further away one goes from the typical symptom formation—for example, abstinence from food and emaciation—the more variable become the personalities and biographies of these patients. It is pointless to enumerate individual characteristics, but meaningful to use the cause of the symptoms as a point of departure. In this connection Freud (1916-1917, p. 366) has spoken of "individual" symptoms, which can be referred to roots in the patient's life history, and of "typical" symptoms, which have biographical sources, but owe their content and form to the psychic dynamics and structure. There is no fundamental difference between "individual" and "typical" symptoms; this becomes obvious during psychoanalytic psychotherapy, when it is possible to relate the typical symptoms to the biographical situation, bring them into *statu nascendi* by means of transference, and, ideally, cause a change in the *form* of the psychic experiencing of unconscious *content*.[1] There is a difference in viewpoint between the psychological test examination given by Palmer et al. and our procedure. We placed the main emphasis on the symptom formation and the question of why these patients do not eat normally. Our examinations also showed that there is no uniform picture of the character traits which are independent of the symptoms. Palmer et al., however, seem to have focused their attention on such character traits and not on the patterned symptom formation. However, if one attempts to

---

[1] Parenthetically, in view of the character of this technique it is overlooked in, and especially outside of psychoanalysis, that the basic theme in psychoanalytic theory is that of the organized relationship between instinctual, representative content and form (see Freud, 1900, pp. 506-507, n. 2).

place the latter in the center of the psychological test examination, there appears a far-reaching congruence with our psychodynamic diagnosis, as is shown by the psychodiagnostic results of Dr. Vogel[2] (see cases 1 and 5). In any case, the Rorschach test is based upon psychodynamic principles, so that one would expect a certain agreement between psychoanalytic and psychodynamically oriented psychological test diagnoses. For this reason, control tests which have no bias for psychodynamics of psychoanalytic viewpoints would be justified. This situation is similar to that which we discussed in regard to comparison of therapies (see Chapter 3, "Results of Psychotherapy").

In our attempt to make complete delineations of the biographical conditions for the emergence of the typical syndrome, we were forced to give extremely detailed case histories. Obviously, we cannot refer to the biographical details of the background here; rather we must proceed schematically. From time to time we shall also have to use psychogenetic and psychodynamic formulas in our discussions. Of course this does not do justice to the full experience of our patients. It is clear to us that abstractions can only be a shadow of reality. But because of this one does not want to abandon all theories and make no attempts to formulate a drive disturbance—and there is such a disturbance in anorexia nervosa, insofar as one is permitted to speak of a drive in human beings.

In order to facilitate understanding of our schematic representation, we think it is desirable to introduce occasional remarks about the general study of neuroses and about psychoanalytic theory itself. In a dynamic method of observation, the phenomenology is observed in connection with function. As Freud wrote (1916-1917): "We seek not merely to describe and to classify the phenomena, but to understand them as signs of an interplay of forces in the mind as a manifestation of purposeful intentions working concurrently or in mutual opposition. We are concerned

---

[2] At that time, clinical psychologist at the Psychosomatic Department of Heidelberg University; now Professor of Clinical Psychology at the Psychoanalytical Institute of Frankfurt.

with a *dynamic view* of mental phenomena. In our view, the phenomena that are perceived must yield in importance to trends which are only hypothetical" (p. 67).[3]

Therefore, if we want to follow Freud's advice on the theme of anorexia, we should differentiate the following steps: (1) The phenomena of abstinence from food should be described and, taking into consideration other psychopathological signs, nosologically classified (psychotic or nonpsychotic refusal of food); (2) To the extent that there is no basic physical illness which causes the abstinence, we should investigate the psychic motivation.

We have learned that human experience is full of subtle conflicts, and that psychopathological phenomena appear and disappear in connection with these conflicts. In abstinence from food, which will be discussed first, conflicting tendencies as such are not immediately apparent, but there are good grounds for postulating them. Closer observation reveals actual goal-seeking tendencies, such as hunger fantasies. However, some kind of resistance prevents the satisfaction of need, and restlessness, anxiety, or guilt feelings are caused by any drive breakthrough which might occur. This resistance, as well as behavioral changes in thought and action, indicate that there are unconscious defense mechanisms at work, which can be neither recognized nor experienced as such by the patients themselves. On this basis, symptoms which would otherwise seem incomprehensible can be understood in terms of their functional context—for example, the abstinence from food in anorexia nervosa. The relationship between instinctual representatives, anxiety, defense mechanisms of the ego, and symptoms is the focal point of all "psychodynamic cross-sectional studies" (Hartmann and Kris, 1945).

[3] It seems important to indicate the context of this quotation. Freud is speaking about the analysis of *parapraxes* and advises the reader to keep in mind the manner in which these phenomena were handled as a model for psychoanalytic psychology. The three sentences quoted here follow. Many years earlier Roffenstein (1923) expected "a phenomenologie which would profit from the Freudian applications and the Freudian method" (p. 48).

Anna Freud's description of the resolution of pathological conflicts at puberty, as quoted at the beginning of this chapter, also proceeds from a psychodynamic cross-sectional view. This is not an etiological explanation, as Redlich (1952) so rightly emphasizes, but it is a valuable starting point for the far more difficult psychogenetic reconstruction. In the case of the latter, we must try to explain why, "in past situations of conflict, a specific solution was adopted; why the one was retained and the other dropped, and what causal relation exists between these solutions and later developments" (Hartmann and Kris, 1945, p. 17). Therefore it is not sufficient to establish which infantile (pregenital) needs come to the surface at puberty and are defended against (in Anna Freud's sense); it must also be made quite clear why it happened that this particular fixation was activated at puberty. However, since we cannot achieve this ideal, "we must be content if we can explain what has happened" (Freud, 1927, p. 154). We must also refrain from characterizing the family environment of the anorexia nervosa patient and its etiological influence on the pathogenesis of this symptomatology. Of course our observations about the mother–child relationships of these patients would be worthy of mention in the case histories, but they cannot yet be generalized.[4]

B. Precipitating Causes of Illness and Constitution

Since "phantasies possess *psychical* as contrasted with *material* reality, and we gradually learn to understand that *in the world of the neuroses it is psychical reality which is the decisive kind*" (Freud, 1916-1917, p. 368), mental conflicts cannot be adequately

---

[4] Here I would like to express my grateful thanks to Professors F. Redlich and T. Lidz, who gave me the opportunity of working for a year as assistant in the Psychiatric Clinic of Yale University in New Haven. There I became aware of what preparations would have to be made in order to be able to make any valid generalizations whatsoever on the "family environment" (of schizophrenics). While collecting material for this book, I realized that it would be impossible to accomplish the same for my anorexia nervosa patients, and decided to confine my discussion to the psychotherapy of the patients themselves.

explained by external events, in regard to their contents and form. Still, it is useful to inquire into the precipitating causes of illness insofar as anorexia nervosa is brought about in a typical way.

Freud (1912b) once drew distinctions among four main "precipitating causes of falling ill." In the first category, the patient becomes ill because of an *experience*; in the second, as a result of *a developmental process*. "In the first case he is faced by the task of renouncing satisfaction, and he falls ill from his incapacity for resistance; in the second case his task is to exchange one kind of satisfaction for another, and he breaks down from his inflexibility. In the second case the conflict, which is between the subject's efforts to remain as he is and the effort to change himself in order to meet fresh demands from reality, is present from the first" (p. 233). Freud's third category is like an exaggeration of the second: the patient falls ill from an *inhibition in development*. As Freud put it, "There is no theoretical reason for distinguishing it, but only a practical one; for those we are here concerned with are people who fall ill as soon as they get beyond the irresponsible age of childhood ..." (p. 235). Finally, he describes a fourth precipitating cause: "We see people fall ill who have hitherto been healthy, who have met with no fresh experience and whose relation to the external world has undergone no change, so that the onset of their illness inevitably gives an impression of spontaneity. A closer consideration of such cases, however, shows us that nonetheless a change *has* taken place in those whose importance we must rate very highly as a cause of illness. As a result of their having reached a particular period of life, and in conformity with regular biological processes, the *quantity* of libido in their mental economy has experienced an increase which is in itself enough to upset the equilibrium of their health and to set up the necessary conditions for a neurosis" (pp. 235-236). As examples of this, he cites the biological changes of puberty and the menopause.

Later in the same work, Freud wrote, "Pathology could not do justice to the problem of the precipitating factors in the neuroses so long as it was merely concerned with deciding whether those affections were of an 'endogenous' or 'exogenous' nature. . . . Psycho-analysis has warned us that we must give up the unfruitful contrast between external and internal factors, between experience and constitution, and has taught us that we shall invariably find the cause of the onset of neurotic illness in a particular psychical situation which can be brought about in a variety of ways" (pp. 237-238).

Nearly all of our patients fell ill as the result of the second, third or fourth of these "precipitating causes." Only one (Case 27) fell ill immediately after a dramatic experience. In most of the cases, it was the developmental processes as such that led to mental conflict. It made no difference whether the ego had been made aware of the bodily changes at puberty by a teasing remark, or whether this had happened spontaneously.

From the psychoanalytic point of view, this remarkable absence of dramatic external conflicts—except for the battles at mealtimes —indicated a withdrawal from the instinctual object relationship which extends far beyond the normal introversion of the adolescent. Conflicts are no longer worked out openly in the world of reality; the patients generally try to conquer them inwardly, indirectly, through symptom formation. In severe cases the patients are unwilling to start a conversation, and contact is often established only after a considerable time, or sometimes not at all. "They reject the doctor not with hostility but with indifference." Freud was referring here (1916-1917, p. 447) to the narcissistic neuroses, but this indifference is equally frequent among anorexia nervosa patients. Although the special circumstances of puberty increase the difficulties of treatment, the prospects of a spontaneous improvement are more favorable, since the anorexia nervosa patients' narcissistic attitudes have not necessarily become set in a permanent character deformation.

In view of the lack of external occurrences to which the illness could be linked as an abnormal reaction, if one used the alternatives endogenous–exogenous and had an experimental method based upon this (see Zutt, 1948, it would be quite easy to attribute the decisive etiological meaning to endogenous factors.

When it has been shown that there is no endogenous–internal secretory etiology, it must be considered whether endogenous considerations, in the sense of the constitution, have an essential influence on the pathogenesis of anorexia nervosa.

However, the arguments on this topic are unacceptable for several reasons. In connection with the fourth "precipitating cause of illness," the one that makes an impression of spontaneity, Freud attributed a special meaning to quantitative–biological factors, and gave puberty as an example. Some authors (Feuchtinger; Kretschmer; Sheldon, 1937; Stäubli-Frölich) have assumed constitutional anomalies of all sorts and special organ inferiorities of the diencephalic–pituitary system in connection with anorexia nervosa. The thesis of an organ inferiority brings the weak assumption of an internal secretory etiology of anorexia nervosa back into a modified and indefinite form. However, the "principle of localization" (Oehme), the search for a *sedes morbi*, has entrenched itself very deeply into medical thinking.

This kind of organ inferiority, as Sheldon (1937) concluded after examining three cases—he reversed his opinion in 1939—is indicated by a small physical size, the late appearance of puberty, an infantile uterus, overweight at puberty, and other symptoms. The loss of appetite is supposed to originate from this constitutional background, as a reaction to a psychological need. Kretschmer (1958) reported the case of a female patient who was 24 at the time of treatment, but who had fallen ill with "puberal dystrophy" at the age of 17. Menstruation, which had been regular since she was 12, stopped abruptly. As it pertains to our present theme, Kretschmer's explanation is most interesting. He suggests that the patient, who was a premature baby of seven months, was "born with a latent constitutional insufficiency." He said further, "without a fully developed diencephalic anlage ... the panic-like defensive reaction to the inadequate sexual excitation is just as understandable as the irradiations emanating from it" (p. 49). "Puberal dystrophies are often given the inadequate name of anorexia nervosa. In fact, in classical cases, we are dealing with a stubborn cessation of constitutional maturation occurring in every aspect of development at puberty. It is frequently characterized physically, for example, by persistent lanugo hair, and, as is the case here, occasionally by extensive hypoplasia in the genital area" (p. 50). "A dogmatically inclined somatologist who saw nothing more than 'pretense' here," Kretschmer continues, "would betray an astonishing disregard for the need to find causes—as would be true in the reverse situation, if these things were given a purely psychoanalytical interpretation, with no consideration of the extensive developmental and constitutional background" (p. 51).

We must arrive at another interpretation, one which takes into consideration the psychoanalytic relief of symptoms in general, and, specifically, the constitutional anomaly of anorexia nervosa. It is easy to explain why the repeated emphasis on "somatic compliance" (Freud, 1905a, p. 40) and the interaction of "limitations" have been ignored in the etiology of psychic illness. Freud said that doctors had "transferred what is a characteristic of the technique onto the theory itself. It is the therapeutic technique alone that is purely psychological; the theory does not by any means fail to point out that neuroses have an organic basis ... " (1905a, p. 113). Nevertheless, *positive* statements about a "somatic compliance" peculiar to anorexia nervosa cannot be supported in the light of our investigations. Rather, they cover up an actual ignorance. The height and weight of the average anorexia nervosa patient before illness, as calculated from 29 female patients, did *not* vary greatly from the norm; seven cases were slightly overweight (2-13 lbs). At the menarche the average age was 13 (see Tables 8-10). Individual instances of delayed menarche, obesity before the illness, or less than average height—without the usual correction of such which is made during the investigation of a large number of cases—do not allow for an immediate assumption of diencephalic organ inferiority.[5] Even the lanugo hair does

---

[5] Schreier (1959) reported that in the University Child Clinic in Heidelberg, 180 cases with more than 15 per cent overweight have been admitted since the currency reform. Since 1950 there has been no single case of a purely pituitary, adrenal, or ovarian cause of adipositas. In 12 cases the case histories at admission seemed to indicate an obesity possibly caused by prenatal or postnatal cerebral damage (debility, imbecility, epilepsy, after-effects of meningitis).

not indicate a constitutional variant; in most cases, it seems to be as much a symptom of the disease as genital hypoplasia (Altschule, 1953; Decourt, 1944). In fact, it is the illness which leads to the "constitutional change." Decourt has described the physical changes of anorexia nervosa in "morphogrammes," which are comparable to those of still undeveloped girls. But these changes are not the result of an organ inferiority—not, at least, according to my observations. Responsibility for them must be given to the processes that have limited the satisfaction of hunger and disturbed normal menstruation. "Developmental inhibitions" are certainly very complex processes. However, the case described by Kretschmer (1958) provides a good illustration of the principle on which they are based. In this instance, after a real danger (a threatened rape), the patient showed a "defense," which "here as in many similar cases, followed a primitive hypobulic pattern" (p. 49). In most anorexia nervosa cases, the defense is not directed against an external danger. It is the developmental processes themselves that are experienced as dangerous, independently from any massive external cause. Although the particular form it takes varies from case to case, it is the nature of defense to follow "hypobulic," i.e., preconscious or unconscious sequential patterns. This is what is understood by "defense mechanisms" in psychoanalysis.

It would be extremely useful for psychoanalytic theory if it were possible to explain, in terms of their (neuro) physiological function and (cerebral) location, the defense mechanisms that are determined through their manifestations in normal, and particularly abnormal thought and behavior. Here we are dealing with the theme of the relationship of the "mental apparatus" to the organic, cerebral substratum. Some explanation would be appropriate here since the phrase "mental apparatus" has been the cause of so much misunderstanding.

After Freud had proposed his ideas in *The Origins of Psychoanalysis* (1887-1902), "for merging the study of neuroses and normal psychology with brain physiology" (Kris, 1950), the psychoanalytic theory in *The Interpretation of Dreams* (Freud, 1900) found its original and pioneering expression, especially in the

discussion in Chapter VII. Here the "mental apparatus" is used
specifically as a "model" in order to allow the spatial representation of mental functions. From then on this model served to elucidate the *psychological* theories of psychoanalysis; from the beginning Freud always wanted to "carefully avoid the temptation
to determine psychical locality in any anatomical fashion"
(p. 506). He had repeatedly emphasized that a "model" must be
implicitly understood in connection with the term "psychic apparatus" (1905b, 1916-1917, 1925a, 1940). In the work "The Unconscious" (1915d) there was an especially thorough discussion
about how one should imagine the location of the psychical
topography: "Research has given irrefutable proof that mental
activity is bound up with the function of the brain as it is with no
other organ. We are taken a step further—we do not know how
much—by the discovery of the unequal importance of the different parts of the brain and their special relations to particular
parts of the body and to particular mental activities. But every
attempt to go on from there to discover a localization of mental
processes, every endeavour to think of ideas as stored up in nerve-
cells and of excitations as travelling along nerve-fibres, had mis-
carried completely. The same fate would await any theory which
attempted to recognize, let us say, the anatomical position of the
system *Cs.*—conscious mental activity—as being in the cortex and
to localize the unconscious processes in the subcortical parts of the
brain. There is a hiatus here which at present cannot be filled,
nor is it one of the tasks of psychology to fill it. Our psychical topography has, for the present, nothing to do with anatomy; it has
reference not to anatomical localities, but to regions in the mental
apparatus, wherever they may be situated in the body" (pp.
174-175).

The model of the "psychical apparatus" serves as a spatial representation in the psychoanalytic theory called "metapsychology"[6] in which mental, especially psychopathological phenomena

---

[6] Rapaport (1960) has written a systematic presentation of psychoanalytic
theory, which is the only one of its type.

are described from dynamic, topographical, genetic, and economic viewpoints. It is not surprising, especially in view of the strong character of the summons to hypostasis which emanates from the "mental apparatus," that frequently the concept was taken for the thing itself. Also there was frequent anthropomorphization of the topographical division in three stages, which are defined by function and quality, and designated as Id, Ego, and Superego.

The psychoanalytic theory of instinctual drives groups the somatic excitatory processes together under the designation "source of an instinct," and considers them from the economic viewpoint. With hunger, Freud (1900, p. 565) outlined simple models for his theory of affect, ideation, and behavior, which are obviously extremely significant for any research into anorexia nervosa. The physiological regulatory mechanism—in psychoanalytical terminology, the processes at the source of an instinct—that give rise to hunger as a "need" and a "pressure" for "satisfaction" (Freud, 1915a, p. 122) are complex in nature (Ebbecke, Glatzel, Janowitz and Grossman). The discovery that important regulatory centers for hunger and menstruation lie in the hypothalamus—and thus that the reflectory (Cannon and Washburn, 1902) humoral and hormonal theory of hunger described only a fraction of the process—tended to discourage psychosomatic theories of anorexia nervosa. In consequence, the theory of an organ insufficiency was made functional to a certain extent and the complex phenomenon of the refusal of food was reduced to the status of a functional disturbance of the hypothalamus.

Decourt's explanation is a good example of this kind of hypothesis. His theory, in brief, is as follows:

The hypothalamus is seen as a kind of collecting bowl for emotional stimuli, and as a regulatory organ for instinctual and affective life—in control of neurovegetative and endocrine functions. It is understood that the "drama of puberty"—Decourt calls anorexia nervosa a psychoendocrinal cachexia of maturation (1953) —can be enacted at this level; it is expressed both physically and mentally, in mood and behavior, hunger and nutrition, sex instinct and gonad function. Here we are dealing with simultaneous aspects of a disturbance which is supposed to have its center in the hypothalamus. According to Decourt, the two levels intersect one another, but are nevertheless inseparable. Thus it would be impossible to distinguish whether, for instance, the amenorrhea was determined by physical or by endocrinal factors. In the case of the instinctual impulse, the question would be whether the pathogenic shock of an instinctual inhibition comes from the body or from the mind. Is the cessation of menstruation caused by a regulatory dysfunction of the pituitary gland, or by an inhibition of cortical origin? Does refusal of food arise from a functional disturbance of some appetite center, or is it a conscious hunger strike?

This is certainly true: "How the psychic factor works is basically a metaphysical question. At least at present we are not yet able to describe this process in terms of a ceaseless flow of waves of excitation in the central neural chains. But nevertheless we ourselves see this process from within, without having any method of bridging the gap between subjective experience and objective event" (Schaefer, 1955, p. 18). However, Decourt confines his "drama" to the hypothalamic centers, and his reference to cortical inhibitions remains in the realm of neurophysiology. He is not concerned with the region of subjective experience, and pays no attention to which conscious or unconscious barriers are blocking the satisfaction of the instinct. The test of Decourt's theories is found in his therapeutic measures: isolation and forced feeding. The psychological treatment should be "synthetic[7] rather than analytic. The usual course of psychoanalysis is hardly indicated for these patients" (1953, p. 1663). There is very little we can do with Decourt's mainly negative recommendations—what the psychological treatment should *not* be, without an explanation of

---

[7] Freud made an extremely thorough and, we believe, convincing reply to the objection that there was no synthesis in his analysis. He remarked, after a discussion of this criticism, that he felt justified in saying "it was nothing but an empty phrase" (1919, p. 161).

what actually constitutes the "synthetic" method. Thus his questions remain purely rhetorical, and have been quoted only as an example.

Apart from the definition of an instinctual drive as a "concept on the frontier between the mental and the somatic" (Freud, 1915a, pp. 121-122), psychoanalysis has tended to leave the problem of metaphysics alone, and has developed a diagnostic therapeutic technique. It is clear that a *purely psychological* method can have little to tell us about the biological excitatory processes at the source of the instinct itself—in this case, hunger—as a physiological event. At the same time, psychoanalysis had always emphasized the dependency of the mental apparatus on its physical substratum. Anorexia nervosa patients—and they are not the only ones—give an excellent example of the degree to which the mental representations of drives, in this case "hunger," can be modified under the influence of affect and imagination. They prove how loosely even the hunger drive is attached to its object. This is a quality, according to Freud, of all instinctual drives. On the pathways which lead in one way or another from the neuro–hormonal–humoral–secretory excitation to the experience of hunger, and finally to a consummatory action, there are many possibilities of interruption. An obvious example would be the shifting of the satisfaction of hunger under the influence of revulsion. Revulsion itself is a good illustration of the general principle: "without that something we generally call 'psyche,' many of the regulatory processes cannot be fully described. And this 'psychic' factor always influences the regulatory processes when the organism is interacting with its environment, and thus when its homeostasis,[8] its equilibrium, must be determined from the environment" (Schaefer, 1955, p. 107; *my italics*).

Psychogenetic points of difficulty of the illness lie in this area of the functional cycle "hunger," which may be regarded as the disruption of the instinctual object relations with the environment. Nevertheless, we believe we have shown that: a) a constitutional

[8] There are several points of contact between "homeostasis" (Canon) and Freud's pleasure–reality principle (cf. Flugel, 1953).

organ inferiority cannot be demonstrated, and b) there is no "transmission disturbance" in the sense of a localizable pituitary–diencephalic functional disturbance[9] (Bahner). However, it can be positively determined through which processes the hunger is disturbed in the *subjective* realm of its functional cycle. Thus, in the usual terminology, with anorexia nervosa we are dealing with a psychogenic illness (Gëro, 1943).

C. Development and Regression

Anorexia nervosa patients themselves can tell us nothing about the "endopsychic processes" (Freud, 1916-1917, p. 284) which have led to this general developmental inhibition, and particularly the symptom formation. Many of these processes have remained unconscious. Others have been dimly perceived and forgotten. The rest is kept secret. Actually, it is not merely an inhibition in development that we have here, but a regression,[10] and, as Freud pointed out, "certain regressions are characteristic of certain forms of illness" (1933, p. 130). I would like to suggest that in anorexia nervosa, the patients have abandoned the genital-sexual stage of development, both subjectively and objectively.

[9] We have chosen this expression in order to point out the incongruity which exists when *one* section of a functional cycle—here the regulation of hunger—is attributed a pathogenetic significance, *without* demonstrating a local disturbance. This theme was fully discussed by Oehme, Siebeck, and Vogel at the Heidelberg Medizinischen Gesellschaft in 1944.

[10] In the general sense, the concept of regression implies a "return from a higher to a lower stage of development." To this extent, "repression too can be subsumed under the concept of regression, for it too can be described as a return to an earlier and deeper stage of the development of a psychical act" (Freud, 1916-1917, p. 342). In the specific sense, three kinds of regression—"topographical, temporal, and formal"—should be distinguished (Freud, 1900, p. 548). The aspect which is primitive in form is also the oldest chronologically. We know from L. Binswanger, Brun, Kris, Rapaport, Spehlmann, Stengel, and Vogel that Freud started by introducing Jackson's concepts (involution and disinvolution) into his investigations on aphasia. He then made an application to *psychopathology* of Jackson's conception of functional retrogressions in the regression concept.

In many cases, it is the amenorrhea which represents the first sign of involution. Sexual impulses vanish from consciousness. Thought becomes dominated by material from the oral stage, so that the patient's behavior toward their mothers shows every sign of oral ambivalence, although it does not appear in an obvious or simple form. We must not forget that these patients are regressed adults or adolescents, not ordinary children, even though some of them begin using their childhood spoons and forks again; and, in rare cases, encopresis appears (Case 9).

The oral ambivalence, however, is not only obscured by layers of material from later developmental stages; it is also covered over by defensive processes which lead to an unusual ego modification. Perhaps these changes have something in common with the "ego regressions" described by Freud, which go back "to the stage of hallucinatory satisfaction of wishes" (1916-1917, p. 223). In any case, anorexia nervosa patients make themselves almost completely independent of food and of their environment by their negativism and their unawareness of illness, that is their refusal to be sick and in need of help. They seem to have no more needs, and every offer of help is experienced as a danger which could threaten the perfection and security which they have achieved through partial disavowal of reality. They appear unmoved by their own physical deterioration; this can be traced back to a delusional belief that they are capable of living on their own substance, in a kind of autarchy (see case history 1).

"The passive helplessness of the ego in the face of the persistent and inexorable demands of hunger" (Kunz, 1946b, Vol. I, p. 85) is a terrifying sensation for these patients, and one which leads them to use defenses. For in hunger we experience fully the ego's dependence on nature, on our own bodies, and, particularly in childhood, on the care and assistance of some other person. It is true that there is also an oral autoeroticism (Abraham, Rado); but there is no self-satisfaction of hunger. In other words, while genital masturbation may relieve the inner sexual impulse and result in physical satisfaction, "oral" masturbation can lead only to a ficitive, illusive, or hallucinatory satisfaction[11] (see case history 5).

Anorexia nervosa patients are therefore always hungry and always unsatisfied. Their greedy, compulsive eating, which often alternates with periods of ascetic abstinence, leads only to physical satiation, and leaves a psychic emptiness. Even the most appetizing delicacies are not satisfying substitutes for the object relationships abandoned during the regression. Thus there is a growth of the latent unconscious feelings of resentment for not having received enough from the mother; later on no one can make food meaningful enough to replace love, marriage, and a career.

Our next question is how and why regression occurs, and in what way it becomes bound up with a premorbid developmental disturbance (fixation) in the symptom formation. According to psychoanalytic theory, there is a complementary relationship here, somewhat like the interaction of constitutional and exogenous factors in the etiology of mental illnesses. While we cannot make any positive statements about the constitutional factors in anorexia nervosa, with a thorough knowledge of each case history it is possible to establish, at least in extreme cases, whether the chief emphasis lies on the "fixation" or the "regression." For diagnostic and therapeutic reasons, however, it is extremely important that the effects of the regression, together with the present psychic conflict, never be underestimated.

The descriptive account of a psychophysical retrogression must include a few remarks on the psychodynamics. Actually it is the "transformations" and "new arrangements" (Freud, 1905d, pp. 207–208) of puberty which lead to the anxiety and defensiveness that occur when sexual maturity becomes, or threatens to become,

---

[11] A report of the so-called Minnesota Experiment, in which 39 volunteers lived on 1,570 calories a day for six months, speaks of a kind of nutrition–masturbation. The subjects were interested only in food, cookbooks, dietary recommendations, and some even planned to become chefs. They could never make up their minds whether to play with their rations for hours or to gobble them up all at once (Franklin et al., 1948). The same is true of anorexia nervosa patients, who often care for other patients, mothering and spoiling them. Case history 5 illustrates especially how complicated the structure of this mothering is.

a psychic reality. Biological maturation, psychosexual and psycho-social differentiation between men and women are processes which are connected, but can fall away from one another, as we see especially with the perversions. Thus, the menarche is not so much a precipitatory factor as it is a chronological starting point for the onset of the illness, which lets the "transformations" become an anxiety-cathected experience. Our experiences with anorexia nervosa patients confirm the psychoanalytic observations which led to the introduction of the psychoanalytic psychology of the ego, and the revision of the theory of anxiety which occurred in the early twenties. The following theoretical points will make it easier to understand the symptom formation: "The ego is the actual seat of anxiety" (Freud, 1926a, p. 140). The defense mechanisms avoid or alleviate unpleasure and anxiety. The chief types of anxiety—moral anxiety, fear of the power of an instinct, and realistic fear—can be related to the dependence of the ego on the superego, the id, and the outside world. As Freud expressed it, "symptoms are created so as to avoid a *danger-situation* whose presence has been signalled by the generation of anxiety" (1926a, p. 129; Freud's italics). In extreme cases, patients fail to recognize reality to such an extent that instead of fearing death by starvation, they regard it with apparent indifference, seeing a far greater potential danger in the satisfaction of their nutrition drive. This confusion is the result of a long chain of defense processes which also eventually lead to diminished reality testing.

At the time when the symptoms are developing, the defense against the affective and ideational representatives goes along with an ego modification. The different kinds of anxiety mentioned above can be observed in the following examples: Henriette A. (Case 1) suffered from a severe fear of blushing; this symptom disappeared as soon as she began to lose weight, and she became totally free of anxiety. Sabine B. (Case 2) feared she was going to be poisoned when a young man gave her something to eat; after an attack of diphtheria, anorexia nervosa developed. It is remarkable how many levels even initial symptoms have,

from a psychodynamic point of view. In every case, it is a fundamental principle that tensions intolerable to the ego are allayed
by the defense processes. These are always connected with a change
in the patient's interpersonal relationships in general or the psychic functions in particular. Henriette A.'s fear of blushing is a
good example. At first she tried to relieve the blushing by avoiding the real danger; she exposed herself to the view of her schoolmates as little as possible. Sabine B. also simply refused to accept
anything from a young man. In her case, however, there was a
concurrent disturbance of the ideational representative of the
object. The fear of being poisoned indicated that either an oral
fixation was present or that a regression began simultaneously
with the symptom formation, as a result of which the object was
perceived in a distorted form. The fact that a token of love assumed such a threatening aspect shows the revival of an early oral
ambivalence. The aggressive and destructive part of her own impulses were overcome through projection. It must be understood
that we have occasionally pointed up various aspects when we
spoke of the superego, the id, and reality, and their relationships
to anxiety. For this situational fear of poisoning comprises, in
brief, an instinctual fear, a superego fear, and a realistic fear, and
thereby provides an excellent vantage point for the consideration
of the psycho-physical changes that occur during the warding
off of fear.

   In view of the modifications of the experience in the course of
the symptom formation, one cannot expect that patients develop
a consistent picture of their anxieties. "Fear of growing up" (Janet, 1908; Leibbrand, 1939) is too general an interpretation. When
sexual maturity threatens to become a psychic reality, a severe
inner crisis results, because the ego ideal and the body ego are not
consistent. In Schilder's view (1923), every person has a certain
mental image of himself. If this is so, then the anorexia nervosa
patients' mental image and ego ideal would be described as "boyish." Fear of adulthood inevitably results when a girl cannot tolerate her actual feminine development, because it does not con-
form to the desired physical ideal. However, the ego ideal alters
during the course of the illness. The desire to be a boy is gradually

replaced by the ideal of being a pure, sexless being (H. Müller, Sommer, Weizsäcker).

In psychodynamic terms, the fear of being neither boy nor girl, which Janet mentions in his case "Nadia," belongs to the complete animosity toward the instincts which is characteristic of "asceticism at puberty" (A. Freud, 1936, p. 172). In this instance, Anna Freud is describing the innate hostility between ego and instinct, which is indiscriminate, primary and primitive, and which rejects all sexual impulses at puberty before a qualitative differentiation has even begun. Actually, there develops a condition of both a physical (see section B of this chapter) and a mental sexuality, or, to put it more accurately, every positive wish, whatever the content, is unconsciously warded off and consciously disavowed or negated. The indiscriminate antagonism toward everything instinctual is resolved, one might say, through an affectation of complete neutrality and an attempt to be beyond all human feelings. In the regressive state which leads to a transformation of the ego ideal, the wish to be a boy (penis envy is obscured by oral content. Since this oral content also falls prey to the ascetic ideal formation, the patient appears to have a complete lack of wishes.

Some of the difficulties encountered during therapy help us to make further inferences about the significance of the indiscriminate hostility between ego and instinct that is shown by so many anorexia nervosa patients, particularly those who disavow everything and who refuse to eat, without allowing any insight into their motivation. This denial of motive is caused by the influence of a law of "all or nothing." They are afraid of falling into a state of "total emotional surrender" and therefore cling desperately to their allegedly unmotivated, desireless negativism (A. Freud, 1952). (A discussion of this problem can be found in case history 5.)

Even those of the patients who lacked appetite or who believed that their anorexia was caused by stomach or digestive troubles were conscious that they were definitely trying to lose weight. They maintained that they were taking this course of their own free will, without any feeling of fear or compulsion. Their object, as one patient expressed it, was to attain an ever purer spiritual devotion or to merge with the cosmos.

This short description of the defense processes, the changes in the ego, and the ideal formation may have given the impression that the anorexia nervosa patient is actually capable of becoming asexual and free from need. In fact, the opposite is true; these patients are involved in a perpetual struggle, and their efforts to set themselves beyond good and evil are destined to fail from the start. The "fatal inevitability of the sense of guilt" (Freud, 1930, p. 132) at the root of ambivalence is a psychic reality; it exists independently of the patient's attempts to express or to deny love or hate. These remarks have no relation to an equation of "illness" with "guilt." They refer to an important psychodynamic process which occurs at the beginning of the illness. The ambivalence becomes primarily orally experienced—that is, linked with bodily functions; this then leads to anxiety and, on a higher plane, to guilt feelings. The abstinence from food thus serves as self punishment, and represents a vain attempt to evade guilt feelings by avoiding certain actions or by automatically inhibiting certain functions. This transitory relief is achieved at great cost. The symptom formation leads to an actual performance loss, and the guilt feelings arising out of unconscious striving and conscious fantasies are reinforced by self-accusations of weakness and worthlessness. Many anorexia nervosa patients try to take refuge from their feelings in an obviously overdetermined hyperactivity, which can give little true satisfaction. A good example of this is the excessive care with which many anorexia nervosa patients mother members of their families or other patients. This form of altruism was described by Anna Freud (1936). The fifth case history shows how a patient may strive in this way to satisfy hunger through imagination.

D. *Ambivalence, Object Relations, and Identification*

Lore Berger, an anorexia nervosa patient who later committed suicide, wrote an autobiographical novel in which she described her feelings after having committed some petty thefts. Stealing is "something primitive like eating, loving, killing" (p. 214). This is almost exactly what Freud (1915a) said about the relationships between incorporation, love, and annihilation of the object (pp. 138-139). Freud felt that these contradictory emotional attitudes could be included under Bleuler's concept of ambivalence, and he showed that this ambivalence is connected with physical functions (oral ambivalence = incorporation, love, annihilation). Certainly anorexia nervosa patients do not experience ambivalence only at an oral level; or rather, they do not ward off only the conscious experience of the tender and aggressive oral strivings which they direct alternately or simultaneously at the same person. Nevertheless, the best means of understanding these patients' disturbances in interpersonal relationships and problems in identification is to proceed from the oral ambivalence.

We do not wish to make any decisive statements here about the applicability of Melanie Klein's theory that depressive and paranoid positions preceded this ambivalence as well as the reaction formations and defense mechanisms which can most certainly be identified in the psychodynamic cross-section. In view of the well-founded criticisms by Glover (1945) and Waelder (1936), however, and the problems of interpretation at preverbal phases of development, we felt justified in emphasizing the role of regression in the previous section. Here I am relying on my own observations and can say without hesitation that an oral ambivalence is the basis of the symptomatology and that the defense mechanisms mold the entire picture of anorexia nervosa. Since these observations were made on patients already in a state of regression, statements about early infantile forms of ambivalence and defense processes can be made only with the caution which is necessary with every psychogenetic reconstruction.

From a psychodynamic point of view, a primitive experience is affecting these patients. Freud describes it in the following words: "At the very beginning, in the individual's primitive oral

phase, object-cathexis and identification are no doubt indistin-
guishable from each other" (1923, p. 29). These patients do not
achieve the primary narcissism[12] which, according to Spitz, is still
dominant in the third month: "At the three-months stage primary
narcissism is dominant, the sense of separateness and the capacity
for ideation are non-existent" (1959, p. 120). This narcissism is
unconsciously reactivated in the course of the regression. The
patients' manifest behavior is in contradiction to their unconscious yearning for union with the mother. All relationships are
avoided, and an intense desire for solitude and negation is used
to safeguard the "ego boundaries" (Federn; Freud, 1930). Because
it is precisely oral relationships that become full of conflict as a
result of the regression, anorexia nervosa patients avoid communal meals. Freud has shown that identification may be created by
meals eaten in common (1921, p. 110). The English and French
words, "companion" and "compagnon," illustrate this connection
since both originally denote a person who shares or eats the same
bread (Latin, *panis*). Thus eating is experienced as an especially
intimate process by these patients (see Chapter 4, stage 7).

At this point I would like to summarize in a simple way what
has been discussed in the first, second, and fifth case histories.
"If we ask ourselves why the avoidance of touching, contact, or
contagion should play such a large part in this neurosis and should
become the subject-matter of complicated systems, the answer is
that touching and physical contact are the immediate aim of the
aggressive as well as the loving object cathexes. Eros desires contact because it strives to make the ego and the loved object one,

[12] Both Balint (1960a) and Bing et al. (1959) have recently pointed out that
Freud never gave a conclusive definition for "primary narcissism." In the stage
of primary narcissism the infant has not yet begun to distinguish between the
ego and the outside world. "The antithesis between subjective and objective
does not exist from the first" (Freud, 1925b, p. 237). In practice, however, a
relationship to the object does exist from the very beginning, as Freud demonstrated in the case of the acceptance of food (1905d). This has nothing to do
with whether, when, and what mental representations are being made of the
objects. Balint (1935) Kunz (1942, 1946) and Müller-Braunschweig (1936) have
all emphasized that, in view of the object relationship which is in fact present,
we should speak of primary narcissism only in the sense that an infant makes
no distinction between subject and object (see also Freud, 1921, p. 130; 1940).

to *abolish all spatial barriers between them"* (Freud, 1926a, pp. 121-122; *my italics*). Hence we can see how the incorporation of nourishment abolishes the spatial barriers between the ego and the object. At the same time, even from a physiological point of view, a gradual transformation takes place and the object choice becomes an identification. An ambivalent attitude toward the object (nourishment = mother) means that the removal of boundaries is experienced as a dangerous process. Danger is avoided by the abstinence from food; at the same time, an estrangement is created. This symptom can easily be understood from the fact that the oral object relationship, in ontogenetic terms, represents the prototype of the object choice (Freud, 1905d). A few words about the concept of orality will clarify this point.

To avoid the use of clichés we would like to recall a means of expression used by Abraham. He compared his list of the stages in the organization of the libido and the development of object love to a "timetable of express trains in which only the larger stations at which they stop are given" (1924, p. 496). In reality, "the oral zone is only the focal point of an early method of approaching things," and the "mode of incorporation" is connected with skin contact and grasping with the hands (Erikson, 1961). This "mode of incorporation" can spread from the oral zone to sensitive zones all over the surface of the body. According to Erikson, the "mode of incorporation" embraces the biting oral-retentive, oral-eliminative and oral-penetrative auxiliary modi. From the biological matrix, "social modalities" evolve—for example, receiving, grasping and taking what is given. These remarks have a direct relevance to the chief symptom of anorexia nervosa. A feeling of emptiness develops because the patients avoid not only object choice confined to the oral zone, but every form of actual or emotional proximity, including tenderness, skin contact, receiving, and taking. The severer the depressive components of the illness, the more pronounced the introjection processes which are typical for the depressive structures (Abraham, Freud). Courchet, Gëro, Meng, Meyer, Weinroth, and Scott have all given precise descriptions of the depressive components from the psychoanalytic point of view. The avoidance of proximity and touch result inevitably in isolation. Hyperactivity and bulimia are not effective escapes; they are merely substitute satisfactions, which bar the way to realistic, and therefore also psychic satisfaction. This trait gives to the clinical picture all the characteristics of an addiction, a feature which was first noticed by Wulff (1932). Binswanger also drew attention to it in "The Case of Ellen West" (1957). Even when the patients stuff themselves with food, their sensations of emptiness do not disappear, because no amount of surreptitious eating can replace the abandoned interpersonal relationships. *Mutatis mutandis,* the same is true for hunger and overeating as for thirst and drinking as an addiction (Mitscherlich, 1947, p. 68).

Isolation and emptiness concealed behind hyperactivity result in a general mood of mild depression; it is a sign of the patient's retreat from an ambivalent object cathexis. Therapeutically, the difficulties are increased when depressive structures, in the narrow sense, are present. In case histories 2 and 5 there is a discussion of the introjection processes which are essential for the understanding of depressive experience.

The following dream description provides a concrete example of the relationships which have been presented in our psychoanalytic scheme—that is, the choice of an object and identification, estrangement, the loss of an object, and depressive structural changes.

Martha E. (5) dreamed that she was drawing closer and closer to a girl friend until finally she became fused with her. The way in which the approach and the fusion happened was never made quite clear, and the patient herself produced no associations. This resistance is as important as the manifest content of the "Identification Dream" itself.

The latent dream-thought of an identification with the mother is easily identified from the suppressed longing to become united with a friend, even though the conscious experience and actions are dominated by an opposing reaction formation. Actually, few anorexia nervosa patients have either a friend or an affectionate relationship with their mothers. By the time their illness starts, they have all begun to place themselves at a distance and to behave like strangers toward their families. As soon as the patients' ties with reality become weaker and regression has begun, a vicious circle seems to develop which drives them further and further into isolation. This process can be schematically described in the following way: tender, sexual, or aggressive strivings, or other acts which can be consciously performed, are submerged into the unconscious by automatically functioning defense processes. Since the acts in question are psycho-physical in nature, it is not surprising that anorexia or other inhibitions ensue when they are submerged. At the same time need-tension develops, which presses the patient into producing dreams of an infantile type. As Freud commented in this connection, "These are the dreams which all through life are called up by imperative bodily needs—hunger, thirst, sexual need—and are wish-fulfillments as reactions to internal somatic stimuli" (1916-1917, p. 132). Archaic forms of expression are revived in these dreams. The vicious circle consists of the fact that the growing instinctual tension causes primitive forms of (dream) thought and activity to become manifest (see section G. of this chapter), while in the sphere of the defense mechanisms of the ego, a rigidity is formed to prevent disintegration. Thus the refusal of every emotional relationship corresponded to the "Identification Dream" on the level of experience and behavior.

It will be easier to understand this pathological negativism if we look at it from the point of view of the "transformations" which normally occur at puberty and the corresponding changes in the psychic structure. Anorexia nervosa patients are afraid, theoretically speaking, of an ego loss, as the "Identification Dream" illustrated so vividly. Here the spatial barriers were removed; it is difficult to decide whether the fear was generated more by the erotic or the aggressive components of the action. These patients in fact experience the demands of their love as destructive, fearing love as something which removes the separate existence of others, as in the "Identification Dream," where the type and means of the union was shown. This process may be linked with various functions and means of experiencing. A distinction was made between the different stages and functional phases which lead from the choice of an object finally to an identification. Often the tender desire for skin contact is mixed with homosexual or aggressive urges, and this confusion complicates every relationship. Consciously the patients avoid what they unconsciously seek. Martha E.'s excessive and annoying tickling of her mother is a good example of the kind of outlet that these patients find for their tender-aggressive urges. Typically, this ambivalent relationship was abandoned at the onset of the illness.

There are other aspects which should be considered for an understanding of the psychogenesis of the fear of physical contact in general, and specifically the avoidance of food. A fraction of a process, or a single unconscious content, can attract all the anxiety to itself. Thus, the fear of sexual conception is transferred to oral receptivity, and is defended against in that region by the refusal of food (Waller, Kaufmann, and Deutsch, 1942). The special significance that receptivity has in a woman's life accounts for the fact that it is almost exclusively girls who develop anorexia nervosa. Henriette A.'s thoughts on this subject, as quoted earlier, are particularly interesting in this context. She defined receiving as a specifically feminine function, and attributed first an oral, then a sexual content to it. The initial and continually effective uneasiness can be caused as much by the *function* or by its psychic representatives, as by the changes in *form* or in the body image. However, it is not only the fantasy of oral impregnation that leads to a disturbance of function; other contents play a part. These are the feminine qualities which are incompatible with the ego ideal. The lone male patient under treatment was affected in exactly the opposite way. He did not feel that he was a "real boy" and his illness was precipitated by a burst of growth in height.

Either an ambivalent object cathexis prevents a real gratification, or certain essential psychic contents in the manifest form of experience is lacking and a feeling of emptiness results. Identification entails a partial object loss, but in the unconscious union there is a narcissistic-depressive-masochistic cycle. The ambivalence of the original relationship with the girl friend-mother causes a "good" and a "bad" image to be introjected and erected in the ego, or the superego, whenever an identification arises. The step by step changes in the patients' relationship to reality are often easy to trace. Martha E. for instance, ceased tickling and openly annoying her mother before the beginning of the illness. At the same time she stopped hitting herself, in hate for a bad mother image, and stopped imagining a suicide to punish her family. The particular changes in the ego that result from identifications depend upon which appeal is the strongest.

The structural theory of psychoanalysis is useful here for understanding why these patients condemn themselves in a depressive manner and deny the danger of death in an absolutely hypomanic way (Lewin, 1951). The self-accusations really represent accusations against the "object" that the ego has assimilated. This explanation coincides with the introjection process described by Freud (1917). The autarchy and freedom from anxiety discussed in the previous section of this chapter should be seen as an unconscious union with the imaginary picture of the beloved person. The patients live as though they were still unconsciously united to a nursing mother. Sabine B. (2), for example, dreamed about both a cannibalistic incorporation and being herself in the belly of a big fish (directly after the death of her mother). These two aspects of her identification intensify the ambivalence directed toward the same person (mother) and produce the depressive self-accusation mentioned above (I am bad, evil) and the illusion of autarchy (I am good, perfect and inexhaustible, like mother).

These patients often claimed with delusional insistence that they were "their own providers," and thus were not dependent on any actual food supplies. Because of their unconscious identification, several of the patients also adhered to the idea of parthenogenesis in order to be able to replace their desires for relationships of a sexual nature with an unconscious sense of omnipotence.

Of course, the ambivalence described above does not become inactive because of ego changes. Its progress can be observed clearly, particularly among those patients who exerciese strict control and discipline to prevent anything dangerous from approaching them. It regularly occurs that ideational or affective representations intolerable to the ego are warded off and attach themselves to other object representatives. In this way, conscious awareness of instinctual danger can be prevented and overcome in projection: various anxiety contents are concentrated in the fear of eating. Danger can be avoided through a severe restriction of "intake," an interchange of emotional intensity, and in other ways. When transference is successful, and these structures begin to alter, the original fears are released; it then becomes possible to observe the relationship between ambivalence, object relationship, and anxiety *in statu nascendi.*

The conflict for anorexia nervosa patients is active on two planes, which are connected, in spite of attempts to keep them apart. Thus, danger is sometimes experienced more as internal, sometimes more as outward. In the "external field," the dangers are embodied in the form of food. In the "region of internal experience," the instinctual anxiety is concentrated in and concealed in and concealed by the fear of being or becoming fat. At the same time, on the positive side of the ambivalence, a union is being sought; thus food becomes a very dear commodity. The final effect of the identification processes is that the patients believe themselves in a condition of perfection.

Masochism and narcissism, self-hate and self-love exist simultaneously because of an ambivalent identification. "Many of them neglect their appearance in every way. They are unwashed and smeared with dirt, their hair tousled and unkempt, their clothing neglected. . . . Others are inordinately vain, powdering and adorning themselves in secret, spending hours on their clothes or taking to their beds in lace-trimmed nightgowns, with their hair neatly combed and arranged, *as if they were preparing for some solemn occasion. One might almost think that they were lying in state"* (Bahner, 1954, p. 1134; *my italics;* see also the case history of Sabine B.).

In this account of the typical way in which an oral ambivalence in states of regression determines the object relationships and pathologically changes the identification processes, I have omitted any discussion of childhood development and the special role of the mother. One reason for this is that my investigators were chiefly confined to the patients themselves, and no accurate picture of their family relationships was recorded. Although it is safe to claim that maternal behavior often exacerbated the conflicts, no general rules can be made. Simplifications are generally not true to reality, unless it is possible to give the other family members as thorough a psychological examination as Lidz and his fellow workers did with their schizophrenic patients' families.

Smirnoff (1958-1959) has suggested that the source of anorexia nervosa lies in a primary disturbance of the mother-child unit and the symbolic relationships, and that tracing the illness back to various conflict situations does not provide a satisfactory explanation. We do not agree, however, and offer the following example. Sabine B. grew more and more angry in transference; she declared that she wanted to kill the analyst and at the same time, eat him up with love. As she said this, her own fear of being bitten or devoured increased, to the point where she grew afraid that "the cloth on the couch might bite me." In fact, under the influence of conflict, her field of mental perception was changing amidst severe aggressive tension. It would be misleading to discuss only the symbolic relationships, without regard to the conflict.

If we proceed from the "psychodynamic cross-sectional picture" (Hartmann and Kris, 1945), as it appears during therapy of a well-known patient, it is feasible to make positive statements about the relationship between wish and anxiety images and their defense reactions, as well as changes in thought, action, and symbol formation. In our view, there are very important consequences for the technique of treatment and the formation of theory if one proceeds from a primary disturbance of the mother-child duality, rather than using the present conflicts as the starting point. Hartmann (1950) has criticized such simplifications, which take one part from the whole, and base whole theories on isolated factors. He calls them "theories by reduction." One could make such simplifications as the fact that mothers are not always "good," responsible for all later ill health. If we were to accept as true the words of Kafka's "Hunger artist" that he had to fast because "there was no food that was appetizing to him," we might be tempted to attempt the naïve task of providing a "good" mother to feed the patients. However understandable such a naïve notion is, there is nothing to be gained from taking overt or hidden complaints against the mother as absolute truths and constructing a method of treatment around them. In fact, the consequences might even be disastrous (cf. Freud, 1933, p. 156).

E. Vomiting and Gastroenteric Symptomatology

The anorexia nervosa patients' secret vomiting is interesting in more ways than one. It is often artificially produced by the patients themselves, who induce retching with a finger. In this way they are always in a position to reverse the results of satisfying their hunger. At first, vomiting has to be initiated, but gradually it begins to happen after only a little retching, or even spontaneously. Here again, the situation is due to the patients' ambivalence; indeed, their attitude has always been ambivalent at this physiological level. We could almost borrow from one of Freud's early essays (1892-1893, p. 41) and call it a "perversion of the will." Revulsion and anorexia are governed by a "counter-will" (loc. cit.) which has taken charge of the patient's ego. Nevertheless, the patients themselves do not feel that they are at the mercy of their "counter-will"; they are positive that their neurotic intentions are something they have formed of their own volition. In actual fact, the vomiting can be explained only on the basis of changes in the ego, with the enthronement of the "counter-will" as the controlling force. The mechanisms of the conversion neurosis come to light only after several more layers have been peeled off.

In nervous vomiting, the symptom is demonstrative, relative to the situation, and structured like a conversion neurosis; the patients are easy subjects for transference, their resistance being based mainly on repression. In these cases, vomiting takes the "place of a psychical act" (S. Freud, 1895, p. 297). In Freud's case, an image that the ego could not tolerate was not "talked away"; instead, some of the physiological innervations (nausea and/or vomiting) joined in the "conversion" (p. 296). It was cases such as these which led Freud to suggest that there was a special form of defense at work in this conflict, namely, a *conversion*. With reference to Darwin, Freud spoke of an "expression of the emotions" (1895). The essential feature of this defense is that the emotionally colored ideational contents always take second place to the formal occurrence. Nausea and vomiting thus do not symbolize a stable ideational content (S. Freud, 1895, p. 89; 1900, p. 570). This is true even though we know that unconscious wishes for and fears of pregnancy can usually be established in cases of hysterical vomiting.

A case was also reported recently in our clinical seminar, in which the relationship between attacks of nervous vomiting and acknowledged desires for pregnancy and the rejection of sexuality became obvious during the first interview. The symptom then disappeared abruptly, after having lasted for three and a half years (unpublished paper by Dr. Clemens de Boor).

Another eighteen-year-old patient had been subject to frequent attacks of nervous vomiting since the age of eight, which eventually became so serious that she was unable to go to work. A prolonged course of psychotherapy disclosed that, when she was eight, she had eavesdropped on her parents' lovemaking. This incident was followed by phantasies of fellatio accompanied by vomiting whenever she saw anything unpleasant, or had to touch or eat anything repellent. The symptom grew even more acute during one period, when she had to take care of an infant. Using the methods of experimental psychology, Beech also established that oral modes of experience had a sexual connotation for an anorexia nervosa patient of long standing. In my experience, these images or symbols do not belong to the same levels in nervous vomiting and anorexia nervosa, since there is such an enormous difference in the respective patients' capacity for consciousness.

The vomiting of anorexia nervosa takes place in secret, is often voluntarily induced and, because of changes in their egos, the patients are frequently reluctant in transference, showing a so-called "superego" resistance. This last derives chiefly from an unconscious sense of guilt or need for punishment (S. Freud, 1924, p. 166), which is intensified by the subterfuges the patients employ to dispose of food and vomitus unnoticed, or to counterfeit an increase in weight. "The vomiting," as Bahner has said, "follows the meals as punishment and penance follow a crime" (p. 1133); the attempt to undo the evil deed is aided and abetted by the "counter-will." When all is said and done, it makes very little difference whether these patients vomit on purpose, or whether vomiting happens involuntarily, as the primary or secondary result of nausea or revulsion. In both cases, negativism provides the common denominator: in the first, the act is self-contained and logical; in the second, a biological function has achieved autonomy.

Vomiting thus has similarities to anorexia, which also lies on the borderline between "will not" and "cannot." This similarity becomes more obvious when we consider it in the light of Freud's important work *Negation*. In this essay, Freud discusses the function of judgment and its origins. "The attribute to be decided about may originally have been good or bad, useful or harmful. Expressed in the language of the oldest—the oral—instinctual impulses, the judgment is: " 'I should like to eat this,' or 'I should like to spit it out,' and put more generally: 'I should like to take this into myself and to keep that out.' That is to say: 'It shall be inside me' or 'It shall be outside me' " (1925b, p. 237).

Judgment in this case is a development of the way in which the ego "took things into itself or expelled them." Its polarity "appears to correspond to the opposition of the two groups of instincts which we have supposed to exist. Affirmation—as a substitute for uniting—belongs to Eros; negation—the successor to expulsion—belongs to the instinct of destruction" (1925b, p. 239).

In this instance, Freud is not primarily concerned with negation as a purely logical act of judgment, but as a reaction which has its wellspring in a conflict situation. Spitz has recently given a comprehensive account of this. In my opinion, however, there is a relationship between the "oral expulsion," the vomitus, and the patient's negativism, and I should like to make a short excursion into the problem of the "origin of an intellectual function from the interplay of the primary instinctual impulses" (loc. cit.).

The fact that "the symbol of negation has endowed thinking with a first measure of freedom from the consequences of repression" (loc. cit.) was confirmed time and time again during interviews with at least the more seriously ill among the anorexia nervosa cases. Naturally, this negation makes it even more difficult to reach the unconscious ideational content, and to free the destructive impulses that are interwoven with the negativism and the vomiting. Considerable ground must be won before fantasies with aggressive contents are produced, and not until then can relationships be reestablished that have been broken off during the period of the negativistic behavior. If the patients' nihilistic attitudes and symptoms do begin to change during the process, then we are justified in inferring that there were indeed destructive impulses at work. In this way, we also gain some insight into "perversion of the will" and its source in the primary instinctual impulses. As Kunz so rightly puts it, "The greatest proportion of a human being's aggression is not clothed in motor activity, but in thought, ideation and fantasy" (1946a. p. 34). He suspects, on the other hand, that "in cases where negation has set in a chronic habit, whether it takes the form of aggression, negativism or even nihilism on principle, there are definitely aggressive and destructive impulses at work" (loc. cit.). This can be observed in anorexia nervosa.

The next problem that arises is the question of the changes which occur within the patients at an ego-psychological level. As we have already seen, the frustration of the normal satisfaction of hunger encourages the development of imperative needs and eventually sets up a vicious circle. The oral aggression that has been warded off leads to a regressive activation of unconscious images of cannibalism and, by the reverse process, to a vigorous refusal of food. We may assume that the unpleasant experience of not getting enough to eat reawakens infantile feelings of frustration at not having been given enough, and the ego takes over the "no" of the frustrating object. As Spitz has described it, "The aggressor is in this case the frustrating object against whom his own 'no' is hurled" (1959, p. 47). The anorexia nervosa patients' defiance safeguards their immediate environment from open aggression and also from their excessive desire for love. Negativism and vomiting are also reaction-formations, or, in some cases, the results of ambivalence at the relevant stages of development. If we are to judge these symptoms with regard to the prognosis as well, we must also take the normal manifestations of puberty into account, the normal emotional aloofness and intellectualization of the teenager. It is hardly a coincidence that the problem of freedom of the will is generally debated more hotly during puberty than at any other age. Indeed anorexia nervosa patients cling tenaciously to their voluntary—that is, unmotivated—negativism which has its physiological counterpart in the refusal of food and vomiting. As soon as they have proven to themselves that they can master their physiological needs, the extreme forms of the reaction-formation are alleviated, and even spontaneous recoveries may occur.

It may seem surprising to approach the psychosomatic aspect of the vomiting in anorexia nervosa from the point of view of negation, but it was the observation that patients often induced the reflex voluntarily which led to the choice of "perversion of the will" as a starting-point. For treatment and for psychodynamic theory alike, it is of the greatest importance to know that these patients not only conceal their vomiting with unparalleled ingenuity, but are also extremely unwilling to discuss their motives for so doing. With other patients whose vomiting is psychically determined—for instance, hysterical vomiters—it is often possible to establish the relationship between nausea and vomiting, convince the patient, and thus accomplish the first step of the treatment. But anorexia patients are completely inaccessible; they even withdraw from the feeling of revulsion.

In an interpretation of Sartre's novel, "La Nausée," V. von Weizsäcker spoke of negation as a defense mechanism. The negation dissociates itself more and more from the life of the body, until it becomes an entity in its own right (1944, p. 496). In principle, this sequence of events is the same as that described by Freud in *Negation*: irreconcilable instinctual impulses lead to repression-revulsion as a reaction-formation, and finally to negation, as the patients attempt to remove themselves from the proximity of the physical experience of revulsion (both the instinctual impulses and their object-directed nature). In the case of Sartre's hero, Antoine Roquentin, the "nausée"—the revulsion—developed from a pathological desire to touch. Von Uexküll's impressive study of the effects of nausea and the unloosening of an emotional bond is directly relevant at this juncture. His exhaustive analysis of nausea showed that "discomfort, revulsion, dizziness, vomiting and so on appear only when nausea has reached a high degree of intensity" (1951-1952, p. 418) and, in mitigated forms, only when there is some inhibition of activity in the stomach and of the feeling of hunger.

In a state of revulsion conditioned by an experience—and in vomiting—danger, the feeling of being overpowered, is not experienced in the same way as it is in a state of anxiety. Wolf suggests that there is interference here from a predetermined biological pattern in nausea, which serves the purpose of ejecting harmful material from the stomach (quoted by T. von Uexküll, 1951-

1952, p. 423). This ejection of *harmful* material may well be at the root of the anorexia nervosa patients' vomiting, their gastro-enteric symptoms including their excessive use of laxatives, and the complicated purification ceremonies some of them are compelled to carry out. Indeed, they experience the feeling of having overcome danger by vomiting or excessive enemas, as a tremendous liberation, a conquest. It is as if they look upon eating as a far more dangerous menace than starvation. The symptom of rumination gives a particularly vivid example of the methods used, especially by gravely ill patients, to achieve a state of apparent independence, the state which gives them their greatest illusion of satisfaction.

The act of negation weakens the intensity of the sensation of physical revulsion, and helps the patients to overcome their fear of harmful materials, but in a phobic way—for they are particularly wary of fat, whether in the form of body fat or fatty foods. At the same time, their gastrointestinal symptoms reinforce the ambivalence and the defensive measures, particularly in two directions: the patients either have to make up ailments in order to avoid having to eat, or they must endure intolerable physical sensations arising out of their hypochondriacal fears or, in some cases, out of their own instinctual urges. Constipation, often extremely persistent, increases the feeling of fullness, and again a vicious circle is set up. A large number of my patients took to the use of laxatives, and one chronically ill girl had been swallowing up to 100 laxative pills every day. Although the constipation is undoubtedly aggravated by the mechanical effects of a reduced intake of food and liquids, it does confirm the "anal character" of the anorexia nervosa patients' psychogenetic constitution, for they are indeed "orderly, parsimonious and obstinate."

F. Amenorrhea

The pathophysiology and the clinical features of amenorrhea have already been fully discussed in Chapters 2 and 3. As far as the psychosomatic aspects of the symptom are concerned, there is little to add to the remarks in the first case history, at the point where the patient had an attack of *angina tonsillaris* (Chapter 4). According to Alexander's definition of psychosomatic symptoms, amenorrhea would not be a symbolic expression, but is correlated with sudden or persistent emotional tensions. Rejection of the female sexual role undoubtedly played a large part in the patients' lives, and it would be reasonable to conclude that this state of mind has a physiological counterpart. But, as Kelley emphasized, there was no constant, common form of expression or specific relationship, in the sense that these patients had stopped menstruating because, and only because, they were refusing to be feminine. Women often cease to menstruate in circumstances in which they fear for their safety or their lives. Thus the anorexia nervosa patients' organisms could be said to be responding as if a (real) danger were at hand; in other words, the reaction has been turned inward in order to banish from consciousness the experience of anxiety. It is tempting to compare the amenorrhea that occurs in situations of mortal danger with the amenorrhea of anorexia nervosa, since in both cases the cessation of the menses is due to psychic factors, and is aggravated by undernourishment and cachexia. Again, both conditions feature ovarian insufficiency and a reversible atrophy of the gonads. Further observation of both examples, however, shows that the neurohormonal processes that control the menstrual cycle during moments of great danger are not subject to the individual's psychophysical capacity for reaction, and can be independently disturbed. One of Freud's "complementary series" can be built from the following series of statements. In the case of the amenorrhea of a woman under sentence of death, exogenous factors are all-pervading. The situation of refugees and of the inmates of concentration camps leaves more scope for the individual's personal capacity to react, although their amenorrhea is definitely related to the fate that threatens them, a danger from outside. In the case of anorexia nervosa, the position is exactly reversed; the amenorrhea is now connected with the patients' frame of mind.

A formula as generalized as this, although limited in some respects, does have the advantage of providing one all-embracing concept for both mental and somatic phenomena—the word "attitude." "Excitation," "mood," "behavior," "tension" and "instinct" are similar "portmanteau-concepts." On the other hand, these rather ambiguous terms have little significance for the empirical investigation of, for instance, the patients' general behavior, with particular reference to the menstrual cycle. In both these cases, it is impossible to avoid methodological and empirical dualism, and concepts that purport to comprehend a personality in all its psychosomatic complexity are usually only describing a stretch of the psyche's and soma's mutual journey in holistic phraseology (Thomä, 1958-1959c, p. 887). Even in the realm of everyday conscious human experience, there are those states which we describe as bodily and those which we describe as mental.

However certain we may be that "defective" menstruation is a side-effect of a "defective" mental attitude, it is still extremely difficult to isolate the various components on the subjective-objective side and to estimate their relative importance. In the section on precipitatory causes of illness (this chapter), it could be shown that loss of appetite and amenorrhea cannot be reduced to a mere functional disturbance of the hypothalamus. "It is sheer speculation to base an argument on impulses coming from the cortex, diencephalon or pituitary and impinging upon the ovaries. Although it is widely known that these kinds of pathways are undoubtedly involved, we do not yet know more than that they 'play a part.'" With these words Bahner (p. 1136), has summed up our present position. The same is true, *mutatis mutandis*, for the psychosomatic side of my thesis. It can be taken for granted that fending-off of the feminine sexual role, the "displacing" of imaginative activity to oral contents, the finding of gratification in an urge for activity, and the setting of exaggeratedly high standards—all these are among those features of the illness that eventually caused the amenorrhea. Nevertheless, no special prominence should ever be attached to any one particular fragment of a mental process. In view of the uniformity of the anorexia nervosa syndrome, it will probably be more helpful to keep the comprehensive and more general concept of regression in the fore.

Although, like Freud, we must still avoid the ever-present temptation to locate psychoanalytic systems in the brain, we must not lose sight of the radically biological nature of the processes of regression. With this in mind, we can thus make a definite distinction between conflicts whose elements of form and content are typical as far as the case history and individual pattern are concerned, and changes in experience and neurohormonal regulation in the course of a regression due to conflict. The discovery that amenorrhea is one of these changes, obviously in conformity with some biological law, is not so much an explanation as a description. There is no purpose in seeking explanations in isolated causal chains, when they can be found only in the psychosomatic situation as a whole. The facts bear this out: not until the patients' attitudes had altered, and their conflicts were at least on the way to being resolved, did the menses reestablish themselves. Hormone treatments were either useless or superfluous (see Chapter 3).

G. *The Urge for Activity and Kleptomania*

The delusion of autarchy also manifests itself in another guise —the desire to appear as a kind of perpetual motion machine, and to produce tremendous results with minimal energy expenditure. The fact was that the capacity for effort that many of the patients forced themselves to show was only relatively great; they simply would not admit to fatigue or exhaustion. Nevertheless, they managed to pull the wool over their own and their families' eyes, and to conceal the fact that their exaggerated show of liveliness was only an outlet for the tension generated by their need for food, which they were so vigorously warding off. As was mentioned above, Freud himself used hunger as a good example of the relationship of physiological excitation (the objective side of

hunger) to perceptual experience and the experience of satisfaction, on the one hand, and to restlessness (in some cases, hallucination), on the other (1900, p. 565). Although he makes no reference to Freud, Katz would seem to agree with this: "Tensions
are generated in hunger; as long as they are not discharged, they
cause bursts of movement either in the realm of the imagination,
or the more primitive muscular system" (1932, p. 13). The psychoanalyst would call it a "regressed cathexis of motility." Eventually, awareness of the object that is really being sought for—
food—recedes into the background. In the language of V. von
Weizsäcker's principle of equivalence (for definition, see Chapter
4), it could be said that the real purpose of the movement has
been disavowed, and that it is now being used as a substitute for
(goal-seeking) perception. It is finally also possible to trace a connection between many of these patients' actions, in terms of the
instinctual economy, and the modern behaviorists' concept of
"displacement activists" (Lorenz). A "consummatory action"
(Craig) is avoided, and "appetitive behavior" takes over (Craig;
see Tinbergen, 1952).

The urge to keep moving and the tendency toward kleptomania are both responses to hunger pangs, which have taken the
form of motor activity. Although ruminating and vomiting, or
mental participation in other people's meals, may seem to quiet
these pangs, the other links in the biological reaction-chain "hunger"—i.e., restlessness and grasping—gradually gain ascendancy.
The ensuing hypermotility and kleptomania have been fully
discussed in case histories 1 and 5 respectively. There is nothing
new to be said as far as the defense processes are concerned, but a
few words should be added on the subject of restlessness, kleptomania, and confessions of clandestine raids on the larder, known
as "larder anecdotes," and their psychoanalytic significance.

According to the laws of mental economy, the biological energy
aroused by the excitatory processes at the source of a drive will always strive toward an outlet. A study of anorexia nervosa substantiates this, even if we disregard the problem of quantity and
quality, for as tension mounts and as satisfaction is warded off, the

level of modes of action and experience sinks, exactly as the psychoanalytic theory of regression would predict. The patients no longer eat, they gobble, and it seems as if a "grasping instinct" has taken over. In many cases, they have reacted under the influence of the full force of their hunger, rather like the cats in Brügger's experiments, whose eating and chewing reflexes were released by stimulation of seventeen points in the area of Vicq d'Azyr's bundle (1943). Hess' experiments are also interesting in this context. He found that the stimuli described above evoked a goal-seeking feeding response, in terms of which the cats would approach even the most inappropriate objects—such was their excitement—merely in order to discharge the "tension generated by the arousal of an instinct" (1944-1946, p. 138).

The patients themselves suffer greatly from any breakthrough of their drives, but their restlessness provides them with a compensating "pleasure in movement" (Abraham, 1924, p. 162). The sequence of events is as follows: first, the act of warding off normal satisfaction or, in this case, the appearance of the instinctual representations in consciousness, is followed by the triumph of having achieved autarchy and the possibility of deluding themselves that they are "perpetual motion machines." As a result of this, the patients finally experience pleasure in movement as such, because it does not impinge upon the ego; at the same time, their bodies are purified, and they lose another few pounds. In this way, satisfaction and punishment are achieved at a single stroke.

It would be neither constructive nor in keeping with psychoanalytic principles to draw up a list of the symbolic objects that the patients are searching for in the larder, in the solitude of nature, or when they steal. It is more to the purpose to inquire why their normal actions are thus disturbed and why they feel impelled to seek this secret or unconscious symbolic satisfaction.

The "larder anecdotes" provide a good illustration of the way in which symbols and symptoms form during mental conflict. One need not be a psychoanalyst to understand that these patients eat in secret because they are hungry, yet wish to conceal the fact. Why are they so concerned about maintaining the impression of being anorectic? It is hardly satisfactory to suggest that they are perhaps embarrassed at the thought of admitting their needs, even though these really exist.

It has already been established that, in anorexia nervosa, anxiety and a sense of guilt have caused the warding off of oral demands, which have been regressively reinforced and overlaid. Eventually the refusal of food increases oral envy, adding fuel to the flame of the oral aggression that originally motivated the anorexia. Under such circumstances, it is hardly surprising that the patients feel very uneasy at mealtimes, and that they avoid the family table with all its latent conflicts and rivalries. Instead, the inward tensions are discharged as described above, and the objects which the patients grasp or devour with such greed become symbols for all the things they are consciously avoiding and unconsciously seeking.

As for the symbols, whatever they may be, we can be sure that the furtively enjoyed food serves as a mother-substitute (see case history 2). But, apart from this, food can have the strangest variety of unconscious psychic contents projected onto it, especially since it is practically the only object for which the patients feel any attachment. This is undoubtedly due to the fact that the eating process is regressively disturbed. The schematic picture can be broken down into the following components. An asexual ego ideal—*I am neither boy nor girl*—acts as a reaction-formation to give sure protection against sexual desires becoming conscious. The unconscious accusation that nature (mother) has not given the patient enough—love, food, money, beauty, and so on—becomes confused with warded-off envy of all those (father, mother, siblings) who possess the unconsciously desired object—food, breast, penis, or whatever it is. As a consequence of regression, oral incorporation and manual grasping are imbued a particularly aggressive (castrative) character, which is more than consciousness can bear. The resultant repression leads to an inhibition of function and a repression of the ego, which is reinforced by the formation of a special set of ideals. Eventually an impulsive act is committed, a theft, and at last the pent-up excitation can be discharged in a manner that is remote from the ego, empty of image or fantasy. To call this act a "symbolic theft" is really an oversimplification, since it can be understood psychoanalytically only in its triple aspect. This comprises: first, the *topical* aspect (conscious asexual ideal, unconscious wishes with widely differing contents); secondly, the *dynamic* aspect (conflict); thirdly, the *economic* aspect (discharge of excitation). All three are fully discussed in case history 5.

Anorexia nervosa patients are lonely souls, and it is characteristic that their favorite companion is often an animal. Dorothy Burlingham summed up these real or imaginary friendships with animals when she wrote: "There is nothing that this dumb animal cannot understand; speech is quite unnecessary, for understanding comes without words" (1945, p. 206). It is an essential part of these relationships that no conflicts arise, and that they seem to represent a pre-ambivalent state: inseparability without disillusionment, but with infinite scope for make-believe. Sabine B. (2), who was bedridden, had the same kind of feeling for her teddybear that she did for a baby. Even though the experience of pleasure in movement, a pleasure remote from the ego, or a cosmic "surrender to the wind" are not really very much like the sensation of swimming in water, they undoubtedly have something in common. The patients encounter stirrings of an "oceanic feeling," as Freud described it in *Civilization and its Discontents*: "A feeling of an indissoluble bond, of being one with the external world as a whole" (1930, p. 65). It is no coincidence that these sensations are so vague as to be almost impersonal or remote from the ego; they provide just the kind of pleasure that anorexia nervosa patients, in their regressed state, can permit themselves to accept.

H. Development of a Personality or Process

In his *General Psychopathology* (1963), Jaspers makes an important distinction between "developments" and "processes."

For Jaspers, the "development"—for example, of a neurotic personality—can be "understood" psychologically, whereas the
"process" of a psychotic illness can only be "explained"—that is,
inferred—from somatic causes. From a descriptive and psychopathological point of view, he draws a sharp division between, for instance, a delusion of jealousy and neurotic or psychopathic jealousy. Thus, in Jaspers' terminology, a delusion of jealousy, and
all other psychotic symptoms, can at best be "explained" from
organic causes, whereas neurotic jealousy can be "understood."
Jaspers gives a critical assessment of various concepts, theories
and methods of psychiatry on the basis of this twofold psychopathological definition. Mayer-Gross et al. (1954) claim that the
first edition of *General Psychopathology,* which appeared in 1913,
"did much to clear the air for the successful development of scientific psychiatry in Germany, France, Holland and Scandinavia
between the two wars" (p. 16).

This is a rather subjective judgment. Jaspers and the psychiatrists who were influenced by his methodological definitions (e.g.
Gruhle, Mayer-Gross, K. Schneider) have done little to transform the vague "understanding" of psychopathological "developments" into a scientific method. Indeed, psychotherapy was in
danger of being choked off by the clear air of this "scientific
psychiatry." It is typical of the movement that its adherents have
made no serious psychotherapeutic investigations, but instead
have filled the gap with criticisms of psychoanalysis. (For readers
not familiar with German psychiatry, it might be helpful to
know that K. Schneider is the chief exponent of Jaspers' principles.) It would also be interesting to note how a case of
anorexia nervosa is diagnosed and handled when the principles
of "descriptive psychiatry" are applied in a pure and untram-
meled form.

In Chapter 3, there was some discussion of the cognitive significance of psychotherapy, and the fact that this useful tool had
hardly ever been applied to anorexia nervosa, except in studies
already inspired by psychoanalysis. An example of this kind of
omission is provided by a case reported by Schottky (1932), on

which he based an important contribution to the nosological-diagnostic problem, and to Jaspers' basic psychopathological problem of the "development of a personality or process." Schottky, who was then working at the German Institute for Psychiatric Research under K. Schneider, dealt with a typical case of anorexia nervosa, by diagnosing it as "unusual impulsive behavior during a disturbance of development due to a process." Here is a short summary of the case.

> After years of uneventful, indeed "good psychosomatic development"—that is, without any obvious psychopathic tendencies before the illness began—this girl developed anorexia nervosa at the age of 15. The crux of the trouble was her fixed idea of "reducing her weight in any and every possible way" (height, 5 foot 4 inches; weight, 71 pounds). She set to work with laxatives and a stomach pump that had once been applied by the doctor and was now operated by the patient herself. She vacillated between bulimia and loss of appetite, between an unusual urge for activity and kleptomania, under the force of which she stole useless objects, as well as food. Eventually she came before the courts for larceny. Since there was no apparent logical connection between her mania for slimness and the thefts, the court medical officers refused to ask for leniency. However, the judge let her off. She was eventually run over and killed by a car, as she was crossing the road, "in the act of greedily gulping down a sausage she had just begged from somebody" (p. 45).

Schottky begins by examining the differences between obsessive and compulsive drive-ridden behavior. He then discusses whether the thefts, the stomach-pumpings and the enemas can be interpreted symbolically; without further hesitation, he concludes that "even though this kind of psychoanalytical interpretation is valid in many cases, it has little reference to the case in hand" (p. 51). From this brief review of the more obvious features of the case, he plunges rapidly "into the middle of the causal connections, as far as they are compatible with a somatic explanation" (p. 52). He eventually decides that the amenorrhea was due to acute sexual underdevelopment, and substantiates his opinion with a description of the gynecological findings. This assumption of an underlying state of general degeneration, with an emphasis on sexual underdevelopment, enables Schottky to explain away an entire complex of experiences (such as impulsive behavior) which would otherwise be incomprehensible. As his title suggests, he traces the personality changes as a whole, back to a moment when "something snapped," "which can usually be observed only after a psychotic break" (p. 54).

In Jaspers' terminology, then, the "psychic process" would be said to lead to a split (not necessarily schizophrenic), a kind of snapping-off. Something new and mysterious appears on the scene. Personality developments, on the other hand, as well as psychopathic variations, are easy to understand because they are formed by a specific disposition (*Anlage*) interacting with a milieu. Jaspers demonstrated the difference by using the example of jealousy: on the one side, the eruption of symptoms of jealousy is process-determined; on the other, it is the result of the paranoiac development of a psychopath, jealous because he is so unsure of himself. However, even Jaspers himself concedes that there are some cases which cannot be explained by these two alternatives. "Personality-disorder or process, decidedly abnormal personality or schizophrenic transformation (deterioration) of a previously quite different being are two diagnoses in opposition, yet opposed in such a way that not only do difficult cases occur, but, because of such cases, the basic concepts are themselves in question and their limitations constantly felt" (p. 706).

In Schottky's case, however, it was established that the patient was in a good state of psychosomatic maturity before the illness, so that by definition it could scarcely have been caused by a quantitative increase in preexisting individual eccentricities, and thus by the "development of a personality."

After a description of the obsessive symptoms, a nonschizophrenic process ("in the sense of a snapping-off, not in the sense of a progressive deterioration") was diagnosed, as was noted above.

This case gives a particularly good demonstration of the limitations of a diagnostic procedure which pays no heed to psychoanalytic methods. In Jaspers' sense of the words, Schottky presumably considers that he has "explained" the physical changes of anorexia nervosa, although I myself have found throughout that these changes can be understood only as primarily psychosomatic, or, in some instances, as the secondary effects of prolonged loss of appetite. Schottky also gives a purely static description and classification of any psychopathological phenomena which may exist. Little scope is left either for the postulation or the understanding of any psychodynamic relationships that may occur between the symptoms. Surely this methodological purism has been too dearly bought, for it leads only to theoretical sterility. It is interesting, however, that Jaspers himself has pointed out how a purely static psychopathology could be overcome; his remarks (quoted in Chapter 3) are unexpected, but most enlightening.

How incongruous it seems, considering the trend of thought in his *General Psychopathology*, to find Jaspers comparing his static, phenomenological psychopathology with investigations based on psychotherapeutic intervention! K. Conrad and K. Schneider bewail the stagnation of clinical psychopathology: "For years no advance has been made" (Conrad, 1958, p. 4); "The phenomena have been reaped, gathered and garnered, and it is hardly likely that there is much more for us to see or learn" (J. Schneider, 1949, p. 343). This unsatisfactory state of affairs is certainly due to the psychopathologists themselves and the way in which they have fought shy of the "dangers" inherent in psychotherapeutic experimentation that Jaspers spoke of. (This has surely not happened only in the field of anorexia nervosa!) The *General Psychopathology*, as such, cannot be held solely responsible for the fact that a purely static method of understanding isolated phenomena gained the upper hand—what Conrad called the "tedious process of splitting up a phenomenon." On the other hand, Jaspers' criticism of the theoretical side of psychopathology and the ambiguous position of his understanding of psychology—poised as it is between empirical psychology, the psychology of "as if" understanding experiences (p. 132), and philosophy—inevitably placed the onus on static understanding. In addition, as Ruffin (1953-1954) emphasizes, Jaspers' methodology lacked the essential ingredients for a system of psychological therapy.

It is thus hardly surprising that no progress was made beyond a system of phenomenological analysis—which, although important for clinical diagnosis, could only deal with the phenomena as isolated entities. Schottky's description of a case of anorexia nervosa is typical of this method. Admittedly, he provides an accurate working distinction between "explaining" and "understanding," in Jaspers' sense of the words and, like Schneider, he reaps, gathers, and garners the phenomena, one by one. But of those facts that were left ungathered and ungarnered, disturbingly enough, there is no trace; from my own observations of similar cases, I feel compelled to conclude that, of all the facts, it was precisely the most vital ones that were left behind.

Freud once spoke of the "secret of hallucination" (1916-1917, p. 231), which cannot be explained by regression alone. We have certainly not yet grasped the full psychodynamic significance of the particular form taken by regression in anorexia nervosa, nor of the changes in the ego. The patients confuse wish-perceptions of the food with realistic fulfilments, but the disturbance of their sense of reality seems more like self-deception than hallucination. For the present, we must content ourselves with the established fact that the regression of anorexia nervosa does not appear hand in hand with a schizophrenic disturbance of the ego (Eissler, 1943). Even though the problem of content and form in the psychogenesis of various psychiatric and psychosomatic clinical pictures has, as yet, many undiscovered facets, the concept of regression rules out descriptive psychopathology's "development" or "process." As far as anorexia nervosa is concerned, these "fundamental concepts" have turned out to be not only of questionable value, but as Schottky's report showed, actually obstructive.

The chief objection to the "development" or "process" dichotomy is that both definitions have proven to be far too narrow. Obviously, some distinction must be made between psychogenetic factors and secondary physiological or somatopsychic changes in anorexia nervosa; otherwise the same kind of confusion might arise as in the phrase "organ psychosis," which was coined by Meng (1934). Meng diagnosed anorexia nervosa as an organ psychosis because he assumed that it was caused by a pituitary deficiency. As we now know, there is *no* pituitary deficiency, so that the "psychosis" has had the "organ" taken out "from under its feet"! The validity of Meng's psychoanalytic description of anorexia nervosa, however, remains unchallenged. Moreover, Meng backed up his "organ psychosis" with a speculative development of the concept of regression. In the meantime, Margolin and Grinker, working quite independently, have introduced a similar generalization as a new hypothesis for psychosomatic medicine. My own observations of anorexia nervosa do not corroborate this hypothesis, and I feel sure that criticisms of the concept of "psychophysiological" regression, made by Mendelson, Hirsch, and Weber are thoroughly well-founded.

I. Existential Analysis and Anorexia Nervosa

Roland Kuhn (1953) was the first existential analyst to publish a study concerned explicitly with anorexia nervosa. Boss (1957) has also contributed to this particular field of research with a critical assessment of Kuhn's studies. We are thus in an excellent position to compare the views of two existential analysts on a subject of essential importance to our theme: the problem of "spatiality." Since our enquiry must be confined to a few salient points, we shall begin with Kuhn's case, where we are at least on diagnostically safe ground. In L. Binswanger's "The Case of Ellen West," there remains some uncertainty as to whether the patient was suffering from anorexia nervosa or schizophrenia simplex (L. Binswanger 1957, p. 18; Schultz-Hencke, 1952; Zutt,

1948). This is a problem that can be left to one side for the time being.

The subject of Kuhn's first study was an innkeeper's daughter, who consulted the psychiatrist of her own accord after two years of illness, but showed no interest in his attempts to help her. She complained of palpitations as well as the usual symptoms. She also suffered from anxiety dreams (of burglars, thieves, and murderers), did not believe that dreams had any meaning, and could not be persuaded to produce any free associations. She declared that she could think of nothing to say, and "after she had described her symptoms, every interview petered out in nothingness" (p. 11). The customary psychotherapeutic practice —Kuhn's own words–of approaching a patient from the biographical angle, led nowhere in this and other cases of anorexia nervosa. For Kuhn, the "biographical" approach included questions about "causes" and "effects," "how it came about," "when" some incident occurred, what was "remembered," and what "forgotten." "All these questions require the patient to talk about the *chronological* [*my italics*] structures of her existence, and this is something which seems quite impossible for young girls with anorexia nervosa. They are equally inaccessible from the temporal aspect of their existence" (p. 11).

Communication did not become easier until Kuhn introduced the concept of "spatiality," and questioned his patient about the *spatial* structures of her existence: for instance, "where" something had happened, and what the relationships were between "near" and "far," "inside" and "outside." In this way, the emphasis was laid on the "qualities of things" such as "heaviness" and "lightness," "hardness" and "softness," "coldness" and "warmth," "resilience" and "plasticity," "fullness" and "emptiness." The "body" and "touching" (in the sense of "physical approach," as well as "affective stimuli") and, last but by no means least, "eating," were also brought to the surface in this way (p. 11). This new approach aroused the patient's interest and, after 18 psychotherapy sessions spread over a year, she was as good as cured.

Being an innkeeper's daughter, she often came into contact with the customers and had been frightened of being touched for some time past. These fears had caused her to direct all her energies toward keeping people at a distance from her body. Eating acquired the same special significance as it did in my case histories, and since Kuhn's description of this coincides by and large with my own, it can be omitted. However, there is another aspect to this case which does merit further discussion.

During the two years that the illness lasted, there were two temporary spells of improvement, both after operations: the first, a tonsillectomy; the second, a normal appendectomy. Because of a dream "in which the patient's throat was operated on by a doctor with a large instrument like a pair of forceps," Kuhn envisages the operations as a kind of "being touched on the inside," a "violent breach of the security system inside which the patient has barricaded herself" (p. 12). He finds it conceivable that there might be cases where a "similar unique return (surgically induced) to a normal organisation of the world might lead to a permanent cure" (p. 13). Even the patient mentioned above must have been "transported into another world" by the operation. But "since she persevered with her efforts to increase the distance between herself and other people or things, the improvement could not last" (p. 13).

It is probably correct to suppose that, whether it was successful or not, the effects of, for instance, a pituitary implantation (see Chapter 3) would be due to suggestion and in that way related to whatever this surgical intervention signifies in actuality. It may also be true that the patient was transported into another world by being "touched inside" during an operation, or by dreaming of it. On the other hand, we are dealing with an event that can have repercussions at more than one level. A single interpretation is not sufficient.

Kuhn's new method of approach, as described above, seems equally suspect. It is supposed to be the result of the influence of existential analysis, and to have furnished the master-key to this patient's problems. However, it is not accepted practice in psychotherapy to approach patients exclusively from the biographical aspect of their lives. Besides, the question "how it came about" cannot be said to be probing into a purely chronological set of circumstances. In addition, dislike of proximity and physical contact is such a conspicuous feature of anorexia nervosa that it would suggest itself for discussion, even if the patient did not bring it up of her own accord. In fact, Kuhn was extremely fortunate that his patient brought the matter up, of her own accord, by complaining that everything seemed very remote.

It is also a rather common experience, not necessarily only with anorexia nervosa patients, to find that the interview trails off after the patients have described their immediate symptoms, or after clinical anamnesis. This initial and often persistent resistance takes the form of a mere listing of the facts, without any mention of the feelings that accompanied them. There is no point in expecting free associations from a patient who is in this frame of mind. Free associations will be produced spontaneously, within the framework of the individual resistance and transference, as soon as communication becomes a little easier. At first, anorexia nervosa patients are acting under the influence of their defense processes, and their capacity for communicating subjectively to elicit a makeshift clinical anamnesis, and it is probable that Kuhn was referring to traditional clinical anamnesis when he spoke of "accepted psychotherapeutic practice."

The second part of Kuhn's study deals with transference, particularly from the theoretical point of view. He asserts that it is incorrect to "treat the transference situation as an identical copy of some previous relationship, since it represents a completely new, autonomic channel of communication, a fateful encounter ... in the sense of an association between two people," something "truly creative in the life of a human being, as L. Binswanger so rightly asserts (1947, p. 142) in contrast to Freud and the psychoanalytical school of thought" (1953, p. 197). A closer look at Freud's and L. Binswanger's actual words, however, reveals a different state of affairs. In fact, Binswanger does *not* claim, as Kuhn alleges, that the transference situation represents an autonomic channel that is completely new, but rather that communication, the relationship between physician and patient, is not merely a repetition of some previous bond, because it always contains *some new elements*. As Freud showed, communication is a wider concept than transference: "Transference arises spontaneously *in all human relationships,* just as it does between the patient and the physician" (1910b, p. 51; *my italics*). Similarly, Anna Freud gives the following definition: "By transference, we mean all those impulses experienced by the patient in his relation with the analyst which are not newly created, but have their source in early—indeed, the very earliest—object-relations, and are now merely revived under the influence of the repetition-compulsion" (1936, p. 18). There is no doubt that the concept of transference takes precedence over relationship for empirical and methodological reasons; after all, psychopaths are usually unable to approach or communicate with others, they are more or less strongly gripped by a repetition compulsion, and can experience new material in only a very limited form. However difficult it may be to sort out the transferred elements in the physician-patient relationship from the new contents that have been created by means of this relationship, "transference" as a concept is still easy enough to define. There is little to be gained from blurring the distinction between these elements.

In sum, although Kuhn claims that existential analysis is responsible for enlarging the field of psychological knowledge, his arguments do not stand up in the light of closer scrutiny. It is neither accepted psychotherapeutic practice to approach the patient merely on the biographical plane, nor does the concept of transference contain the idea that the relationship between physician and patient is a total facsimile of some earlier relationship.

Kuhn's interpretations seem equally flimsy when put to the test. Fortunately for us, Boss, an avowed representative of one branch of existential analysis, has already challenged Kuhn's position, and his objections pinpoint one of the fundamental

problems of existential analysis. Like Kuhn, Boss begins by describing one aspect of the behavior of anorexia nervosa patients,
but this leads him to continue with an attack on Kuhn's interpretations of a deviation of "spatiality," in the following words:
"This form of spatial dimension is never more than the essential
effect of the patient's specifically defensive and aloof attitude
towards everything that is physical or sensuous. In consequence,
the anorexia nervosa patient's being should not be investigated
primarily from the spatial organisation of his personal world-
structure" (1954, p. 103). Without realizing it, Boss is striking at
the heart of existential analysis. For existential analysis consists
of just this: phenomenological analysis of the primary deviations
of structures and their components—as, for example, the structure
of spatiality. Although space does not permit a lengthy description of the phenomenological method in Husserl's sense, and its
influence on both Heidegger's existential analytic and Binswanger's
existential analysis, a word of explanation will not be amiss.

The emphasis on "being" in existential analysis does not mean
that it is a descriptive phenomenology of "subjective experiences," in Jaspers' or in the ordinary sense of the words. The
existential analyst does not inquire into the psychopathological
deviations from some norm of a patient's subjective experience
of space, but into the primary changes in the *a priori* structure
of spatiality behind the mental structure. By comparison, the psychodynamic method would attribute changes in the patient's
experience of space to unconscious defense processes and conscious aloofness and negation—that is, the processes demonstrated
in the case histories given above, and those to which Boss was referring when he spoke of a "defensive relationship." For in
terminology and content, Boss' interpretation draws heavily upon
the defense mechanisms, as postulated by the theory of psychoanalysis.

1. Although he claims to have superseded psychoanalytic theory
with his existential analysis, he falls back on it time and time again.

2. However, the purpose of existential analysis, as Binswanger

sees it, is not, in contrast to psychoanalysis, to "concern itself with the construction of the framework of the inner life-history, but to interpret the construction of the transcendental framework which is the foundation of all mental frameworks, and a necessary or *a priori* condition of their existence (1947, p. 304). Whenever the words "form of existence," "framework," "structure" and "structural components" are used, they should be understood as referring, in transcendental terms, to *a priori* structures.

In the same chapter, Binswanger also claims that the influence of existential analysis is shown by the fact "that we have... learned to conceive of and describe... the different psychoses and neuroses as definite *deviations* from the *a priori* framework or the transcendental structure of the experience of being human...." (p. 304; *my italics*). In the existential analyst's eyes, the position is as follows: the changes in Kuhn's patient's subjective perception of space are possible only if we presuppose a deviation in her whole spatial world. *But no one has yet been able to discover what kind of relationship exists between a priori and psychological structures, between existential transformations and inhibitions in development.* This problem has still to be solved.

Thus at one moment we find references to the contrast between psychoanalytic and transcendental conceptions of structure, with clear implications that existential analysis (*not* Heidegger's philosophical ontology of existence) describes the *deviations* of the *a priori* or transcendental structures of the psyche. On another occasion (1957, p. 10), perhaps as a reaction to the criticism called forth by his doctrine of "deviations in the a priori structures," Binswanger wrote: "... I must reiterate that there is a considerable difference between Heidegger's ontological existential analytic in philosophy and when it is 'applied' to ontic, empirical events, that is, to definite forms of existence and spans of existence. As here, I have always stressed that this difference is the difference between the *a priori* examination of the structure of existence and the empirical-phenomenological proof of the presence of certain *deviations* in this structure. It should of course be understood that it is not the ontological structure of existence as such which varies or deviates" (*my italics*). If existential analysis is really concerned with definite spans of existence, or lifetimes, and not only with the immutable transcendental structure, then the question of the connection between the existential-analytic and the psychological idiom becomes of paramount importance.

As we mentioned above, the relationship between *a priori* and psychological, like that between ontological and ontic structures, is fraught with complications. Presumably this is because of the difficulty of differentiating between "ontic" and "ontological." L. Binswanger has made several contradictory statements on this point, in spite of the fact that it must be decisive for any systematic method. In one instance, he traces back phenomena in the inner life-history "in advance" to prior changes in the existential structures (1947, p. 206; 1947, p. 294); in another he appears to assume the opposite. This applies to the conditions, the empirical proof and the mode of expression of the phenomena. Thus certain mannerisms are considered to be related to the "covering-up of a biographical weakness, a fear of living or a fear of dying, but also a vulgar aggressivity, controlled only with difficulty" (1956a, p. 114). These mannerisms then serve "to help cover up" these fears.

The problem becomes particularly conspicuous when a deviated structure is being described, and the question of the contributory factors arises. In the life of "Ellen West," for example, the patient's fundamental world-design is supposed to be "existential emptiness." The actual words are: "In case of Ellen West, therefore, no lasting stilling of the hunger occurs, because the hunger is in this case, as with very many toxicomanics, not only a somatically conditioned need, but at the same time the need for filling up the existential emptiness or vacuum. Such a need for filling out and filling up we designate as an existential craving (*Süchtigkeit*). Hence, if Ellen West does not suffer from an addiction in the clinical sense, still her 'life-form' falls under the psychopathological category of existential craving. In this respect, she is close to the life-form of toxicomanics and of many sexual perverts. At the same time, for lack of sufficient material, we had to leave quite unresolved the question of the extent to which her own homoerotic component contributes to her un-fulfilled and unfillable existence" (1957, p. 346).

The Copernican turn of existential analysis is particularly well illustrated by this case history. In the first instance, it postulates a world design or world structure, which has deviated into a "vacuum," one, however, that may be filled (by oral greed). On the other hand, we find a potential homoerotic component which may be contributing to this existential vacuum. It is very hard to see how existential terminology gives a clearer picture of this "emptiness" than does the simple observation that oral incorpora-tion always has homosexual components, which may lead to anorexia or addictive bulimia. This observation has been con-firmed in several similar cases. Indeed it is for this reason, among others, that anorexia nervosa patients can never be satisfied even by the daintiest of morsels. Of course if this "emptiness" were not latent in some form in the individual's "world-design," it could neither arise nor be experienced. But from a psychological point of view, and as long as the "emptiness," in all its guises, is not considered in isolation, there are many contributory factors which can help us to gather up the threads and understand why an "unfillable" vacuum is experienced.

It makes no difference to the problem whether or not "Ellen West's" deviated world was a schizophrenic symptom. To be sure, Binswanger has diagnosed her case as schizophrenia simplex, and has stuck by his opinions in spite of well-argued suggestions that she was suffering from anorexia nervosa (Schultz-Hencke, 1952; Zutt, 1948). For my part, I am more interested in showing, as in the case of the deviated spatiality mentioned above, that the "emptiness" is not primarily an existential, quasi-metaphysical transformation or aberration of a span of existence. It can be un-derstood perfectly well, like the other world, for example, the ethereal or tomb-world of "Ellen West," within the framework of dynamic-genetic methods of investigation—that is, methods that focus on the conflict and its relationship to subjective experience.

As I suggested in a previous publication (1958-1959c, p. 893), the same is true, in principle, of Binswanger's analysis of a hysteric (1947, p. 158; first published 1934), where he found the source and explanation of the existential deviations in an experience of "repression." In actual fact, it is the concept of defense which is the linchpin of existential analysis.

However much we may admire Binswanger's outstanding contributions to this field of research, we must not allow ourselves to be blinded to the defects of the specifically existential-analytic "Copernican turn" (L. Binswanger, 1957, p. 319). This fundamental precept implies that, only when a hole-, tomb-, swamp- or vacuum-world-design is present, will the corresponding somatopsychic characteristics be found (orality, anality). Binswanger once remarked that he could find only one way of improving upon Freud's combination of life-functional-impersonal or systematic and life-historical-personal-comparative methods of representation (especially in the study of mental *conflict*), and that was at the level of the kind of *a priori* examination of existence that occurs in Heidegger's analytic of existence (1957a, p. 49). But what about conflictfulness as a fundamental existential property of existence? Are we to assume that conflicts are essential constituents of the configuration of every "world," and is it proper to investigate formal changes in experiencing, thinking and acting without the frame of reference that would be provided by a psychopathology of conflict? In practice, it would appear that the four constituent concepts of the existential-analytic school of thought—they also embrace, by the way, the existential-analytic theory of schizophrenia—are indeed connected to a psychopathology of conflict.

These are the concepts as defined by Binswanger (1957, p. 13-20); the first and fundamental concept is the "*disintegration of the continuity of normal experiencing, its discontinuity.*" He cites "The Case of Ellen West" as an example of a complete disruption of the ability to see things as they really are. "Ellen" dictates how things are to behave, including her own body, which is not permitted to grow plump, but must stay thin. The *"splitting asunder of the continuity of experiencing into two alternatives, a rigid either-or,"* is the second of these concepts. One side of this parting of the ways is characterized by a rigid formation of high-flown ideals; anything that is incompatible with these ideals branches off. To abandon the exaggerated ideal means, "the dread, the boundless dread of straying into the dominion of the other alternative" (ibid., p. 16). "Another constituent concept for our researches was the concept of *covering-up*. We mean the Sisyphus-like attempt to cover up the warded-off, intolerable side of the alternative in order to prop up the authority of the high-flown ideal" (loc. cit., p. 19). Finally, Binswanger postulates the notion of "the *becoming-chafed* (or harassed) of existence, the culmination of antinomic tensions, of helpless bewilderment, in *resignation* or *withdrawal* from the antinomic situation altogether, taking the form of a *retreat* from the progressive development necessary to existence" (*my italics*).

It is often very difficult to determine whether a term, as used by the existential analysts, has a fundamentally ontological meaning, or a psychological-sociological one. As Kunz pointed out, this is the consequence of the existential psychiatric school's misinterpretation of Heidegger's philosophy (1949, p. 56). The significance of Binswanger's four concepts, however, is clear enough. Freud once spoke of concealed anxiety, from which the ego retreats by obediently carrying out the commands, precautions and penances imposed upon it (1926a, p. 128). Binswanger's "covering-up" seems to be of the same sort. For it incorporates, among other things, "Ellen West's" efforts to prevent obesity by constant movement and excessive use of laxatives. It could be asserted that "being-covered" (Heidegger's "untruthfulness") is existentially one of the necessary conditions of "covering-up" (as a psychopathological process), and that constant movement and excessive use of laxatives, and the struggle not to grow fat are all anchored in the transcendental structures. This tautological use of "covering" may make sense to the existential psychiatrist, but it cannot be disputed that the structure-schema for the understanding of psychopathological symptoms which Binswanger develops in the introduction to his book on schizophrenia, literally pivots on what can only be described as the term "defense, the earliest representative of the dynamic standpoint in psychoanalytical theory" (A. Freud, 1936, p. 45). The emphasis is laid at one moment on the branched-off, the warded-off side; at the next moment, Binswanger is suggesting that the high-flown ideals are mere tools of the fending-off of anxiety, as though they were mannerisms."

In retrospect, it is interesting to note how Binswanger's more recent schema has necessitated the revision of the "Copernican turn," a term which he first applied to an actual case in 1944 in "The Case of Ellen West." Nevertheless, I fail to see how his four constituent concepts indicate primary deviations in *world-designs*, although it must be admitted that world-designs as such have begun to become far more comprehensible since Binswanger pointed out the psychological relationship between their individual structural components.[13]

This vacillation among the basic concepts of existential analysis not only makes it difficult to understand what is meant by the word "structure" every time it is used, but also reveals an underlying problem. In fact, the more minutely we examine the chief differences between fundamental ontological and psychopathological methods of investigation, the more obscure existential-analytical statements about psychopathological structures become; one might almost say that closer scrutiny of the existentialia shows just how impossible they really are.

Existential-analytic psychopathology and existential psychotherapy have become, to give a modern twist to the phrase *philosophia ancilla theologiae,* "handmaidens" of philosophy. They destroy one another because they are being made to serve two masters: the patient and the structure of his symptoms, and the philosopher and the structure of his existentialia. Of course,

---

[13] But this indicates implicitly a return to psychodynamic theory and the abandonment of the "Copernican turn."

even though they may prefer to disregard the world of reality, these philosophers are fully entitled to examine the *a priori* structures in their symposia; yet, for the "handmaidens," reality cannot be put aside, and the crumbs that fall from the philosophers' tables are not existentialia, but empirical "ontic" problems. For example, "worry" about the daily bread that is so despised by anorexia nervosa patients is said by philosophizing psychiatrists to be derived from "worry" as a basic structure of existence. The physician, however, quite naturally wonders why the "worry" that is anchored in the instinct of nutrition is thus pushed into the background. Certainly, it is possible to describe the phenomenon of refusal to eat in existential-analytical terminology, even though its vocabulary has been enriched with snatches of philosophy; *de omnibus disputandum est* (Kierkegaard). However, this would involve a rearrangement in the definition of some concepts, and Heidegger's exegesis is not exactly the place to go rummaging for criteria by which to judge the validity of psychopathological statements. As Jaspers has said, "Our interest in this ontology of human existence, however, is its possible value as a theory *when applied to psychology* (and what it may help to produce in the way of empirical knowledge); also whether it has value as a possible construct for particular meaningful connections" (p. 777; *my italics*). These conclusions have a decisive significance for the assessment of existential analysis and its interpretations.

Disregarding for the moment in whatever relationship of "fruitful misconception" it may stand vis-a-vis Heidegger's philosophy, we are now in a position to compare existential analysis —though it purports to be beyond them—with other psychopathological theories. It has already been shown how the existential-analytical sketch-map of schizophrenia circumscribes the psychoanalytic concept of defense, and it would be beyond the scope of this book to delve deeper into the question of whether the four principles of organization really increase our understanding of typical schizophrenic structures. Doubtless, the basic concepts of "disintegration," "splitting asunder," "covering-up" and "be-

coming chafed" help us to pigeonhole psychopathological phenomena, but they do little to make it easier to understand the
nature of a typical schizophrenia. In fact, the sketch-map mentioned above really gives an outline of the changes in structure
that can be found in anorexia nervosa, without offering any new
ideas that are not already comprised in the psychoanalytic psychopathology of conflict.

This conclusion, which was reached after consideration of the
psychological content of the existential-analytic concept of structure, is not original. Szilasi, "who has contributed most to the interpretation of my methods" (Binswanger, 1957, p. 27), antici-
pated it with a similar comment. "If the prevailing structure
configuration is to be independently reconstructed out of the observed symptoms, there will be more than enough latitude for
subjectivity in the interpretation. Furthermore, this method
would not pave the way for new knowledge but, at best, a new
categorization as, for example, when instead of a phobia's being
explained as the result of an overstrong tie with the mother (by
Binswanger), the emphasis is laid on the realization that this
kind of overstrong tie with the mother could only be possible if
we presuppose a category of connectedness, cohesion, continuity"
(Szilasi, 1951, p. 75). So long as it follows "correct" procedure
and does not try to reconstruct the structure formation from the
observed symptoms of illness, Szilasi attributes to existential
analysis "methods that have heights of perceptiveness all their
own" (p. 77).

It is not my intention to criticize the philosophical problem
of the "heights" of the "pathways and structures" of existential-
analytical methods, and the even "higher heights" (Szilasi's expression) of Heidegger's fundamental ontology. On the other
hand, sufficient evidence has been given to show that, as far as the
practical side of its methodology is concerned, existential analysis cannot maintain the high levels Szilasi ascribes to it. It is also
true that the construction of psycho- (patho)-logical structures
occasionally proceeds from the top downwards. Löwith has indicated a series of factors that were of no small importance for

Heidegger's influence on his contemporaries: the predominant "pathos of the mystery of a concealed revelation, its negative relationship to the rationality of the 'empirical' *sciences* . . . and on the other side its positive relationship to poetry . . ." (1960; *my italics*). It looks as if these are the factors that take the lead in existential-analytical analyses of psychopathological phenomena.

It should be pointed out, in conclusion, that even the existential analyst is liable to objectivize, and rarely takes his stand outside the subject-object split. Thiel has given a remarkably apt description of the pretensions and self-deceptions of this school; "They do not merely observe, but also enact. They disclose, they stand in the open space of Being, they shed light, integrate, realize, are historically concrete and so on. They claim that their way of thinking has broken through all previous barriers of knowledge, and that their communication with the patient has complete immediacy. The concept of consciousness is—deliberately—waived. An *a priori* statement can be made about this: it is self-deception. Naturally the existential analyst is confined within the framework of the subject-object split—as long as he thinks at all, that is" (1954, p. 297).

This self-deception, however, exercises a strange appeal, all the stronger because it is probably due to a mystic longing for union. No wonder that the gradual receding of "immediate" life creates an increase in the yearning for paradise lost. The revelation of a tacit understanding in a state of inexpressible immediacy has something curiously spellbinding about it. Perhaps this is why existential analysis, as Boss understands it, provided the "practising psychoanalyst with almost no new words, concepts or terms of reference, but 'only' a mute, and therefore [!] all the more fundamental and wise attitude and approach to the sick human being, and the events during the course of the treatment" (1957, p. 129). Existential analysis would be essentially meaningless were it really only trying to prove the wisdom of the old saw, "Silence is golden," in psychotherapeutic practice. Silence on the part of the patient and the analyst during psychotherapy has always been of the greatest significance, but surely not because "the muter, the wiser"! On the other hand, there can be no doubt that even existential analysis must use the common coinage of words.

To sum up: if we examine the methodological and conceptual premises of existential analysis, it becomes obvious that these premises, and the connection between existential analysis, Heidegger's analytic of existence, and Husserl's phenomenology have never been satisfactorily explained. Boss' contradictory statements alone are proof enough. But it does not really matter which existential-analytical writer neglected to give an adequate interpretation of these philosophical premises. Inasmuch as existential analysis sets out to be an empirical discipline, its propositions cannot be measured against the yardstick of the correct or incorrect deductions and interpretations of contemporary philosophers. I prefer to echo Jaspers' opinion of existential analysis, and call it a theory which needs to be confronted with the area of reality it professes to describe. Existential-analytical thought will arrive at a satisfactory comprehension of psychopathological phenomena only when Binswanger's "Copernican turn" is either put into reverse or not performed at all. The example of "emptiness" made it obvious that, where this "turn" reached its first climax, in the case of "Ellen West," the relevant psychopathological circumstances of the case were definitively upset. In contrast, the "reversed turn" that is present in the existential-analytical schema of schizophrenia, is rooted in the psychopathology of conflict. The concept of "covering-up," therefore, also shows how empirical existential-analytical knowledge of psychopathological interconnections leans on the guiding principles of the "mechanism of defense." Indeed, Binswanger has frequently emphasized how little existential analysis can dispense with the tried and tested methods of psychotherapy, and above all psychoanalysis. It is only too obvious from existential-analytic interpretations of anorexia nervosa that this group has cut itself off from the main body of psychotherapeutic thought all too soon. For example, Binswanger's interpretation of "Ellen West" was formed almost entirely from the patient's own writings, poems, and diaries.

In conclusion, the existential analysts' claim that they have discovered a fundamental way of extending the horizon of psychiatric and psychotherapeutic understanding does not survive the test of anorexia nervosa.

J. Further Critical Points

It is the anorexia nervosa patient's antagonistic attitude that has proved the chief stumbling-block for every investigator since Gull and Lasègue. Indeed this attitude has made it difficult, almost impossible, for any of them ever to produce a satisfactory description of the "phenomenology of the subjective experience" (Jaspers) of their patients. Nor have they been able to understand how the outward symptoms fitted in with this particular frame of mind. Nobody could construct a coherent psychodynamic or psychogenetic theory under these conditions.

The method of psychoanalysis was developed on the basis of observations of the phenomena of *resistance* and *transference,* and the theory of psychoanalysis is an attempt to account for these two "striking and unexpected facts of observation which emerge whenever an attempt is made to trace the symptoms of a neurotic back to their sources" (S. Freud, 1914a, p. 16). The empirical findings thus antedate the hypotheses based upon them. Indeed, any physician who is not content with a description of the immediately obvious symptoms can easily observe resistance and transference for himself. In the case of anorexia nervosa, experience and understanding of these phenomena is all-important. In fact, the success or failure of any new researches into the subject is largely determined by the extent to which the author uses or neglects these phenomena. Unfortunately, most writers have not paid enough attention to them, nor to the particular form that they take in anorexia nervosa. It is hardly surprising that anorexia nervosa is still such a bone of contention in many quarters.

However, as H. Hartmann (1944) has pointed out, psychoanalytic and phenomenological psychology should not be thought of as opponents, but rather as partners, the one complementing the other in an essential way, and my own observations lead me to agree with him.

Thus it is rare indeed to find an account of anorexia nervosa which transcends the boundaries of the classical case. All too many studies go astray on one of the following points, although these are all-important for both pathogenesis and therapeutic procedure alike.

1. There is either an inconclusive description of the psychodynamic situation or none, and psychoanalysis is rejected out of hand or without sufficient explanation (Decourt, 1944; Ryle, 1936; see also this Chapter).

2. The idea that certain symptoms—in Schottky's case, thefts, stomach pumpings, or enemas—might be interpreted in terms of psychoanalytic symbolism is entertained, but it is also rejected and without reasonable grounds.

3. Psychoanalytic descriptions that give special emphasis to this or that theoretical vantage point are singled out. For example, Kay (1953) oriented his psychotherapeutic procedure around the theoretical formula of Waller et al., which, in brief, traced refusal to eat back to a phobic defense against unconscious fantasies of oral conception. It is hardly surprising that the results of Kay and his fellow workers at the Maudsley Hospital were largely negative. It is impossible to make a fair test either of the rich resources of psychoanalytic methods of treatment or of psychoanalytic theory in this way. For one thing, it is technically incorrect to found a method of treatment on such circumscribed premises and, for another, psychoanalytic theory rightly requires the investigation of every conceivable facet of the psychogenetic background. This was completely overlooked.

Kay et al. (1954) showed rare restraint, however, in not developing their own psychodynamic theory of anorexia nervosa. It is far commoner to find that the process of "forming a theory by reduction," as Hartmann calls it, is pursued to its bitter end. In this case, the writer borrows a few ideas from psychoanalysis' "wealth of motives" (Freud)—for instance, the "instinct of power, the ethical conflict, the mother, genitality etc." (1933)—and remodels them into an essential principle. Thiemann (1957) evolved an ostensibly original theory of anorexia nervosa in just this way. He believed that "traditional" analysis attributed too much importance to the fear of pregnancy expressed by two of his 22 patients, and used this example to show the alleged bias and narrowness of "traditional" analytic interpretations (p. 62). He suggested that anorexia nervosa was more likely the outcome of a lack of recognition and reassurance (on the part of the mother), which took the form of an oral protest (p. 58). He saw the real nucleus of the illness as "false attitudes" and "false values," which must be torn down and rebuilt by psychotherapy. The kind of "false value" he quotes as typical of anorexia nervosa patients is the great store they set upon the masculine role, and their attempt to be the equals of boys. This is Thiemann's interpretation of his observations: "but if these attempts are made to further the interests of an identification with the male they cannot but fail, because a personal value is being replaced by an alien value, a judging by other people's standards. This kind of identification must prove mistaken in the long run, because the qualities that are considered to distinguish between men and women in our society are ultimately taken for granted, and are not seen as the effect of conditioning by our particular climate of cultural beliefs and standards" (1958, p. 55).

Quite apart from the fact that the search for a model is a perfectly natural process, especially during the years of development, Thiemann's strangely worded interpretation is wide of the point. The difference between men and women is not ultimately taken for granted only in our society. True, masculine and feminine roles can vary widely from culture to culture, but the difference between the sexes has been laid down once and for all, which is why Freud could say: "Anatomy is destiny" (1910a, p. 189). The reason why a young woman's masculine identification is "mistaken," is not that the ultimate standards are cultural. On the contrary, an identification with the masculine role, as it appears in our age and social climate, is "mistaken" when it contradicts the *reality* of a feminine body and feminine sexual characteristics. This discrepancy is the source of a fundamental conflict which can be resolved in a wide variety of ways. It is easy to recognize the effects of the defense processes in the formal changes in experience and behavior, and in the fact that certain wish-contents have been relegated to the unconscious—for example, the wish to be a boy, penis desire, or penis envy. My patients also evinced attitudes and wishes, such as the wish for an operation to change their sex, without becoming aware of their basic conflict, even though the desire was so unambiguously expressed. Since it must be assumed from Thiemann's not-so-unambiguous explanations that he regards one's masculinity or femininity not as an absolute, but as a function of cultural adjustment, we cannot expect him to have recognized the penis desire or penis envy which lies at the root of this identification.

The same is true of Catel's statement (1958, p. 1371) that, like Hoche, he had been unable to discover any penis envy among girls during three decades of child study. There is no doubt that social and familial factors determine whether or not the little girl's frequent desire to have a penis and be able to urinate like a boy will assume pathogenic significance (cf. Waelder, 1960, p. 116). The fundamental conflicts that are created by the fact that there are two sexes, as well as their solutions, are always colored by the particular cultural climate in which they occur, and to this extent Freud's observations and interpretations of the special role of penis envy are rooted in the mores of his time. However, there can be no question that the desire to be a boy has a definite, though limited, influence on the psychogenesis of anorexia nervosa. We can thus be confident that a suitable investigator would be able to show the presence of this fundamental conflict in the four cases of Simmonds' syndrome reported by Catel (1940). All these patients were girls who were presumably suffering from anorexia nervosa.

Of course the difficulty of defining the boundaries of psychoanalytic technique and theory is a problem in its own right, and one that should never be underestimated. There is a "close relationship between theoretical outlook and therapeutic practice" (S. Freud, 1933). However, I am proposing to ignore the question here, since the last thing anybody could object to in the anorexia nervosa literature is the *narrowness* of psychoanalytic theory. Thus it is all the more remarkable how many difficulties arise when there is no psychoanalytically oriented investigation, when no use is made of the psychodynamic or psychogenetic approach to clinical pictures, when the enormous resources of psychoanalytic theory are left untapped, or when new theories are constructed without due attention to definitions. Upon closer observation, these last often prove to be composed of ideas borrowed from the "wealth of motives" of psychoanalysis which have been rechristened. It can only be that Thiemann's statements are due to his ignorance of psychoanalytic theory. This is substantiated by the fact that he overlooks the relationship between "false values" and the "ethical conflict," and its significance in the theory of psychoanalysis.

Another neo-psychoanalytic schema attacks the problem of anorexia nervosa from a different angle; propounded by Schultz-Hencke, it has been upheld by Dührssen and Binswanger, who have based their work on his studies of the neuroses (1951, p. 293 ff.; see also 1952, p. 282). Schultz-Hencke contrasts the "traditional psychoanalytical formula"—"unconscious rejection of fatness as equal to pregnancy"—with his neo-psychoanalytic conception "that we must interpret anorexia nervosa as captative-oral in core and retentive-anal in derivation" (p. 298); the contradictory appearance of the clinical picture as a whole is supposed to be due to something like a dozen further "conditions." What a misleading impression he succeeds in giving! How rigid the allegedly orthodox interpretations of psychoanalysis seem when contrasted with this all-embracing elasticity, with its nuclear process and covey of conditions! In reality, the "traditional analytical formula" to which he refers is Schultz-Hencke's own fabrication. There is very little point in asking whether any known psychoanalyst has ever actually offered this interpretation. It is only interesting to speculate whether this explanation of loss of appetite has ever corresponded to the theoretical position of psychoanalysis and, if so, when and whether psychoanalytic theories were ever so narrowly defined that this formula offered the only possible solution.

Schultz-Hencke's conclusion also implies that such narrow-mindedness was still prevalent in 1950, which itself contains the suggestion that psychoanalysts have clung to the same dogma decade after decade, and that original work in this field has been hampered and constrained. Neither assumption is true. The oldest psychoanalytic formulation of anorexia nervosa was put forward in 1895 by Freud himself, who had concluded that it was a "melancholia with undeveloped sexuality." In the *Three Essays on the Theory of Sexuality* (1905d)—and particularly the third edition, which appeared in 1915 and included the introduction of the so-called pregenital stages in the development of the libido —the importance of *grasping* and *finding an object* was stressed, *inter alia,* in terms of their being part aspects of the oral phase of development. The contributions of Abraham (1907-1920) and Freud (1917) to the theory of depression, now classics on the subject, also did much to increase our understanding of neurotic and psychotic inhibitions of the nutrition instinct, including grasping, object-finding, and the rest.

With the "captative-oral" and "retentive-anal" inhibitions of anorexia nervosa patients, Schultz-Hencke is describing a symptom complex that is only too easy to observe. Nobody is quarreling about the presence or absence of these inhibitions, since they are a *sine qua non* of the syndrome. Differences of opinion arise only during the theoretical interpretation of these data, when the question is asked whether the captative-oral inhibition is really the focus of disturbance in anorexia nervosa, and how and why this inhibition has come about. A brief outline of Schultz-Hencke's[14] theory will help us to understand his neo-psychoanalytic

---

[14] Schultz-Hencke's neo-psychoanalysis has little in common with the other neo-psychoanalytic movements (cf. H. Thomä, 1962).

answers. Neo-psychoanalysis recognizes six kinds of impulse that have some bearing on the psychology of the neuroses, and five neurotic structures. The six impulses are the captative-oral, retentive-anal, aggressive, recognition-seeking, urethral and loving-sexual instinctual experiences. The neurotic structures are supposed to originate in the "nuclear process of the inhibition" of one or more of these. If we inquire how an inhibition comes into being, we are told that "the logical inference is that something inhibiting is obstructing the impulses and needs. For only when that is the case, can the process of inhibition be set in motion" (Schultz-Hencke, 1951, p. 42). The inhibiting factors that lead to the initiation of a neurotic structure in the first five years of life are, according to Schultz-Hencke, chiefly *strictness* and *pampering* (loc. cit.). The neurotic symptomatology is manifested in situations of temptation or despair, when the previously inhibited, latent urges and needs break through. "The neurotic symptomatology is only a fragment of the complete drive-regulated experience *(Antriebs-erlebnes)*" (loc. cit., p. 112).

Although there is not enough space to devote individual attention to each of the connecting links between neo-psychoanalytic and classical psychoanalytic theory, there are one or two points that must be pursued further, since they shed more light on the psychodynamics of anorexia nervosa. There can be no doubt that the process of inhibition is related to "repression." Schultz-Hencke, however, does not raise any points of either similarity or dissimilarity, and "repression" does not figure in his index. He gives no particular reasons for believing that there is any advantage to speaking of "inhibition" rather than "repression." From the point of view of both the terminology and the patients, the introduction of a "process of inhibition" seems to have decided disadvantages. It means that no distinction is made between the many-layered *symptoms* of an inhibition like anorexia, and the mechanisms (e.g., the repression) that lead up to it (see Freud 1925a). The fact that strictness and pampering during the first five years are considered to be the chief *inhibitory* factors clinches the argument.

Of course these factors play their part. But the inhibition, or repression of impulses, as it should be called, is essentially an intrapsychic process. External factors can only release it. To find the prelude to the whole of this process, we must seek among those intrapsychic states that are in a position to inhibit impulses. Schultz-Hencke's attempt to endow the agonistic-antagonistic nature of drive-regulated experiences, and hence the drives themselves, with the function of directing and inhibiting is a contradiction in itself. For an inhibition to take place, it is logically necessary, as Schultz-Hencke himself says, for there to be something to obstruct the impulses. Logically and psychologically, this conclusion is of the utmost importance. It has resulted in the theory of defense mechanisms and has led to the psychoanalytic psychology of the ego. Yet in this neo-psychoanalytic theory it is practically ignored!

However, there is little point in inquiring here how much unspoken ego psychology is contained in Schultz-Hencke's micropsychological descriptions. It is merely interesting to find out whether or not the realization that there must be something which acts as an obstacle to the impulses has any place in the theory. One glance at the index of Schultz-Hencke's book (1951) suffices to show that it has not. The "ego" is not listed and there is only one reference to the concept of "defense." It appears on page 116 in the context of a suggestion that the inhibited drive fragment becomes manifest in consciousness at weak points in the structure of the neurosis. Schultz-Hencke then states: "To this extent (on the basis of a corresponding developmental history with a typical structure), we are therefore dealing with fragments of *fears* and fragmentary guilt-feelings, fragments of the antagonistic and directive factor, and thus of 'defense' " (*author's italics*).

In brief, the neo-psychoanalytic theory of the neuroses propounds a *single* schema with variations (pampering and/or strictness leading to inhibition of one or more of six types of impulse and four or five forms of neurosis); it is, in other words, a patchwork of fragments from the theory of psychoanalysis, as it was before the introduction, around 1920, of ego psychology. It is certainly no coincidence that Schultz-Hencke has almost completely ignored the "inhibitive element" in the process of inhibition. In fact, his theory is nonsense without the framework of ego psychology, and in order to make sense of it, Schultz-Hencke would have had to bring in the dynamic, topical, structural, genetic, economic, and adaptive aspects, and thus precisely that kind of "metapsychology" that neo-psychoanalysts are so anxious to discard. In fact, Schultz-Hencke let it be known that he had abandoned "metapsychology" (1951, p. vi) in order to be able to devote himself to "psychology in the real sense" (loc. cit., p. 21). However, theoretical speculations are always with us, and we can regard these "witches" (Freud, 1937) how we will. Whether burnt at the stake or forgotten, they have a tenacious grip on life, and usually manage to return in some less conspicuous form, wreaking ever greater damage now that they can do it incognito. One of these forgotten witches has been brought to life again in the neo-psychoanalytic theory of structure.

It would be unjust to say that the neo-psychoanalytic nuclear process of the captative-oral inhibition does not give a satisfactory explanation of at least *one* psychodynamic condition of the illness. Apart from the description of the symptoms, it does. But no explanation is given as to why, since it is almost only girls who suffer from this disease; this kind of inhibition of the grasping instinct does not happen to boys. There is an abundance of firsthand evidence indicating that it is often a dread of accepting that leads to a captative inhibition. In any case, the captative-oral inhibition formula only skims the surface of that which lies between these patients' refusal of food and the inhibitive factors of pampering and excessive severity. Schultz-Hencke himself pointed this out when he wrote that "we must, in principle, take a broad view of the determining factors of loss of appetite. On one side it is a question of an existential reaction, a negation of progress, maturation, the future, and of life itself" (loc. cit., p. 298). The narrower the schema and the pithier the nucleus of a structure, the greater the danger that it is not the observations which have given rise to the theory, but the other way around.

Rigidity in the terms of reference, premature categorization of the data, dogmatism and orthodoxy lie in wait at every turn, and it is hard enough to keep a scientific discussion free from "red herrings." As far as possible, however, I have tried to do this. Nevertheless, as soon as I felt certain that psychoanalytic methods and theories provided a better means of plumbing the hidden depths of anorexia than any others, I realized that comparative studies of other systems would provide an excellent yardstick for my own success or failure as well as my theoretical interpretations, and were therefore essential, whether they were entirely relevant or not.

K. *Various Problems of Treatment*

The severity and the course taken by the clinical picture in anorexia nervosa are largely governed by the degree of psychopathological disturbance. According to the condition of the patients, certain typical transference and countertransference constellations can be observed. I shall conclude by describing some of these, with emphasis on the more general aspects, choosing examples mainly from the initial phases of the psychotherapy. Any problems which arose during the course of an analysis were discussed at the appropriate moment during the case histories.

The anorexia patient's attitude to life arouses an almost automatic countertransference of a characteristic kind. For one thing, all the physician's prescriptions and recommendations are frustrated by the patient's rejection. From the very first moment, objective judgments and considerations are overshadowed by the sheer conflict of the situation, and it is not long before the shadows have lengthened and obscured sense and reason. One physician will try to help with kindness, another experiments with strict diets; neither does any good. It is hardly surprising that the physician soon realizes his own helplessness and the futility of all his efforts in the face of the patient's alarming cachexia. His concern arouses his own defense mechanisms and releases a certain kind of countertransference. Without intending to, Heydt-Gutscher has given an impressive description of what can happen in psychotherapy when the therapist (in this case a woman) is no longer able to control her countertransference, and her kindliness turns into excessive indulgence. This is supposed to prove to the patient that she is an "infinitely loving mother." But no good can come of this division of the mother-image into two, a bad half—the real mother—and a good half—the ideal psychotherapist. It must be utterly confusing for the patient when the ideal becomes visibly angry. Of course there is always the chance that punishment may have a "therapeutic" effect, especially since anorexia nervosa patients are decidedly masochistic. Indeed, Heydt-Gutscher has described how a box on the ears delivered in a fit of exasperation worked wonders with a patient whom she had hitherto handled with a self-denial bordering on saintliness.

Although there is not enough space here to discuss the significance of punishment as a therapeutic aid, it is clear that the act mentioned was dictated by countertransference, which has led to exactly the same situation that Lasègue described so vividly (see Chapter 1). In extreme cases, this situation is an exact repetition of the way in which the patients' families have behaved toward them. As soon as we lose track of why the patients behave like this, why they do not eat and so on, the treatment becomes disoriented, governed more and more by the mood of the moment. It is interesting to note how, in the extremes of countertransference, precisely those emotions of the physician come into play which these patients are incapable of accepting or acknowledging in themselves. Instead of becoming aware of any positive or negative transference, they try to lure the physician into assuming certain roles. The more successful they are in inducing him to pamper or punish them, the more chaotic the situation becomes. For in "counteraction," the analyst now represents those very emotional impulses which the patients have to fend off within themselves.

Another typical danger is as follows: since the patients do their utmost to conceal their condition, either by trickery or by the unconscious processes of disavowal and negation discussed above, many therapists tend to do the same. They either underestimate the true seriousness of the situation, or hide their heads in the sand and refuse to draw the obvious conclusions. Again and again, reports of anorexia nervosa cases show how the therapist was tempted, against his better judgment, to follow a wish-thought and whitewash the facts. This is particularly well illustrated in Heydt-Gutscher's case. Here a severely cachectic patient was not required to lie in the classical position on the couch. "I accepted her," writes Heydt-Gutscher (1960), "as an undoubtedly *dangerously* [*my italics*] ill, but busy, happy, active schoolgirl," and while sitting opposite one another (this was an ambulant case), "we talked about her school life and the other themes she herself brought up" (p. 80).

This sort of procedure may well have curative results in some individual cases, but it would not be wise to base a general rule on it. Anorexia nervosa patients who are chronically or dangerously ill should be treated in a hospital, even though they pull every string they can to stay outside. It is not reasonable to expect interpretations to have an immediate positive effect, but there should be some attempt to reveal to these patients a few of the more outstanding motives of their resistance. Under no circumstances should the therapist join his patients in "glossing things over," for they are past masters at it. The patients' confidence is not increased when the therapist pretends to believe their lies about their normal appetites.

At first, interpretations should be directed toward those factors of which the patients are quite clearly aware, but which they conceal and disavow. I am, however, unable to see any contradiction between "fact-finding" and "motivational interpretations," as Bruch does. Surely it is in accordance with a well-established psychoanalytic rule to proceed from the conscious to the unconscious layers, although motivational interpretations will probably go in one ear and out the other, so long as other essential elements are allowed to lie undisturbed. For instance, the secretiveness and the denial of being ill, so characteristic of anorexia nervosa patients, are only outposts of their line of resistance, and this fact must be recognized before the respective motives can be interpreted. But it is certainly not true that the odd behavior of these patients is due to a "basic defect in their personalities, namely the inability to know what they themselves feel." Nor is Bruch (1952) correct in his further assumption that only their mothers "know" how they feel, or that this alleged defect can be exacerbated by motivational interpretations. On the contrary, interpretations of any kind are intended to give the patients insight into their behavior or motives, and if this is not done, their feelings of anxiety and guilt really do gain the upper hand; the result is a vicious circle which makes for greater confusion. To discuss schoolroom problems with a sick girl is one thing; it is quite another to recognize that these themes, and this happy and active attitude toward life, are merely camouflage for the serious illness and helplessness that lie beneath. If the physician is not guided in deed and word by an awareness of the defensive nature of such camouflage, the patient will feel misunderstood. And in this situation, there is material for a circle vicious enough to drive the analyst into a state of concealed anxiety, which then manifests itself as excessive indulgence or open aggression, just as Heydt-Gutscher described.

Since anorexia nervosa patients also deny being either ill or in need of help, the invitation to lie on the analyst's couch seems to them like a great imposition. However, I preferred to analyze my patients in the classical position, whenever this was feasible. This does not necessarily mean that they have to lie on the couch and produce free associations, while the analyst remains silent and impassive in the background, as the cartoonists seem to think. To quote Anna Freud, "We see then that what concerns us is not simply the enforcement of the fundamental rule of analysis for its own sake, but the conflict to which this gives rise. It is only when observation is focused now on the id and now on the ego and the direction of interest is twofold, extending to both sides of the human being whom we have before us, that we can speak of psychoanalysis, as distinct from the one-sided method of hypnosis" (A. Freud, 1936, p. 15).

The wider the breach made by the defense processes in normal feeling, thinking, and acting, the less the patients can comply with the instructions to give "free" vent to their thoughts. Technique must always play second fiddle to the attempt to understand the patients' "battle." If their dread of regression is too great, they cannot be expected to be able to lie down on the couch, before at least some interpretations have been made. External changes—such as treatment in a sitting position instead of lying down, play-therapy with painting and modelling, and other innovations—must be related to the twofold direction of interest described by Anna Freud. If it is impossible to incorporate the play-therapy within the transference and resistance analysis, or at least to understand it in this context, it will probably have little therapeutic value. Until their defenses had at least begun to crumble, few of my patients could either paint, model, or play. In spite of frequent encouragement, Martha E. (5) modelled only one clay figurine, a penitent woman. Sabine B. (2) painted several interesting pictures, but only after her compulsion had been worked over for some time. In other cases (13, 15, 16, 17, 18) no definite claims about the effects of this combination procedure can be made. On the other hand, "lying dreams," a kind of "obliging dreams" (S. Freud, 1920 occurred, and also "lying and obliging" games with dolls and blocks. After a preliminary, extremely coarctitive scene, Waldraud K. produced a series of scenes which, taken at face value, represented a tremendous advance. In reality, they were only "lying or obliging" scenes, designed to help her resist transference and to protect her conflicts from prying eyes.

As a final thought, I feel that it is important to consider the matter of the acting out that occurs during countertransference and to see how much it differs from measures dictated by a real knowledge of the facts. During acting out, in brief, unconscious motives or affects criss-cross the objective and realistic considerations which should be guiding the therapist. Anorexia nervosa patients provoke this. It is really difficult to give directions for, or to apply, such necessary measures as parenteral infusions or forcible feeding without complicating the relationship, because the patients are always on the lookout for punishment. It gives them new material to bolster up their submerged aggressivity. This can be avoided by arranging for some other member of the staff to carry out any such measures.

Precautions like these make it easier for the psychotherapist to keep his sense of proportion and to lessen the risk of falling into a state of "counteraction." But, as Ruffler (1953-1954, p. 532) has shown, fear of countertransference itself may hamper a physician in an objective and valuable course of action. In fact, the task of harmonizing theory and practice is one that meets us afresh every day.

References

Abraham, K. (1907-1920), *Klinische Beiträge zur Psychoanalyse aus den Jahren 1907-1920*. Leipzig, Vienna, Zurich: Internat. Psychoanal. Verlag, 1921.

——— (1924), A Short Study of the Development of the Libido viewed in the light of Mental Disorders. *Selected Papers*, New York: Basic Books, 1953.

Acconero, F. (1943), L'anoressia mentale. *Rivista Sperimentale di Freniatria e Medicine Legale delle Alienazioni Mentale*, 67:447.

Aggeler, M., Lucia, S. P., and Fishbon, H. M. (1942), Purpura Due to Vitamin K Deficiency in Anorexia Nervosa. *Amer. J. Dig. Dis.*, 9:227.

Albeaux-Fennet, M. et al. (1959), Étude des fonctions hormanales dans 29 cas d'anorexie mentale et de maigreur fonctionelle des jeunes filles. *Sem. hôp. Paris*, 35:1000.

Aldrich, C. A. (1944), A Common Type of Anorexia Seen in Run About Children. *Bull. Menninger Clin.*, 8:185-187.

Alexander, F. (1935), Über den Einfluss psychischer Faktoren auf gastrointestinale Störungen. *Internat. Z. ärztl. Psychoanal.*, 21:188-219.

Alexander, G. H. (1939), Anorexia Nervosa. *R. I. Med. J.*, 22:189.

——— (1951), *Psychosomatic Medicine*. New York: Norton, 1950.

Allison, R. S. and Davies, R. P. (1931), Treatment of Functional Anorexia. *Lancet*, 1:902.

Altschule, M. D. (1953), Adrenocortical Function in Anorexia Nervosa before and after Lobotomy. *N. E. J. Med.*, 248:808.

Amelung, W. and Brandt, A. (1943), Voraussetzungen und Möglichkeiten der Behandlung hypophysärer Kachexie und verwandter Zustände von Magersucht ("Inkretorische Magersucht"). *Ergebn. phys.-diät. Ther.*, 2:45.

Aschoff, J. (1959), Zeitliche Strukturen biologischet Vorgänge. *Nova Acta Leopoldina*, 21:147.

Augier, P. and Cossa, P. (1936), Anorexie mentale et anthéhypophyse. *J. med. franc.,* 25:356.

Aurimond, R. (1930), *Contribution à l'étude de l'anorexie psychopathique.* Thesis. Toulouse.

Axenfeld, A. and Huchard, H. (1883), *Traité des névroses.* Paris: Baillière, Tindall, & Cox.

Baeyer, W. von (1959a), Diskussionsbeitrag. *Nervenarzt,* 30:507.

—— (1959b), "Metabletica"—Bemerkungen zum gleichnamigen Werke von J. H. van den Berg, zugleich zum Problem der Pubertätsmagersucht. *Nervenarzt,* 30:81.

Bahner, F. (1954), Fettsucht und Magersucht. *Handbuch der Inneren Medizin,* 7 (1). Berlin: Springer.

Balduzzi, E. (1953), Schemi psicopathologici della anoressia mentale. *Archivio Generale di Neurologia, Psichiatria e Psicoanalisi,* 14:176.

Balen, G. F. van (1939), Anorexia nervosa und hypophysäre Magerkeit. *Acta med. scand.,* 101:433.

Balint, M. (1935), Critical Notes on the Theory of the Pregenital Organisations of the Libido. *Primary Love and Psycho-Analytic Technique.* London: Hogarth, 1952.

—— (1951), Changing Therapeutic Aims and Techniques in Psycho-Analysis. *Yearbook of Psycho-Analysis,* 7:175-188. New York: International Universities Press.

—— (1960a), *Thrills and Regressions.* New York: International Universities Press, 1959.

—— (1960b), Primary Narcissism and Primary Love. *Psychoanal. Quart.,* 29:6-43.

Ballet, G. (1907), L'anorexie mentale. *Rev. gén. clin. théra.,* 21:293.

Bally, G. (1959), Das Diagnosenproblem in der Psychotherapie. *Nervenarzt,* 30:481.

Bansi, H. W. (1940), Zur Klinik und Pathogenese der Fettsucht. *Med. Welt,* 162.

—— (1949), *Das Hungerödem und andere alimentäre Mangelerkrankungen.* Stuttgart: Enke.

—— (1955), Magerkeit als ganzheitsmedizinisches Problem. *Med. Klin.,* 50:49.

Baraldi, M. (1952), Contributo allo studio della anoressia mentale. *Revista Sperimentale di Freniatria e Medicina Legale delle Alienazioni Mentali,* 76:381.

Barber, H. (1870), Cases of Long Continued Abstinence from Food. *Brit. Med. J.,* 1:544.

Bargues, R. and Neuvéglise, D. (1950), A propos d'un cas d'anorexie mentale. *Évolut. psychiat.,* 2:293.

Bartels, E. D. (1946), Studies on Hypometabolism, I. Anorexia Nervosa. *Acta med. scand.*, 124:185.

Bartlett, W. M. (1928), An Analysis of Anorexia. *Amer. J. Dis. Child*, 35:26.

Bartstra, H. K. G. (1948), Een geval van anorexia nervosa. *Ned. T. Geneesk.*, 92:750.

Bass, F. (1947), L'amènorrhée au camp de concentration de Térézin (Theresienstadt). *Gynaecologia*, 123:211.

Beck, J. C. and Brøchner-Mortensen, K. (1954), Observations on the Prognosis in Anorexia Nervosa. *Acta med. scand.*, 149:409.

Beech, H. R. (1959), An Experimental Investigation of Sexual Symbolism in Anorexia Nervosa Employing a Subliminal Stimulation Technique. *Psychosom. Med.*, 21:277-280.

Benedek, T. (1936), Dominant Ideas and their Relation to Morbid Cravings. *Internat. J. Psychoanal.*, 17:40-56.

———— and Rubenstein, B. B. (1939), The Correlations Between Ovarian Activity and Psychodynamic Processes. *Psychosom. Med.*, 1:245-270, 461-485.

Benedetti, G. (1950), Zur Kenntnis der Fett- und Magersucht. *Schweiz. med. Wochenschrift*, 80:1129.

Berger, L. (1944), *Der barmherzige Hugel.* Zurich: Buchergilde Gutenberg.

Bergmann, G. von (1934), Magerkeit und Magersucht. *Dtsch. med. Wochenschrift*, 60:123, 159.

———— (1938), Das Streben nach Synthese—wissenschaftliche Medizin und natürliche Heilweisen. *Dtsch. med. Wochenschrift*, 64:455.

———— (1944), Die psychogene Magersucht. *Med. Z.*, 1:41.

Bergstrand, H. (1939), Ein Obduktionsfall von Morbus Simonds. *Acta chir. scand.*, 82:227.

Berkman, J. M. (1930), Anorexia Nervosa, Anorexia, Inanition and Low Basal Metabolic Rate. *Amer. J. Med. Sci.*, 180:411.

———— (1939), Functional Anorexia and Functional Vomiting: Their Relation to Anorexia Nervosa. *Med. Clin. N. Amer.*, 23:901.

———— (1943), Some Clinical Observations in Cases of Anorexia Nervosa. *Proc. Mayo Clin.*, 18:81.

———— (1945), Anorexia Nervosa: The Diagnosis and Treatment of Inanition Resulting from Functional Disorders. *Ann. Intern. Med.*, 22:679.

———— (1948), Anorexia Nervosa, Anterior Pituitary Insufficiency, Simmonds' Cachexia and Sheehan's Disease. *Postgrad. Med. J.*, 3:237.

————, Owen, C. A., and Magath, T. B. (1952), Physiological Aspects of Anorexia Nervosa. *Postgrad. Med. J.*, 12:407.

———, Weir, J. F., and Kepler, E. J. (1947), Clinical Observations on Starvation Edema, Serum Protein and the Effect of Forced Feeding in Anorexia Nervosa. *Gastroenterology*, 9:357.

Berlin, I. N., Boatman, M. J., Sheimo, S. L., and Szurek, S. A. (1951), Adolescent Alternation of Anorexia and Obesity, Workshop 1950. *Amer. J. Orthopsychiat.*, 21:387-419.

Berman, L. (1935), The Treatment of Malnutrition (Simmonds' Disease-like) with Prepituitary Growth Hormone. *N. Y. State J. Med.*, 35:916.

Bernfeld, S. (1934), Die Gestalttheorie. *Imago*, 20:32-77.

Betzendahl, W. (1939), Körper-seelische Wechselwirkungen bei organischen Psychosen. *Gegenwartsprobleme psychiatrisch-neurologischer Forschungen*, Ed. C. Roggenbau. Stuttgart: Enke.

Bhattacharya, S. and Sem, P. C. (1945), Post-Mortem Studies of Starvation Cases. *Ann. Biochem.*, 5:117.

Bickel, G. (1936), L'insuffisance antéhypophysaire (hypopituitarisme antérieur). *Presse méd.*, 44:1204.

Biema, H. D. van, Koek, H. C., and Schreuder, J. T. R. (1941), Hysteric Anorexia Resembling Simmonds' Disease: Case. *Ned T. Geneesk*, 85:58.

Bilz, R. (1936), *Psychogene Angina*. Leipzig: Hirzel.

Bing, I. F., McLaughlin, F., and Marburg, R. (1959), The Metapsychology of Narcissism. *The Psychoanalytic Study of the Child*, 14:9-28. New York: International Universities Press.

Binswanger, H. (1952), Psychiatrische Aspekte zur Anorexie mentale (Pubertätsmagersucht). *Z. Kinderpsychiat.*, 19:141, 173-180.

Binswanger, L. (1947), *Ausgewählte Vorträge und Aufsätze*, Vol. I. Bern: Francke.

——— (1956a), *Drei Formen missglückten Daseins: Verstiegenheit, Verschrobenheit, Manieriertheit*. Tübingen: Niemeyer.

——— (1956b), *Der Mensch in der Psychiatrie*. Pfullingen: Neske, 1957.

——— (1957), The Case of Ellen West. *Existence*, ed. R. May et al. New York: Basic Books.

——— (1964), *Being in the World: Selected Papers*. New York: Basic Books.

Birnie, C. R. (1936), Anorexia Nervosa Treated by Hypnosis in Out-patient Practice. *Lancet*, 1:1331.

Bleuler, M. (1954), *Endokrinologische Psychiatrie*. Stuttgart: Thieme.

Bliss, E. L. and Migeon, C. (1957), Endocrinology of Anorexia Nervosa, *J. Clin. Endocrinol.*, 17:766.

——— and Branch, C. H. (1960), *Anorexia Nervosa*. New York: Hoeber.

Blitzer, J. R., Rollins, N., and Blackwell, A. (1961), Children Who Starve Themselves: Anorexia Nervosa. *Psychosom. Med.*, 23:269.

Boenheim, F. and Heymann, F. (1930), Beitrag zur Klinik der Hypophysären Kachexie. *Dtsch. med. Wochenschrift,* 56:18.

Bom, F. (1940), Simmondssche Krankheit (endogene Magersucht) bei einem Paar eineiiger Zwillinge. *Nord. Med.,* 8:2506.

Bond, D. D. (1949), Anorexia Nervosa. *Rocky Mt. Med. J.,* 46:1012-1019.

Boss, M. (1954), *Einführung in die psychosomatische Medizin.* Bern and Stuttgart: Hans Huber.

———— (1957), *Psychoanalyse und Daseinsanalytik.* Bern and Stuttgart: Hans Huber.

Boutonnier, J. and Lebovici, S. (1948), Rôle de la mère dans la génèse de l'anorexie mentale. *Cah. Psychiat.,* 3.

Brenman, M. and Knight, R. (1945), Self-Starvation and Compulsive Hopping with a Paradoxial Reaction to Hypnosis. *Amer. J. Orthopsychiat.,* 15:65-75.

Broser, F. and Gottwald, W. (1955), Symptomatische Psychosen bei Magersucht, *Nervenarzt,* 26:10.

Brosin, H. W. and Appelbach, G. (1941), Anorexia Nervosa: Case Report with Autopsy Findings. *J. Clin. Endocrinol.,* 1:272.

Brown, W. L. (1931), Anorexia Nervosa. *Lancet,* 1:864.

Bruch, H. (1952), Psychological Aspects of Reducing. *Psychosom. Med.,* 14:337-346.

———— (1961), Transformation of Oral Impulses in Eating Disorders: A Conceptual Approach. *Psychiat. Quart.,* 35:458.

———— (1962), Perceptual and Conceptual Disturbances in Anorexia Nervosa. *Psychosom. Med.,* 24:187.

Bruckner, W. J., Wies, C. H., and Lavietes, P. H. Anorexia Nervosa and Pituitary Cachexia. *Amer. J. Med. Sci.,* 196:663

Brügger, M. (1943), Fresstrieb als hypothalamisches Symptom. *Helv. physiol. pharmacol. Acta,* 1:183.

Brull, L. (1950), Syndromes pseudo-hypophysaires. *Rev. méd. Liège,* 5:433.

Brun, R. (1936), Sigmund Freuds Leistungen auf dem Gebiet der organischen Neurologie. *Schweiz. Arch. Neurol. Psychiat.,* 37:200-207.

Büchmann, G. (1942), *Geflügelte Worte.* Berlin: Paschke.

Burlingham, D. (1945), The Fantasy of Having a Twin. *The Psychoanalytic Study of the Child,* 1:205-210. New York: International Universities Press.

Cahane, M. and Cahane, T. (1936), Sur un cas de mélancolie associé avec un syndrome fruste de Simmonds. *Ann. méd. psychol.,* 2:798.

Calder, R. M. (1932), Anterior Pituitary Insufficiency (Simmonds' Disease). *Bull. Johns Hopkins Hosp.,* 50:87.

Cameron, A. T. and Carmichael, J. (1946), The Effect of Acute Starvation on the Body Organs of the Adult White Rat, with Special Reference to the Adrenal Glands. *Canad. J. Res. E.,* 24:37.

Cannon, W. B. (1898), The Movements of the Stomach Studied by Means of the Röntgen Rays. *Amer. J. Physiol.,* 1:38.

―――― and Washburn (1902), Alimentary Peristalsis. *Amer. J. Physiol.,* 29:144.

Cany (1932), Note sur un cas grave d'anorexie mentale amélioré à la Bourboule. Gain de 30 kilos en six mois. *J. méd. Bordeaux,* 109:524.

Carmody, J. T. B and Vibber, F. L. (1952), Anorexia Nervosa Treated by Prefrontal Lobotomy. *Ann. Intern. Med.,* 36:647.

Carrier, J. (1939), *L'anorexie mentale. Trouble instinctive-affectif.* Paris: Le François.

Catel, W. (1940), Das Simmondssche Syndrom im Kindesalter. *Mschr. Kinderheilklinik,* 84:36.

―――― (1958), Die Gegenwartssituation unserer Kinder. *Münch. med. Wochenschrift,* 100:1369-1374.

Cervera, L., Folch, A., and Benaiges, B. (1937), Cachexie hypophysaire et anorexie mentale. *Rev. franç. endocr.,* 15:291.

Charcot, J. M. (1892), *Poliklinische Vorträge,* Vol. I, trans. S. Freud. Vienna and Leipzig: Hans Deuticker, 1894-1895.

Chatagnon, P. and Scherrer, P. (1939), L'anorexie mentale et son traitement d'urgence. *Presse méd.,* 47:1277.

Clow, F. E. (1932), Anorexia Nervosa. *N.E.J. Med.,* 207:613.

Codet, O. (1948), A propos de 3 cas d'anorexie mentale. *Rev. franç. psychanal.,* 12:81-100.

Collins. W. J. (1894), Anorexia Nervosa. *Lancet,* 1:202.

Comby, J. (1909), Anorexie nerveuse. *Arch. méd. enf.,* 12:926.

―――― (1912), Anorexie nerveuse chez les nourissons. *Arch. méd. enf.,* 15:697.

―――― (1927), Anorexie infantile et juvénile. *Presse méd.,* 1:40.

―――― (1938a), L'anorexie mentale chez les enfants et les adolescents. *Bull. Soc. Méd. Paris,* 62:1754.

―――― (1938b), Maladie de Simmonds et anorexie mentale. *Arch. méd. enf.,* 41:638.

Conrad, A. (1937), The Attitude toward Food. *Am. J. Orthopsychiat.,* 7:360.

Conrad, K. (1952), Die Gestaltanalyse in der Psychiatrie. *Stud. Generale,* 5:503.

―――― (1958), *Die beginnende Schizophrenie.* Stuttgart: Thieme.

—————(1959), Das Problem der "nosologischen Einheit" in der Psychiatrie. *Nervenarzt,* 30:488.

Conybeare, J. J. (1930), A Fatal Case of Anorexia Nervosa. *Guy's Hospital Report,* 80:30.

Courbon, P. and Rondepierre (1929), Anorexie émotionelle révélatrice de demande précoce en régression. *Bull. soc. méd. ment. Paris,* 17:12.

Courchet, J. L. (1947), Etude analytique d'un cas d'anorexie mentale grave. *Evolut. psychiat.,* 1:43-59.

Cremieux, A. (1942), *Les anorexies mentales.* Comptes-rendus de Congrès des Aliénistes et Neurologistes de langue française, Montpellier. Paris: Masson.

Cross, E. S. (1939), Diagnosis and Treatment of Anorexia Nervosa. *Clin. N. Amer.,* 23:541.

Curschmann, H. (1930), Über postpartuale Magersucht. *Monatschrift. Geburtsh, Gynäk.,* 86:252.

————— (1939), Über hypophysare Kachexie. *Munch. med. Wochenschr.* 86:317.

————— (1950), *Differentialdiagnose Innerer Krankheiten.* Berlin, Gottingen, Heidelberg: Springer.

Dally, P. I. and Sargant, W. (1960), A New Treatment of Anorexia Nervosa. *Brit. Med. J.,* 1:1770-1773.

Damm, G. and Zur Horst-Meyer, H. (1950), Über die Behandlung mit Hypophysentransplantation. *Dtsch. med. Wochenschr.,* 76:267.

Davis, H. P. (1939), Anorexia Nervosa. *Endocrinology,* 25:991.

Debre, R., Mozziconacci, P. and Doumic, A. (1950), Etude psychosomatique de l'anorexie nerveuse. *Sem. hôp. Paris,* 26:455.

Decourt, J. (1944), A propos des aménorrhées d'origine psychique—les aménorrhées pithiatiques, curables par la persuasion. *Presse méd.,* 52:116.

————— (1951), Nosologie de l'anorexie mentale. *Presse méd.,* 59:797.

————— (1953), Die Anorexia nervosa: Psycho-endokr. Kachexie der Reifungszeit. *Dtsch. med. Wochenschrift,* 78:1619-1661.

—————, Jayle, M. F., Lavergne, G. H., and Michard, J. P. (1950), L'aménorrhée des anorexies mentales: notions cliniques; étude biologique et biochemique. *Ann. endocrinol. Paris,* 11:571.

————— and Michard, J. (1949), Les rapports de l'anorexie mentale et de la maladie de Simmonds: aperçu historique et position actuelle du problème. *Sem. hôp. Paris,* 25:3343.

Déjérine, J. and Gauckler, E. (1911), *Les manifestations fonctionelles des psychonevroses, leur traitement par la psychothérapie.* Paris: Masson.

Delay, J. (1949), La narco-analyse d'une anorexie mentale. *Presse méd.,* 57:577.

Deniau, L. (1883), *De l'hystérie gastrique.* Thesis. Paris.

Donnadieu, M. J. A. (1932), *L'anorexie mentale.* Thesis. Bordeaux.

Dowse, T. S. (1881), Anorexia Nervosa. *Lancet,* 1:827.

Dubois, F. A. (1949), Compulsion Neurosis with Cachexia (Anorexia Nervosa). *Amer. J. Psychiat.,* 106:107.

Dubois, F. S. (1950), Anorexia Nervosa, A Re-evaluation of the Problem. *J. Insur. Med.,* 5:1.

Dubois, R. (1913), De l'anorexie mentale comme prodrome de le démence précoce. *Am. méd.-psychol.,* 10:431.

Dührssen, A. (1950-1951), Zum Problem der psychogenen Essstörung. *Psyche,* 4:56-720.

Dunn, C. W. (1937), Anorexia Nervosa. *Lancet,* 1:723.

Durand, C. (1955), Psychogénèse et traitement de l'anorexie mentale. *Helv. med. Acta,* 22:368.

Ebbecke, U. (1955), Hunger, Durst, Sättigung, Übelkeit, Ekel von der physischen und psychischen Seite betrachtet. *Acta neuroveg.,* 10:409.

Edge, A. M. (1888), A Case of Anorexia Nervosa. *Lancet,* 1:818.

Eiff, A. W. von (1957), *Grundumsatz und Psyche.* Berlin, Göttingen, Heidelberg: Springer.

Eissler, K. R. (1943), Some Psychiatric Aspects of Anorexia Nervosa. *Psychoanal. Rev.,* 30:121-145.

———— (1958), Notes on Problems of Technique in the Psychoanalytic Treatment of Adolescents: With Some Remarks on Perversions. *The Psychoanalytic Study of the Child,* 13:223-254. New York: International Universities Press.

———— (1959), On Isolation. *The Psychoanalytic Study of the Child,* 14:29-60. New York: International Universities Press.

Eitinger, L. (1951), Anorexia Nervosa. *Nord. Med.,* 45:915.

Elst, R. van der (1927), L'anorexie nerveuse. *Presse méd.,* 1:40.

Erhardt, K. and Kittel, C. (1937), Zur Behandlung hypophysärer Störungen durch Hypophysenimplantation. *Z. Klin. Med.,* 132:246.

Erikson, E. H. (1961), *Childhood and Society.* New York: Norton, 1950.

Escamilla, R. F. (1944), Anorexia Nervosa or Simmonds' Disease? *J. Nerv. Ment. Dis.,* 99:583.

———— and Lisser, H. (1942), Simmonds' Disease: A Clinical Study with Review of the Literature; Differentiation from Anorexia Nervosa by Statistical Analysis of 595 Cases, 101 of which were Proved Pathologically. *J. Clin. Endocrinol.,* 2:65.

Evans, J. C. G. (1939), Anorexia Nervosa. *Lancet,* 1:268.

Ewald, G. (1954), *Neurologie und Psychiatrie.* Munich and Berlin: Urban & Schwarzenberg.

Ey, H. (1952), Grundlagen einer organo-dynamischen Auffassung der Psychiatrie. *Fortschr. Neurol. Psychiat.,* 20:195.

Faber, K. (1926), Anorexia Nervosa. *Arch. Verdau. Kr.,* 37:17.

Falstein, E. I., Sherman, C., Feinstein, S. C., and Judas, I. (1956), Anorexia Nervosa in the Male Child. *Amer. J. Orthopsychiat.,* 26:751-772.

Falta, W. (1927), Die endogene Magerkeit. *Handbuch der Inneren Medizin,* 4:2. Berlin: Springer.

———— (1940), Hypophysäre Krankheitsbilder. *Wien. Arch. inn. Med.,* 33:277.

Farquharson, R. F. and Hyland, H. H. (1938), Anorexia Nervosa: A Metabolic Disorder of Psychological Origin. In: *Evolution of Psychosomatic Concepts,* ed. M. R. Kaufman and M. Heiman. New York: International Universities Press, 1964, pp. 202-226.

Federn. P. (1956), *Ichpsychologie und die Psychosen.* Bern: Huber.

Fenichel, O. (1945), Anorexia. *Collected Papers of O. Fenichel,* Vol. II. London: Routledge and Kegan Paul.

Ferenczi, S. (1924), Theory of Genitality. *Psychoanal. Quart.,* 2:361-403.

Feuchtinger, O. (1942a), Die diencephal-hypophysäre Fett- und Magersucht. *Dtsch. Arch. klin. Med.,* 180:377.

———— (1942b), Hypothalamus, vegetatives Nerven system und innere Sekretion. *Wein. Arch. inn. Med.,* 36:248.

———— (1943), Konträre und paradoxe Reaktionen als Folge diencephal-hypophysärer Regulations störungen. *Nervenarzt,* 16:428.

———— (1946), *Fettsucht und Magersucht.* Stuttgart: Enke.

Flugel, I. C. (1953), The Death-Instinct, Homeostasis, and Allied Concepts. *Internat. J. Psychoanal.,* Suppl.

Forchheimer, F. (1907), Anorexia Nervosa in Children. *Arch. Pediat.,* 24:801.

Franklin, J. C., Schiele, B. C., Brozek, J., and Keys, A. (1948), Observations of Human Behavior in Experimental Semistarvation and Rehabilitation. *J. Clin. Psychol.,* 4:28.

Freud, A. (1936), *The Ego and the Mechanisms of Defense.* New York: International Universities Press, 1946.

———— (1946), The Psychoanalytic Study of Infantile Feeding Disturbances. *The Psychoanalytic Study of the Child,* 2:119-132. New York: International Universities Press.

———— (1952), A Connection Between the States of Negativism and of Emotional Surrender. *Internat. J. Psychoanal.,* 33:265.

——— (1958), Adolescence. *The Psychoanalytic Study of the Child,* 13:255-278. New York: International Universities Press.

Freud, S. (1892-1893), A Case of Successful Treatment by Hypnotism with some Remarks on the Origin of Hysterical Symptoms through "Counterwill." *Collected Papers,* 5:33-46. London: Hogarth, 1950.

——— (1895), Studies on Hysteria. *Standard Edition,* 2:1-305. London: Hogarth, 1955.

——— (1887-1902), *The Origins of Psychoanalysis. Letters to Wilhelm Fliess, Drafts and Notes: 1887-1902.* New York: 1954.

——— (1900), The Interpretation of Dreams. *Standard Edition,* 4/5:xxxii + 1-621, 687-751. London: Hogarth, 1953.

——— (1905a), Fragment of an Analysis of a Case of Hysteria. *Standard Edition,* 7:7-122. London: Hogarth, 1953.

——— (1905b), Jokes and Their Relation to the Unconscious. *Standard Edition,* 8:9-238. London: Hogarth, 1960.

——— (1905c), On Psychotherapy. *Standard Edition,* 7:257-268. London: Hogarth, 1953.

——— (1905d), Three Essays on the Theory of Sexuality. *Standard Edition,* 7:125-245. London: Hogarth, 1953.

——— (1910a), Contributions to the Psychology of Love. *Standard Edition,* 11:163-208. London: Hogarth, 1957.

——— (1910b), Five Lectures on Psychoanalysis. *Standard Edition,* 11: 3-55. London: Hogarth, 1957.

——— (1910c), The Psychoanalytic View of Psychogenic Visual Disturbance. *Standard Edition,* 11:141-151. London: Hogarth, 1957.

——— (1911), Formulations on the Two Principles of Mental Functioning. *Standard Edition,* 12:218-226. London: Hogarth, 1958.

——— (1912a), Recommendations to Physicians Practicing Psychoanalysis. *Standard Edition,* 12:109-120. London: Hogarth, 1958.

——— (1912b), Types of Onset of Neurosis. *Standard Edition,* 12:229-238. London: Hogarth, 1958.

——— (1912-1913), Totem and Taboo. *Standard Edition,* 13:vii-xvi, 1-161. London: Hogarth, 1955.

——— (1914a), On the History of the Psycho-Analytic Movement. *Standard Edition,* 14:3-66. London: Hogarth, 1957.

——— (1914b), On Narcissism: An Introduction. *Standard Edition,* 14:73-102. London: Hogarth, 1957.

——— (1915a), Instincts and their Vicissitudes. *Standard Edition,* 14:117-140. London: Hogarth, 1957.

——— (1915b), Observations on Transference-Love. *Standard Edition,* 12:157-171. London: Hogarth, 1958.

———— (1915c), Repression. *Standard Edition,* 14:146-158. London: Hogarth, 1957.

———— (1915d), The Unconscious. *Standard Edition,* 14:159-215. London: Hogarth, 1957.

———— (1916-1917), A General Introduction to Psychoanalysis. *Standard Edition,* 15, 16. London: Hogarth, 1963.

———— (1917), Mourning and Melancholia. *Standard Edition,* 14:243-260. London: Hogarth, 1957.

———— (1919), Lines of Advance in Psycho-Analytic Therapy. *Standard Edition,* 17:159-168. London: Hogarth, 1955.

———— (1920), The Psychogenesis of a Case of Homosexuality in a Woman. *Standard Edition,* 18:147-172. London: Hogarth, 1955.

———— (1921), Group Psychology and the Analysis of the Ego. *Standard Edition,* 18:69-143. London: Hogarth, 1955.

———— (1922), Certain Neurotic Mechanisms in Jealousy, Paranoia and Homosexuality. *Standard Edition,* 18:223-232. London: Hogarth, 1955.

———— (1923), The Ego and the Id. *Standard Edition,* 19:12-66. London: Hogarth, 1961.

———— (1924), The Economic Problem of Masochism. *Standard Edition,* 19:159-170. London: Hogarth, 1961.

———— (1925a), An Autobiographical Study. *Standard Edition,* 20:7-76. London: Hogarth, 1959.

———— (1925b), Negation. *Standard Edition,* 19:235-239. London: Hogarth, 1961.

———— (1925c), Some Additional Notes upon Dream-Interpretation as a Whole. *Standard Edition,* 19:131-134. London: Hogarth, 1961.

———— (1926a), Inhibitions, Symptoms and Anxiety. *Standard Edition,* 20:77-175. London: Hogarth, 1959.

———— (1926b), Psycho-Analysis. *Standard Edition,* 20:259-270. London: Hogarth, 1959.

———— (1927), Fetishism. *Standard Edition,* 21:152-157. London: Hogarth, 1961.

———— (1930), Civilization and its Discontents. *Standard Edition,* 21:57-146. London: Hogarth, 1961.

———— (1933), New Introductory Lectures on Psycho-Analysis. *Standard Edition,* 22:3-182. London: Hogarth, 1964.

———— (1937), Analysis Terminable and Interminable. *Standard Edition,* 23:211-233. London: Hogarth, 1964.

———— (1940), An Outline of Psychoanalysis. *Standard Edition,* 23:141-207. London: Hogarth, 1964.

Fuchs, E. (1930), Verweigerte Nahrungsaufnahme. *Z. Psychanal. Pädiat.*, 4:128.

Gagel, O. (1941), Hypophysenzwischenhirn und Fettstoffwechsel. *Wien Arch. inn. Med.*, 39:217.

Galdston, I. (1956), Some Historic, Holistic, and Psychosomatic Implications in Tuberculosis. In: *Personality, Stress and Tuberculosis*, P. J. Sparer, ed. New York: International Universities Press.

Gallavan, M. and Steegman, A. T. (1937), Simmonds' Disease (Anterior Hypophyseal Insufficiency). Report of 2 Cases with Autopsy. *Arch. Intern. Med.*, 59:865.

Gebsattel, V. von (1947), *Christentum und Humanismus*. Stuttgart: Klett.

————(1954), *Prolegomena einer medizinischen Anthropologie*. Berlin: Springer.

————(1960), Medizinische Anthropologie. *Jahrbuch Psychol. Psychother. med. Anthropol.*, 7:193.

Geldrich, I. (1939), Simmondssche Krankheit im Kindesalter. *Monatschrift Kinderheilklinik*, 80:103.

Gennes, L. de (1936), Un cas de cachexie hypophysaire. *Presse méd.*, 44:1900.

Georgi, R. and Levi, R. (1951), Zur Pathophysiologie und Therapie der sogennanten Pubertätsmagersucht. *Nervenarzt*, 22:365.

Gero, G. (1943), The Idea of Psychogenesis in Modern Psychiatry and in Psychoanalysis. *Psychoanal. Rev.*, 30:187-211.

———— (1952-1953). Ein Äquivalent der Depression: Anorexie. *Psyche* (Stuttgart), 5:641-652.

Gilbert-Dreyfus and Mamou, H. (1947), Cachexie cerebro-hypophysaire d'origine fonctionelle et à évolution mortelle sans alterations histologiques à l'autopsie. *Ann. endocrinal*, 8:540.

Gilles de la Tourette, G. (1895), *Traité clinique et thérapeutique de l'hystérie*. Paris: Plon.

Gillespie, R. D. (1931), Treatment of Functional Anorexia. *Lancet*, 1:995.

Girou, J. (1905), Anorexie, suite d'arrêt voluntaire de l'alimentation. *Rev. neurol.*, 13:145.

Glatzel, H. (1954a), Ernährungskrankheitern. *Handbuch der Inneren Medizin*, 6:2. Berlin, Göttingen, Heidelberg: Springer.

———— (1954b), Ernährungs-therapie. *Handbuch der Inneren Medizin,* 6:2. Berlin, Göttingen, Heidelberg: Springer.

Glazebrook, A. J., Matas, J. and Prosen, H. (1956), Compulsive Neuroses with Cachexia. *Canad. Med. Ass. J.*, 75:40.

Glover, E. (1945), Examination of the Klein System of Child Psychology. *The Psychoanalytic Study of the Child,* 1:75-118. New York: International Universities Press.

———— (1956), *On the Early Development of Mind.* London: Imago.

Godard, P. (1937), Les diverses formes d'anorexie. *Schweiz. med. Wochenschrift,* 18:1233.

Goitein, P. L. (1942), The Potention Prostitute: Theory of Anorexia in the Defense against Prostitutional Desires. *J. Crim. Psychopath.,* 3:359.

Gottesfeld, B. H. and Novaes, A. C. (1945), Narcoanalysis and Subshock Insulin in Treatment of Anorexia Nervosa. *Dig. Neurol. Psychiat.,* 13:486.

Greenwald, H. M. (1928), Anorexia Nervosa. *Amer. Med.,* 34:875.

Grimshaw, L. (1959), Anorexia Nervosa: A Contribution to its Psychogenesis. *Brit. J. Med. Psychol.,* 32:44-49.

Grinker, R. R. (1953), The Problem of Specificity in the Psychosomatic Process. In: *The Psychosomatic Concept in Psychoanalysis,* ed. F. Deutsch. New York: International Universities Press, pp. 37-62.

Grote, L. R. and Meng, H. (1934), Über interne und psychotherapeutische Behandlung der endogenen Magersucht. *Schweiz. med. Wochenschrift,* 64:137.

Gull, W. W. (1868), The Address in Medicine. In: *Evolution of Psychosomatic Concepts,* ed. M. R. Kaufman and M. Heiman, New York: International Universities Press, 1964, pp. 104-131.

———— (1873a), Meeting of the Clinical Society. *Med. Times & Gaz.,* 2:534.

———— (1873b), Anorexia Nervosa (Apepsia Hysterica, Anorexia Hysterica). In: *Evolution of Psychosomatic Concepts,* ed. M. R. Kaufman and M. Heiman, New York: International Universities Press, 1964, pp. 132-138.

———— (1888), Anorexia Nervosa. In: *Evolution of Psychosomatic Concepts,* ed. M. R. Kaufman and M. Heiman. New York: International Universities Press, 1964, pp. 139-140.

Hagedorn, H. C. (1955), Anorexia Nervosa. *Acta med. scand.,* 151-201.

Haider, M. (1951), Psychische Energie und geistige Leistung. Versuch einer hirntheoretischen Energetik. *Stud. Generale,* 4:435.

Hamburger, W. W. (1958), The Occurrence and Meaning of Dreams of Food and Eating. *Psychosomat. Med.,* 20:1-16.

Hansen, O. E. (1956), Behandling af anorexia nervosa. *Ugeskr. Laeg.,* 118:1368.

Hartmann, H. (1944), The Psychiatric Work of Paul Schilder. *Psychoanal. Rev.,* 31:287-298.

—— (1950), Comments on the Psychoanalytic Theory of the Ego. *The Psychoanalytic Study of the Child,* 5:74-96. New York: International Universities Press.

—— and Kris, E. (1945), The Genetic Approach in Psychoanalysis. *The Psychoanalytic Study of the Child,* 1:11-30. New York: International Universities Press.

Heilmeyer, L. (1946), Hungerschäden. *Med. Klin.,* 41:243.

Heiman, M. (1956), The Relationship Between Man and Dog. *Psychoanal. Quart.,* 25:568-585.

Heni, F. (1951), Die primär psychogene Magersucht (auch Anorexia nervosa bzw. endokrine Magersucht genannt) und ihre Behandlung. *Endokrinologie,* 28:28.

Hermann, I. (1936), Sich-Anklammern—Auf-Suche-gehen. *Internat. Z. Psychoanal.,* 22:349-370.

Hermann, K. (1934), Neuere Erfahrungen mit der Simmondsschen Krankheit. *Münch. med. Wochenschrift,* 81:1460.

Hertz, H. (1952), Nervous Anorexia. *Acta med. scand.,* 266:523.

Hess, W. R. (1944-1946), Von den höheren Zentren des vegetativen Funktionssystems. *Bull. Schweiz. Akad. med. Wiss.,* 1:138.

Heydt-Gutscher, D. (1960), Psychotherapie einer Magersüchtigen. *Zeitschrift psychosom. Med.,* 6:77.

Hirschmann, I. (1954), Instinktmechanismen im menschlichen Nahrungsverhalten. *Stud. Generale,* 7:285.

Hoff, F. (1957), *Klinische Physiologie und Pathologie.* Stuttgart: Thieme.

Hoffer, W. (1949), Mouth, Hand and Ego-Integration. *The Psychoanalytic Study of the Child,* 3/4:49-56. New York: International Universities Press.

—— (1950), Development of the Body-Ego. *The Psychoanalytic Study of the Child,* 5:18-23. New York: International Universities Press.

—— (1951), Oral Aggressiveness and Ego Development. *The Yearbook of Psychoanalysis,* 7:123-131. New York: International Universities Press.

Hosemann, M. (1946), Die Behandlung der Amenorrhoe. *Ärztl. Wochenschrift,* 1:19.

Hotop, H. (1934), Verhandlungsbericht der medizinisch naturwissenschaftlichen Gesellschaft Münster i. W. *Dtsch. med. Wochenschrift,* 60:1153.

Huchard, see Axenfeld, A.

Huebschmann, H. (1959), Über phagisches Verhalten. *Nervenarzt,* 30:494.

Hurst, A. (1939), Discussion. *Proc. Royal Soc. Med.,* 32:744.

Israel, S. (1959), The Onset of Menstruation in Indian Women. *J. Obstet. Gynaec. Brit. Emp.*, 66:311.

Janet, P. (1908), *Les obsessions et la psychasthénie.* Paris: Alcan.

Janowitz, H. D. and Grossmann, M. E. (1949), Hunger and Appetite: Some Definitions and Concepts. *J. Mt. Sinai Hosp.*, 16:231.

Jaspers, K. (1910), Eifersuchtswahn. Ein Beitrag zur Frage: Entwicklung einer Persönlichkeit oder Prozess? *Z. ges. Neurol. Psychiat.*, 1:567.

———— (1948), *General Psychopathology.* New York: Manchester University Press, 1963.

Jessner, L. and Abse, D. W. (1960), Regressive Forces in Anorexia Nervosa. *Brit. J. Med. Psychol.*, 33:301.

Jores, A. (1955), Krankheiten der Hypophyse und des Hypophysenzwischenhirnsystems. *Handbuch der Inneren Medizin*, 7:1. Berlin, Göttingen, Heidelberg: Springer.

Jost, F. (1961), Die Anorexia nervosa—ein funktionelles Pubertätssyndrom der Frau. *Med. Welt*, 1:1202, 1254.

Kafka, F. (1952), The Judgment. *Selected Short Stories.* New York: Modern Library.

Kalk, H. (1934), Zur Frage der Beziehung zwischen Hypophysenvorderlappen und Nebennierenrinde. *Dtsch. med. Wochenschrift*, 60:893.

Katz, D. (1932), *Hunger und Appetit.* Leipzig: Barth.

———— (1935), Zur Grundlegung einer Bedürfnispsychologie. *Acta Psychol.*, 1:122.

Katzenstein-Sutro, E. (1953), Über einen Fall von Pubertätsmagersucht. *Schweiz. med. Wochenschrift*, 83:1526.

Kay, D. W. K. (1953), Anorexia Nervosa; A Study in Prognosis. *Proc. Royal Soc. Med.*, 46:3.

———— and Leigh, D. (1954), Natural History, Therapy and Prognosis of Anorexia Nervosa, Based on a Study of 38 Patients. *J. Ment. Sci.*, 100:411.

Kelley, K., Daniels, G. E., Poe, J., Easser, R., and Monroe, R. (1954), Psychological Correlations with Secondary Amenorrhea. *Psychosom. Med.*, 16:129.

Kissel, A. (1896), Ein Fall einer schweren hysterischen Anorexie (Anorexia Nervosa) bei einem 11-Jährigen Mädchen. *Arch. Kinderheilklinik*, 20:382.

Klein, M. (1934), A Contribution to the Psychogenesis of Manic-Depressive States. *Contributions to Psychoanalysis 1921-1945.* London: Hogarth, 1950.

———(1940), Mourning and its Relation to Manic-Depressive States. *Contributions to Psychoanalysis 1921-1945.* London: Hogarth, 1950.

Klinefelter, H. F., Albright, F., and Griswold, G. C. (1943), Experience with a Quantitative Test for Normal or Decreased Amounts of Follicle Stimulating Hormone in the Urine in Endocrinological Diagnosis. *J. Clin. Endocrinol.,* 3:529.

Knipping, H. W. (1935), Über die Entstehung der Magersucht *Dtsch. med. Wochenschrift,* 61:1075.

Köhler, A. (1957), Psychische Faktoren bei Gewichtsverschiebungen. *Z. psychosom. Med.,* 3:109.

Kolle, K. (1955), *Psychiatrie.* Munich and Berlin: Urban & Schwarzenberg.

Koller, T. (1954), Pubertätsmagersucht. *Geburtsh. u. Frauenheilk.,* 14:668.

Korbsch, R. (1934), Zum Krankheitsbild der Magenschleimhautatrophie. *Dtsch. med. Wochenschrift,* 60:356.

——— (1936), Die Magersucht im Gefolge der akuten Magenschleimhautatrophie junger Mädchen als eigenes Krankheitsbild. *Dtsch. med. Wochenschrift,* 62:1948.

Krauel, G. (1942), Zur Behandlung der Simmondsschen Kachexie mit Transplantation von Kalbshypophysen. *Med. Welt,* 16:999.

Krause, F. and Müller, O. H. (1937), Über schwere Hypophysenvorderlappen-Insuffizienz und ihre Behandlung. *Klin. Wochenschrift,* 16:118.

Kretschmer, E. (1958), *Hysterie, Reflex und Instinkt.* Stuttgart: Thieme.

Kris, E. (1950), Introduction to: S. Freud, *Aus den Anfängen der Psychoanalyse.* London: Imago.

Kubie, L. S. (1953), The Central Representation of the Symbolic Process in Psychosomatic Disorders. *Psychosom. Med.,* 15:1-7.

Kuhn, R. (1953), Zur Daseinsanalyse der Anorexia mentalis. *Nervenarzt,* 22:11, 24:191.

Kunstadter, R. H. (1938), Pituitary Emaciation (von Bergmann). *Endocrinology,* 22:605.

Kunz, H. (1942), Zur Theorie der Perversion. *Mschr. Psychiat. Neurol.,* 105:1-104.

——— (1946a), *Die Aggressivität und die Zärtlichkeit.* Bern: Francke.

——— (1946b), *Die anthropologische Bedeutung der Phantasie,* Vols. I and II. Basel: Recht und Wissenschaft.

——— (1949), Die Bedeutung der Daseinsanalytik Martin Heideggers für die Psychologie und philosophische Anthropologie. *Martin Heideggers Einfluss auf die Wissenschaft.* Bern: Francke.

—— (1951-1952), Das Problem des Geistes in der Tiefenpsychologie. *Psyche*, 5:241-269.

Kütemeyer, W. (1956), Anthropologische Medizin in der Inneren Klinik. *Der Arzt im Irrsal der Zeit*. Göttingen: Vandenhoeck & Ruprecht.

—— (1959), Medizin in Bewegung. *Medicus Viator*. Stuttgart: Thieme.

Kylin, E. (1935), Die Simmondssche Krankheit. *Ergn. inn. Med.*, 49:1.

—— (1937), Magersucht in der weiblichen Spätpubertät. *Dtsch. Arch. Klin. Med.*, 115:180.

—— (1943), *Die Klinik der hypophysären Erkrankungen*. Leipzig: Barth.

Laboucarié, J. and Barres, P. (1954), Les Aspects cliniques, pathogéniques et thérapeutiques de l'anorexie mentale. *Évolut. psychiat.*, 1:119.

Labré, P. L. A. (1952), L'anorexie mentale. Données récentes sur sa pathogénie. *Acta neurol. belg.*, 52:164.

Lafora, G. R. (1927), La anorexia psicogenética de las mujeres adolescentes. *Arch. Neurobiol.*, 7:121.

Landgrebe, L. (1956), Seinsregionen und regionale Ontologien in Husserls Phänomenologie. *Stud. Generale*, 9:313.

Langdon-Brown, W. (1937), Anorexia Nervosa. *Lancet*, 1:473.

Lasègue, E. C. (1873), On Hysterical Anorexia. In: *Evolution of Psychosomatic Concepts*, ed. M. R. Kaufman and M. Heiman. New York: International Universities Press, 1964, pp. 141-155.

Lehmann, E. (1949), Feeding Problems of Psychogenic Origin: A Survey of the Literature. *The Psychoanalytic Study of the Child*, 3/4:461-488. New York: International Universities Press.

Leibbrand, W. (1939), *Der göttliche Stab des Aeskulap*. Salzburg and Leipzig: Otto Müller.

Leichtentritt, B. (1932), Pubertätsneurose, Hungerzustand und Niereninsuffizienz. *Med. Klin.*, 11:355.

Leonhard, C. E. (1944), Analysis of a Case of Functional Vomiting and Bulimia. *Psychoanal., Rev.*, 31:1.

Lesser, L. C. et al (1960), Anorexia Nervosa in Children. *Amer. J. Orthopsychiat.*, 30:572-580.

Lewin, B. D. (1951), *The Psychoanalysis of Elation*. London: Hogarth.

Lidz, T. et al. (1959-1960), The Family Environment of Schizophrenic Patients. *Amer. J. Psychiat.*, 106:332-345.

Linn, L. (1958), Psychoanalytic Contribution to Psychosomatic Research. *Psychosom. Med.*, 20:88-98.

Loch, W. (1959-1960), Begriff und Funktion der Angst in der Psychoanalyse. *Psyche* (Heidelberg), 8:801-816.

Loeper, M. and Fau, R. (1936), Cachexie hypophysaire et anorexie mentale. *Monde méd.,* 46:921.

Löffler, W. (1955), Die Anorexia nervosa. *Helv. med. acta,* 22:351-367.

Loo, P. (1958), L'anorexie mentale. *Ann. méd. psychol.,* 116:734-750.

Lorand, S. (1943), Anorexia Nervosa: Report of a Case. *Psychosomat. Med.,* 5:282-292.

Lövey, E. and Bona, E. (1947), Anorexia nervosa. *Z. ges. inn. Med.,* 12:749-753.

Low, M. B. (1936), Anorexia in Children. *N. E. J. Med.,* 214:834.

Löwith, K. (1960), *Heidegger, Denker in dürftiger Zeit.* Göttingen: Vandenhoeck & Ruprecht.

Lublin, A. (1929), Lipogene und antilipogene Hormonwirkungen als Ursache endogener Fettsucht und Magersucht. *Klin. Wochenscrift,* 2276.

Lucke, H. (1932), Hypophysäre Magersucht und Insulin. *Klin. Wochenschrift,* 1988.

Lukas, H. (1956), Therapie einer Magersüchtigen. *Z. Psychother. med. Psychol.,* 6:159-173.

Lurie, O. R. (1941), Psychological Factors Associated with Eating Difficulties in Children. *Amer. J. Orthopsychiat.,* 11:452-466.

Lutz, J. (1947-1948), Kombination einer Neurose bei Pubertätsmagersucht mit katatönieartigem Zustandsbild. *Z. Kinderpsychiat.,* 14:68.

Mach, R. S. and Durand, C. (1952), Anorexie mentale, troubles digestifs et ACTH. *Praxis,* 41:1038.

Mackenzie, S. (1888), On a Case of Anorexia Nervosa vel Hysterica. *Lancet,* 1:613-614.

Magendantz, H. and Proger, S. (1940), Anorexia Nervosa or Hypopituitarism? *J.A.M.A.,* 114:1973-1983.

Mahler, M. (1952), On Child Psychosis and Schizophrenia: Autistic and Symbiotic Psychosis. *The Psychoanalytic Study of the Child,* 7:286 305. New York: International Universities Press.

Margolin, S. G. (1953), Genetic and Dynamic Psychophysiological Determinants of Pathophysiological Processes. In: *The Psychosomatic Concept in Psychoanalysis,* ed. F. Deutsch. New York: International Universities Press, pp. 3-36.

Margolis, P. M. and Jernberg (1960), Analytic Therapy in a Case of Extreme Anorexia. *Brit. J. Med. Psychol.,* 33:291.

Marshall, C. F. (1895), A Fatal Case of Anorexia Nervosa. *Lancet,* 1:149-150.

Martini, P. (1953), *Methodenlehre der therapeutisch-klinischen Forschung.* Berlin, Göttingen, Heidelberg: Springer.

Martius, H. (1946), Fluchtamenorrhoe. *Dtsch. med. Wochenschrift,* 71:81.

Marx, H. (1941), Die hypophysäre Kachexie (Morbus Simmonds). *Handbuch der Inneren Medizin,* 6:1. Berlin, Göttingen, Heidelberg: Springer.

Massermann, J. H. (1941), Psychodynamism in Anorexia Nervosa and Neurotic Vomiting. *Psychoanal. Quart.,* 10:211-242.

Mayer, A. (1957), Zur Psychologie der weiblichen Pubertätsmagersucht —die Pubertätsmagersucht als "Schicksalskrankheit." *Med. Klin.,* 52:2185.

Mayer-Gross, W., Slater, E., and Roth, M. (1954), *Clinical Psychiatry.* London: Cassell.

McCullagh, E. P. and Tupper, W. R. (1940), Anorexia Nervosa. *Ann. Intern. Med.,* 14:817-838.

Meierhofer, M. (1963), Die Mutter-Kind Beziehung bei einem Fall von Anorexia Nervosa. *Schweiz. med. Zeitschrift,* 93:71.

Mendelson, M., Hirsch, S., and Webber, C. S. (1956), A Critical Examination of Some Recent Theoretical Models in Psychosomatic Medicine. *Psychosom. Med.,* 18:363-373.

Meng, H. (1934), Das Problem der Organ-Psychose. *Internat. Z. ärztl. Psychoanal.,* 20:439-458.

——— (1935), Organische Erkrankung als Organ-Psychose. *Schweiz. Arch. Neurol. Psychiat.,* 26:271-283.

Menze, W. (1947), Über der Einfluss des Hungerns auf die Keimdrüsen. *Endokrinologie,* 24:159.

Meyer, B. C. and Weinroth, L. A. (1957), Observations on Psychological Aspects of Anorexia Nervosa. *Psychosom. Med.,* 19:389-398.

Meyer, H. H. (1938), Über Magersucht. *Dtsch. med. Wochenschrift,* 64:1400.

Meyer, J. E. (1961), Das Syndrom der Anorexia nervosa; Katamnestische Untersuchungen. *Arch. Psychol. u. Z. ges. Neurol.,* 202:31.

Meyer, W. C. (1938), Untersuchungen und Beobachtungen an Fällen von hypophysärer Magersucht (Simmonds) und deren Behandlung, insbesondere durch Hypophysenimplantation. *Dtsch. Arch. klin. Med.,* 182:351.

Meyler, L. (1938), Simmonds' Disease (Hypophysary Emaciation). *Acta med. scand.,* 96:157.

Michel-Hutmacher, R. (1955), Das Körperinnere in der Vorstellung der Kinder. *Schweiz. Z. Psychol.,* 14:1.

Milner, M. (1944), A Suicidal Symptom in a Child of Three. *Internat. J. Psychoanal.,* 25:53-61.

Mitscherlich, A. (1947), *Vom Ursprung der Sucht.* Stuttgart: Klett.

———— (1949-1950), Über die Reichweite psychosomatischen Denkens in der Medizin. *Psyche.*, 3:342-358.

———— (1957), Pubertät und Tradition. *Verhandl. des 13. Deutschen Soziologentages.* Cologne and Opladen: Westdeutscher Verlag, p. 65

———— (1958-1959), Rationale Therapie und Psychotherapie. *Psyche,* 12:721-731.

Mollaret, P. and Péron, N. (1938), Anorexie mentale à forme grave. Nécessité vitale de la cure d'alimentation. *Bull. Soc. méd. hôp. Paris,* 62:1716.

Möller, E. (1924), Quantitative Verhältnisse des Stoffwechsels bei Unterernährung, illustriert durch 4 Fälle von nervöser Anorexie. *Klin. Wochenschrift,* 3:1575.

Moore, B. E., Friedman, S., Simon, B., and Former, J. (1948), *The Frontal Lobes.* Baltimore: Williams & Wilkins.

Morton, R. (1689), *Phthisiologia seu exercitationum de phthisi.* Ulmae: Daniel Bartholomae, 1714.

Moulton, R. (1942), A Psychosomatic Study of Anorexia Nervosa, Including the Use of Vaginal Smears. *Psychosom. Med.,* 4:62-74.

Mühle, G. W. (1956), Rückgriff und Regression. Ein Beitrag zur Psychologie der Gestaltung. *Stud. Generale,* 9:561.

Müller, H. (1956), Die Pubertätsmagersucht der jungen Mädchen. *Med. Klin.,* Berlin, 51:209-212.

Müller, H. A. (1948), Menarche und Menstruationscyklus. *Klin. Wochenschrift,* 26:621.

Müller-Braunschweig, C. (1936), Die erste Objektbesetzung des Mädchens in ihrer Bedeutung für Penisneid und Weiblichkeit. *Internat. Z. ärtzl. Psychoanal.,* 22:137-176.

Musso, E., Borth, H., and Mach, R. S. (1952), Étude des effets biochemiques et cliniques d'une nouvelle préparation d'hormone adrénocorticotrope (ACTH). *Schweiz. med. Wochenschrift,* 82:642.

Naudeau (1789), Observation sur une maladie nerveuse accompagnée d'un degout extraordinaire pour les aliments. *J. Méd. Chir. Pharmacol.,* 8:197.

Nemiah, J. C. (1950), Anorexia Nervosa: A Clinical Psychiatric Study. *Medicine,* 29:225-268.

———— (1958), Anorexia Nervosa: Fact and Theory. *Amer. J. Digest. Dis.,* 3:249-274.

Neyroud, M. (1954), L'anorexie de l'enfant et la médicine psychosomatique. *Praxis,* 43:47.

Nicolaeff, L. (1923), L'influence de l'inanition sur la morphologie des organes infantiles. *Presses méd.,* 31:1007.

Nicolle, G. (1938a), Pre-psychotic Anorexia. *Lancet,* 2:1173.

—— (1938b), Pre-psychotic Anorexia. *Proc. Boy. Soc. Med.*, 32:153-162.

Nonnenbruch, W. and Feuchtinger, O. (1942), Über den Wechsel von Fett- und Magersucht als Ausdruck diencephal-hypophysärer Regulations-törungen. *Dtsch. med. Wochenschrift*, 68:1045.

Oberdisse, K. (1959), Die Fettsucht und die Magersucht. *Med. Kongressbericht*, 1835.

Odlum, D. (1938), Discussion. *Lancet*, 2:1173.

Oehme, C. (1944), Lokalisationsprizip und Funktionsanalyse im vegetativen Gebiet. *Dtsch. med. Wochenschrift*, 70:263.

Osgood, E. E. (1938), Pituitary Cachexia? *Endocrinology*, 23:656.

Palmer, G. B. (1951), Three Cases of So Called Anorexia Nervosa. *N. Z. Med. J.*, 50:57.

Palmer, H. A. (1931), Beriberi Complicating Anorexia Nervosa. *Lancet*, 1:269.

Palmer, H. D. and Jones, M. S. (1939), Anorexia Nervosa as a Manifestation of Compulsive Neuroses. *Arch. Neurol. Psychiat.*, 41:856.

Palmer, J. O., Mensh, I. N., and Matarazzo, J. S. (1952), Anorexia Nervosa: Case History and Psychological Examination Data with Implications for Test Validity. *J. Clin. Psychol.*, 8:168-173.

Pardee, I. H. (1939), "Cachexia Nervosa," a Psychoneurotic Simmonds' Syndrome. *Arch. Neurol. Psychiat.*, 41:841.

—— (1941), Cachexia (Anorexia) Nervosa. *Med. Clin. N. Amer.*, 25:755-773.

Peltz, H. D. (1956), Kritisches zur Pubertätsmagersucht. *Ärztliche Wochenschrift*, 11:781.

Perloff, W. H., Lasche, E. M., Nodine, I. H., Schneeberg, N. G., and Vieillard, C. B. (1954), The Starvation State and Functional Hypopituitarism. *J.A.M.A.*, 155:1307.

Péron, N. (1938), Défense de l'anorexie mentale. *Paris méd.*, 2:65.

Pfister, O. (1952-1953), Karl Jaspers als Sigmund Freuds Widersacher. *Psyche*, 6:241-275.

Plügge, H. (1950-1951), Die Wirkung des Nichts. *Psyche*, 4:321-334.

Porot, M. (1947), Le test de Rorschach dans l'anorexie mentale. *Algérie méd.*, 50:60.

Querido, A. (1948), De pathophysiologie van anorexia nervosa. *Nederl. tschr. Geneesk.*, 92:660-663.

Rado, S. (1926), The Psychic Effects of Intoxication; Attempt at a Psychoanalytic Theory of Drug Addiction. *Internat. J. Psychoanal.*, 7:396-413.

Rahman, L., Richardson, H. B., and Ripley, H. S. (1939), Anorexia Nervosa with Psychiatric Observations. *Psychosom. Med.*, 1:335-365.

Rangell, L. (1959), The Nature of Conversion. *J. Amer. Psychoanal. Assn.*, 7:632-662.

Rank, B., Putnam, M. C., and Rochlin, G. (1948), The Significance of the "Emotional Climate" in Early Feeding Difficulties. *Psychosom. Med.*, 10:279-283.

Rapaport, D. (1960), The Structure of Psychoanalytic Theory: A Systematizing Attempt. *Psychol. Issues*, Monogr. 6. New York: International Universities Press.

———— and Gill, M. M. (1959), The Points of View and Assumptions of Metapsychology. *Internat. J. Psychoanal.*, 40:153-162.

Redlich, F. C. (1952), The Concept of Schizophrenia and Its Implication for Therapy. *Psychotherapy with Schizophrenics*. New York: International Universities Press.

Régis (1896), Discussion. *Proc. Cong. de med. Alienistes et Neurol. France*, 2:360.

Reifenstein, E. C. (1946), Psychogenic or "Hypothalamic" Amenorrhea. *Med. Clin. N. Amer.*, 30:1103.

Reiss, M. (1943), Unusual Pituitary Activity in a Case of Anorexia Nervosa. *J. Ment. Sci.*, 89:270-273.

Reye, E. (1926), Das klinische Bild der Simmondsschen Krankheit (Hypophysäre Kachexie) in ihrem Anfangsstadium und ihre Behandlung. *Münch. med. Wochenschrift*, 73:902.

———— (1928), Die ersten klinischen Symptome bei Schwund des Hypophysenvorderlappens (Simmondssche Krankheit) und ihre erfolgreiche Behandlung. *Dtsch. med. Wochenschrift*, 54:696.

Richardson, H. B. (1939), Simmonds' Disease and Anorexia Nervosa. *Arch. Intern. Med.*, 63:1-28.

Richter, H. E. (1957-1958), Über Formen der Regression. *Psyche*, 11:275-285.

Roch, M. and Monnier, M. (1941), Anorexia mentalis und Simmondssche Krankheit. *Schweiz. med. Wochenschrift*, 71:1009.

Roffenstein, G. (1923), *Das Problem des Unbewussten*. Vienna: Püttmann.

Rolland, C. F. (1953), Anorexia Nervosa. *Proc. Nutr. Soc.*, 12:153.

Rose, J. A. (1943), Eating Inhibitions in Children in Relation to Anorexia Nervosa. *Psychosom. Med.*, 5:117-124.

Ross, C. W. (1938), Anorexia Nervosa with Special Reference to the Carbohydrate Metabolism. *Lancet*, 1:1041-1045.

Rossier, P. H., Staehelin, D., Bühlmann, A., and Labhard, A. (1955), Alkalose und Hypokal: ämie bei Anorexia nervosa ("Hunger-Alkalose"). *Schweiz. med. Wochenschrift*, 85:465-468.

Rüegg, M. (1950), Zum psychischen Bild der Pubertätsmagersucht. Discussion. Zurich.

Ruffin, H. (1953-1954), Die Leistung Sigmund Freuds für die Psychopathologie. *Freiburger Dies Universitatis*, Vol. II. Freiburg: Schulz.

Ruffler, G. (1953-1954), Grundsätzliches zur psychoanalytischen Behandlung körperlich Kranker. *Psyche*, 7:521-560.

Ryle, J. A. (1936), Anorexia Nervosa. *Lancet*, 2:893-899.

—— (1939), Discussion on Anorexia Nervosa. *Proc. Royal Soc. Med.*, 32:735-746.

Sanford, R. N. (1936), The effect of Abstinence from Food upon Imaginal Processes: A Preliminary Experiment. *J. Psychol.*, 2:129.

Sargant, W. (1951), Leucotomy in Psychosomatic Disorders. *Lancet*, 2:893.

Sartre, J. P. (1938) *Nausea*. New York: New Directions.

Saurer, A. (1942), Zur hormonalen Behandlung der Magersucht. *Schweiz. med. Wochenschrift*, 72:281.

Schaefer, H. (1955), Vom Speisen. *Die Grundlagen unserer Ernährung*. Stuttgart: Kröner.

—— (1957), Einige Probleme der Kreislaufregelung in Hinsicht auf ihre klinische Bedeutung. *Münch. med. Wochenschrift*, 99:69.

Schaffer, D. and Keiser, S. (1949), Undisguised Oral Mechanisms. *Psychoanal. Rev.*, 36:370-375.

Scheler, M. (1957), *Gesammelte Werke*, Vol. X. Bern: Francke.

Scheulen, C. (1931), Menstruationsängste. *Zeitschrift psychoanal. Päd.*, 5:223-225.

Scheunert, G. (1959-1960), Zum Problem der Gegenübertragung. *Psyche*, 13:574.

Schiele, B. C. and Brozek, J. (1948), "Experimental Neuroses" Resulting from Semistarvation in Man. *Psychosom. Med.*, 10:33.

Schilder, P. (1923), *Das Körperschema*. Berlin: Springer.

—— and Wechsler, D. (1935), What do Children Know about the Interior of the Body. *Internat. J. Psychoanal.*, 16:355-360.

Schilling, F. (1948), Selbstbeobachtungen im Hungerzustand, *Beiträge aus der allgemeinen Medizin*, Vol. VI. Stuttgart: Enke.

Schmideberg, M. (1933), Psychoneuroses of Childhood: Their Etiology and Treatment. *Brit. J. Med. Psychol.*, 13:313-327.

Schmied, M. (1936), Ess-störung und Verstimmung vor dem 3. Lebensjahr. *Zeitschrift Psychoanal. Päd.*, 10:241-250.

Schneider, K. (1949), Notiz über Ichstörungen und entfremdungen. *Fortschr. Neurol. Psychiat.*, 17:343-347.

Schneider, R. (1947), Störungen der Ernährungstriebe. *Schweiz. Arch. Neurol. Psychiat.*, 58:315.

Schnyder, L. (1913), Anorexie-Formen des Pubertätsalters. *Korrespond. Blatt der Schweiz. Ärzte, 43.*

Schottky, J. (1932), Über ungewöhnliche Triebhandlungen bei prozessafter Enwicklungsstörung. *Z. ges. Neurol. Psychiat.,* 143:38.

Schreier, K. (1959), Adipositas im Kindesalter. *Dtsch. med. Wochenschrift,* 84:1297.

Schultz-Hencke, H. (1951), *Lehrbuch der analytischen Psychotherapie.* Stuttgart: Thieme.

——— (1952), *Das Problem der Schizophrenie.* Stuttgart: Thieme.

Schüpbach, A. (1936), Zur Hormonbehandlung der Simmondsschen Krankheit und verwandter asthenischer Zustände. *Schweiz. med. Wochenschrift,* 17:1245.

——— (1951), Postpartuales Myödem und Simmondssche Krankheit. *Schweiz. med. Wochenschrift,* 81:610.

Schur, M. and Medvei, C. V. (1937), Über Hypophysenvorderlappeninsuffizienz. *Wien. Arch. inn. Med.,* 31:67.

Scott, W. C. M. (1947-1948), Notes on the Psychopathology of Mental Anorexia Nervosa. *Brit. J. Med. Psychol.,* 21:241-247.

Scouras, P. (1950), Anorexie mentale d'origine complexuelle. Action combinée de l'électrochoc et de la narcoanalyse. *Encéphale,* 39:545.

Searles, H. F. (1955), Dependency Processes in the Psychotherapy of Schizophrenia. *Collected Papers on Schizophrenia and Related Subjects.* New York: International Universities Press, 1965, pp. 114-156.

Seeman, W. F. (1950-1951), Über Hungerreaktionen von Kriegsgefangenen. *Psyche,* 4:107.

Selling, L. S. and Ferraro, M. A. (1945), *The Psychology of Diet and Nutrition.* New York: Norton.

Selye, H. (1947), *Textbook of Endocrinology.* Montreal: Acta.

Sewell, W. H. and Mussen, P. H. (1952), The Effects of Feeding, Weaning and Scheduling Procedures on Childhood Adjustment and the Formation of Oral Symptoms. *Child Devel.,* 23:185-191.

Sexton, D. L. (1950), The Diagnosis and Treatment of Anorexia Nervosa. *Ann. West. Med. Surg.,* 4:397-401.

Sheehan, H. L. (1937), Postpartum Necrosis of Anterior Pituitary. *J. Path. Bact.,* 45:189.

——— (1939), Simmonds' Disease Due to Postpartum Necrosis of Anterior Pituitary. *Quart. J. Med.,* 8:277.

——— and Summers, V. K. (1949), The Syndrome of Hypopituitarism. *Quart. J. Med.,* 18:319.

Sheldon, J. H. (1937), Anorexia Nervosa with Special Reference to Physical Constitution. *Lancet,* 1:369.

———— (1939), Discussion on Anorexia Nervosa. *Proc. Roy. Soc. Med.,* 32:735.

———— and Young, F. (1938), On the Carbohydrate Metabolism in Anorexia Nervosa. *Lancet,* 1:257.

Sherman, I. C. and Sherman, M. (1929), Birth Phantasy in a Young Child. *Psychoanal. Rev.,* 16:408-419.

Siebeck, R. (1942), In: *Lehrbuch der Inneren Medizin,* Vol. I, ed. G. von Bergmann. Berlin: Springer.

———— (1944), Vegetatives System und Stammhirn. *Dtsch. med. Wochenschrift,* 70:543.

———— (1949), *Medizin in Bewegung.* Stuttgart: Thieme.

Siebenmann, R. E. (1955a), Über eine tödlich verlaufende Anorexia Nervosa mit Hypokaliämie. *Schweiz. med. Wochenschrift,* 85:468-471.

———— (1955b), Zur pathologischen Anatomie der Anorexia nervosa. *Schweiz. med. Wochenschrift,* 85:530-537.

Sifneos, P. E. (1952), A Case of Anorexia Nervosa Treated Successfully by Leucotomy. *Amer. J. Psychiat.,* 109:356-360.

Silver, S. (1933), Simmonds' Disease (Cachexia Hypophyseopriva). Report of a Case with Postmortem Observations and Review of Literature. *Arch. Intern. Med.,* 51:175.

Simmonds, M. (1914), Über Hypophysisschwund mit tödlichem Ausgang. *Dtsch. med. Wochenschrift,* 40:322.

———— (1916), Über Kachexie hypophysären Ursprungs. *Dtsch. med. Wochenschrift,* 42:190.

Small, S. M. and Milhorat, A. T. (1944), Anorexia Nervosa: Metabolism and its Relation to Psychopathologic Reactions. *Amer. J. Psychiat.,* 100:681-685.

Smirnoff, V. N. (1958-1959), Kritische Bemerkungen zum Problem der Anorexia mentalis. *Psyche* (Heidelberg), 12:430-446.

Smith, J. W. (1946), Anorexia Nervosa Complicated by Beriberi. *Acta psychiat. neurol.,* 21:887-900.

Sollier, P. (1891), Anorexie hystérique (sitieirgie hystérique). *Rev. Med.,* 11:625.

Soltmann, O. (1894), Anorexia cerebralis und centrale Nutritionsneurose. *Jahrbuch Kinderheilklinik,* 38:1.

Sommer, B. (1955), Übertragungsprobleme in der Behandlung der Pubertätsmagersucht. *Acta psychother.,* 3:383.

———— (1955-1956), Die Pubertätsmagersucht als leib-seelische Störung einer Reifungskrise. *Psyche* (Stuttgart), 9:307-327.

Souques, A. (1925), Une cause provocatrice de l'anorexie mentale des jeunes filles. *Rev. neurol.,* 2:562.

Speer, E. (1958), Magersucht und Schizophrenie. *Meterdimensionaler Diagnostik und Therapie, Festschrift zum 70. Geburtstag von E. Kretschmer.* Stuttgart: Thieme, pp. 194-197.

Spehlmann, R. (1953), *Sigmund Freuds neurologische Schriften.* Berlin, Göttingen, Heidelberg: Springer.

Spiegel, L. A. (1951), A Review of Contributions to a Psychoanalytic Theory of Adolescence: Individual Aspects. *The Psychoanalytic Study of the Child,* 6:375-394. New York: International Universities Press.

Spitz, R. (1959), *No and Yes.* New York: International Universities Press.

Staehelin, J. E. (1943), Über präschizophrene Somatosen. *Schweiz. med. Wochenschrift,* 73:1213.

Stäubli-Frölich, M. (1953), Probleme der Anorexia Nervosa. *Schweiz. med. Wochenschrift,* 83:811-817, 837-841.

Stengel, E. (1954), A Re-evaluation of Freud's Book "On Aphasia." Its significance for Psychoanalysis. *Internat. J. Psychoanal.,* 35:85-89.

Stephens, D. J. (1941), Anorexia Nervosa: Endocrine Factors in Undernutrition. *J. Clin. Endocrinol.,* 1:257.

Stephens, L. (1895), Case of Anorexia Nervosa. *Lancet,* 1:31.

Stieve, H. (1940), Nervös bedingte Veränderungen an den Geschlechtsorganen. *Dtsch. med. Wochenschrift,* 66:925.

Stoerr, E. E. (1932), *L'anorexie mentale.* Thesis. Strasbourg.

Stokvis, B. (1944), Organneurosen und Organpsychosen. *Schweiz. med. Wochenschrift,* 74:943.

—— (1952), Die "Organpsychose" (Meng) in ihrer Bedeutung für die psychosomatische Medizin. *Psyche,* 6:228-240.

Stroebe, F. (1936), Die Simmondssche Krankheit. *Med. Klin.,* 32:859.

——(1938), Zum Problem der endogenen Magersucht. *Zbl. inn. Med.,* 59:97.

Stunkard, A. (1959), Obesity and the Denial of Hunger. *Psychosom. Med.,* 21:281-290.

Sydenham, A. (1946), Amenorrhea at Stanley Camp, Hong Kong, During Internment. *Brit. Med. J.,* 2:159.

Sylvester, E. (1945), Analysis of Psychogenic Anorexia in a Four-Year-Old. *The Psychoanalytic Study of the Child,* 1:167-188. New York: International Universities Press.

Szilasi, W. (1951), Die Erfahrungsgrundlage der Daseinsanalyse L. Binswangers. *Schweiz. Arch. Neurol. Psychiat.,* 67:74.

Thannhauser, S. J. (1929), Endogene Magerkeit. *Verh. dtsch. Ges. Verdau- und Stoffwechselkr.,* 9:96.

Thiel, M. (1951), Die Distanzproblematik in der Philosophie. *Stud. Generale*, 4:271.

—— (1954), Philosophie und Psychotherapie. *Jahrbuch Psychol. Psychother. med. Anthropol.*, 2:297.

Thiemann, E. (1957), *Die Pubertätsmagersucht als überwiegend psychisch bedingte Erkrankung.* Stuttgart: Schattauer.

Thomä, H. (1957-1958), Männlicher Transvestitismus und das Verlangen nach Geschlechtsumwandlung. *Psyche*, 11:81-124.

—— (1958-1959a), Die organisch Kranken in tiefenpsychologischer Diagnostik. *Psyche*, 12:497-510.

—— (1958-1959b), Review of: A. W. Eiff, Grundumsatz und Psyche. *Psyche*, 12:750.

—— (1958-1959c), Sigmund Freud—ein Daseinsanalytiker? *Psyche*, 12:881-900.

—— (1962), Bemerkungen zu neuen Arbeiten über die Theorie der Konversion. *Psyche*, 16:801-813.

Thorn, G. W. et al. (1950), The Clinical Usefulness of ACTH and Cortisone. *N. E. J. Med.*, 242:783.

Tiemann, F. (1958), Das Krankheitsbild der Anorexia nervosa, seine Differentialdiagnose und Behandlung. *Med. Klin.* Berlin, 53:329-335.

Tinbergen, N. (1952), *The Study of Instinct.* London and New York: Oxford University Press, 1951.

Trefzer, C. (1939), Hungerstreik im Kindesalter. Discussion. Zurich.

Tucker, W. L. (1952), Lobotomy Case Histories, Ulcerative Colitis and Anorexia Nervosa. *Lahey Clin. Bull.*, 7:239-243.

Tustin, F. (1959), Anorexia Nervosa in an Adolescent Girl. *Brit. J. Med. Psychol.*, 31:184-200.

Uexküll, T. von (1951), Untersuchungen über das Phänomen der "Stimmung" mit einer Analyse der Nausea nach Apomorphingaben verschiedener Grösse. *Zeitschrift klin. Med.*, 149:132.

—— (1951-1952), Das Problem der "Befindensweisen" und seine Bedeutung für eine medizinische Phänomenologie. *Psyche*, 5:401-432.

Venables, J. F. (1930), Anorexia Nervosa: A Study of the Pathogenesis and Treatment of Nine Cases. *Guy's Hosp. Rep.*, 80:213-226.

Villinger, W. (1950), Zur Pathologie, Anamnese und Psycho-Pathologie der Pubertätsmagersucht. *Zbl. ges. Neurol. Psychiat.*, 108-312.

Vogel, P. (1944), Beiträge zur Frage des vegetativen Systems und Stammhirns. *Dtsch. med. Wochenschrift*, 70:548.

—— (1956), Der Wert der neurologischen Studien Sigmund Freuds für die Gehirnpathologie und Psychiatrie. *Schweiz. Arch. Neurol. Psychiat.*, 78:274.

Volhard, E. (1939), *Kannibalismus, Studien zur Kulturkunde,* 5. Stuttgart: Strecker & Schröder.

Voss, H. E. (1952), Die Therapie hypophysär bedingter Störungen mit heteroplastischer Hypophysenimplantation. *Ärztliche Wochenschrift,* 7:266.

Waelder, R. (1936), The Problem of the Genesis of Psychical Conflict in Earliest Infancy. *Internat. J. Psychoanal.,* 18:406-473.

———— (1960), *Basic Theory of Psychoanalysis.* New York: International Universities Press.

Wahlberg, J. (1935), Asthenia gravis hypophyseogenea. *Acta med. scand.,* 84:550.

Wall, J. H. (1956), Anorexia Nervosa. *Bull. N. Y. Acad. Med.,* 32:116-126.

Waller, J. V., Kaufman, M. R., and Deutsch, F. (1942), Anorexia Nervosa: A Psychosomatic Entity. *Psychosom. Med.,* 2:3-16.

Wallerstein, R. S. et al. (1956), The Psychotherapy Research Project of the Menninger Foundation. *Bull. Menninger Clin.,* 20:221-278.

Walter, K. (1953), Zur Psychopathologie der Pubertätsmagersucht. *Wien. Arch. Psychol.,* 3:101.

Weiss, E. and English, O. S. (1949), *Psychosomatic Medicine. The Clinical Application of Psychopathology to General Medicine Problems.* Philadelphia and London: Saunders.

Weitbrecht, H. J. (1959), Das Syndrom in der psychiatrischen Diagnose. *Fortschr. Neurol. Psychiat.,* 27:1.

Weizsäcker, V. von (1937), Über Träume bei sogenannter endogener Magersucht. *Dtsch. med. Wochenschrift,* 63:253, 294-297.

———— (1946), *Studien zur Pathogenese.* Wiesbaden: Thieme.

———— (1948-1949), Der Widerstand bei der Behandlung von Organkranken. *Psyche,* 2:481-498.

———— (1950), *Der Gestaltkreis.* Stuttgart: Thieme.

Whytt, R. (1767), *Observations on the Nature, Causes and Cure of those Disorders which have been commonly Called Nervous Hypochondria or Hysteric: To which are Prefixed Some Remarks on the Sympathy of the Nerves.* London: Becket & de Hondt, Edinburgh: Balfour.

Wilson, R. R. (1954), A Case of Anorexia Nervosa with Necropsy Findings and a Discussion of Secondary Hypopituitarism. *J. Clin. Pathol.,* 7:131-136.

Wisdom, J. O. (1959), On a Differentiating Mechanism of Psychosomatic Disorder. *Internat. J. Psychoanal.,* 40:134-146.

Wissler, H. (1941), Die Pubertätsmagersucht. *Monatschrift Kinderheilklinik,* 85:172.

Wittekind, D. and Mappes, G. (1957), Beitrag zur Kasuistik der Hypophysenvorderlappeninsuffizienz. *Z. klin. Med.*, 154:494.

Wulff, M. (1932), Über einen interessanten oralen Symptomenkomplex und seine Beziehung zur Sucht. *Int. Z. ärztl. Psychoanal.*, 18:281-302.

Zondek, H. and Koehler, G. (1928), Über cerebral-hypophysäre Magersucht. *Dtsch. med. Wochenschrift*, 54:1955.

Zutt, J. (1946), Psychiatrische Betrachtungen zur Pubertätsmagersucht. *Klin. Wochenschrift*, 24:21.

———— (1948), Das psychiatrische Krankheitsbild der Pubertätsmagersucht. *Arch. Psychiat. Nervenkr.*, 180:5-6.